Racial and Ethnic Groups in America

Second Edition

Juan L. Gonzales Jr.

California State University, Hayward

KENDALL/HUNT PUBLISHING COMPANY
2460 Kerper Boulevard   P.O. Box 539   Dubuque, Iowa 52004-0539

DEDICATION

In Memory of
Alfred F. Garcia

Copyright © 1993 by Kendall/Hunt Publishing Company

ISBN 0-8403-8553-6

Printed in the United States of America
10 9 8 7 6 5 4 3 2 1

Contents

Preface

As we enter the mid-1990s we have to wonder what the future of race relations will be in the United States. Some are of the opinion that conditions for ethnic and racial groups have improved over the past decade and that race relations will improve by the turn of the century. But others are quick to point to some of the disturbing acts of racial violence and urban unrest that have occurred during the first half of the 1990's. These events have caused great consternation and concern in the American public. As a result many Americans are troubled by the future of race relations in the United States.

The objective of this book is to provide an academic background for understanding the history, culture, and social relationships that constitute the day-to-day life in ethnic communities. The hope is that with an exposure to some basic facts about American ethnic groups that people will arrive at a new level of understanding and cooperation. It is my belief that education can provide the key to understanding ethnic and racial diversity in American society and that such an understanding will promote greater tolerance and acceptance of cultural diversity.

While the genesis of this book is the sociological tradition, and therefore sociological theory and methodology serves as its academic superstructure, the scope and orientation of this book is based on the multicultural perspective and therefore reflects a strong interdisciplinary approach. Consequently our survey of American ethnic groups has a strong historical orientation but also relies on the sociological method to examine the social issues of the day, the economic conditions, and the political life of American minorities.

As a result of the interdisciplinary approach of this book the reader will learn to appreciate the work and the research findings of scholars from various academic backgrounds. For this reason racial and ethnic groups are studied from the perspective of the sociologist, the historian, the economist, demographer, political scientist, and the psychologist.

The first section of the book provides an overview of the major theories of race relations. While the focus is on prejudice and discrimination, the complexities of assimilation of both established minorities and recent immigrants are examined. Assimilation is viewed as a long term process and is considered one of the many options available to American ethnic groups today.

With an emphasis on the immigration experiences and historical circumstances of minorities as a backdrop, each chapter in this book captures the unique social, economic, and political experiences of each group. Five major ethnic groups are the focus of study, the Asian Americans, the Latinos, the white ethnics, Native Americans and the African Americans. In addition one chapter is devoted to minority women and women as minorities in American society.

I am certain that students will appreciate the clear writing style of the book and the systematic presentation of ideas and information in each chapter. As students read about the lives of ethnic and racial minorities they will gain an appreciation for their struggle to survive in American society. Each chapter provides a wealth of demographic and economic data to help students understand the past and current socio-economic position of ethnic and racial groups in society. Tables and graphs are used extensively in each chapter and the box readings and chronological overviews serve to highlight specific characteristics of each group.

Instructors will find the multicultural-interdisciplinary approach of the book refreshing. The organization and presentation of materials in each chapter is based on years of teaching experience at the community college level, the university, and at the graduate level. Instructors will discover that they can key their lectures to the topics presented in each chapter and still emphasize the theories or topics that they feel are most important for their students to learn and absorb.

Many instructors will find that this book can serve as the primary text for their race relations course in either the quarter or semester systems. In addition the cultural diversity of the groups that are examined in the book will give instructors the option of spending more time on certain groups and less time on others.

Instructors will find the extensive reference list at the end of each chapter particularly useful, as these references can serve as a working bibliography for student papers and research projects. The list of important names and key terms found at the end of each chapter will help students focus on the important concepts and ideas presented in each chapter. In addition the sample test questions provided at the end of each chapter can serve as the basis for mid-term and final examination questions. These sample test questions will also reduce the concerns and anxieties that students typically have regarding the type of questions that will be asked on tests. In fact some instructors may even decide to select their test questions from the list of sample test questions provided at the end of each chapter.

In addition to the clear academic orientation of the book, the general reader will discover a distinct ethnic feeling in the presentation of facts and information. This strong cultural sensitivity and awareness derives from my personal knowledge of and feeling for ethnic and racial groups. For it should be clear that this book is not only the result of many years of formal education, research, and teaching, but also derives from the life experiences of an individual who has lived the culture.

Juan L. Gonzales Jr.

Acknowledgments

I would like to thank my friends and colleagues who took time from their busy schedules to offer their insights, suggestions, and constructive comments on my manuscript. Marjorie Donovan (Pittsburg State), Edward Murguia (Texas A & M University), and Terry Jones (California State University) were kind enough to read several chapters of my work and they deserve a special note of appreciation.

The presentation of these diverse and complicated ideas was improved as a result of the helpful comments of several of my distinguished colleagues: Mario Barrera (U.C. Berkeley), Bob Blauner (U.C. Berkeley), Edna Bonacich (U.C. Riverside), Jorge Bustamante (El Colegio de la Frontera Norte), Bruce Chadwick (Brigham Young University), Jose Cobas (Arizona State University), Leonard Gordon (Arizona State University), Michael Kearney (U.C. Riverside), Stanford Lyman (Florida Atlantic University), Phylis Martinelli (St. Mary's College), Michael Messner (University of Southern California), Basil Sherlock (California State University), and William Wei (University of Colorado).

For his good cheer and moral support during the long hours of writing I would like to thank my very good friend and colleague, Robert Dunn. For the preparation of the art work I would like to thank Alice Guerrero. And I would also like to extend my most sincere gratitude to my research assistant Rosa Gonzales.

Finally, I would like to thank my wife for her understanding, assistance, personal support, and encouragement during the long and arduous task of writing this book.

Part I

★ ★ ★

Theories of Race and Immigration

Chapter 1

The Origins of Racial and Ethnic Groups

Race Relations in America

Sociology is the study of people interacting in groups, and the primary focus of sociological research is the observation of group behavior. In an applied setting sociology is based on the objective observation of individual behavior as it occurs in a group setting. In their observations of group behavior sociologists study and analyze the organizational structure of informal and formal groups, the relationships that develop among the members of the group, and the influence of the group on individual behavior. At the macro level of analysis, sociology is the scientific study of social groups, but at the micro level sociology is based on the analyses of the effects of the group on the individual.

The French philosopher August Comte (1798-1857) is considered the founding father of sociology. Comte was given this unique distinction in recognition of the fact that he was the first to develop a systematic approach to the study of society and human relationships. When he discovered this new approach to the study of society Comte referred to this new discipline as social physics, as he wanted to emphasize his scientific approach to the study of group behavior. Comte's positivist approach, that is the rigid application of systematic procedures to the study of human interaction in groups, served as the basis for the creation of modern sociology (Coser, 1971).

Today sociologists study every conceivable aspect of group behavior and social interaction. The fact that distinguishes the observations of sociologists from those of the average person on the street is that they apply the scientific method to their research and observations. Historically sociologists have used the scientific approach to study specific issues or social problems that affect society. Therefore it should come as no surprise to discover that one of the first areas of sociological research and observation in the United States focused on race relations.

Among the first American sociologists to apply the scientific method to the study of race relations were Robert E. Park and Ernest W. Burgess. Today they are recognized as the founding fathers of the Chicago school of sociology (Faris, 1967). When they began their sociological studies in the early 1920's, the city of Chicago was an ideal laboratory for the observation of human behavior, as the city was growing and there were dozens of ethnic communities spread throughout the metropolis. While they encouraged their graduate students to study a whole host of social problems in the city, such as crime, poverty, homelessness, and urbanization, they also focused on race relations.

Park and Burgess observed that the city of Chicago grew and expanded from a central core, and from this core the businesses, industries, and neighborhoods expanded outward and formed easily recognized concentric circles that radiated from the central business district. Within these circles the residential location of specific racial and ethnic groups could be delineated. They also observed that newly arrived immigrants invariably settled in the ethnic enclaves near the central business district. But as they experienced social mobility they gradually moved away from the central city and settled in the more desirable suburban neighborhoods.

As a result of their observations Park and Burgess theorized that all ethnic groups would enter the city at the soft spot, that is at the point of least resistance. Furthermore they hypothesized that these immigrants would settle in one of the natural areas (i.e., an ethnic ghetto) of the city and that eventually they would move out of the ethnic enclaves and blend into the surrounding suburbs. But as we shall see, their theory of ethnic settlement patterns, residential segregation, social mobility, assimilation, and suburbanization only applied to the white ethnic groups living in the city of Chicago.

Despite some minor flaws in their concentric circle theory and Park's failure to recognize that not all groups would blend into the fabric of American society, their contributions to the scientific study of race relations were invaluable. Of greater importance they provided their graduate students with the research skills and knowledge that eventually allowed them to conduct dozens of studies on specific racial and ethnic groups living in urban areas throughout the country.

What is a Minority Group?

Since the cultural revolution of the sixties the definition of a minority group has undergone a series of revisions and modifications in the minds of most experts. In general the term minority group can be applied to any recog-

4

nizable racial, ethnic, religious, or gender group that has suffered a historical disadvantage as a result of an ingrained pattern of prejudice and discrimination. Following a consistent pattern of discrimination, the minority group experiences social isolation and segregation. Ultimately the members of the minority group are avoided and rejected by the dominant society. Over the long term these acts of discrimination and the acceptance of racial segregation are institutionalized and legalized because of social pressure, political action, and social legislation.

Those scholars who have studied race relations in the United States would agree that there are five fundamental characteristics that determine minority group status (Wagley and Harris, 1958):

1. a minority group must have a history of unequal treatment,
2. a minority group must have distinctive physical or cultural characteristics,
3. their membership in the group must be involuntary,
4. they experience ingroup marriage,
5. and they must be aware of their minority status.

History of Unequal Treatment

A minority group must have a history of being the object of prejudice, discrimination, segregation, racism, sexism, xenophobia, or homophobia. Their unequal treatment is based on the fact that the majority group, that is those who wield power in society, has the means to discriminate against them and the social will and political ability to do so. Once minorities are selected for special treatment, the effects of prejudicial attitudes and the development of stereotypes insures their unequal treatment. This pattern of long term discrimination is translated into laws and social policies that guarantee their segregation and social isolation. In the end the legal institutions reflect their unequal treatment and ultimately justify their subordination.

An excellent example of the close relationship between the unequal treatment of minorities and the development of laws and social policies that discriminate against them is the experience of the Chinese in California. Following the discovery of gold in the Sierra foothills the Chinese began to arrive in large numbers. After an initial welcome, several local groups agitated against their immigration. Before long, bands of unemployed white workers were rioting in the streets of San Francisco. The hapless Chinese were the victims of innumerable acts of mob violence. Eventually these race riots prompted the state legislature to pass laws prohibiting further immigration from China. Likewise the city of San Francisco passed a series of ordinances that made life very difficult for them. These discriminatory laws were obviously racist and based on the spurious observation that the presence of Chinese immigrants often resulted in mayhem and violence in the streets.

Distinctive Characteristics

Perhaps the most important characteristic of our definition of a minority group is that they must have some physical or cultural characteristic that differentiates them from the majority group. This provision only seems logical in view of the fact that if you intend to discriminate against a particular group then you must select a unique physical or cultural characteristic of the group and focus attention on it. This is essential since a way must be found to pick them out of a group in order to discriminate against them. If no such characteristic is visible or available, then you must devise a way by which you can distinguish them from the other members of society.

Historically, societies that have subjugated minorities have always found ways to make them appear different. In their zeal to discriminate against minorities some societies have even gone as far as to make them appear subhuman. Even when there are no obvious physical or cultural distinctions available an effort is made to apply a social stigma to the group. This concocted stigma or fabricated blemish is attached to the minority group in an effort to make them appear different. This explains why the Jews in Nazi Germany were required to sew the Star of David on their coats. Eventually Hitler ordered all the Jews tattooed.

The best historical examples of using physical attributes to distinguish one group from another are skin color, facial features, color and texture of hair, body build and size, and sexual differences. Language, religious differences, family and kinship patterns, and manner of dress are the most frequently used cultural characteristics to draw a distinction among groups (Zenner, 1991:19-26). The record shows that distinct physical attributes and cultural characteristics are often used in combination to enhance the impact of racism. This combined approach contributes to the development of strong racial stereotypes that often serve to justify the original acts of prejudice and discrimination. The end effect of this established pattern of discrimination is that minorities are stigmatized, that is they carry the stigma of race.

The Labeling Theory of Race

The dynamics of racial discrimination can best be understood in terms of the labeling theory of race, which is based on the use of socio-racial terminology (Mörner, 1967:56-60). In its most basic form the labeling theory of race holds that if we perceive someone as different, that is based on racial and cultural differences, then we immediately began to treat them differently. Over a short period of time our unequal treatment of people becomes a self-fulfilling prophecy. Gunnar Myrdal has referred to this insidious social-psychological process as cumulative causation (1944:25-28). In brief, cumulative causation describes the vicious circle of prejudice and discrimination that feeds upon itself, since prejudice leads to discrimination and discrimination supports prejudicial attitudes.

The labeling theory of race is based on five basic steps:

1. We establish a perception of racial or cultural differences between ourselves and the members of a recognized minority group.
2. We make a judgement or evaluation of the identity of the minority person.
3. We make a decision as to how we are going to relate to this person.
4. We develop an attitude toward that person and the group that he/she represents.
5. We put our ideas into action. Once we take action our relationship with the minority person is very much as we expected, hence we are the victims of our own self-fulfilling prophecy.

Involuntary Membership

The basis for involuntary membership in a minority group is simply the fact that membership is an accident of birth. Therefore membership is an ascribed status, since individuals are born into a minority group and minority membership identifies the individual in society. Other well known examples of ascribed statuses are sex, which is also an accident of birth, and age, which is bestowed in good time. Therefore an individual does not choose to be Asian or white, male or female.

The most important thing to remember about minority group status is that a person is only a minority because society has arbitrarily defined membership in a particular group as having negative social consequences. The positive or negative characteristics associated with a particular set of physical attributes simply reflects society's definition of a minority group. For example, the fact that a person is born with dark pigmentation will have certain social consequences for a person born in Nigeria, different ramifications for someone born in New York City, and yet another set of consequences for a person born in Montgomery. Obviously the accident of birth does have profound consequences for minorities, as minority group status has a direct impact on a person's life chances.

Ingroup Marriage

The propensity for ingroup marriage is another important characteristic of minority group status. Endogamy refers to the tendency of minorities to marry within their group. The opposite of endogamy is exogamy, or intermarriage. In the United States minorities have historically practiced endogamy during their early period of settlement, when they often experience high levels of social isolation and segregation. But as minorities gain social acceptance their level of exogamy increases. For this reason the rate of exogamy among minorities is often used as an indication of their level of social acceptance and their degree of assimilation.

The fact that endogamy is endemic to America's minorities is clear when we consider that they have historically been the victims of racism and the assumption is that they would be spurned as marital partners by the majority group. Indeed some states (especially those in the South) actually passed anti-miscegenation laws to prevent legal marriages from occurring between African Americans and whites and between Mongolians (i.e., Asians) and whites. In some states county clerks even refused to process marriage licenses for Mexican Americans who wanted to intermarry with whites. Since the late sixties all anti-miscegenation laws have been expunged from the books of all states (Sickels, 1972:64-110).

Awareness of Subordinate Status

The final characteristic of minority group membership is the simple fact that minorities must recognize that they are minorities. While this may seem self evident, it happens that minority group status is not always recognized or even accepted by all the members of the group. However, the acceptance of minority group status often results in greater social cohesiveness among minorities. Social psychologists have found that strong identification with their minority status results in a "consciousness of kind" among minorities. The sociologist Franklin Giddings (1924) referred to consciousness of kind as a feeling of identification with others who are similar to oneself. As a result minorities often develop an *esprit de corps*, that is a sense of brotherhood, a feeling that "we have a shared historical experience" (Northcott, 1948).

During the Civil Rights Movement the awareness of ethnic consciousness and group identification was particularly evident. It was also during this period that many minorities became aware of their ethnic history and culture. Strong ethnic identification is also likely to occur when minorities find that they are outnumbered or socially isolated, as often happens to African American and Latino students in a college environment. From the perspective of the majority group this close identification with their group may be interpreted as clannish behavior on the part of minority students.

At the other end of the social spectrum some individuals reject their ethnicity, as they make every effort to expunge or disguise their minority status. The attempt by some minorities to escape the stigma of race and avoid victimization is not uncommon today. The most effective attempt to escape their minority identification is known as passing. Passing means that an individual has managed to lose, or in various ways disguise, the most obvious characteristics of racial identification and has gained acceptance into the majority group. In the most successful cases the minority person is fully accepted by the majority group as one of their own. Passing usually requires individuals to alter their physical appearance (by means of plastic surgery, skin bleaching, hair straightening), lose a distinctive accent, physically move into the majority group's cultural milieu, and (sometimes) marry a person from the dominant group (Dominguez, 1986).

Types of Minority Groups

In view of the social and cultural diversity that is such an important part of the social fabric of our society it is sometimes difficult to categorize all the minorities who are a part of the American cultural environment. But in spite of the heterogeneity of American society most minorities can be assigned to one of five basic groups:

- A Racial Group
- An Ethnic Group
- A Nationality Group
- A Religious Group
- A Gender Group

Racial Groups

Because of our unique historical experience racial groups are the most noticeable minorities. The concept of racial groups is based on the premise that people are different because of observed physical differences and because these physical differences result in specific social consequences for the members of these racial groups. Obviously the idea of racial differences automatically implies that basic biological differences do exist among people. The criteria used by anthropologists to define racial groups is often based on commonly observed physical differences, such as body size and shape, skin color, facial features, and the structure and color of hair (Banton, 1983:32- 59).

However, there are two important factors to consider in any discussion of racial classifications. The first is that any single physical characteristic is not statistically exclusive to any racial group. Therefore any physical characteristic that is used to identify a racial group, such as skin color, tends to overlap from one racial group to another. The second point is that while these racial distinctions are strictly arbitrary classifications, they are nonetheless important because they produce social consequences. In effect, observed physical differences are only important because society has made them important and our culture has given them social significance.

Ethnic Groups

While the concept racial group is strictly a biological concept, ethnic group is a cultural concept. The concept ethnic group is based on the distinctive cultural characteristics of a particular group. The most common tangible aspects of a culture are its language, religion, social customs, folklore, historical origins, community traditions, manner of dress, and traditional cuisine (Thompson, 1989:21-46).

As distinct from a racial group, an ethnic group is defined by its unique cultural characteristics and not by its physical characteristics. Therefore it is possible to have an ethnic group that is also a recognized racial group. For example, the concept Asian refers to a large group of individuals who share a common gene pool, while the distinctions between the various Asian groups would represent the specific cultural differences that exit between them, such as those that exist between the Japanese, Chinese, and Koreans. Therefore while each of these groups is culturally distinct, they are all genetically related. However, many Americans find that it is convenient to refer to all people from the Far East as Asians. This is a good example of how people often use a racial category, in this case Asians, as a convenient way of relating to a group of individuals who are culturally distinct. The use of the term Asians is a cultural crutch that is often used by individuals who are ignorant of the distinct ethnic differences among Asians.

Nationality Groups

Historically the term nationality group was applied to those immigrants who arrived in America during the latter part of the nineteenth century. Today the term nationality group is still applied to those Americans who identify themselves as English, Irish, Germans, Italians, etc. As a concept, nationality group is a broad based term used to describe citizens of a particular country. The term nationality group derives from a person's political allegiance to, or origin from, a particular nation. Hence the term is a political concept and is not necessarily synonymous with any particular ethnic or racial group, although sometimes it is.

The popular use of the term, and its tenacity in the culture, derives from the fact that people from the same nationality group often share a common history, language, customs, and traditions. But this is not always the case. On this point caution must be taken not to confuse nationality group with the cultural term ethnic group. Sometimes the two terms are congruent in reference, but this is not always the case. For example, a common mistake is to refer to someone as Spanish, simply because they happen to speak the Spanish language. But the term Spanish should only be applied to a person when it is used as a nationality concept and never as an ethnic concept. In fact Spanish speaking people in the United States, such as Mexican Americans, are often offended by this oversight.

Religious Groups

The recognition of religious groups as minority groups is particularly important when a religious group is in the numerical minority in any given society. For example, Catholics would be considered a religious minority in the United States, since most Americans are Protestants. For it was not many years ago that Catholics were a persecuted minority in this country. In general when we think of religious minorities today we usually think of such groups as the Jews, Mormons, Hutterities, and the Amish.

Sometimes the religious minority within a society is recognized for its ethnic or racial composition, to the extent that the religious group is synonymous with an ethnic or racial group. For example, during the great migration of Irish-Catholics this was the case. Other religious groups in American society like the Jews, the Sikhs, and the Nation of Islam have very strong racial and ethnic attachments. Therefore care must be taken in designating one group or another as either a religious group, an ethnic group, or a nationality group. In other countries it is not unusual for one group to have all the characteristics of a religious group, an ethnic group, and a nationality group. For example, this is true in some Middle Eastern nations.

Gender Groups

The last minority group discussed in this section is a numerical majority in the United States, since women represent approximately fifty-two percent of the population. As a group women are a minority in American society since they have experienced both prejudice and discrimination, they have a long history of unequal treatment, they clearly have distinctive physical characteristics, they are aware of their minority group status, and their membership in the group is involuntary. The minority status of ethnic and racial women is particularly significant in American society as these women are the victims of "double jeopardy." This means that minority women suffer from discrimination because they are women and because they are members of an ethnic or racial group.

Evolving Minorities

Since the early seventies several minority groups have emerged and have managed to gain social recognition and a degree of political power. Although these groups do not meet all the criteria for minority group membership, it is nonetheless true that they do exhibit the more important characteristics.

Over the past twenty years the elderly have managed to obtain social and political recognition as a minority group in American society. Today they represent about fifteen percent of the population. Because of improved health care and the gradual increase in the life expectancy of the average American, their numbers will continue to climb. As a minority the elderly have also suffered from prejudice and discrimination, particularly in housing and in the labor market.

Another group that has also gained national attention in recent years as an emerging minority are the physically challenged (disabled) Americans. The physically challenged have a long history of discrimination in American society. Only as a result of their organizational efforts have they managed to change many of the laws that have made life difficult for them. With the elimination of the most blatant discriminatory laws and the availability of new opportunities in higher education and employment, their quality of life has improved. Their access to new opportunities has also given them a chance to make their mark in the world. This has resulted in the development of more positive attitudes toward the physically challenged in all areas of American society. To improve their access to the opportunity structure many physically challenged individuals have joined local, state, and national organizations that strive to represent their interest and concerns.

Since the late sixties the gay community has carried on a courageous struggle to obtain equal rights under the law. As is true of the history of other recognized minorities, gays have also been the victims of senseless acts of violence and blatant discrimination (Comstock, 1991; Herek, 1992). It is only in the past ten years that the most blatant discriminatory laws against gays have been changed to assure that they have equal access to the opportunity structure. Most of these laws guard against discrimination in the labor market or in housing. Unfortunately these positive steps have only been taken in more liberal cities in the nation. To this day federal laws do not protect gay rights (Mohr, 1988). The most recent example of the failure of the federal government to protect gay rights has occurred in the military, where men and women with distinguished service records have been discharged simply because of their sexual orientation.

The most recent group to strive for recognition as a minority within American society are the homeless. While many are well aware of the vicious cycle of poverty, the nation has failed to recognize the plight of those who have fallen through the safety-net of the welfare system. Homelessness is often the end result of a life of poverty, unemployment, or family disorganization. It is only in the past ten years that the government and the public have become aware of the homeless problem and the social and economic conditions that have transformed so many Americans into a minority of homeless men, women, and children.

The Creation of Minority Groups

Social groups are subjected to any number of forces that affect their standing in the community. Depending on the circumstances and the historical period, a minority group can move up or down the social scale and also can gain acceptance into the larger society or remain on its fringes. These social forces result in the modification and change of minority groups over time. Historically there are five fundamental methods by which minority groups are created:

1. Voluntary Migration
2. Involuntary Migration
3. Political Annexation
4. Colonial Expansion
5. Internal Colonialism

Voluntary Migration

In all the experiences of immigration it is not unusual for new arrivals in a host society to be treated as outsiders, foreigners, and immigrants. This is the first step in the creation of a new minority by the method of voluntary migration. The history of our country is replete with dozens of examples of voluntary migration.

Obviously the reason that new arrivals are treated as minorities is that they are aliens in the host society and need time to adjust to the needs and expectations of the new society. But as they integrate into the host society and blend into the culture they often relinquish their minority status as they learn the new language, dress like the others in the host society, settle into integrated neighborhoods, and eventually as their children intermarry. This is the process of assimilation.

But the process of acceptance and integration of immigrants into the host society is not always so smooth or so easy. As a result some immigrants will retain their minority status for decades. Usually the second generation, that is the children born in America, will began the process of assimilation. The third generation will intermarry and blend into the culture.

Involuntary Migration

The distinction between voluntary and involuntary migration is not always clear-cut, as not all immigrants who arrive as voluntary migrants really emigrate on their own volition. For example, the Irish Catholics were voluntary migrants but they did not emigrate because they had a strong desire to leave their homeland, rather they were forced off their land and emigrated to avoid the death grip of poverty. On the other hand, the African slaves who were brought to this country in chains were certainly involuntary migrants.

Another example of involuntary migration to America was the indentured servants whose passage was paid by farmers and businessmen during the colonial period. As their only means to repay their masters for their passage they had to sign a contract promising to work for them for five to seven years. Once they completed their period of service they were given their freedom (Franklin, 1967:72). In fact more than half the colonists who came to America during the colonial period were indentured servants (Zinn, 1980:43-44).

Some would consider any form of contract labor as a type of involuntary migration. The use of contract laborers was a common practice during the nineteenth century and was used extensively with Chinese, Japanese, and Filipino farm workers in California and Hawaii. They were required to sign a three-year labor contract. When their obligation was fulfilled they were allowed to return home, although some chose to remain in America and work as free laborers (Frazier, 1957).

Political Annexation

Historically it is common for those who are victorious in battle to claim the land of the vanquished. Under these circumstances the defeated people are relegated to an inferior status and often become minorities in their society. In the process they are subjected to the most virulent forms of racism. Their imposed minority status can remain in effect for many years or their inferior position in society may pass to the next generation and remain attached to the group indefinitely.

American history is replete with examples of territorial domination following a military victory. For example, the Treaty of Guadalupe Hidalgo (1848) ended the war between the United States and Mexico and forced Mexico to relinquish vast territories in the Southwest. The Mexicans living in these territories were considered racially inferior and were the victims of an untold number of acts of racism and violence.

Another example of political annexation in American history occurred when the United States signed the Treaty of Paris in 1898, ending its war with Spain. In return the United States obtained the Philippines, Puerto Rico, and several islands in the Pacific. The people of Puerto Rico and the Philippines were subjugated and treated as racial minorities in their homeland.

Colonial Expansion

Most history books refer to the period of colonial expansion as the period of Exploration and Discovery. This refers to that historical period when the

14

Europeans set out to claim and conquer all the territories in the New World. While their objective was to obtain more land, they also wanted to extract the raw materials from the conquered territories, ship them to the mother country, and increase their wealth. The key to their success was their ability to press the indigenous populations into forced labor. The Europeans were successful because they had superior military force, an advanced technology, and a sophisticated political structure. An additional advantage in their drive to subdue the native populations was the cooperation of the major religions, who provided the missionaries whose job it was to Christianize and civilize the savages.

The fact that these indigenous groups were all People of Color was particularly significant, as the European culled from a variety of racial theories to justify the subjugation of indigenous people throughout the world. If people could be made to believe that they were inferior, and their only purpose in life was to serve as a source of cheap labor, obviously this made it a lot easier for those who were intent on their subjugation.

Internal Colonialism

The internal colonial model of race relations derives from the characteristics of classic colonialism. Under the system of internal colonialism there is no longer a need to create new minorities in foreign lands to take advantage of their cheap labor, rather these groups are now attracted to the mother country and are segregated within the society where their labor is exploited. In a real sense internal colonies are created within the mother country and these labor reservations are popularly known as ghettos and barrios.

According to Robert Blauner (1969), who refined this theory, there are four basic characteristics of internal colonialism:

1. The colonized have the social system imposed on them.
2. The native culture is modified or destroyed.
3. The internal colony is controlled from the outside.
4. Racism prevails.

Even though the internal colonial model can be applied to several American ethnic groups, Blauner selected the African Americans as his working example. According to Blauner, African Americans were brought here against their will and their culture was almost destroyed. Today their communities are politically powerless and are controlled from the outside by a group of politicians and administrators who do not represent them or look after their best interest. They are also controlled by the police, who are bent on keeping the social problems and disruptions confined within the African American community. Blauner's last point regarding the prevalence of racism is based on historical experience and is also supported by current social and economic conditions in American society.

The Origins of Social Darwinism

The importance of Charles Darwin's contribution to our understanding of evolution was monumental, as his book *On the Origin of Species* (1859) gave the world the theory of evolution. With this publication Darwin refuted the archaic theory of the multiple origins of the human species (Gossett, 1965). He not only changed forever the basis for the theory of racial differentiation, he also demonstrated that all human races evolved from a single species.

It was also significant that Darwin provided a detailed scientific explanation for the process of change and adaptation in the natural world, which he called natural selection. It did not take long for someone to adopt his idea of natural selection and apply it to the human condition.

The fact that is surprising to most people is that it was not Darwin who applied the idea of the survival of the fittest to the human condition, rather it was Herbert Spencer, an English sociologist. Contrary to popular belief Darwin did not coin the phrase "survival of the fittest," rather Spencer was the one who drew the analogy between conflict in the biological world and the struggle for existence between the various groups in society. Spencer even applied the theory of evolution to the conflict between nations. In his view the human condition was ruled by the laws of competition and conflict, with natural selection serving to eliminate the weak and reward the strong (Peel, 1972).

Spencer went as far as to suggest that warfare had a useful eugenic effect, since it served to kill off inferior races. In his book *Principles of Sociology* (1896), Spencer argues against intermarriage, as he felt it would result in the degeneration of the human stock. He also argued against public education, for he believed that only those who could afford an education should receive an education. For the same reason he wanted to see the postal service and public libraries eliminated. Spencer also believed that providing assistance to the poor would only exacerbate things in the future. He supported the theory of laissez-faire economics and his motto was the less government the better. Many of his positions on social issues were later adopted by the modern libertarian party.

Early Explanations for Racial Differentiation

One of the riddles that has plagued societies from the dawn of civilization is the question of how to account for the physical differences that exist among the various people in the world. For it is obvious that racial differences exist, but what is not always so clear are the social ramifications of these basic biological differences.

The Egyptians were the first to classify groups of people. Their classification was simplistic as it was based on differences in skin color. They considered themselves red, their enemies from the east were yellow, those living to the north were considered white, and black was used to describe the various tribes in Africa (Gossett, 1965:4).

The Bible states that the descendants of Canaan and Ham were punished by being made black. Greek mythology holds that the son of the sun god lost control of his chariot as he traversed the sky and he burned a whole nation of people. The first person to account for racial differences on the basis of climate and geography was Hippocrates. Aristotle believed that both physical and temperamental characteristics were caused by climate, particularly very cold or hot climates.

During the Age of Discovery and Exploration a plethora of ideas were generated to account for the great variety of racial groups that were discovered. Like the Greeks, Leonardo Da Vinci (1452- 1519) was convinced that physical differences among people could be attributed to environment. The Swiss physician Philippus Paracelsus (1493-1541) believed that the descendants of Adam and Eve only occupied a small part of the earth and that Africans, and other races, had a wholly separate origin. The Italian philosopher Giordano Bruno (1548-1600) proclaimed that no thinking person could imagine that the Ethiopians had the same ancestry as the Jews. Jean Bodin (1530-1596), the French political philosopher, believed that geography, climate, and astrology could account for racial differences. In 1655, Isac De La Peyrere declared that there were two separate creations, as he believed that a race of people existed before Adam and Eve.

Perhaps the first serious attempt to establish a human classification system was made by Francois Bernier (1684), a French physician. But his classification was rudimentary as it consisted of four groups: the Lapps, the Africans, the Europeans, and the Far Easterners. The most famous of these catalogers was the Swedish botanist Linnaeus (1707-1778). To his credit he held that all races were varieties and not separate species. But his credibility suffered when he devised a politically sensitive system of four racial groups: Homo Europaeus, Homo Asiaticus, Homo Afer, and Homo Americanus.

Without any doubt the most influential person during this period of racial classification was the French naturalist George Buffon (1707-1788). Following the publication of his 44 volumes on *Natural History*, Buffon concluded that the "white race" is the norm for mankind and all other races are simply exotic variations. It was Johann Blumebach (1752-1840), a German professor of medicine, who coined the term "Caucasian." As part of a research project Blumebach collected skulls from around the world and he felt that one particularly large skull from the Caucasian mountains (in Russia) closely resembled the crania of the German people. Blumebach divided the human races into five basic groups: Caucasian, Mongolian, Ethiopian, American, and Malay.

The debate over the origin of the species was also a topic of great interest among the elites in American society. Benjamin Rush (1745-1813), a physician and one of the signatories of the Declaration of Independence, believed that the blackness in Negroes was a mild and apparently uncontagious form of a disease, perhaps leprosy. Thomas Jefferson (1743-1826), the nation's third President, considered Negroes ugly and believed that they were inherently inferior to whites in both mind and body (Gossett, 1965:41-44).

Obviously these racial theories were simply self serving explanations for the belief that white Europeans were racially superior to any other race. Understandably these ideas were particularly popular in America, as the leaders of our great nation attempted to justify the existence of slavery.

Racial Theories and Racial Diversity

Over the years a plethora of theories have evolved in an attempt to account for the racial differences as they occur around the world. In an attempt to make sense of these explanations it is instructive to collapse these theories into a manageable number of approaches. In general these theories fall into one of seven categories:

1. The Environmental Theory—these are probably the most simplistic, as they are based on such variables as climatic conditions and geographical location.
2. The Monoginist Theory—the belief that humankind originated at one place and at one point in time. Everyone evolved from a common set of ancestors and racial variety occurred over time.
3. The Polygynist Theory—held that there were separate origins throughout the world and the races constitute separate species.
4. The Religious View (the Biblical account)—based on the idea that Adam and Eve were the first humans and that racial differences are the result of sinful behavior and punishment for transgressions against the laws of God.
5. The Concatenated Theory—a more scientific view that held that there was a sequential development of the species, so that at different levels in the evolutionary process various species evolved.
6. The Anatomical View—this view has a long history and holds that the structure of the human body developed in response to the attempts of human beings to adapt to disparate environmental conditions. Therefore as groups adapt to new environments their physical characteristics change accordingly.
7. The Genetic View—this is the most recent and sophisticated of all the racial theories. It holds that the structure and combination of genes is the most important variable in accounting for observed racial differences. The problem with this theory is that it attempts to explain racial diversity and social behavior by referring to inbred genetic differences.

Today the various academic disciplines have provided their approach and interpretation of the origins of humankind (See Figure 1.1). It is obvious that each discipline attempts to answer the question of racial heterogeneity. As in the past, it is also a common practice for these authorities to use a combination of theoretical approaches, that is an eclectic theoretical approach, in their attempts to account for racial diversity (Ehrlich and Feldman 1977:13-34). But in the final analysis racial differences are only important in the minds of certain individuals.

Figure 1.1
Basis for Racial Distinctions in Various Disciplines

Discipline (Approach)	Method of Transmission	Basis for Discrimination
Biology	Genetics	Physical Characteristics
Anthropology	Ethnocentrism	Ethnic Groups
Sociology	Prejudice	Ideology of Race
Psychology	Genetic	I.Q. Differences
Political Science	Patriotism	Nationality Groups
Philosophy	Rationalization	Correct Reasoning
Psychiatric	Authoritarianism	Inferiority-Superiority
Religion	Religious Dogma	Religious Beliefs
Economics	Laissez-Faire	Success and Mobility

The Concept of Race

For over two centuries anthropologists and others have taken the concept of race for granted. In brief, this means that they have accepted the concept of race without providing an adequate operational definition, with the result that some experts in the field have created more than two hundred racial categories (Garn, 1971). Obviously it is impossible to settle upon an all inclusive definition of any racial category. The reason for this academic quagmire is that all racial definitions are arbitrary and the degree and frequency of overlap between adjacent categories is so great as to render the established categories meaningless (Ehrlich and Feldman 1977:32-34).

In application this means that for any given variable used to define a racial group, for example skin color, you can find sufficient overlap between designated groups to render the original definition of race meaningless. In our example this would mean that you would find enough people at the extremes of any two categories, based on the variable of skin color alone, that would overlap with one another. Therefore at the extremes of any given category a person could be placed in one or the other racial category (Davis, 1991). This phenomenon is supported by common sense observation.

In this regard Ashley Montagu has made the observation that the concept of race has been treated as an omelet, for just as many things are dropped into an omelet, so it is a common practice to average and total racial characteristics (1964a:6). This arbitrary procedure has rendered the omelet concept of race meaningless, simply because it is not applicable to anything in the real world. The only logical conclusion is that the concept of race is a total fabrication. In Montagu's opinion the concept of race is not only artificially created and formalistic, it is also arbitrarily circumscribed and defined (1964b:24-26).

Obviously logic would tell us that instead of starting with the concept of race, whose definition is predetermined, it would be more propitious to study a given population and then arrive at a set of conclusions. For this reason the noncommittal term ethnic group is far more appropriate, since it raises questions and prompts an investigation to discover the facts. Furthermore the term ethnic group encourages the individual to move from a state of ignorance to a position of thoughtful investigation and contemplation of the issues. As a general term, the concept of ethnic group leaves all questions of definition open and available for study (Banton, 1988:30-43).

On the other hand the term race only takes for granted that which remains to be demonstrated and therefore closes the mind to further investigation. Even more important the term race is a value laden word that is bound up in a whole series of emotional responses. In practice the term race is so familiar to us that we take a noncritical perspective and often rely on our own private meaning of the term. The sequence of events in this social psychological process is very interesting (See Figure 1.2).

Chapter Summary

Since the turn of the century the principles and methods of sociology have been used to obtain a better understanding of race relations. To this end sociologists have taken their skills into ethnic communities to observe the relationship between diverse groups of people.

In order for a group to be considered a minority certain characteristics must define the group. The group must have a history of unequal treatment, be physically different, membership must be involuntary, members must practice endogamy, and the minorities must be aware of their subordinate status.

Figure 1.2
From Race to Racism: Sequence of Events

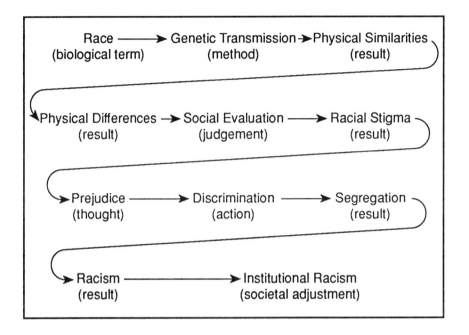

Most sociologists recognize five basic types of minorities: racial groups, ethnic groups, nationality groups, religious groups, and gender groups. While the number of minority groups has remained constant over time, new groups are evolving as a result of the rapid rate of social change.

Minority groups are created in several ways, either by voluntary migration, involuntary migration, political annexation, colonial expansion, or as a result of internal colonialism. Sometimes new minority groups are created as a result of the interaction of two or more of these processes.

It is now established that race is a biological concept and ethnic group is a cultural concept. The use of the term ethnic group forces people to ask questions and results in further investigation, while the term racial group allows people to fall back on their old stereotypes.

References

Banton, Michael
    1988   *Racial Consciousness.* London: Longman.

Blauner, Robert
    1969   "Internal Colonialism and Ghetto Revolt." Social Problems
              16:393-408.

Comstock, Gary D.
    1991   *Violence Against Lesbians and Gay Men.* New York:
              Columbia University Press.

Coser, Lewis A.
    1971   "August Comte 1798-1857". In Lewis Coser (ed.) *Masters of
              Sociological Thought.* New York: Harcourt Brace Jovanovich.

Darwin, Charles
    1958   *On the Origin of Species.* New York: New American Library.

Davis, F. James
    1991   *Who is Black? One Nation's Definition.* University Park, PA:
              Pennsylvania State University Press.

Dominguez, Virginia R.
    1986   *White by Definition: Social Classification in Creole Louisiana.*
              New Brunswick, NJ: Rutgers University Press.

Ehrlich, Paul R. and S. Shirley Feldman
    1977   *The Race Bomb: Skin Color, Prejudice, and Intelligence.*
              New York: Quandrangle.

Faris, Robert E.
    1967   *Chicago Sociology 1920-1932.* Chicago: The University of
              Chicago Press.

Franklin, John Hope
    1967   *From Slavery to Freedom.* New York: Vintage Books.

Frazier, E. Franklin
    1957   *Race and Culture Contacts in the Modern World.* New
              York: Alfred A. Knopf.

Garn, Stanley
    1971   *Human Races.* Springfield, IL: Thomas.

Giddings, Franklin
    1924   *The Scientific Study of Human Society.* Chapel Hill,
              NC: University of North Carolina Press.

Gossett, Thomas F.
    1965   *Race: The History of an Idea in America.* New York:
              Schockenooks.

Herek, Gregory M. (ed.)
1992 *Hate Crimes: Confronting Violence Against Lesbians and Gay Men.* Newbury Park, CA: Sage Publications.

Mohr, Richard D.
1988 *Gays/Justice: A Study of Ethics, Society, and Law.* New York: Columbia University Press.

Montagu, Ashley
1964a "The Concept of Race in the Human Species in the Light of Genetics." In *The Concept of Race.* Ashley Montagu (ed.), London: Collier Books. Pp. 1-11.
1964b "The Concept of Race." In *The Concept of Race.* Ashley Montagu (ed.), London: Collier Books. Pp. 12-28.

Mörner, Magnus
1967 *Race Mixture in the History of Latin America.* Boston: Little, Brown and Company.

Myrdal, Gunnar
1944 *An American Dilemma.* New York: Harper & Row.

Northcott, Clarence H.
1948 "The Sociological Theories of Franklin Henry Giddings." In *An Introduction to the History of Sociology* (Abridged Edition). Harry E. Barnes (ed.), Chicago: The University of Chicago Press.

Peel, John David
1972 *Herbert Spencer on Social Evolution.* Chicago: The University of Chicago Press.

Sickels, Robert J.
1972 *Race, Marriage and the Law.* Albuquerque, NM: The University of New Mexico Press.

Spencer, Herbert
1896 *The Principles of Sociology.* New York: Appleton.

Thompson, Richard H.
1989 *Theories of Ethnicity: A Critical Appraisal.* New York: Greenwood Press.

Wagley, Charles and Marvin Harris
1958 *Minorities in the New World: Six Case Studies.* New York: Columbia University Press.

Zenner, Walter P.
1991 *Minorities in the Middle: A Cross-Cultural Analysis.* Albany, NY: State University of New York Press.

Zinn, Howard
1980 *A People's History of the United States.* New York: Harper & Row.

Important Names

Robert Blauner	Ernest W. Burgess	August Comte
Charles Darwin	Franklin Giddings	Thomas Jefferson
Ashley Montagu	Gunnar Myrdal	Robert E. Park
Benjamin Rush	Herbert Spencer	

Key Terms

concentric circles	ethnic enclaves	soft spot
natural areas	prejudice	discrimination
segregation	racism	sexism
xenophobia	homophobia	vicious circle
labeling theory of race	endogamy	ascribed status
cumulative causation	exogamy	stigma of race
self-fulfilling prophesy	passing	tangible culture
involuntary membership	Racial Group	Ethnic Group
anti-miscegenation laws	Nationality Group	Religious Group
consciousness of kind	Gender Group	gene pool
double jeopardy	safety-net	Voluntary Migration
Involuntary Migration	Political Annexation	Colonial Expansion
Internal Colonialism	indentured servants	Treaty of Paris
survival of the fittest	natural selection	Genetic View
laissez-faire economics	Environmental Theory	Monoginist Theory
Polygynist Theory	Religious View	Concatenated Theory
Anatomical View	Treaty of Guadalupe Hidalgo	

1. List five characteristics of a minority group, and provide a brief description of each.
2. List and provide a brief description and one example of five types of minority groups.
3. What role did Charles Darwin and Herbert Spencer play in the development of the "concept of race."
4. Provide a brief discussion of five ways in which minority groups are created.
5. Provide four characteristics of the internal colonial model.
6. Discuss four major contributions that Robert Park and Ernest Burgess made to our understanding of race relations in America.

Chapter 2

The Nature of Prejudice and Discrimination

The Definition of Prejudice

Prejudice refers to any unfavorable or negative attitude directed toward any person or group based on a set of assumed characteristics. Therefore prejudice exists when any hostile attitude is directed toward a particular individual or group. Prejudice is a universal phenomenon and occurs in all societies. No one is free of prejudice.

Prejudice is usually based on a hostile or negative attitude toward a minority person held by a member of the majority group. Although prejudice occurs in both minority and majority groups and can be directed from one group toward the other, the social consequences of prejudice are more deleterious when held and acted upon by members of the majority group. This relationship prevails since the majority group has the power to act upon their negative attitudes and beliefs. But on the other hand, it would be fallacious to believe that the majority group has a monopoly on prejudice.

While prejudice is an individual characteristic reflecting certain psychological and social needs, it also reflects the values of society. Therefore while prejudice is the result of the socialization process, it is also a significant part of our immediate social environment and an intrinsic characteristic of the society in which we live. Prejudicial attitudes are often held by the individual because they are the result of social expectations and tend to support the status quo. In brief, prejudice is maintained because it,

1. is a part of the conventional morality of society,
2. upholds and supports the self-respect of the individual and society,
3. maintains cultural, ethnic, and racial differences in society and allows for categorization of groups,
4. is often based on irrational fear (xenophobia),

5. is sometimes based on envy, which sometimes result in ingroup conflict and violence,
6. is usually learned in the formative years and can be learned when the victims of prejudice are absent,
7. is often the result of competition between groups,
8. is sometimes supported by the social and legal institutions of society,
9. is based on power, that is the subjugation of one group by another (Perlmutter, 1992:20-45).

Prejudice is strongly associated with any negative or hostile attitudes that a person may have against another person or group of individuals because of some perceived or assumed differences based on (1) race, (2) ethnic origin, (3) religious identification, (4) gender, (5) social class, (6) age, or (7) sexual orientation. Prejudice is often based on inaccurate information or inflexible generalizations.

In sum, prejudice is most likely to occur among those individuals who are (1) rigid in their thinking, (2) ignorant of racial and ethnic differences, and (3) are unwilling to accept those who are different from themselves. The likelihood of changing a prejudiced person is difficult because prejudice is often a rigid attitude that the prejudiced person will defend at all costs.

Characteristics of Prejudice

One of the primary reasons that prejudice is such a strongly held attitude is that is makes life less complicated and therefore easier to manage. But more important, prejudicial attitudes are maintained because people who cling to these beliefs are rewarded for their negative attitudes and hostile feelings. According to Gordon Allport (1954), the persistence and tenacity of prejudice is based on five characteristics that serve to perpetuate negative attitudes: (1) over-categorization, (2) misconceptions, (3) prejudgments, (4) rationalization, and (5) value judgements.

Over-Categorization

Over-categorization is based on the methodological fallacy of inductive reasoning. This simply means that a person takes one example, or one experience, and then generalizes that experience to all the members of a particular group. The psychological error that is committed in over-categorization is simply that the individual, either consciously or unconsciously, applies the unique characteristics of one individual to a whole group of related individuals. In the process the person is guilty of judging group behavior, or the characteristics of a whole group, on the observations made of one individual from that group. As an example, over-categorization occurs when someone draws the conclusion that one individual is shiftless and lazy and then assumes that all members of that group are also shiftless and lazy. It is obvious that over-categorization represents a simplification of the facts. And it is this very characteristic of over simplification that makes the persistence of prejudicial attitudes convenient. If people are willing to hold onto such sweeping generalizations, then life in a multi-cultural world is greatly simplified.

Misconceptions

Misconceptions occur when people make a mistake in the organization of their facts. Essentially this means that a prejudicial attitude is based on the organization of erroneous information, which serves to mislead our thinking. For example, if we believe that people living in a certain area of the city are naturally prone to violence, then we would be guilty of judging a whole group based on erroneous information. However, if people are willing to rectify their erroneous perceptions in the light of new information or facts, then they are not prejudiced.

Prejudgments

When a person evaluates the characteristics of an individual or a group before all the facts are in, then that person is guilty of making a prejudgment. In application this occurs when a person is willing to form an opinion about a group and is willing to act on that opinion before all the facts are known. This reaction is most likely to occur in those situations where a person receives information about a particular minority group from a third party. An important distinction is that while prejudice is based on a prejudgment, not all prejudgments are based on prejudice.

Prejudgments are only one aspect of prejudice if our opinions about a minority are based on strongly held personal views to which we are emotionally attached and are unwilling to change or abandon. Sometimes people will maintain their prejudicial attitudes even when confronted with new or contradictory information. However, if people are willing to correct or adjust their attitudes based on new information, then they do not have an irrational attachment to their prejudicial beliefs.

Rationalization

Rationalization occurs when people make every effort to integrate new or contradictory facts into their old ways of thinking. This means that a prejudiced individual can maintain their hostile and negative attitudes toward a minority group while they simultaneously absorb new or contradictory information. For example, if a person believes that members of a particular ethnic group are bad drivers, but then discovers that the data on highway accidents does not support this belief and they fit this new (but contradictory) information into their established prejudice, then they are guilty of rationalization.

Rationalization represents the determined effort by the bigot to maintain an old prejudice in spite of new evidence or contradictory information. In their daily lives confirmed bigots can absorb new information that would otherwise render their prejudices erroneous and make this new information fit into their overall prejudicial attitude. In this regard rationalization is often a sign of a very insecure person. For these individuals fear that their whole world of negativity and hostility will collapse around them if they ever allow the slightest bit of contradictory information into their conception of the world.

Value Judgments

It is universally true that every person has a set of value judgment by which they make decisions regarding what is right and what is wrong. A value judgment is a personal statement about what is desirable or worth while. The problem with value judgments occurs when they force a person into holding rigid attitudes, when they succumb to narrow thinking, and when they rely on dogmatism. Value judgments should be avoided since they exclude or obscure the facts. For the prejudiced individual value judgments have a profound effect on their perception of social and cultural diversity in society.

Theories of Prejudice

A fundamental characteristic of prejudice is that it is pervasive throughout society and every member of society is affected by it. Prejudice is unavoidable because it is learned in the family, within our peer groups, and in the general society.

In an effort to understand the origins and tenacity of prejudice sociologists have developed several theories regarding the existence and persistence of prejudice. While there are dozens of theories that attempt to explain the pervasiveness of prejudice in society, there are five basic theoretical approaches that serve as the basis for our understanding of prejudice, namely:

1. The Exploitation Theory
2. The Scapegoating Theory
3. The Authoritarian Personality Theory
4. The Ecological Theory
5. The Linguistic Theory

The Exploitation Theory

The exploitation theory is most likely to take hold in those societies where there is a significant disparity in the power relationship between the majority group and various minority groups. This theory is applicable when one group dominates and takes advantage of another. It requires that the selected inferior groups in the society must be kept in their proper place and they must bend their will to the needs and desires of the dominant group. This relationship creates tension and conflict between the majority and minority groups in society. Karl Marx viewed this as the systematic economic exploitation of the working classes.

Marx believed that the pervasiveness of prejudice in society was used by the capitalist to keep certain groups in subordinate positions. Of greater importance for capitalist societies is the fact that prejudice (1) serves to justify the exploitation of minorities, (2) it makes minorities feel inferior, and (3) it keeps minorities in their place.

In this regard Marx recognized that the exploitation of the working classes and class conflict guaranteed the success of capitalism. He believed that prejudice would serve to divide the working classes and create conflict between them. These hostile racial feelings between the working classes would then allow their employers to play one group off against the other. Because of the strong prejudicial attitudes within the working classes employers could always use the threat of hiring another group of workers who would be willing to work for less as a means of keeping wages at their lowest possible level. In sum, employers realized that maintaining a high level of prejudice in the work place was profitable for their businesses (Bonacich, 1990:197-200).

Another advantage to the employers in maintaining a high level of prejudice in the work place, according to Marx, was that it greatly reduced the possibility that these workers would cooperate and organize themselves to improve their wages and working conditions. Prejudice and conflict between the workers also meant that one group could always be brought into the labor market during a strike and thereby prevent unions from using their most effective bargaining chip.

The use of prejudice to maintain class conflict in American society has a long and troubled history. For example, the exploitation of slaves found strong support and justification among white landowners, who reaped enormous profits from their free labor. The attitude that slaves were inferior to whites served as a justification for their exploitation (Banton, 1983). Similarly the view of the Chinese as coolie labor served as a justification for their exploitation. And the introduction of Korean, Filipino, and Mexican farm workers into California at the turn of the century insured conflict in

31

the fields. Today the prejudice that many Americans hold toward undocumented Mexicans insures employers of a continuous source of cheap labor.

Scapegoating Theory

Scapegoating occurs when someone places blame for their problems on some convenient, but powerless and innocent person or group. The scapegoating theory holds that those who are unwilling to accept personal blame for their misfortunes will find another person or group to blame for their problems. Obviously they are unwilling to accept their personal shortcomings. A good example of scapegoating occurred shortly after the Chinese arrived in San Francisco, when unemployed Irish immigrants took out their frustrations on the powerless Chinese laborers, whom the Irish blamed for their economic hard times. Similarly people are quick to blame undocumented workers for the lack of jobs and the low wages that are offered in certain industries today.

The term scapegoating is derived from the practice among the ancient Hebrews who observed an annual ritual of symbolically placing all their sins on a goat, who was then driven out into the wilderness. This purification rite served to rejuvenate the moral and religious health of the Jewish community.

A closely related theory is the frustration-aggression hypothesis, proposed by John Dollard (1937). Dollard suggested that the frustration-aggression hypothesis served to explain the psycho-dynamics of scapegoating. Essentially his theory held that when individuals are frustrated in their attempts to achieve a strongly desired goal, they tend to become aggressive. If they cannot retaliate against the source of their frustration, either because they cannot identify the source of their frustration, the source is considered too powerful, or they fear the consequences, then they will direct their growing frustration at some weaker or less threatening person or object. From the psychological perspective prejudice is considered a form of aggression and is viewed as a universal response to frustration.

Therefore when the efforts of a group to reach a specific goal are frustrated, they are likely to respond with aggression. However, when the source of their frustration is too powerful to attack, then a substitute is found. History reveals that from time to time various minorities were targets of frustration and were the victims of aggression and violence. The best known example of this was the mass extermination of the Jews in Nazi Germany. Hitler used the Jews as scapegoats for all the social ills of pre-war Germany.

Authoritarian Personality

A well known approach to the study of prejudice in American society is the authoritarian personality studies. While the personality approach to the study of prejudice began in German during the early 1930's, it was not systematically studied until the end of the Second World War. In view of the horrors of Nazi Germany, social scientists were particularly interested in understanding the basis for strongly held prejudicial attitudes and the development of racial hatred.

The hallmark of these postwar studies dealing with the origins of prejudice appeared in the publication of *The Authoritarian Personality* in 1950. Theodore Adorno, the principal author of this study, and his colleagues at the University of California administered more than 2,000 interviews and psychological tests and found that approximately ten percent of all Americans revealed strong authoritarian characteristics. Thirty percent demonstrated a strong propensity for authoritarianism.

At the conclusion of their massive study they found that the authoritarian personality is represented by a personality type noted for (1) extreme conformity, (2) rigid thinking, (3) superstition, (4) toughness, (5) suppression of emotions, (6) strong adherence to convention, (7) submissiveness to authority, and (8) arrogance toward those whom they considered inferior. They found that authoritarians are very insecure and seek security in social hierarchies and in strong identification with the group. They were also very ethnocentric, that is adamant in the belief that the values and goals of their group were the best and judged all other groups by the standards of their group.

It is curious that the authoritarian personality is shaped by fear of authority. Today psychologists believe that this personality type develops in a highly structured and disciplinary relationship between parent and child. A domineering father who makes harsh demands and arbitrary decisions in his relationship with his child is also a key characteristic of this personality type. Physical punishment and rigid rules of behavior dominate the child's environment. Therefore any children reared in such a strict family environment will likely respond to all persons in authority as if those people were their parents.

As adults they are likely to refine these authoritarian characteristics. They are quick to treat everyone whom they perceive as inferior with distrust and disdain. They also rank high on Adorno's "F-scale" (Fascism scale), a psychological test used to measure levels of personal prejudice against others. A high score on the F-scale demonstrates a high correlation with anti-Semitic attitudes.

The Ecological Theory

The ecological theory holds that the immediate social environment has a direct impact on peoples attitudes and perceptions. Therefore if a person lives in surroundings where prejudice is part and parcel of everyday social intercourse, then they are likely to share prejudicial attitudes, political perspectives, religious beliefs, and life goals.

An excellent example of this phenomenon was observed by Thomas Pettigrew (1959), who observed that whites in the South were more prejudiced against Blacks, than whites in the North were. But his most interesting finding was that when Southern students moved North to attend college they accepted the more liberal attitudes of their fellow Northern students as their own. On the other hand, when Northern students transferred to Southern universities, they very quickly accepted the more prejudicial attitudes of their Southern classmates.

In their ground breaking research in social ecology Deutsch and Collins (1951) studied the relationship between residential location and the development and perpetuation of prejudicial attitudes. As hypothesized, they found that the immediate housing environment and the racial attitudes that existed in either segregated public housing units or in integrated units had a very dramatic effect on the level of prejudice exhibited by these groups. One of their most salient findings was that if integrated housing and social equality was promoted by those in authority, then the level of prejudice was significantly reduced. However, if segregation was allowed and those in authority did not play a leadership role in promoting racial harmony, then the groups tended to maintain a high level of suspicion and hostility toward one another.

A more specific application of the ecological theory is the observation that racial attitudes are not only affected by regional differences, but also by organizational membership. This would include membership in segregated social, community, civic, recreational, and business organizations. These organizations have a profound effect on people's social, political, and racial attitudes.

Just as private organizations affect a person's racial attitudes, it is also true that the work environment has a significant impact on the maintenance of prejudicial attitudes. For this reason the expression of prejudicial attitudes and the willingness to discriminate are situation specific, that is people may express prejudicial attitudes and discriminate in one situation, but will not do so in another situation. Most bigots will select a safe place to discriminate. African Americans, in particular, are very much aware of this closet bigotry (Sigelman and Welch, 1991:47-66).

For example, individuals may not express prejudicial attitudes at work for fear of the negative sanctions that will follow. But they may be very prejudiced among their close friends. In reality some environments allow for, and even encourage the expression of prejudicial attitudes, while others do not. The reason for this difference is that our involvement in various organizations does not involve our total self or personality. Usually people are very selective about revealing their prejudices. It is also true that people will tolerate a certain level of prejudice in one situation, but are not so tolerant in another (Bethlehem, 1985:136-167).

The Linguistic Theory

The linguistic theory is based on the premise that our language and cultural environment have a direct impact on our way of thinking and affects the development of our ideas and opinions. Edward Sapir (1921) and Benjamin Whorf are the researchers who developed the linguistic theory and promoted the renown, Sapir-Whorf hypothesis. At its essence the Sapir-Whorf hypothesis holds that the language we use is more than just a medium for interpersonal communication, but more importantly by learning a language we also develop a framework for interpreting social reality. As a result language plays a very significant role in determining the social reality that we know and experience (Deutscher, 1973).

The significance of language is that it serves as a symbolic representation of our consciousness, for without symbols it would be impossible to form ideas and opinions. Therefore if the language and the symbols that we use in everyday life foster prejudice, then it becomes very difficult to change our attitudes and opinions about other people. In order to address the issue of prejudice in our everyday lives we must consider the language and the symbols that we use and the meaning that they have for us. A basic check is to consider the types of ethnic slurs or sexist remarks that we use in our daily conversations that are part of our linguistic repertoire.

The integration of ethnic slurs and disparaging remarks in our repertoire is known as an ethnophaulism. Even the use of essentially neutral words in our conversations sometimes has positive or negative connotations. The symbols that are conveyed by our words are very important in sorting out and eliminating prejudicial attitudes from our own lives. For example, the word "black" has historically conveyed a negative connotation, as witches are black, death is associated with the color black, evil magic is black magic, and when someone is ostracized we often say they are blacklisted or blackballed. On the other hand the color white has always had positive connotations, such as in purity, bridal gowns, and even in soap (Moore, 1988:269-279). Similarly Asians have been portrayed as yellow people, which has the negative connotation of being a coward, tricky, or untrustworthy (Moore, 1988:270-271). Women have also had to deal with negative appellations, such as, girl, broad, sister, chick, fox, and even bitch (Baker, 1988:280-295).

The Sapir-Whorf hypothesis holds that the connotation of words become a part of our cultural environment. Therefore our attitudes and opinions are affected by our use of particular words to describe certain groups or by our association of specific words with certain negative characteristics or experiences. Today we can think of words that are commonly used to describe either male or female characteristics. An evaluation of the words that we use to describe men and women reveals that we tend to use words that have positive connotations when referring to men and words that have negative connotations when we talk about women.

Stereotypes and Prejudice

The ability to sustain prejudicial attitudes over a long period of time is a reflection of an individual's dependence on stereotypes, which is a characteristic of prejudiced thinking. For without stereotypes, prejudice cannot exist. Stereotypes refer to any set of biased generalization about an individual or group that are (1) unfavorable, (2) exaggerated, and (3) oversimplified.

Stereotypes are mnemonic devices since they allow the individual to sort people into certain slots based on a set of preconceived notions. While the use of stereotypes can make life less complicated, there are a number of serious problems with the use of stereotypes. Stereotypes can lead to many pitfalls, because they can (1) mislead us with false conceptions, (2) are often based on negative or biased information, (3) are emotionally anchored, (4) are difficult to change (even in the light of new information), and (5) they are easily adopted into our personality and psychological make-up (Stroebe and Insko, 1989:4-30). Even though a person may realize that their stereotypes are incorrect or baseless, they are nonetheless maintained because they represent the shared beliefs of the community (Pettigrew, 1982:7-14).

The first scientific studies of stereotypes were conducted in the early 1930s by David Katz and Kenneth Braly. Katz and Braly asked 100 Princeton undergraduates to list the most distinctive personality traits of Jews. The Jewish stereotypes that appeared with the greatest frequency were these: shrewd, mercenary, industrious, grasping, intelligent, ambitious, and sly. What was most revealing was that most students had never even met a Jewish person. This finding demonstrates that stereotypes are simply just pictures in our head. Almost twenty years later this study was replicated among students at the University of California and the results were very similar (Centers, 1951; Gilbert, 1951). The same results were also obtained in a replication of the study in 1967 (Karlins, et al., 1969).

The interesting thing about stereotypes is that they change over time. For example, the Chinese were described as superstitious and sly by one-third of the Princeton students in 1933, but only seven percent of the students in a replication study, conducted 34 years later, expressed these opinions (Karlins, 1969, et al.). Stereotypes held about Jews, Blacks, and Mexicans were also modified over the same period.

Since these early studies the relationship between prejudice and stereotypes has been examined in great detail and it is now clear that stereotypes have five basic characteristics:

1. Stereotypes are Self-Fulfilling

   Because the social structure allows little room for change in the lives of some minorities, their lives become very predictable. For example this is true of the poor, who have limited lifestyle options. Therefore their daily lives are monotonous and predictable and are often self-fulfilling.

2. Stereotypes are Based on Selective Perception

   Once a person accepts the credibility of a stereotype, they create a mind-set and search for characteristics that fit the original stereotype for that particular group. For these reasons stereotypes often become self-fulfilling prophecies.

3. Stereotypes are often Negative

   Historically when stereotypes are associated with racial and ethnic groups they are usually negative. This is the reason that the maintenance of stereotypes supports prejudicial attitudes.

4. Stereotypes Result in Rejection and Social Isolation

   Since stereotypes are often negative, they encourage a policy of avoidance and rejection, which leads to social isolation. In practice a strong belief in a stereotype causes people to alter their behavior. This results in rejection and social isolation of the group that is stereotyped, since we no longer want to associate with individuals from that group.

5. Stereotypes are Based on a Kernel of Truth

   Sometimes stereotypes are created and are accepted because they are based on a kernel of truth. Sometimes an anomalous characteristic of the group is selected and then projected to all members of that group. For example, the belief that some women in the women's movement are lesbians is often generalized to all women in the National Organization for Women.

Measuring Prejudice

In their book, *Introduction to the Science of Sociology*, Park and Burgess (1921) introduced the concept of social distance. They used the term to describe the tendency of people to avoid those whom they perceived as different from themselves and they also observed that the greater the distance between two groups, the greater the likelihood they would develop avoidance behavior. But it was Emory Bogardus (1925), a sociology professor at the University of Southern California, who designed an elaborate research plan to study the relationship between social distance and prejudice.

The social distance scale developed by Bogardus represents the first serious attempt to measure the strength and tenacity of prejudice. His original scale consisted of sixty statements about which people were asked to express an opinion on how willing they would be to interact with a variety of racial and ethnic groups in American society. Each social situation depicted by these statements described varying degrees of social distance, that is intimacy, that existed between diverse ethnic groups. In all 39 ethnic and racial groups were included on his list, from Armenians to Greeks, Hindus to Jews, Mexicans to Russians, etc. (Bogardus, 1925, 1933, 1968).

In all Bogardus used sixty statements in his original study. He arranged the items on the scale in a descending order of intimacy or closeness, thereby providing an ever increasing level of social distance. He asked each respondent to express an opinion whether they would be willing to interact with each of the 39 groups listed in his survey. A sample of some of his survey statements are provided below (not all statements are listed):

1. Would be willing to marry.
2. Would be willing to have my son or daughter marry.
3. Would have a minority in my social club or fraternity.
4. Would have as my regular friends.
5. Would have merely as speaking acquaintances.
6. Would entertain overnight in my home.
7. Would allow one family, only of their group, to live in my city block.
8. Would debar from my neighborhood.
9. Would take as my guests at church.
10. Would have as my teachers (Bogardus, 1933).

Based on his results Bogardus was able to determine with statistical accuracy the groups that his respondents were willing to have contact with and those they preferred to avoid. Those groups with whom they were willing to have close or intimate contact with were perceived as being of an equal or higher status than they themselves had. It was also clear that the more willing they were to have contact with a group, the lower their level of prejudice toward that group (Bethlehem, 1985:202-204; Ehrlich, 1973:71-80).

Richard LaPiere (1934) also designed a study to investigate the nature of prejudice in the early 1930's. As the focus of his research LaPiere traveled throughout the United States with a Chinese couple in an attempt to measure the reaction of merchants to their appearance. Despite the harsh racial climate of the day, LaPiere found that in all but one of the 251 establishments where they were guests, the owners of the restaurants and hotels that they visited were very courteous toward them. This positive treatment of his Asian companions caused LaPiere to wonder why they did not experience any obvious prejudice or discrimination.

When LaPiere returned home he sent questionaires to each establishment they had visited, to inquire if they would be willing to accept a Chinese couple as guests. To his surprise ninety percent said they would not, although they had already visited each of the businesses he had contacted. He concluded that there was a clear distinction between having a prejudicial attitude and acting upon that prejudice when involved in face-to-face contact (Linn, 1965).

Types of Discrimination

Discrimination occurs when an act or behavior excludes specific individuals from certain rights, opportunities, or privileges. Therefore discrimination is an act that results in the unequal treatment of an individual or a group based on race, ethnicity, religion, gender, sexual orientation, age, or social class.

Discrimination can take two forms: it can either appear as individual discrimination or as institutional discrimination. When individuals act upon their prejudices, this is known as individual discrimination, or active racism. However, when an institution or an organization discriminates against minorities, this is called institutional discrimination or more appropriately as institutional racism.

The term institutional racism was introduced by Carmichael and Hamilton (1967) in their book, *Black Power*. In their analysis of race relations they used the term institutional racism to describe all acts of discrimination committed against an entire group that have the support of existing laws and social policies. This simply means that discrimination in society is sometimes given official sanction and is supported by the laws of the state or the official policies of an organization.

By definition discrimination means that certain individuals or groups are treated one way, while others are treated another way. The ability to give an individual or group a preference or an advantage, means that discrimination is usually an act of unequal treatment practiced by someone who has the power to discriminate against those who are powerless. The relationship between power and the occurrence of discrimination is a universal phenomenon since only those who can make decisions over the lives of others can practice discrimination.

When discrimination occurs it is based on an existing prejudice, since discrimination is the tangible expression of prejudice. However, it is possible for a person to discriminate without being prejudiced and it is also possible to be prejudiced without discriminating. But when prejudice is acted upon it is transformed into discrimination and this means that the victims of discrimination will experience some negative consequences.

Discrimination is well known to all minorities as it affects them each day of their lives. The interest in the study of discrimination is related to the fact that unequal treatment and the deprivation of opportunities is so clear and the impact is so immediate that it cannot be ignored. Therefore it is instructive to focus on the best known examples of discrimination, these include, (1) economic, (2) labor market, (3) educational, (4) housing, and (5) sex discrimination.

Economic Discrimination

Economic discrimination occurs when laws, public policies, or corporate policies have a differential impact on certain groups that put them at an economic disadvantage. The most blatant form of economic discrimination occurs in the determination of the wage structure. All the economic studies to date demonstrate that minorities and women have suffered, and continue to suffer, from a wage gap differential. This simply means that minorities and women are paid less for doing the same type of work. Because of wage discrimination women typically receive about sixty percent of the wages that men receive for doing the same type of work. African American and Latino workers also suffer from the wage gap differential.

The nation's banking and mortgage institutions are also guilty of economic discrimination. Historically these financial institutions have viewed women and minorities as bad credit risks. For example, economic discrimination is likely to occur when minorities apply for home loans, since mortgage companies are very reluctant to finance homes in certain neighborhoods. In the past few years some major banks and mortgage companies have been convicted of red-lining. Red-lining occurs when lending institutions carve out certain sections of the city where they refuse to make home loans. These are usually areas of the city that are known for their heavy concentration of African Americans and Latinos, as they are considered bad credit risks, and these neighborhoods are considered bad investments.

The need for automobile, home, and life insurance also places minorities at a severe economic disadvantage. Various studies of the insurance industry have demonstrated that African Americans and Latinos usually pay more for all their insurance needs. One of the most abusive practices by the insurance industry is their policy of setting automobile insurance rates according to the zip code areas. Therefore the rates that minorities pay for auto insurance are keyed to the high rate areas of the city. Sometimes minorities pay fifty to a hundred percent more for their automobile insurance. The auto insurance burden is even more severe on those minorities who live in states that mandate auto insurance for all drivers (Gonzales, 1991).

The very same discriminatory policies are used by insurance companies in setting their rates for home insurance policies for minorities. Again the insurance premiums are always higher in designated minority neighborhoods. The working assumption is that minorities must pay more since they are often concentrated in the less desirable areas of the city (Yinger, 1978).

Institutional racism also occurs in the multi-million dollar life insurance industry. The discrimination that occurs against African American men is particularly blatant and abusive, since they have classified them as a high risk category. The result of these policies is that African American men not only find it difficult to secure life insurance coverage but they also discover that their premiums are higher than they would be for a white male of similar age, health, and socioeconomic status.

Examples of economic discrimination also can be found when minorities shop for the necessities of life. Various studies conducted by consumer groups across the country have found that supermarket prices are always higher in ethnic neighborhoods for comparable products purchased in the more affluent areas of the city. Even the same products purchased at the same chain store located in the two different neighborhoods reveal that the poor pay more for their food. Since many chain stores have abandoned these ethnic neighborhoods, minorities are often forced to purchase their grocery items at convenient stores or in local mom and pop markets. It is also a well known fact that these stores always charge a premium for their products. Low income families living in these neighborhoods have no alternative but to pay higher prices, since many do not have cars and taking public transportation to the nearest supermarket is impractical. One study of this economic problem concluded that African Americans living in the inner cities were the victims of a prison economy, for just like prisoners their physical mobility is restricted and their consumer options are very limited (Alexis, et al., 1980:93).

Labor Market Discrimination

Even though the hiring practices of employers are carefully scrutinized to insure that they comply with government regulations regarding anti-discrimination provisions, it is still true that not all employers follow the rules and regulations. In fact, the best examples of the long term effects of institutional racism are most apparent in the hiring practices of employers. One of the first areas of hiring discrimination can be seen in the role of employers as gate keepers, in that they always have the option of applying certain rules and regulations as they see fit. This results in blatant acts of discrimination in the labor market.

In view of the high unemployment rates and the depressed economy today, the labor market can best be described as an employer's marketplace. The primary reason that employers have the advantage is the simple fact that there are more people looking for work than there are jobs. Consequently employers can be very selective in whom they hire. Under these conditions they can raise the hiring standards for all their positions, especially for entry level jobs. One result of raising the standards beyond the actual job requirements is that the advertised requirements for the job are not always consistent with the tasks that need to be performed. The second major impact of these hiring policies is that many people who would otherwise qualify for the job are eliminated from the competition. In the end, exaggerated job requirements simply serve as screening devices to eliminate certain people from the initial application process.

Other examples of these measures are educational requirements that exceed the actual level of knowledge or skills required for the job, such as requiring a two year degree for a gardener's position. Sometimes employers require excessively long periods of previous experience on the job, this is the continuous employment snag. Employers are also prone to write very specific job descriptions for a particular position. The problem with this is that only those who are already working in that specific office or operation will be eligible to apply for the position. This tactic is often found in those inside hire situations where the new position is tailor made for a person who is already working for the company. When this tactic is used it allows employers to advertise the availability of the position and meet all the affirmative action guidelines and still hire the person that they intended to hire in the first place. In these situations it is not uncommon to find that a few minorities are always invited for job interviews, just so the employer can comply with federal affirmative action laws.

In the end, minorities are adversely affected by these discriminatory hiring practices. These hiring policies are discriminatory because they automatically eliminate a higher proportion of African American and Latino applicants from the qualified labor pool. Employers realize that even if they only require a high school diploma for a particular job, this will automatically eliminate half the Latino applicants and about forty percent of the African American applicants, while only affecting 20 to 25 percent of the white applicants. If employers require a two-year college degree, then the impact on these minorities increases exponentially.

The tactic of requiring several years of on the job experience is another way that employers can eliminate minority applicants. This tactic places many minorities in a "Catch 22" situation, that is since they are barred from certain jobs they will never have the opportunity to establish a continuous record of employment. The employer's position is, "Why discriminate, when you can eliminate?"

The Split Labor Market Theory

A theory that explains the relationship between the needs of the labor market, the competitive nature of American society, and its system of racial stratification is known as the split labor market theory. This theory was introduced in the early seventies to explain the relationship between wages, working conditions, and the segmentation of the labor market on the basis of racial discrimination (Bonacich, 1972). According to this theory the labor market consists of two segments: the primary labor market and the secondary labor market.

42

The primary labor market is recognized for offering better working conditions, higher wages, a variety of benefit packages and vacation plans, various profit-sharing and retirement programs, and employees are usually represented by a collective bargaining contract. In contrast those individuals who are employed in the secondary labor market are payed at a lower rate, receive minimal benefits, their working conditions are less desirable, rarely receive retirement or pension plans, are only allowed one or two weeks of vacation per year, are not represented by a union, and suffer from periodic unemployment. Consequently their opportunities for social mobility are very limited. It is also important to note that many minorities are concentrated in the secondary labor market, while the primary labor market remains predominantly white.

Obviously the American labor market is highly segmented by race and ethnicity, as certain occupations are monopolized by whites and others are recognized for their over-representation of minorities. Secondary labor market jobs tend to be low paying, dead-end jobs, with the result that the life chances of minorities who are concentrated in these jobs are very limited. And by its very nature the secondary labor market limits their access to the opportunity structure. Those who are employed in the secondary labor market will experience periodic layoffs, work long hours for low wages, and will probably never qualify for a home mortgage. In addition, they are more likely to suffer a serious injury on the job and will never build up a retirement program.

The reason minorities spend their lives working in these low paying dead-end jobs is that they have no other options and the tactics used by employers to eliminate them from the primary labor market are also used by the gate keepers to insure that only a few minorities will escape the consequences of the secondary labor market. Clearly, those minorities who are employed in the secondary labor market serve as a source of cheap labor. Marx referred to them as the surplus labor force, as they serve to keep the competition for these jobs at a high pitch and they maintain a continuous downward pressure on wages (Jiobu, 1990:163-187).

A careful analysis of the labor market today reveals that there is a third, or tertiary labor market (Gonzales, 1984). In the tertiary labor market employees are paid at or below the minimum wage and they lack job security. They are often hired on a daily basis, work in unsafe conditions, and their civil rights are often ignored. Tertiary labor market conditions usually flourish in the assembly line industries, sweat shops, and in the agricultural industry. These jobs are recognized for their high concentration of undocumented aliens.

Because of the cheap labor that is available in the tertiary labor market employers accumulate enormous profits and American consumers also benefit because they pay far less for their essentials, such as food, clothing, labor markets in the American economy is very instructive (See Figure 2.1).

43

Figure 2.1
The Split Labor Market

Comparative Variable	Primary Labor Market	Secondary Labor Market	Tertiary Labor Market
Wages (1993)	$15-$30 Per Hr	$6-$12 Per Hr	$4-$6 Per Hr
Working Conditions	Very Safe	Unsafe	Unsafe-Dangerous
Medical Benefits	Many	Very Few	No Benefits
Vacations	2-5 Weeks	1-2 Weeks	No Vacations
Labor Organization	Unionized	Non-Union	Non-Union
Educational Opportunities	Sponsored	Very Limited	None Available
Job Promotions	Open-Many	Very Few	None Available
Job Security	Guaranteed	Little Security	Hired by the Day
Labor Rights	Labor Contract	Very Limited	Widely Ignored
Retirement	Excellent Benefits	Minimum Support	No Plan

When the characteristics of each of these labor markets are compared, it is unmistakable that the level of exploitation increases as one moves from the primary to the tertiary labor market. It is also apparent that a move from the top of the labor market to the bottom results in a higher concentration of minorities. Therefore minorities are not only over-represented in the secondary and tertiary labor markets, they are systematically channeled into these less desirable jobs.

Educational Discrimination

In 1954 the Supreme Court ruled in *Brown v. the Board of Education* that it is illegal to distinguish among racial groups for purposes of institutional discrimination in public schools. The Court also ruled that separate educational institutions were inherently unequal and by definition discriminatory. Despite the high Court's ruling public schools remained highly segregated throughout the sixties and the seventies. To this day, almost forty years after the Court's decision, most of the nation's schools remain segregated (Meier, et al., 1989:49-57). The history of American education reveals that segregated schools produce a substandard educational experience for minority students (Meier, et al., 1989:108-135).

Another serious problem facing the nation's education system is the inordinately high drop-out rate among minority students. If the number of students who graduate from high school today is any indication of the success of public education, then we can only conclude that the system has failed to provide a quality educational experience for minorities (See Table 2.1).

Table 2.1
High School Completion Rates Among
Anglos, African Americans, and Latinos
1975-1991

Year	Total	Anglos	African Americans	Latinos
1975*	81.9	83.6	67.5	53.4
1976	82.3	83.6	71.4	51.5
1977	83.6	84.9	72.0	56.2
1978	84.6	85.9	74.4	55.0
1979	85.0	86.3	74.7	54.3
1980	85.4	86.7	76.4	56.1
1981	85.9	86.8	78.6	54.9
1982	86.3	87.3	79.7	56.6
1983	86.7	87.6	80.2	57.5
1984	86.8	87.9	79.9	58.9
1985	86.3	87.2	80.7	59.4
1986**	74.7	76.2	62.3	48.4
1987	75.7	76.9	63.5	50.9
1988	76.2	77.6	63.4	50.9
1989	76.9	78.4	64.6	51.0
1991	78.4	79.9	66.7	51.3

* Ages 25 to 34 (1975 to 1985)
** Persons 25 and over (1986 to 1991)
Source: U.S Census, Statistical Abstract, 1976-1992

With fewer minority students completing high school it is no surprise to discover that even a smaller number are going on to college. And the number of those who apply for college and are rejected is well above the national average. This reflects the lack of preparation that many minority students receive in the secondary schools and the fact that even those who graduate from high school are ill prepared for college. Their low college admission rate also can be attributed to the biased admission tests that filter out many minority applicants (Fraga, et al., 1986).

Housing Discrimination

The history of urbanization in America is also the history of housing segregation, for as our nation became more urbanized, it also became more segregated. According to all the housing studies, America is more segregated today than ever before (Draden, 1986). The very high level of residential segregation today demonstrates that the anti-discrimination laws in housing are ineffective (Jiobu, 1988:107-148). Residential segregation is the norm in American society today as it is not uncommon to find African American families with above average incomes living in areas where the property values are far below what would be expected statistically (Gonzales, 1988; 1989). In contrast it is difficult to locate white families living in neighborhoods where the housing values are so incongruous with their income levels and their level of education (Jackman and Jackman, 1986).

It is important to remember that until the end of the Second World War it was a common practice for homeowners to sign legally binding contracts, called restrictive covenants, that prohibited property owners from selling their homes to certain undesirable individuals. According to the conclusion of one of the most important studies of residential segregation, the real estate industry and the bankers insured that housing for People of Color would be restricted to certain areas of the city (Helper, 1969).

Over the years the real estate industry has sought to maintain property values in selected neighborhoods and therefore considers the settlement of minorities in certain areas of the city as a serious economic threat to property values. For these reasons, banks and other mortgage lending institutions have also worked to maintain property values and have engaged in various discriminatory practices that have promoted residential segregation. Their goal is to insure that certain undesirable elements do not enter the more desirable neighborhoods of the city and adversely affect property values.

Several studies and investigative reports have found that these banks and lending institutions have been involved in red-lining. This refers to the banking industry's practice of not making home loans to minority applicants in neighborhoods where they might adversely affect property values or refusing to make loans in minority neighborhoods that have lost their economic potential (Pol and Guy, 1982).

Sex Discrimination

Even though women constitute a majority of the nation's population, at 52 percent, nonetheless they are a minority group and have historically experienced a wide range of discriminatory practices. Since the dawn of civilization women have been considered the subordinate sex and have been treated as second class citizens (Chafetz, 1974, 108-152; Epstein, 1988).

Perhaps the best known area of sex discrimination occurs in the area of wages and compensation for work (Mezey, 1992:91-108). In view of a long history of discrimination against working women and the fact that women's work has never been given the same value as men's work, it is not surprising that women are still payed less than men for doing the same work (Chafetz,

1990:45- 63). Even the most recent income data reveal that women earn about sixty percent of what men earn, for doing the same kind of work and with the same level of experience and education (Cherry, 1989:135-150; McCrum and Rubin, 1987). As in the past women continue to serve as a source of cheap labor for American entrepreneurs.

Besides being paid less than men for comparable work, women are also segregated in certain occupations, such as secretaries, school teachers, health care workers, domestics, assembly line workers, and operatives (See Table 2.2). These jobs have historically offered the lowest wages and the fewest benefits for the skill levels and education required. More recent comparative studies have also found that when men are employed in these pink collar jobs, they are usually paid more and they tend to experience more rapid and consistent promotions (Reskin and Hartmann, 1986).

Table 2.2
Highest Concentration of Women
in Segregated Jobs, 1990

Occupation	Percent	Occupation	Percent
Secretaries	99.0	Data Entry Keyers	93.6
Dental Hygienists	98.6	Welfare Service Aides	92.5
Kindergarten Teachers	98.2	Personnel Clerks	91.1
Dental Assistants	98.1	Bank Tellers	91.0
Practical Nurses	97.0	Bookkeepers	91.0
Child Care Providers	96.9	Dietitians	90.8
Receptionists	96.8	Speech Therapists	90.5
Private Household	96.1	Telephone Operators	90.4
Registered Nurses	95.8	Clerks	88.9
Cleaners and Servants	95.8	Waiters and Waitresses	87.8
Typists	95.6	Hairdressers	88.7
Sewing Machine Operators	94.0	Nursing Aides, Orderlies	88.7
Teachers Aides	93.7	Librarians	87.3

Source: 1991 Census:Table 652

Despite important social gains women are still considered the primary parent in the household. Studies have found that even when women work outside the home (in full-time positions), they are still responsible for the housework and the child care (Blair and Lichter, 1991). One study of dual income families found that eight out of ten (82.9%) of the working mothers performed 20 or more hours of housework per week, compared to less than one out of ten (8.4%) of the working fathers (Coltrane and Ishi-Kuntz, 1992:51). Another study found that women who are employed full-time average an additional 25 to 30 hours of housework per week, compared to gainfully employed men who only spent an additional eight to ten hours a week on domestic chores (Robinson, 1989).

Prejudice and Discrimination

Given our understanding of prejudice and discrimination we would assume that the individual who is prejudiced will always discriminate and the person who discriminates will always have prejudicial attitudes. But in an interesting analysis Robert Merton (1949) has demonstrated that the relationship between thought and action is not always unilateral. Consequently the prejudiced person will not always discriminate and the discriminator is not always a prejudiced person.

Merton began his analysis with the premise that the American creed holds that everyone should have the right of equal access to justice, freedom, and opportunities, despite their race, ethnicity, or religion. But he made the point that the American creed is just a profession of faith, essentially an ideal, that is a part of the American tradition. Merton also correctly points out that there is a real gap between the beliefs of the American creed and race relations in the real world.

In his analysis Merton started out with the assumption that, "Prejudicial attitudes need not coincide with discriminatory behavior." To illustrate his point Merton devised a typology that was based on four ideal types (See Figure 2.2).

Merton said that the Unprejudiced Non-discriminators are the racial and ethnic liberals who follow the beliefs of the American creed and are not prejudiced in their attitudes and do not discriminate. Therefore he gave them a plus sign for being non-prejudiced and non-discriminatory and dubbed them the all-weather liberals. The problem with the all-weather liberals is that while they believe in social equality and practice it, they are content with their behavior and do very little to promote social change. These individuals also lead a privileged life style and are therefore free of any competition or contact with any minorities.

Merton referred to the Unprejudiced Discriminator as the fair weather liberal, a person who is personally free of prejudice, but who is willing to support discrimination when it is easy or profitable to do so. As a result, social pressure and economic conditions may cause this person to discriminate. This is the timid liberal, who Merton says will hesitate to speak up against prejudice or discrimination because he/she fears that they might loose status among their friends. Similarly the fear of losing customers may prevent the fair weather liberal from hiring minorities, as this might be bad for business.

Figure 2.2
A Typology of Ethnic Prejudice and Discrimination

	Attitude Dimension* Prejudice and Non-prejudice	Behavior Dimension* Discrimination and Non-discrimination
Type I: Unprejudiced Non-discriminator (All Weather Liberal)	+	+
Type II: Unprejudiced Discriminator (Fair Weather Liberal)	+	−
Type III: Prejudiced Non-discriminator (Fair Weather Illiberal)	−	+
Type IV: Prejudiced Discriminator (All All Bigot)	−	−

* Where (+) = Conformity to the Creed
* Where (-) = Deviation from the Creed
Source: Merton, 1949:103

The fair-weather illiberal is the reluctant conformist. This is the person who is prejudiced and does not believe in the American creed but who conforms to the creed in practice for fear of social sanctions or litigation. Therefore, while this person is very prejudiced, he will nonetheless hire women for fear of discrimination charges. Timid bigots will not discriminate if they feel that such behavior will receive negative reactions or if they believe that such behavior would be expensive in the long term.

It is interesting to observe that the timid bigot and the timid liberal are in very similar situations. Timid bigots are under stress when they conform to the American creed and likewise timid liberals are under stress when they deviate from the American creed. The psychologist Leon Festinger (1957) would say that they are suffering from cognitive dissonance. This refers to the psychological discomfort that occurs when a person's actions and thoughts are not in harmony.

Merton's last type is the all out bigot, who is consistent in both thoughts and action, since this person is prejudiced and is very willing to discriminate. Bigots do not suffer from any sense of guilt, since they are consistent in their prejudicial attitudes and in their discriminatory behavior. Of Merton's four types, this one is the most difficult to change.

Merton demonstrated that it is possible for a person to be prejudiced and not discriminate or for a person to discriminate and not be prejudiced. The interesting connection between these four types is that Type I and Type IV are similar in that they are both consistent in their thoughts and actions, while Type II and Type III are also similar in that they are inconsistent in both their thoughts and actions.

Chapter Summary

Prejudice occurs in all societies and affects everyone to a certain degree. Prejudice is viewed as a hostile or negative attitude toward a person or a group and is based on over-categorization, misconceptions, prejudgment, rationalization, and value judgments. Many theories have been proposed to account for the existence of prejudice, but there are five major theories, exploitation, scapegoating, authoritarian personality, ecological, and the linguistic theory.

Without the existence of stereotypes, it would be difficult to maintain prejudicial attitudes. Racial stereotypes are pernicious because they are self-fulfilling, based on selective perception, are often negative, result in social isolation, and are usually based on a kernel of truth.

Discrimination is a conscious act that can occur as a result of individual behavior or because of institutional policies or laws. The deleterious effects of discrimination are particularly severe when they occur in the marketplace, in the labor force, or in the educational system.

Robert Merton has demonstrated that the relationship between prejudice and discrimination is not necessarily unilateral or spontaneous. Merton demonstrated that it is possible for a person who is free from prejudice to discriminate and for a person to discriminate without being prejudiced.

References

Adorno, Theodore W., E. Frenkel, D.J. Levinson, and R.N. Sanford
　1950　　　*The Authoritarian Personality.* New York: W.W. Norton
　　　　　　& Company.

Alexis, Marcus, et al
　1980　　　*Black Consumer Profiles: Food Purchasing in the Inner
　　　　　　City.* Ann Arbor: The University of Michigan Press.

Allport, Gordon W.
　1954　　　*The Nature of Prejudice.* New York: Doubleday Anchor
　　　　　　Books. Baker, Robert
　1988　　　" 'Pricks' and 'Chicks': A Plea for 'Persons'." In *Racism and
　　　　　　Sexism: An Integrated Study.* Paula S. Rothenberg (ed.), New
　　　　　　York: St. Martin's Press. Pp. 280-295.

Banton, Michael
　1983　　　*Racial and Ethnic Competition.* London: Cambridge University
　　　　　　Press.

Bethlehem, Douglas W.
　1985　　　*A Social Psychology of Prejudice.* New York: St. Martin's
　　　　　　Press.

Blair, S.L. and D.T. Lichter
　1991　　　"Measuring the Division of Household Labor: Gender
　　　　　　Segregation of Housework among American Couples."
　　　　　　Journal of Family Issues 12:91-113.

Bogardus, Emory
　1925　　　"Measuring Social Distance." *Journal of Applied Sociology*
　　　　　　9:299-308.
　1933　　　"A Social Distance Scale." *Sociology and Social Research*
　　　　　　17:265-271.
　1968　　　"Comparing Racial Distance in Ethiopia, South Africa, and
　　　　　　the United States." *Sociology and Social Research* 52:149-156.

Bonacich, Edna
　1972　　　"A Theory of Ethnic Antagonism: The Split Labor Market."
　　　　　　American Sociological Review 37:547-559.
　1990　　　"Inequality in America: The Failure of the American System
　　　　　　for People of Color." In *U.S. Race Relations in the 1980s and
　　　　　　1990s: Challenges and Alternatives.* Gail E. Thomas (ed.),
　　　　　　New York: Hemisphere Publishing Corporation. Pp. 187–
　　　　　　208.

Carmichael, Stokely and Charles V. Hamilton
　1967　　　*Black Power: The Politics of Liberation in America.* New
　　　　　　York: Random House.

Centers, R.
1951   "An Effective Classroom Demonstration of Stereotypes."
Journal of Social Psychology 34:41-46.

Chafetz, Janet S.
1974   *Masculine/Feminine or Human? An Overview of the
Sociology of Sex Roles.* Itasca, IL: F.E. Peacock.
1990   *Gender Equity: An Integrated Theory of Stability and
Change.* Newbury Park, CA: Sage Publications.

Cherry, Robert
1989   *Discrimination: Its Economic Impact on Blacks, Women, and
Jews.* Lexington, MA: Lexington Books.

Coltrane, Scott and Masako Ishii-Kuntz
1992   "Men's Housework: A Life Course Perspective." *Journal of
Marriage and the Family* 54:43-57.

Deutsch, Morton and Mary E. Collins
1951   *Interracial Housing: A Psychological Evaluation of a Social
Experiment.* Minneapolis: University of Minnesota Press.

Deutscher, Irwin
1973   *What We Say/What We Do: Sentiments and Acts.* Glenview,
IL: Scott, Foresman.

Dollard, John
1937   *Caste and Class in a Southern Town.* New Haven: Yale
University Press.

Draden, Joe T.
1986   "Accessibility to Housing: Differential Residential Segregation
for Blacks, Hispanics, American Indians, and Asians." In
Race, Ethnicity, and Minority Housing in the United States. Jamshid A. Momeni (ed.), New York: Greenwood Press. Pp. 109-
126.

Ehrlich, Howard J.
1973   *The Social Psychology of Prejudice.* New York: John Wiley
& Sons.

Epstein, Cynthia F.
1988   *Deceptive Distinctions: Sex, Gender, and the Social Order.*
New Haven, CT: Yale University Press.

Festinger, Leon A.
1957   *A Theory of Cognitive Dissonance.* Palo Alto: Stanford
University Press.

Fraga, Luis R. et al
1986   "Hispanic Americans and Educational Policy: Limits to Equal
Access." *Journal of Politics* 48:850-876.

Gonzales, Juan L. Jr.
1984   *The Tertiary Labor Force and the Role of Undocumented Mexican
Laborers in the American Economy.* El Paso: The Center for

Inter-American and Border Studies, University of Texas. (December)

1988   "The Pattern of Ethnic Residential Segregation in Oakland, California: 1940-1980." Paper presented at the Annual Meetings of the Western Social Science Association, Denver, CO. (April).

1989   "The Growth of the Black Ghetto in Oakland: A Case of Residential Segregation, 1960-1988." Paper presented at the Annual Meetings of the Western Social Science Association, Albuquerque, NM. (April).

1991   *The Affordability of Auto Insurance Among Low Income Families in Los Angeles.* San Francisco, CA: Consumers Union.

Helper, Rose
1969   *Racial Policies and Practices of Real Estate Brokers.* Minneapolis: University of Minnesota Press.

Jackman, Mary R. and Robert W. Jackman
1986   "Racial Inequalities in Home Ownership." In *Race, Ethnicity, and Minority Housing in the United States.* Jamshid A. Momeni (ed.), New York: Greenwood Press. Pp.39-52.

Jiobu, Robert M.
1988   *Ethnicity and Assimilation.* Albany: State University of New York Press.

1990   *Ethnicity and Inequality.* Albany: State University of New York Press.

Karlins, Marvin, et al
1969   "On the Fading of Social Stereotypes: Studies in Three Generations of College Students." *Journal of Personality and Social Psychology* 13(1):1-16.

Katz, David and Kenneth W. Braly
1933   "Racial Stereotypes of One Hundred College Students." *Journal of Abnormal Sociology and Psychology* 28:280-290.

LaPiere, Richard T.
1934   "Attitudes vs. Actions." *Social Forces* 13:230-237.

Linn, Lawrence S.
1965   "Verbal Attitudes and Overt Behavior: A Study of Racial Discrimination." *Social Forces* 43:353-364.

McCrum, Hanna and Nanna Rubin
1987   "The Eighth Annual Working Woman Salary Survey." Working Woman Pp. 53-64 (January).

Meier, Kenneth J., J. Stewart, Jr. and R.E. England
1989   *Race, Class, and Education: The Politics of Second-Generation Discrimination.* Madison, WI: The University of Wisconsin Press.

Merton, Robert K.
1949   "Discrimination and the American Creed." In *Discrimination and National Welfare*. R.M. MacIver (ed.), New York: Harper and Row. Pp. 99-126.

Mezey, Susan G.
1992   *In Pursuit of Equality: Women, Public Policy, and the Federal Courts*. New York: St. Martin's Press.

Moore, Robert B.
1988   "Racist Stereotyping in the English Language." In *Racism and Sexism: An Integrated Study*. Paula S. Rothenberg (ed.), New York: St. Martin's Press. Pp. 269-279.

Park, Robert E. and Ernest W. Burgess
1921   *Introduction to the Science of Sociology*. Chicago: University of Chicago Press.

Perlmutter, Philip
1992   *Divided We Fall: A History of Ethnic, Religious, and Racial Prejudice in America*. Ames, IA: Iowa State University Press.

Pettigrew, Thomas F.
1959   "Regional Differences in Anti-Negro Prejudice." *Journal of Abnormal and Social Psychology* 59:28-36.
1982   "Prejudice." In *Prejudice*. Thomas F. Pettigrew, et al. (eds.), Cambridge, MA: Harvard University Press. Pp. 1-29.

Pol, Lui and Rebecca F. Guy
1982   "Discrimination in the Home Lending Market: A Macro Perspective." *Social Science Quarterly* 63:716-726.

Reskin, Barbara and Heidi Hartmann (eds.)
1986   *Women's Work, Men's Work: Sex Segregation on the Job*. Washington, D.C.: National Academy Press.

Sapir, Edward
1921   *Language*. New York: Harcourt, Brace & World.

Sigelman, Lee and Susan Welch
1991   *Black Americans' Views of Racial Inequality*. New York: Cambridge University Press.

Stroebe, Wolfgang and Chester A. Insko
1989   "Stereotype, Prejudice, and Discrimination: Changing Conceptions in Theory and Research." In *Stereotyping and Prejudice: Changing Conceptions*. Daniel Bar-Tal, C.F. Graumann, A.W. Kruglanski, W. Stroebe (eds.), New York: Springer-Verlag. Pp. 3-34.

U.S. Census
1991   *Statistical Abstract of the United States, 1991* (111th edition). Washington, D.C.: U.S. Department of Commerce.

Yinger, John
1978   "The Black-White Price Differential in Housing: Some Further Evidence." *Land Economics* 54(2):187-206.

Important Names

Theodore Adorno	Gordon Allport	Emory Bogardus
Edna Bonacich	Kenneth Braly	Stokely Carmichael
Mary Collins	Morton Deutsch	John Dollard
Leon Festinger	Charles Hamilton	David Katz
Richard LaPiere	Karl Marx	Robert Merton
Thomas Pettigrew	Edward Sapir	Benjamin Whorf

Key Terms

prejudice
prejudgments
Exploitation Theory
Linguistic Theory
ethnocentric
Unprejudiced-
  Discriminator
selective perception
Discrimination
frustration-aggression
  hypothesis
inside hire
secondary labor market
residential segregation
Unprejudiced
  Non-discriminator
institutional racism

over-categorization
rationalization
Scapegoating Theory
Authoritarian Personality
Fascism scale
Brown v. the Board
  of Education
social distance scale
individual discrimination
stereotypes
red-lining
split labor market theory
tertiary labor market
restrictive covenants
fair-weather illiberal
Sapir-Whorf hypothesis

misconceptions
value judgments
Ecological Theory
class conflict
ethnophaulism
self-fulfilling
  prophecy
pink collar jobs
institutional
  discrimination
gate keepers
primary labor market
surplus labor force
comparable work
all out bigot
timid bigot

1. List and provide a description of five characteristics of prejudice.
2. Be prepared to provide a definition and an example of five theories of prejudice (i.e. the exploitation, scapegoating, authoritarian personality, ecological, and linguistic theories).
3. What are the five basic characteristics of stereotypes? Be prepared to describe each.
4. Provide a definition of the Split Labor Market Theory and then select five variables and compare the differences between the three labor markets.
5. Robert Merton made a clear distinction between the nature of prejudice and discrimination. List his four types and provide a brief description and example for each of these types.
6. Be familiar with the contributions of the following individuals: Robert Merton, Theodore Adorno, John Dollard, Gordon Allport, Deutsch and Collins, Sapir and Whorf, Emory Bogardus, Richard La Piere, Bonacich.
7. Know the following concepts: the "F Scale", the Sapir-Whorf Hypothesis, the social distance scale, institutional racism, wage-gap differential, prison economy, gate keepers, screening devices, inside hire, life-chances, surplus labor force, *Brown v. Board of Education*, restrictive covenants, red-lining.

Chapter 3

Minority-Majority Relations

The Concept of Assimilation

The most important concept in the study of the social integration of new groups into American society is assimilation. Assimilation refers to the complete merging of two or more groups with separate and distinct cultures and identities into a new group with a common culture and social identity. Under ideal conditions the bounty of the long process of assimilation is the birth of a new nation of people. But the blending that occurs in the assimilation process is not unilateral, as all groups in society are affected.

The historical pattern of assimilation in the United States can best be described as Anglo-centric, since the emphasis has always been on Anglo-conformity. In practice the majority group will make every effort to Americanize minorities by demanding that they relinquish all aspects of their native (i.e., immigrant) culture and adopt the dominant values of society as their own (Gonzales, 1985; 1990).

In contrast, the term acculturation refers to those encounters where a majority culture is modified through contact with one or more minority cultures, but does not experience any significant change. Some believe that acculturation is a true reflection of the American experience, since many ethnic groups have influenced American culture, but no one group has altered the historic Anglo-centric orientation of society. Acculturation also refers to the cultural assimilation of minorities, whereby they adopt the language, customs, and beliefs of the majority group as their own. Some consider the ultimate stage in the process of assimilation as amalgamation, that is the intermarriage or biological blending of the minority group with the majority (Jiobu, 1988:149-177).

A review of the various sociological studies reveals that there are several ways in which new immigrants are integrated into the dominant cultural environment. From a theoretical perspective there are only a few routes by which new arrivals can enter the mainstream of American society. We shall review five of the most important models of assimilation: (1) the Anglo-Centric Perspective, (2) the Melting Pot Theory, (3) Cultural Monism, (4) Cultural Pluralism, and (5) Cultural Nationalism.

The Anglo-Centric Perspective

The Anglo-centric perspective holds that Anglo conformity should be the long term goal of all immigrants. It is based on the belief that Anglo American institutions constitute the basis for American values and culture and these values should be promoted. Anglo conformity has served as the most pervasive ideology of assimilation.

The founding fathers realized that while they needed the labor and talent of thousands of immigrants, they were also threatened by the old world culture and values that immigrants brought with them. For this reason Washington, Jefferson, and Adams were very concerned about the impact that these immigrants would have on the burgeoning American culture. Therefore they insisted on the total rejection of their old values and the rapid absorption of Anglo-Saxon core group values (Gordon, 1964:85). For immigrants to do otherwise was considered un-American. Before long they were enrolled in Americanization programs, with the stated objective of expunging their language, customs, traditions, and political experiences. Their old values were replaced by the Anglo core group values and they were required to learn English, adopt the American lifestyle, and dispose of their traditions and beliefs.

Therefore the Anglo-centric orientation did not allow them to retain any part of their culture, language, customs, or traditions. However, a few of them felt that their immigrant cultures did have something to offer American society. From their perspective cultural diversity was a good idea, as diversity would only enrich the fabric of American society. Unfortunately the idea of encouraging cultural diversity has only become acceptable in the past twenty years.

The Melting Pot Theory

The great American melting pot was supposed to melt down all the ethnic differences in society and bring out the best qualities of each group. Everyone would become a true American as a result of the melting down process and all Americans would be enriched and improved because of the experience. The end result of this process would involve the biological blending of the diverse racial groups in American society and the mixture of diverse cultures.

The belief that the ethnic experience in America was supposed to result in the blending of all groups was very popular at the turn of the century. The vision of America as the melting pot of the world was stamped into the public's imagination by a popular play, called *The Melting Pot*, produced by Israel Zangwill in 1908. It portrayed America as a giant crucible where all ethnic and racial groups would eventually merge and produce a superior stock of people. Unfortunately this view of American society was only a romantic idea that captured the nation's imagination, but in fact it had no relationship to the reality of life in America (Richardson, 1988:108-111; Steinberg, 1989:44-53).

From the theoretical perspective the melting pot approach was plagued with two major flaws. In the first place it is a very conservative view that upholds the values of the dominant cultural group in American society and therefore requires all other groups to relinquish their customs and traditions. In the process the melting pot theory requires all groups to embrace the core group values as their own. The second flaw in this perspective is that it does not apply to People of Color, since People of Color do not melt-down. European immigrants usually assimilated after the second or third generation, as they were successful in blending into Anglo-American society. In contrast, People of Color cannot rid themselves of their facial features or their skin color.

Cultural Monism

Cultural monism is the doctrine that advocates the complete assimilation of all ethnic groups. The melting pot theory and the Anglo-centric perspective are examples of cultural monism. The acceptance of cultural monism as an approach to the integration of minorities into American society would produce a very homogeneous society in which all minorities would be encouraged to adopt the values and the culture of American society.

Cultural Pluralism

The assimilationist view that falls at the opposite end of the spectrum from cultural monism is cultural pluralism. Cultural pluralism holds that cultural heterogeneity or cultural mixture is a goal that should be encouraged in society. Therefore it not only encourages cultural diversity but it also allows for cultural differences within society, that is while these differences do not interfere or conflict with the principal values of the dominant culture.

Those who support cultural pluralism not only believe that cultural diversity is a positive goal for society but feel that cultural heterogeneity should be a part of the fabric of American culture. Cultural pluralism is based on the belief that diverse groups can live in social harmony and work together to build a better society. The key is mutual understanding and respect. This view does not support the blending or the melting of minorities into the core culture but encourages a sharing of values and beliefs. Cultural pluralists do not conceive of American society as a great melting pot of races and cultures, rather they see it as a tossed salad, where minorities intermingle and share in the dominant culture but maintain their culture and do not melt into the dominant culture (Ringer and Lawless, 1989:119-150).

Cultural Nationalism

From a comparative perspective cultural nationalism is a radical version of cultural pluralism. The cultural nationalists believe that racial and ethnic groups should be completely independent and culturally distinct from the core group. Therefore they are very adamant in their belief that minorities should maintain their language, culture, traditions, and religions. In their view American society should consist of diverse racial and ethnic groups who live and work in independent communities and maintain a social existence based on their cultural identities (See Figure 3.1).

Figure 3.1
Comparison of Assimilation Theories

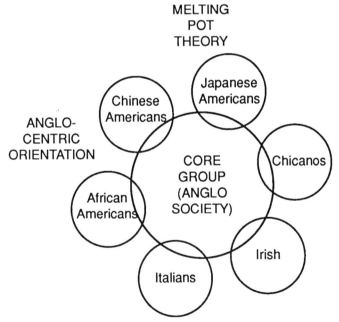

During the sixties cultural nationalism was very popular and produced several groups who promoted the idea as their social philosophy. Some of these groups applied this philosophy to their way of life. For example, the Nation of Islam had a very strong cultural nationalist orientation under the leadership of Malcolm X. Some African American groups that were active during the Civil Rights Movement were also cultural nationalists, as they were strong supporters of African American identity, encouraged a reevaluation of African American history, organized the Black power movement, and some wanted to obtain territorial independence from the United States. Other examples of the application of cultural nationalism occurred among Mexican Americans, with the Chicano movement and the nation of Aztlan, and among Native Americans, with the Pan Indian Movement (See Figure 3.2.).

Figure 3.2
Comparison of Cultural Monism and Cultural Pluralism

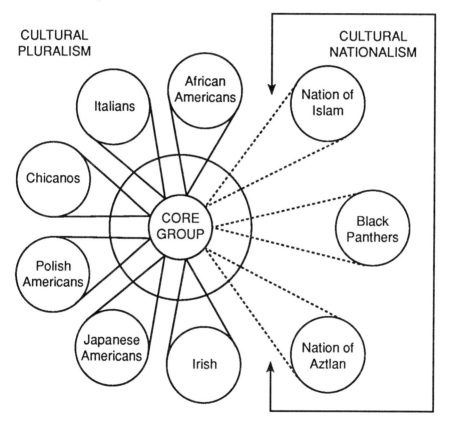

Theories of Assimilation

The research conducted by sociologists at the University of Chicago in the 1920's served as the basis for the original work on the relationship between immigration and assimilation. Since those early days sociologists have always been interested in the dynamics of the assimilation process and have conducted dozens of studies in a variety of settings. Several key studies have come out of these research efforts and have served as the basis for the development of various theories on assimilation.

Park's Contact Theory

Robert Park conducted his first observations on the relationship between racial heterogeneity and assimilation in 1926, while visiting Hawaii. Out of these observations, and other studies conducted in Chicago, he developed his contact theory of assimilation. His theory held that all immigrants move through four stages of adaptation:

1. Contact—the initial period of introduction of an immigrant group into the greater society.
2. Competition and Conflict—the new immigrants and members of the host society compete for scarce resources, primarily jobs and housing. The competition sometimes escalates into open conflict and violence.
3. Accommodation—after a few years the immigrants began to accept the values and goals of American society as their own. By this stage they have established their niche in the greater society and live in relative peace and harmony.
4. Assimilation—it is usually the children of the immigrants who integrate and move into American society, as they speak the language and are socialized to Anglo American culture. In the final stage some intermarry with the members of the majority group.

Unfortunately Park's model of assimilation contains some flaws. In the first place his model establishes assimilation as the ultimate goal for all immigrants and does not allow for other possibilities, such as cultural pluralism. Second, his model is unidirectional, as it holds that social integration can only move in one predetermined direction. Lastly, Park's model is deterministic in that once immigrants start this process, movement through the four stages is irreversible and inevitable. Therefore, from Park's perspective, immigrants who remain isolated in their ethnic communities have failed to achieve the ultimate goal of social integration, that is assimilation.

Bogardus' Immigrant Studies

Following more than thirty years of observation and study, Emory Bogardus observed that following an initial period of contact between two groups a seven step process of racial integration would follow (1959):

1. Curiosity—affects the members of the host society as the immigrants are viewed as peculiar, but interesting.
2. Economic Welcome—the immigrants are considered a valuable source of cheap labor and needed talent.
3. Industrial and Social Antagonism—members of the host society consider the immigrant's competitors, and their frustration often results in social conflict and acts of organized violence.
4. Legislative Antagonism—restrictive immigration laws and discriminatory legislation is passed to prevent further immigration of undesirable aliens.
5. Period of Fair Play—this is marked by a strong reaction to the discriminatory laws passed during an earlier period of social resistance. The opportunity structure is more open and available to minorities during this period.
6. Period of Quiescence—an effort is made by members of the majority group to extend social and political rights to all immigrants and minorities.
7. Crises of Identity—this occurs between the first generation immigrants and their children. The children of immigrants are Americanized and live in a different and alien world from that of their parents.

Park's Marginal Man Theory

The final stage in Bogardus' model of assimilation is very similar to Robert Park's concept of marginality, which describes the experience of second generation immigrants who find that they are caught between two cultures (1928). Park coined the concept of the marginal man to describe the situation of immigrants who are torn between two cultures, that is their traditional cultural values—or those of their parents—and the values of the dominant society. This can result in a state of mental conflict and sometimes creates a serious dilemma for immigrants. Marginal people find that they are not completely loyal or committed to the values and goals of either group, nor can they feel completely accepted by either their group or the majority group. Some conclude that they are really outsiders to both groups. The sense of alienation is pervasive.

Stonequist's Marginal Man Theory

The sociologist Everett Stonequist elaborated on Park's idea of the inevitable alienation of immigrants and wrote a book called *The Marginal Man* (1937). In his study of the marginal man Stonequist not only assigned specific personality traits to the marginal person but he also drew the conclusion that the marginal person suffers from culture conflict. Culture conflict is really a mental conflict that derives from the experience of being torn between two cultures and the feeling of not really being a part of either culture. As a result the marginal person tends to be hypersensitive, exhibits withdrawal tendencies, and suffers from divided loyalties. However, Stonequist failed to consider that not all marginal persons suffer from this mental conflict nor do they always developed these personality characteristics.

Banton's Six Orders of Race Relations

In his book *Race Relations,* Michael Banton provides an alternative view of race relations in which racial contact occurs in six stages (1967):

1. Peripheral Contact—these relationships are short lived and are based on limited contact between two groups.
2. Institutionalized Contact—these relationships are usually based on the need for economic intercourse between two groups.
3. Domination—all the members of the minority group are stigmatized by their race or ethnicity and are subjugated to the will of the dominant group.
4. Paternalism—represents control from the outside and results in the development of caste-like relationships between the majority group and minority groups in society.
5. Integration—after a period of time the racial differences in society begin to lose their importance.
6. Pluralism—the various ethnic and racial groups in society are allowed to retain important aspects of their culture.

The Paternalistic and Competitive Models

The use of the concept of paternalism in race relations was refined by Pierre Van Den Berghe in his book, *Race and Racism* (1978). In this work he developes the idea that all societies can be viewed as either being based on paternalistic relationships or competitive relationships.

Paternalistic relationships are based on the master-servant model of society. In these societies the dominant group is proportionally small but very powerful, as they own the means of production, run the government, regulate the educational institutions, and control the system of rewards and punishments. In these highly regulated societies relationships between the social classes are very rigid and follow the color-line. Race relations constitute the most important relationships in society. The majority group views the subordinate group as childish, immature, irresponsible, and most significantly, inferior. Race relations are based on a caste system and require an elaborate display of social etiquette to maintain.

A major problem with the paternalistic system is that it works best in a preindustrial society, that is in a society based on one of the extractive industries, such as agriculture, mining, timber, or fishing. This model would apply to race relations on the plantations during the Ante-Bellum period, in colonial Africa, and on the encomienda system under Spanish colonialism.

The dramatic changes introduced by the industrial revolution resulted in some significant changes in race relations. The old paternalistic relationships were not compatible with the new methods of production introduced by the industrial revolution. Consequently a new system of race relations evolved, known as the competitive system of race relations. The competitive model is found in industrial societies where a complex division of labor and a sophisticated manufacturing process is required.

In this system of race relations the divisions between racial groups are not as strictly or as clearly defined, since the trappings of caste membership are eliminated in favor of the competition for social positions and prestige that stem from hard work and success in the marketplace. Employers quickly realize that the economic and social costs of maintaining a segregated labor force in an industrial society are more than they are willing to bear. They also discover that competition for jobs between diverse groups plays to their advantage. Entrepreneurs also find that they need to attract educated and skilled workers wherever they can find them, despite their race or ethnicity. In sum, the maintenance of rigid racial barriers in an industrial society is not considered profitable.

Blumer on Race Relations

Herbert Blumer made it clear that the introduction of industrialization and competition would result in the development of a new system of race relations. Blumer felt that the industrial process would force people into new relationships that would have to be based on mutual interest and cooperation. Therefore these relationships would result in the development of a new system of race relations. The changes brought about by industrialization would challenge not only the existing social and economic order, but also the structure of social classes and race relations in society.

In the end, everyone would be forced to compete in the labor force and in the economic marketplace based on their education, skills, and talents, and not on their racial or ethnic origins (Blumer, 1965:226-227).

Employers quickly realized that they could no longer afford to discriminate, since this would result in the loss of their competitive advantage. Industrialization also meant that social mobility would now depend on an individual's preparation and ambition, and not on their race or ethnic background.

Warner on Caste and Race

W. Lloyd Warner held that African Americans in the South represented a social caste and not a social class (1937). He took this position since African Americans had to confront a number of barriers and restrictions on their limited opportunities to improve their social condition. In his view a caste is a social stratum that is based on heredity, and it is the fact of birth into a certain race that determines a person's social position, occupation, residential location, social relationships, and position in the community and society. Therefore their social circumstances and life chances are determined by their racial characteristics and not by their abilities or achievements.

Warner was clearly an optimist, as he predicted that race relations would improve over time and that eventually a person's social class position would be more important in the determination of their success, and not their race or caste position. He believed that eventually the horizontal color bar would move to the vertical position, allowing social class characteristics to determine the nature of race relations and not social caste.

Cox on Caste and Race

In contrast to Warner, Oliver Cox believed that social class was more important in the determination of the social position of African Americans, as opposed to social caste. He felt that the over-emphasis on racial distinctions only served to perpetuate the exploitation of African Americans. On the other hand, the social class analysis that he proposed as an explanation for the role of African Americans in society allowed for an evaluation of their social position based on merit and achievement within the social structure (Cox, 1948:224).

A Comparison of Class, Caste, and Estate

A social class consists of a large category of people who live in an open society and have an opportunity to advance themselves. Members of a class society are different in terms of their level of education, occupational distribution, and incomes.

As distinct from a class society, an estate society is rigid in the determination of social positions. A person's social position in an estate society is determined at birth, and their rights and duties are determined by the laws of the state. The best jobs and educational opportunities are restricted to certain privileged groups in an estate society. The social elites are a select few and the vast majority of the population have limited opportunities for social improvement and advancement.

In contrast, a caste society is very rigid and there are virtually no opportunities for social mobility, as people are born into their social position and die in that social stratum. A handful of elites in a caste society make all the decisions and typically maintain their privileged positions with the assistance of a religious belief system that justifies their position and power in society (Ringer and Lawless, 1989:50-68).

It is instructive to compare these three models of society and take note of the differences that exist in each (See Figure 3.3). The thing that is particularly interesting is that each of these models can be applied to the history of race relations in the United States. The existence of an estate society is closely associated with the institution of slavery in the South, as people were held in bondage and a small social elite controlled the society from above. The caste system of race relations depicts conditions in the United States before the Second World War, when African Americans, Mexican Americans, Japanese Americans, and Filipinos were treated as members of a social caste. And as a result of the Civil Rights Movement a gradual transition was made to a more open and just society.

Figure 3.3
Comparison of Class, Caste, and Estate Societies

Variable	Class Society	Estate Society	Caste Society
1. Opportunity Structure	Open	Closed	Closed
2. Economy	Industrial	Agricultural	Agricultural
3. Intermarriage	Allowed	Prohibited	Prohibited
4. Religion	Free Choice	State Religion	State Religion
5. Education	Open-Competitive	Very Limited	Very Restricted
6. Labor Force	Competitive	Paternalistic	Serfs and Slaves
7. Social	Status Achieved	Ascribed	Ascribed
8. Social Ideology	Freedom of Choice	Master-Servant	Reincarnation
9. Sex Roles	Open-Androgynous	Subordination	Oppression
10. Political Structure	Open-Democracy	Despotism	Theocracy
11. Racial Distribution	Heterogeneous	Homogeneous	Homogeneous
12. Psycho-Personality	Diverse Forms	Stratum	Elites-Slaves

Gordon's Ethclass

Milton Gordon introduced the concept of ethclass as a way to bridge the gap between the social impact of race, social class, and social caste position in American society (1964). His belief was that everyone has a self concept and personal identity based on their position in society. He also observed that minorities belong to a subsociety, that is a subculture that consists of all those racial characteristics that identify the individual in the community. In brief, Gordon's ethclass represents the racial and ethnic characteristics of a group that are intersected by social class differences.

Based on Gordon's theory members of an ethnic group would, as a result of their common history and cultural heritage, have a strong historical identification with one another. But they also would have a strong participational identification with members of the core group, that is based on shared social class characteristics.

The concept of ethclass can explain how a sense of ethnic identification, that is a sense of ethnic consciousness, can cut across social class boundaries. For example, a minority person who is an engineer in a large research firm will have a much closer participational identification with his Caucasian colleagues than he will have with members of his ethnic group, who may be from a lower social class background. However, this person will probably have a strong sense of historical identification with the members of his ethnic group, whereas this would not be the case with his Caucasian colleagues (Banton, 1988:23-25).

Randsford's Class within a Caste Model

In his analysis of the relationship between ethnicity and social class position, H. Edward Ransford made the observation that the standards for judging the social class position for racial and ethnic minorities is different from those that are applied to Anglo Americans (1977). The difference in evaluation of social class position and rank is based on racial and ethnic differences within the minority community.

The first point that Ransford makes is that the definition and rating of social class position is unique to each ethnic group and does not coincide with the definition and rating that is applied in the general population. For example, among Mexican Americans a high school teacher would rank high in the ethnic community's system of social stratification, as school teachers are respected and held in high esteem. Therefore within the ethnic community a high school teacher might be placed in the lower-upper class. The second point he makes is that there is a definite difference between the social class position that people hold in the ethnic community and the position they hold in the greater society. In our example, the Mexican American high school teacher probably would only hold a middle-middle class position in the general system of stratification. This is true since achieving the position of a high school teacher is not as impressive an accomplishment in the greater society, as it is within the ethnic community. As a result ethnic teachers will experience a distinct drop in prestige and social status outside their community.

Assimilation in American Life

Our survey of the various theories that attempt to explain the nature of racial contact and integration in American society demonstrates the complexity of the process. Milton Gordon reminds us that the process of assimilation is composed of a variety of experiences. In brief, Gordon notes that there are seven types of assimilation:

1. Cultural Assimilation—this is sometimes called acculturation and refers to the modifications that minorities make in an attempt to adopt the values of the host society.
2. Structural Assimilation—minorities gain acceptance into the clubs, social organizations, and institutions of the dominant group.
3. Marital Assimilation—refers to the rate of intermarriage that occurs between the various minorities and the majority group.
4. Identificational Assimilation—the development of a sense of peoplehood between the minorities and the majority group.
5. Attitude-Receptional Assimilation—marked by the absence of prejudice in the host society.
6. Behavior-Receptional Assimilation—marked by the absence of discrimination in the host society.
7. Civic Assimilation—marked by an absence of conflict in the political arena and a consensus of social values. In Gordon's opinion the process of assimilation did not have to occur in any particular sequence. But he did believe that some minorities would be more successful with certain types of assimilation. Naturally the success rate of any minority group, within any type of assimilation, will depend upon the degree of acceptance by the host society. Conversely, the greater the level of resistance, then the slower the rate of assimilation.

Factors Affecting the Rate of Assimilation

In order to determine the variables that affect the rate of assimilation we must consider all the social and economic factors that affect the rate of assimilation. A review of these variables reveals that the most important factors affecting the rate of assimilation can be collapsed into six categories:

(1) Racial Factors, (2) Cultural Factors, (3) Human Capital Factors, (4) Sociological-Demographic Factors, (5) Political-Economic Factors, and (6) Geographic Factors.

Racial Factors

In this context racial factors refers to those physical characteristics that draw attention to the individual and the group. These physical characteristics are only important because they serve as the basis for discrimination. As a rule the more distinct or different the individual or group from the members of the host society, the greater the resistance to their introduction. For example, if the immigrants who are integrating into the host society have swarthy complexions and distinctive facial features, then they probably will encounter a high level of resistance, since the ideal phenotype in American society is a light skinned Caucasian (Montalvo, 1991:102-110).

Cultural Factors

The cultural factors or traits that can affect the rate of assimilation of an immigrant group usually include, but are not limited to, language, manner of dress, food, customs, and traditions. Of this group of variables language is probably the most important cultural variable affecting the rate of assimilation of any group. Therefore the ability of an immigrant group to speak English will dramatically increase their rate of assimilation. This is true since the inability to speak English will severely limit the educational, employment, and economic opportunities of the immigrant group.

Religious background also has a direct impact on the rate of assimilation. While religious beliefs and practices are not as significant a factor in the rate of assimilation as they once were, it is nonetheless true that religion can still affect the rate of acceptance of some groups. For example, this would apply to such groups as the Muslims, Sikhs, and Hindus. As a rule it is the consideration of how different a religion is from the majority group's Judeo-Christian beliefs that make them different (Richardson, 1988:126-162).

Cultural factors also would include the customs, traditions, and manner of dress of ethnic minorities. These cultural variables are very important in their acceptance or rejection. Consequently some ethnic groups are the victims of discrimination simply because of the way they dress, the celebrations they observe, the values they hold, or the way they live. In general, the greater the difference between ethnic minorities and the core group, then the greater the resistance to their integration (Fong and Markham, 1991:472-474).

Human Capital Factors

The process of integration into a new society is directly affected by the personal characteristics of the immigrants. These personal factors, sometimes referred to as human capital factors, are an individual's achieved characteristics. For example, the level of education is a human capital factor that can either promote or retard the assimilation process. As a rule, the higher the level of education, the easier the transition to American values and ideas (Zhou and Logan, 1989). Likewise the occupation, skill levels, and entrepreneurial talents of the immigrant group have a direct impact on their rate of assimilation (Butler and herring, 1991:82-83). Those immigrants who have a high score in education and occupation tend to assimilate at a higher rate than those who are lacking in these human capital factors (Scott and Scott, 1989:61-94).

The economic resources that immigrants have at their disposal is another example of important human capital factors. As a rule immigrants who arrive with economic resources will experience a smoother transition than those who do not. For example, many early Cuban and Vietnamese refugees were merchants and professionals who arrived with economic resources and quickly started their businesses and private practices. This accounts, in good part, for their early success in American society. Therefore the higher the socioeconomic status of the new immigrants, as measured by education, occupation, and economic resources, the more rapid their rate of assimilation (Butler and Herring, 1991).

Another variable affecting the rate of assimilation is the individual age of the immigrants upon arrival. As a rule the younger they are at the time of arrival, the smoother the transition to the values and culture of the host society. As a result children assimilate at a faster rate than middle aged adults. The assimilation of adults is slower because they have more difficulty learning the new language, they are more set in their ways, and they still have a strong attachment to their homeland. For this reason the elderly have the greatest difficulty in making the transition.

The reasons for emigration are very important in the assimilation process. Historically immigrants who arrive as sojourners are not strong candidates for assimilation. At the other end of the spectrum political refugees have a very rapid rate of assimilation, since they realize that they probably will never return to their homeland. Political refugees have cast their fate with America and they realize that they must integrate themselves into society as quickly as possible. This explains why Russian and Vietnamese refugees have such a high rate of naturalization.

Sociological-Demographic Factors

Sociological and demographic factors include the size of the immigrant population, their sex-ratio, age distribution, length of residence, and the existence of family and kinship ties. The observation of the settlement patterns of various immigrants over the past thirty years have demonstrated that these variables are among the most important for determining the rate of assimilation among recent arrivals (Portes and Manning, 1986:Table 3).

As a rule the larger the size of the immigrant population and the higher their concentration in ethnic enclaves, then the slower their rate of assimilation. Large immigrant communities are usually self-contained and self-sufficient, as these ethnic enclaves support the culture and limit the contact that new immigrants have with the greater society. The opposite is also true, that is the smaller the immigrant community the more contact recent arrivals have with the greater society and the higher their rate of assimilation. This observation is supported by the adopt a refugee program sponsored by the government for Southeast Asia immigrants. Since many of these immigrants were totally immersed in the American cultural environment, they quickly learn English and the American ways of life.

Historically a skewed sex-ratio has served as a barrier to assimilation. For example, the first wave of Chinese and Filipino immigrants were recognized for their very high concentration of single men, as only two or three percent were women. As a result they had a great deal of difficulty integrating into the mainstream of American society.

The length of time that immigrants have lived in the United States is also important for the assimilation process. Usually the level of assimilation increases as the period of settlement increases, either for the group as a whole or for specific individuals within the group.

The strength of family and kinship ties in the immigrant community can either retard or advance the rate of assimilation. Sometimes family ties in the community can stall the integration process, as new immigrants sometimes become too dependent on their family for support and this limits their contact with the greater society. But if the family is in a position to encourage assimilation, that is if the family has strong ties with the greater society, then the rate of assimilation will increase.

Political-Economic Factors

In the past the United States encouraged immigration, as the labor and skills of immigrants were needed to build this society. During that period the political climate supported the flow of immigrants, as they were viewed as making a positive contribution to the American way of life. In more recent times public opinion has turned against further immigration, as immigrants are often viewed as a threat to American labor and the American way of life. This is an example of how public opinion can affect American immigration policies.

Obviously political and economic factors are important in the assimilation process as public opinion sets the tone for the initial reception of any new group. Political considerations such as the need for skilled labor, the need for unique talent, foreign policy considerations, the form of government of the sending country (i.e., communist, dictatorship, or democratic), and the consideration whether the immigrants are political refugees or victims of a civil war or a natural disaster will often determine whether they are accepted or rejected by the American public. The most recent example of the impact of political considerations on the reception of immigrants occurred in the case of Cuban and Vietnamese refugees.

Geographic Factors

Geographic factors are interesting in that they provide an indication of the impact of physical barriers on the flow of immigrants and their rate of assimilation. For example, distance from the homeland and the ease of return are important geographic considerations since the ability of immigrants to return to their homeland with relative ease will slow the rate of assimilation. In contrast if the immigrants are a long way from their homeland and the return trip would be difficult or dangerous, then this will promote their rate of assimilation.

The ease of travel and the distance from the homeland has a dramatic impact on the return migration and transient migration patterns. Therefore if a significant number of immigrants are making frequent trips to their homeland, this will serve to strengthen the immigrant culture in America. Closely associated with this phenomena is the rate of immigration and the flux and flow of immigrants. For example, immigrants who arrive in large numbers over a short period are sometimes viewed as a potential threat to the host society. But if immigration occurs over a short period, but in small numbers and the flow is suddenly terminated, then the rate of assimilation will increase. The termination of immigration forces the immigrants to adopt to the new society, as they realize that their future will be determined by their ability to succeed in their adopted country.

The size of the immigrant community and the degree of concentration of the immigrant population also will affect the rate of assimilation. When an immigrant community is large and high in density, this results in the development of cultural support systems, which greatly reduce the rate of assimilation. The cultural support system of any ethnic enclave consists of those businesses, institutions, and organizations that supply cultural products and services to the members of the immigrant community. This would include ethnic grocery stores, shops, and restaurants that provide a whole range of products and services. The existence of cultural support systems provides immigrants with a hometown atmosphere. In the long term this means that these immigrants have little incentive to integrate themselves into the dominant culture (Loo, 1991).

It should be clear that the factors affecting the rate of assimilation are not only complex but are also closely related. Therefore the rate of social integration of any immigrant or ethnic group must be considered in light of several complex variables. Only after a detailed study of these variables is it possible to understand the rate of assimilation of any ethnic group in American society.

Chapter Summary

The concept of assimilation is complex and must be approached from several perspectives. The most popular models of assimilation are the melting pot theory and the Anglo-centric perspective. The alternative views to the assimilation experience are cultural pluralism and cultural nationalism, these perspectives were popularized during the 1960's.

Based on the work of Robert Park and Emory Bogardus, sociologists have devised some rather sophisticated theories of assimilation. Most of these models allow for the introduction of contact and competition into the social integration process, while taking into account the dynamics of social change. In a similar vein Milton Gordon provides a revealing insight into the various types of assimilation. He demonstrates that it is possible to achieve assimilation at different levels and in distinct stages.

In conclusion the rate of assimilation is directly affected by several complex social, political, economic, and geographic variables. Consequently, it is difficult to compare immigrants in terms of their rate of assimilation, because the factors that affect their rate of assimilation are complex.

References

Banton, Michael
 1967   *Race Relations.* London: Tavistock Publications.
 1988   *Racial Consciousness.* London: Longman.
Blumer, Herbert
 1965   "Industrialization and Race Relations." In *Industrialization and Race Relations,* London: Oxford University Press. Pp. 220-240.
Bogardus, Emory
 1959   *Social Distance.* Yellow Springs, OH: Antioch Press.
Butler, John S. and Cedric Herring
 1991   "Ethnicity and Entrepreneurship in America: Toward an Explanation of Racial and Ethnic Group Variations in Self-Employment." *Pacific Sociological Review* 34(1):79-94
Cox, Oliver C.
 1948   *Caste, Class, and Race.* New York: Doubleday & Company.
Fong, Eric and William T. Markham
 1991   "Immigration, Ethnicity, and Conflict: The California Chinese, 1849-1882." *Sociological Inquiry* 61(4):471-490.
Gonzales, Juan L. Jr.
 1985   "Introducing Minority Issues and Perspectives into General Education Courses." Paper presented at the Annual Meetings of the Southwestern Social Science Association, Houston, TX.
 1990   "The New Immigration and Refugees in Our Schools." Paper Presented at the Annual Meetings of the California Sociological Association, Carson, CA. (October).
Gordon, Milton A.
 1964   *Assimilation in American Life.* New York: Oxford University Press.
Jiobu, Robert M.
 1988   *Ethnicity and Assimilation.* Albany: State University of New York Press.
Loo, Chalsa M.
 1991   *Chinatown: Most Time, Hard Time.* New York: Praeger.
Montalvo, Frank F.
 1991   "Phenotyping, Acculturation, and Biracial Assimilation of Mexican Americans." In *Empowering Hispanic Families: A Critical Issue for the '90s.* Marta Sotomayor (ed.), Family Service America, Milwaukee, WI. Pp. 97-119.
Park, Robert E.
 1928   "Human Migration and the Marginal Man." *American Journal of Sociology* 33:881-893.

Portes, Alejandro and Robert D. Manning
　1986　　"The Immigrant Enclave: Theory and Empirical Examples."
　　　　　　In *Competitive Ethnic Relations*. Susan Olzak and Joane Nagel
　　　　　　(eds.), New York: Academic Press. Pp. 47-68.
Ransford, H. Edward
　1977　　*Race and Class in American Society*. Cambridge: Schenkman
　　　　　　Publishing Company.
Richardson, E. Allen
　1988　　*Strangers in this Land: Pluralism and the Response to*
　　　　　　Diversity in the United States. New York: The Pilgrim Press.
Ringer, Benjamin B. and Elinor R. Lawless
　1989　　*Race-Ethnicity and Society*. New York: Routledge.
Scott, William A. and Ruth Scott
　1989　　*Adaptation of Immigrants: Individual Differences and Determinants*.
　　　　　　Oxford: Pergamon Press.
Steinberg, Stephen
　1989　　*The Ethnic Myth: Race, Ethnicity, and Class in America*.
　　　　　　Boston: Beacon Press.
Stonequist, Everett V.
　1937　　*The Marginal Man*. New York: Scribner.
Van Den Berghe, Pierre L.
　1978　　*Race and Racism*. New York: John Wiley & Sons.
Warner, W. Lloyd
　1937　　"American Caste and Class." *American Journal of Sociology*
　　　　　　42:234-237.
Zhou, Min and John R. Logan
　1989　　"Returns on Human Capital in Ethnic Enclaves: New York
　　　　　　City's Chinatown." *American Sociological Review* 54:809-820.

Important Names

Michael Banton	Herbert Blumer	Emory Bogardus
Oliver Cox	Milton Gordon	Robert Park
H. Edward Ransford	Everett Stonequist	Malcolm X
Pierre Van Den Berghe	Israel Zangwill	W. Lloyd Warner

Key Terms

assimilation	Anglo-centric	acculturation
amalgamation	Anglo-Centric Perspective	Melting Pot Theory
Cultural Monism	Cultural Pluralism	Cultural Nationalism
People of Color	cultural heterogeneity	Nation of Islam
marginal man	culture conflict	Peripheral Contact
Institutionalized Contact	Domination	Paternalism
Attitude-Receptional-	Behavior-Receptional-	Paternalistic
Assimilation	Assimilation	relationships
paternalistic system	Ante-Bellum period	encomienda system
social caste	social class	horizontal color bar
estate society	social elites	ethclass
Cultural Assimilation	Structural Assimilation	Marital Assimilation
Identificational	Civic Assimilation	human capital
Assimilation	Pluralism	ethnic enclave
Integration	sex-ratio	cultural support system
ideal phenotype		

Sample Test Questions

1. What is assimilation?
2. Be prepared to define and give examples of the following concepts: Anglo-Centric Perspective, the melting pot theory, cultural pluralism, cultural nationalism, Park's Contact Theory, Bogardus' integration theory, the marginal man theory, Van Den Berghe's Model of race relations, Blumer's position on race relations, Oliver Cox's comparison of class, estate, and caste societies, and Gordon's concept of "ethclass", Gordon's seven levels of assimilation, and the factors affecting the rate of assimilation.

Chapter 4

Immigration and the American Mosaic

A Nation of Immigrants

With the arrival of the English Colonists in American in the early 1600's the world witnessed a social experiment on a grand scale. Their arrival in the New World marked the birth of a nation of immigrants. The idea that a nation of people could evolve from such ethnic diversity was something that was unheard of in the whole of human history. Never before had so many people, from such diverse racial and ethnic backgrounds, settled in one place and agreed to live together in peace and harmony.

Since the English were the original settlers, they set the tone for what was to become American culture and society. They provided the language, the religion, a legal system, and a strong sense of history and traditions. But by the eighteenth century millions of others, like the Germans, Scots, Irish, French, Dutch, Italians, Poles, Russians, Scandinavians, Greeks, Chinese, Japanese, and the Spanish were also seeking religious and political freedom and economic opportunities in America. As a result it did not take long for America to become a nation of immigrants (Dinnerstein and Reimers, 1988:15-41).

A consideration of the backgrounds of the immigrants that arrived between 1820 and 1991 reveals that the greatest number came from Germany (7,094,000 or 12.1% of the total number of immigrants), from Italy (5,403,000 or 9.2%), from Great Britain (5,136,000 or 8.7%), from Ireland (4,730,000 or 8.0%), or from Austria-Hungary (4,329,000 or 7.3%). This means that half of the immigrants (45.3%) who have arrived since 1820 came from these five European nations (Hoffman, 1993:397).

In comparison during the same period, that is between 1820 to 1991, only 938,000 (1.6%) immigrants arrived from China, 498,000 (0.8%) from India, 468,000 (0.8%) from Japan, 668,000 (1.1%) from Korea, 1,095,000

(1.9%) from the Philippines, 473,000 (0.8%) from Vietnam, 758,000 (1.3%) from Cuba, 322,000 (0.5%) from El Salvador, 77,000 (0.1%) from Guatemala, and 4,837,000 (8.2%) from Mexico. Therefore the total number of new immigrants only represent 17.1 percent of all the immigrants that have arrived in the United States since 1820 (Hoffman, 1993:397). This represents slightly more than the total number of immigrants that have arrived from Germany alone.

The Causes of Immigration

One of the most popular theories used to describe the process of international immigration patterns is the Push-Pull Migration Hypothesis. This theory holds that people leave their homeland and settle in another country when conditions become uncomfortable or intolerable (the push of immigration) and when conditions in another country are perceived as more favorable (the pull of immigration).

A review of the history of immigration to the United States reveals the push factors of immigration, that is those conditions that make it uncomfortable for people to remain in their homeland. The conditions that make conditions intolerable in their homeland are usually (1) economic conditions, (2) political conditions, (3) social conditions, (4) overpopulation, and (5) natural disasters (Papademetriou, 1991).

Economic push factors are always unfavorable and result in widespread poverty, high unemployment rates, runaway inflation, and business failures on a mass scale. Political push factors such as wars, rebellions, revolutions, and coup d'etats reflect political instability in a society. The social conditions that prompt emigration are the loss of community stability, the failure of the institutions to promote social harmony, and religious persecution. In recent times over population has served as a major push factor. Natural disasters, such as floods, droughts, and earthquakes, often displace large segments of the population, resulting in the loss of land and the development of refugee populations (Massey, 1991:21-27).

The pull factors of immigration are usually the opposite forces involved in the push factors of immigration. This is so since the pull factors are often perceived as the solution to the problems caused by the push factors. Economic pull factors include the availability of jobs, higher salaries (the wage differential), and the opportunity for profitable investments. Sometimes pull factors offer political and religious freedom as a solution to internal problems. In addition to these more obvious push-pull factors of immigration, there is also the consideration of personal or family characteristics, such as gender, age, marital status, personality characteristics, ties to the community, and the desire or motivation for immigration (Scott and Scott, 1989:10-33).

The history of immigration to America reveals that the push-pull factors always work synergistically to encourage immigration. The United States has always been considered the land of opportunity and has historically served as a natural haven for refugees. And our national policy has encouraged immigration. For this reason labor recruitment has played an important role in this process. Historically America has searched for and recruited new sources of cheap labor wherever it was available, as with the indentured servants, the slave trade, the coolie trade, the recruitment of Filipino, Mexican, and Puerto Rican laborers, and the availability of undocumented aliens from Mexico today. These forms of active labor recruitment have had a very dramatic impact on the immigration patterns in America.

An Overview of U.S. Immigration: 1820-1993

The flow of immigrants into America was not officially documented until 1820. A review of the flow of immigrants into the United States reveals distinct historical periods for the arrival of specific groups. The first period of immigration (1820-1880) reflects an open door policy that allowed immigrants to enter the country without any restrictions. Four out of five of all immigrants who arrived during this period came from northwestern Europe, primarily from Germany, Ireland, and Great Britain. These are the so-called old immigrants and they number over 10 million (See Figure 4.1).

The second great wave of immigrants arrived between 1881 to 1920, and are known as the new immigrants. More than 23 million immigrants arrived during this period and were primarily from southern and eastern Europe. Since most came from Italy, they were considered inferior to the true American stock and this resulted in a new wave of resistance to further immigration.

The third period, between 1921 to 1945, was marked by a drastic reduction in the flow of immigrants, as only about five million new immigrants entered during this period. The ravages of the Great Depression and the disruptions caused by the Second World War are the primary reasons for the precipitous reduction in the flow of immigrants. Even so, two out of three of all the immigrants who arrived during this period came from western European nations.

The fourth period of immigration extends from the end of the Second World War to 1964. During this post war period America's immigration policies were designed to accommodate the needs of American citizens and legal resident aliens. This was a period when citizens or legal resident aliens could send for their spouses and children, if they had been separated by the war, and new immigration laws allowed them to marry and bring foreign nationals into the country. Many military personnel took advantage of the war bride provisions approved during this period. These new immigration policies also allowed for the entry of war time refugees (Bennett, 1963).

Figure 4.1
Periods of Immigration to America: 1820-1990

First Period	Old Immigrants	1820-1880
Germany		3,052,126
Ireland		2,829,206
England		962,651
Canada		654,660

Second Period	New Immigrants	1881-1920
Italy		4,114,603
Austria-Hungry		3,925,034
Germany		2,443,565
Ireland		1,529,144
England		1,499,367

Third Period	Depression and War Years	1921-1950
Canada		1,204,760
Germany		752,838
Italy		581,004
England		291,428
Ireland		260,725
Poland		252,331

Fourth Period	Immigration Reform	1951-1970
Canada		791,262
Mexico		753,748
Germany		668,561
Caribbean		593,304
China		577,877
Italy		399,602
England		330,623

Figure 4.1 Continued
Periods of Immigration to America: 1820-1990

Fifth Period	Third World Immigration	1971-1991
Mexico		2,559,300
Philippines		860,500
Korea		603,900
China		568,300
Vietnam		547,100
Cuba		434,900
India		450,700
Dominican Republic		400,000
Jamaica		353,800
Haiti		225,600
Laos		157,800
Cambodia		119,800
Japan		91,000

Source: Arnold, et al, 1987:Table 6.3; Hoffman, 1993:397; INS, 1988:Table 3; INS, 1989: Table 4; U.S. Census, 1990:Table 7.

The most recent period of immigration, between 1965 and 1993, is marked by legislation that attempts to rectify the negative effects of previous immigration policies, that discriminated against immigrants from Third World nations. This most recent period of immigration is recognized for the predominance of immigrants from Asian and Latin American nations.

The 1965 Immigration Reform Act

Over the past twenty-five years the immigration policies of the United States have been affected by and formulated on the basis of four key factors:

1. The public sentiment toward continued immigration,
2. The demands of foreign policy,
3. The interest and goals of elected officials, and
4. The needs of the American economy.

In sum, U.S. immigration policies usually reflect the mood of the American public and the needs of the American economy.

There are many recent examples of how the United States has determined national immigration policies based on need and foreign policy considerations (Reubens, 1987:4-9). With the onset of the Second World War, the government encouraged Mexico to sign a labor agreement that allowed thousands of Mexican aliens to work in the fields and on the railroads in an effort to compensate for the shortage of American laborers. In 1943 Congress repealed the Chinese Exclusion Act, as a reward for China's support of the allied war effort. In 1946, the War Brides Act was passed to insure the reunification of spouses and children of U.S. citizens. During the same year new laws were passed that allowed groups that had previously been barred from American citizenship to secure naturalization rights. In 1952, the McCarran-Walter Act was passed to rectify the inequalities and limitations of the quota system and to provide relief to immigrants from the Asian Pacific triangle.

Without any doubt the most sweeping immigration reforms took place in October of 1965, when Congress passed the Immigration and Nationality Act. The groundwork for this landmark immigration reform was laid by President John F. Kennedy and was signed into law by President Lyndon B. Johnson (Reimers, 1985:63-90). This Act was passed with the intention of achieving five basic goals:

1. To provide for family reunification,
2. To attract skilled and educated aliens,
3. To ease world population problems caused by natural disasters and political unrest,
4. To encourage international exchange programs, and
5. To prevent the entry of aliens with health problems, criminal records, or the indigent.

Besides allowing all nations a quota of 20,000 immigrants per year, the new immigration law also set a ceiling of 170,000, with a cap of 120,000 immigrants per year from the Western hemisphere nations after July of 1968. One of the most significant aspects of the law was the creation of an immigrant preference system, which allowed the government to issue visas based on a seven point system (See Appendix A).

Following the implementation of these new policies the number of Asian immigrants increased dramatically. For example, in 1965 only 17,000 immigrants arrived from all Asian nations. However, since 1981 more than a quarter of a million Asian immigrants have arrived each year. Between 1971 and 1980 one-third (35%) of all immigrants were from Asia and almost half (44%) were from Latin American countries. In effect four out of five of the immigrants who arrived during this period were from Third World nations.

Immigration Reforms Since 1965

Since the early 1960's an important source of new immigrants has come from the flow of political refugees. As early as 1960, the government created the Cuban Refugee Program and allowed more than 800,000 refugees to enter this country between 1960 and 1980. The second largest influx of refugees came from Vietnam, following the fall of Saigon in 1975. Between 1975 and 1979 more than 200,000 Vietnamese settled in the United States. In total more than 700,000 Indochinese refugees arrived between 1975 and 1984 (Bach, 1988). In addition over 616,000 refugees from communist states in Eastern Europe and 113,000 Soviet refugees have arrived in American since the mid-1950's (Kraly, 1990).

In April of 1980 Congress passed the Refugee Act, increasing the limit on refugees to 50,000 and increased the number of immigrants allowed per year from 290,000 to 320,000. The provisions of this Act also gave greater weight to humanitarian concerns in the allocation of immigration slots. In 1980, the Carter administration admitted 130,000 Mariel refugees (Cafferty, et al., 1983:116-125).

Following an extended period of partisan debate over the Simpson-Mazzoli Immigration Bill, Congress passed the Immigration Reform and Control Act (IRCA) in November of 1986. This Act addressed three major issues: (1) the legalization of undocumented aliens, (2) the provision for employer sanctions, and (3) the allowance for temporary agricultural workers (Bean, et al. 1990).

The Immigration Reform and Control Act (IRCA) allowed undocumented aliens who entered the country before January 1, 1982 to adjust their status. During the first eleven months of this program the Immigration and Naturalization Service received more than 400,000 applications (Martin, 1988:7). By August of 1990, 1,300,000 aliens had applied for legalization under the provisions of this Act and only 341 were denied. Of these applicants, 1,230,299 were Mexican nationals (Hoefer, 1991:26-27, 29) In addition another 581,000 applied for legalization under the provisions of the Special Agricultural Workers (SAW) program (Hoffman, 1989:740). During the fiscal year of 1988, a total of 643,000 aliens were granted legal status under the provisions of this act (INS, 1989:1). Under the act the government is also allowed to fine employers who hire undocumented aliens from $250 to $10,000 per alien (Rolph and Robyn, 1990:11-13, 37-40). It is estimated that the flow of undocumented aliens was cut by 2.5 million migrants during the first two years following the passage of IRCA (Espenshade, 1990:74-75).

The Impact of Immigration Reforms: 1960-1993

Those who drafted the Immigration Reform Act of 1965 were very careful to place restrictions on those immigrants who would be allowed to enter the United States. It was the provisions of the third and sixth preferences that stipulated that only the most qualified immigrants from the Third World would be admitted. These provisions also insured that American labor would be protected.

The preferences that were used most extensively by new immigrants were the family reunification preferences and refugee preferences. Under the family reunification provision U.S. citizens and legal resident aliens were allowed to send for immediate family members in the Third World. For the first time in U.S. immigration history the citizens of developing nations, primarily in Asia and Latin America, were given an equal opportunity to emigrate to the United States.

A review of the immigration trends reveals that six out of ten of the immigrants who arrived during the thirty year period before the passage of the Immigration Reform Act of 1965 were from Europe (41% were) or from North America (21% were). In this regard the immediate effect of the Immigration Reform Act of 1965 was to stimulate immigration from Latin America and Asia. For example, half (52%) of the immigrants who arrived between 1961 and 1970 came from Third World nations. But the true demographic impact of these reforms were not felt until the early seventies, when two out of five (43%) of the immigrants were from Latin America and two out of five (43%) were from Asian nations. By the late eighties, the revolution in U.S. immigration policy was complete, as almost nine out of ten (86.4%) of all immigrants were either from Latin America or Asia, and only one out of ten were from Europe (See Figure 4.2).

The changes brought about by the Immigration Reform Act of 1965 are clear when we compare the major sending nations in 1960 with the major sending nations in 1985. In 1960 the top sending nations were Mexico, Germany, Canada, and the United Kingdom. But thirty years later the major sending nations are Mexico, El Salvador, the Philippines, China, Vietnam, and Korea. In fact, not a single Western nation appeared in the top fourteen categories in 1990 (See Figure 4.3).

Overall, the greatest flow of immigrants in 1990 came from Asia (28.6%), Latin America, and the Caribbean. (55.7%). Mexico alone sent 37.1 percent of all immigrants we entered in 1990. In contrast only one out of ten immigrants came from European nations.

Asian Immigration: 1965-1992

Clearly the Immigration Reform Act of 1965 has had the greatest impact on the flow of Asian immigrants. Among the Asian immigrants, the Philippines and China have been the top sending nations since the early 1960's (See Figure 4.3).

A few figures will provide some insight into the dramatic increase in the flow of Asian immigrants. In 1965 the total number of Asian immigrants was only 17,080. Five years later their annual rate of flow had increased by

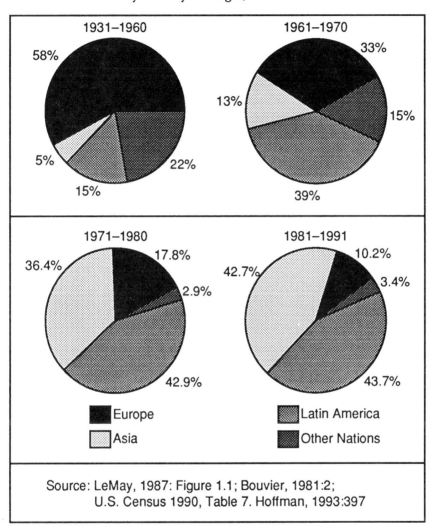

Figure 4.2
Immigrants Admitted to the United States
by Country of Origin, 1931-1991

Source: LeMay, 1987: Figure 1.1; Bouvier, 1981:2;
U.S. Census 1990, Table 7. Hoffman, 1993:397

five times this amount. Ten years after the passage of the Immigration Reform Act their annual rate of flow increased to 119,000. By 1980 their annual rate of flow reached 236,000 (Gordon, 1990). For the remainder of the 1980's their flow stabilized at a quarter of a million per year (See Table 4.1).

Figure 4.3
Major Sources of Immigrants: 1960 and 1991

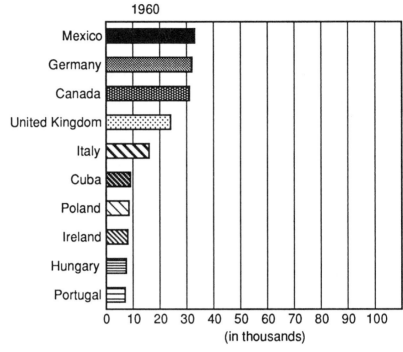

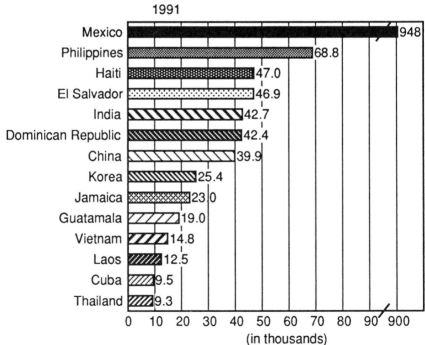

Source: INS, 1960: Table 6; U.S. Census, 1990:
Table 7 Hoffman, 1993: 397.

Table 4.1
Asian Immigration for Selected Years, 1965 to 1991

Year	Number	Year	Number	Year	Number
1965	17,080	1975	118,952	1986	268,248
1966	35,807	1980	236,097	1987	248,300
1967	53,403	1981	264,343	1988	264,465
1968	50,841	1982	313,291	1989	296,400
1969	65,111	1984	256,273	1990	321,900
1970	83,468	1985	264,691	1991	342,200

Source: Arnold, et al, 1987:Table 6.1; Hoffman, 1993:397; INS, 1988:Table 3; INS, 1989: Table 4;U.S. Census, 1990: Table 7.

If we consider the total number of Asian immigrants that arrived between 1960 and 1988, most came from the Philippines and over half a million arrived from Korea and China during this period. These top sending Asian nations are followed closely by Vietnam and India (See Table 4.2).

Table 4.2
Top Ten Sources of Asian Immigrants 1960 to 1991

Sending Nation	Total Immigration 1960-1991	Percent of Total
Philippines	1,036,316	25.1
Korea	672,207	16.3
China	659,359	16.0
Vietnam	566,486	13.7
India	510,762	12.4
Laos	157,810	3.8
Hong Kong	157,439	3.8
Japan	146,461	3.5
Cambodia	119,842	2.9
Thailand	104,823	2.5
Total	4,131,505	100.0

Source: Arnold, et al, 1987: Table 6.3; Hoffman, 1993:397; INS, 1988:Table 3; INS, 1989:Table 4; U.S. Census, 1990:Table 7.

Of all the Asian immigrants that arrived during 1988, half (56% or 147,356) entered as immigrants exempt from numerical limitations. Of this number most arrived as immediate relatives (58%), or as refugees (38%). Of those subject to numerical limitations (117,109), three out of four (78%)

Table 4.3
Immigrants to the United States by Major Occupational Group and
Place of Birth, Fiscal Year 1989

Place of birth	Total	Total reporting an occupation	Professional specialty & technical	Executive, administrative, & managerial	Sales
All places	1.090,924	100.0	9.7	6.2	3.9
Europe	82,891	100.0	24.0	10.0	3.9
Africa	25,166	100.0	21.4	12.9	7.2
Oceania	4,360	100.0	22.9	12.6	6.0
No. America	607,398	100.0	3.3	2.8	3.0
Mexico	405,172	100.0	1.5	2.1	2.6
Caribbean	88,932	100.0	10.8	4.2	3.9
Cen. America	101,034	100.0	3.5	3.3	3.7
So. America	58,926	100.0	11.6	7.4	5.1
Asia (1)	312,149	100.0	22.8	14.2	5.9
Asia (2)	263,459	100.0	22.4	13.7	5.2
Bangladesh	2,180	100.0	16.6	13.8	6.8
Cambodia	6,076	100.0	3.0	1.4	3.3
China	32,272	100.0	15.3	10.7	3.6
Hong Kong	9,740	100.0	23.8	20.5	6.0
India	31,175	100.0	39.2	20.1	3.5
Indonesia	1,513	100.0	24.3	16.6	4.7
Japan	4,849	100.0	22.8	20.7	5.2
Korea	34,222	100.0	23.4	19.0	5.1
Laos	12,524	100.0	2.5	0.5	0.9
Malaysia	1,506	100.0	29.4	18.6	4.7
Pakistan	8,000	100.0	20.9	22.6	8.8
Philippines	57,034	100.0	28.7	12.8	4.3
Singapore	566	100.0	32.5	23.4	8.3
Sri Lanka	757	100.0	41.7	17.6	3.5
Taiwan	13,974	100.0	34.6	24.1	4.9
Thailand	9,332	100.0	13.7	14.8	12.7
Vietnam	37,739	100.0	4.4	1.6	9.2

Table 4.3 (continued)

Administrative support	Precision production, craft & repair	Operator fabricator & laborer	Farming forestry & fishing	Service	No occupation reported
8.0	12.3	29.5	5.5	25.0	47.7
10.1	14.5	15.2	2.2	20.0	51.0
11.9	4.9	12.7	0.4	28.6	44.5
12.7	9.8	9.6	4.5	21.9	48.6
6.2	13.8	37.3	5.7	27.8	39.4
5.1	14.1	42.9	7.3	24.5	36.5
11.0	14.2	18.4	3.3	34.3	57.7
7.5	13.1	28.9	1.4	38.6	33.4
11.2	12.9	26.1	1.4	24.3	52.7
11.6	7.6	13.1	7.4	17.5	62.2
11.9	6.9	13.5	8.6	17.7	62.2
8.0	8.9	8.7	2.5	34.7	54.7
10.4	8.2	54.7	10.9	15.8	77.8
7.6	5.1	18.5	21.0	18.2	42.9
22.7	7.7	5.5	0.2	13.6	48.2
7.9	3.2	3.8	7.6	14.6	63.9
16.7	5.9	7.7	0.4	23.7	53.7
11.9	3.8	2.7	0.9	32.0	62.9
21.3	6.7	10.0	3.0	11.5	78.6
1.1	8.2	63.3	4.5	19.0	81.4
12.6	5.1	5.1	0.4	24.0	49.6
9.7	4.8	8.5	3.0	21.7	57.7
16.9	6.3	6.8	5.7	18.4	56.2
13.9	3.6	1.6	—	16.7	55.5
13.4	3.2	4.5	—	16.1	46.8
14.5	2.1	3.0	4.4	12.3	56.9
15.0	8.0	8.7	1.3	25.8	69.5
2.8	17.8	32.4	12.4	19.5	69.2

Source: U.S. Immigration and Naturalization Service *1989 Statistical Yearbook*, Table 20, p.40.

arrived under the occupational preferences. Therefore most Asian immigrants arrived as a result of the family reunification provisions of the Immigration Reform Act of 1965 (See Table 4.3).

The largest group of Asian immigrants, the Filipinos, rely most heavily on the family preference category, as four out of five (86% of 50,697) entered under this category in 1988. Likewise, nine out of ten Koreans used this category. Overall two out of three (67%) of all Asians who arrived in 1988 entered under the family preference category.

The Vietnamese were most likely to enter as political refugees (83% of 15,789), followed by immigrants from Laos (97% of 10,667), Cambodia (96% of 9,629), and Thailand (52% of 6,888) (See Table 4.5). In total, one out of five (21%) of all Asian immigrants arrived as political refugees. Many of these Asian refugees arrived as the so-called Boat People and despite many hardships and obstacles they have managed to integrate themselves into the economic structure of American society (Caplan, 1989). Refugees have a strong propensity to adjust their status to that of permanent resident aliens (Hein, 1991:69-71). Between 1961 and 1988 a total of 432,306 Vietnamese, 142,798 Laotians, and 111,436 Cambodians did so (Jasso and Rosenzweig, 1990:341-342). It is also true that refugees have a high rate of naturalization, that is when compared to all other immigrants (Portes and Rumbaut, 1990:116-126). As a group Asians also have the highest rate of naturalization (75%), when compared to immigrants from other regions like Africa (52%), the Caribbean and Central America (21%), Europe (27%), and South America (25%) (Jasso and Rosenzweig, 1990: Table 2.1; Portes and Rumbaut, 1990: Table 13).

Asian Population Projections: 1980-2030

The 1980 population of 3.5 million Asian Americans increased to 6.5 million in 1990 and it is estimated that it will increase to ten million (9,850,364) by the turn of the century. By the year 2030 the Asian American population will increase to almost 20 million (Bouvier and Agresta, 1987:Table 12.1).

Among Asian Americans the Chinese had the largest population in America (812,178) in 1980, followed by the Filipinos (781,894), the Japanese (716,331), the Asian Indians (387,223), and the Koreans (357,393). In 1990 the Filipinos were the largest Asian group in America (1,405,146), followed closely by the Chinese (1,259,038), the Koreans (814,495), and the Japanese (804,535). And while they are not as large, the Vietnamese and the Koreans are growing at a much faster rate than all the other Asian groups (Gardner, 1985).

Population projections reveal that the Vietnamese will continue to be the fastest growing Asian group in the United States until the year 2030. Forty years from now the Filipinos will be the largest Asian group, whose population will reach four million (3,963,710), followed closely by the Vietnamese (3,934,661), the Koreans (2,946,986), the Chinese (2,779,127), and the Asian Indians (1,919,163) (Bouvier and Agresta, 1987:Table 12.2).

Historically, immigrants tend to settle in certain cities and in certain regions of the country (Portes and Rumbaut, 1990:34-47). This is a clear pattern among the Asian immigrants today. For example, of the 25,841 Chinese immigrants admitted in 1987, one out of four (27%) settled in New York City, fifteen percent in San Francisco, and one out of ten (11%) in the Los Angeles-Long Beach metropolitan area. Among Filipinos the main area of settlement is California, with sixteen percent selecting the Los Angeles-Long Beach metropolitan area, seven percent San Francisco, and seven percent San Diego. The Vietnamese are also heavily concentrated in California, with one out of ten (11%) living in the Anaheim-Santa Ana metropolitan area, nine percent in Los Angeles-Long Beach, and seven percent in San Jose. Korean immigrants tend to settle in either the Los Angeles-Long Beach area (16%) or in New York City (8%) (INS, 1988:Table 18).

Among all immigrants, three out of ten select California as their intended state of residence, followed by New York (17%), Florida (10%), Texas (7%), New Jersey (5%), and Illinois (4%). Overall these five states account for the intended residence of more than 70 percent of all immigrants admitted in 1988 (INS, 1989:Chart 1).

Of the estimated 9.8 million Asians living in the United States by the turn of the century, half (53%) will be living in the west. Half the Chinese (51%) will be living in the west, as will seven out of ten (69%) Filipinos, half (45%) of the Koreans, eight out of ten (80%) Japanese, and half (53%) of the Vietnamese (Bouvier and Agresta, 1987:Table 12.2; Table 12.5). Most of the Asian Americans living in the west will settle in California, with their heaviest concentration in the Los Angeles-Long Beach metropolitan area, followed by Anaheim-Santa Ana, San Diego, San Francisco, and San Jose.

Chapter Summary

An overview of the total number of immigrants that arrived between 1820 and 1990 reveals that the total number of immigrants arriving from Third World countries is actually small, that is when compared to the total number of immigrants that have arrived from all countries. When the total number of immigrants that have arrived from both Asian and Latin American countries is compared to all the immigrants that have arrived since 1820, the total number of German immigrants exceeds all immigrants that have arrived from both of these areas of the world.

The most significant changes in U.S. immigration laws occurred in 1965, when President Lyndon B. Johnson signed the Immigration Reform Act. For the first time this law allowed People of Color to enter the United

States on an equal footing with all other immigrants. Perhaps the most important provision of the Immigration Reform Act of 1965 was the family reunification provision.

The 1980's are now recognized as a period of dramatic change in the immigration laws and in the flow of immigrants. The result has been a dramatic shift in the flow of immigrants from European nations to Asian and Latin American nations. The flow of Asian immigrants has already had a dramatic impact on the lives of all Americans and on the development of certain cities that are now recognized as primary settlement areas for the new Asian immigrants. The demographic predictions suggest that California and New York will remain the areas of heaviest Asian American settlement beyond the turn of the century.

References

Bach, Robert L.
1988   "State Intervention in Southeast Asian Refugee Resettlement in the United States." *Journal of Refugee Studies* 1:38-56.
Bean, Frank D., T.J. Espenshade, M.J. White, and R.F. Dymowski
1990   "Post-IRCA Changes in the Volume and Composition of Undocumented Migration to the United States: An Assessment Based on Apprehensions Data." In *Undocumented Migration to the United States: IRCA and the Experience of the 1980s.* Frank D. Bean, B. Edmonstron, and J.S. Passel (eds.), Santa Monica, CA: Rand Corporation. Pp. 111-158.
Bennett, Marion T.
1963   *American Immigration Policies: A History.* Washington, D.C.: Public Affairs Press.
Bourvier, Leon F. and Anthony J. Agresta
1987   "The Future Asian Population of the United States." In Pacific Bridges: *The New Immigration from Asia and the Pacific Islands.* James T. Fawcett and Benjamin V. Carino (eds.), Staten Island, NY: Center for Migration Studies. Pp. 285-301.
Cafferty, Pastora, et al.
1983   *The Dilemma of American Immigration: Beyond the Golden Door.* New Brunswick: Transaction Books.
Caplan, Nathan, J.K. Whitmore, and M.H. Choy
1989   *The Boat People and Achievement in America: A Study of Family Life, Hard Work, and Cultural Values.* Ann Arbor: University of Michigan Press.
Dinnerstein, Leonard and David M. Reimers
1988   *Ethnic Americans: A History of Immigration.* New York: Harper & Row.
Espenshade, Thomas J.
1990   "Undocumented Migration to the United States: Evidence from a Repeated Trials Model." In *Undocumented Migration to the United States: IRCA and the Experience of the 1980s.* Frank D. Bean, B. Edmonstron, and J.S. Passel (eds.), Santa Monica, CA: Rand Corporation. Pp. 159-181.
Gardner, R.W., et al.
1985   "Asian Americans: Growth, Change, and Diversity." *Population Bulletin* 40(4): October.
Gordon, Linda W.
1990   "Asian Immigration Since World War II." In *Immigration and U.S. Foreign Policy.* Robert W. Tucker, C.B. Keely, and L. Wrigley (eds.), Boulder, CO: Westview Press. Pp. 73-98.

Hein, Jeremy
1991   "Do 'New Immigrants' Become 'New Minorities'?: The
        Meaning of Ethnic Minority for Indochinese Refugees in
        the United States." *Pacific Sociological Review* 34(1):61-77.
Hoefer, Michael D.
1991   "Background of U.S. Immigration Policy Reform." In *U.S.
        Immigration Policy Reform in the 1980s: A Preliminary Assess-
        ment.* Francisco L. Rivera, S.L. Sechzer, and I.N. Gang
        (eds.), New York: Praeger. Pp. 17-44.
Hoffman, Mark S.
1993   *The World Almanac.* New York: Pharos Books.
Immigration and Naturalization Service (INS)
1960   *Annual Report: Immigration and Naturalization Service.*
        Washington, D.C.: U.S. Department of Justice.
1981   *Annual Report: Statistical Yearbook 1981.* Washington, D.C.:
        U.S. Department of Justice.
1988   *1987 Statistical Yearbook of the Immigration and Naturaliza-
        tion Service.* Washington, D.C.: U.S. Department of Justice.
1989   *Immigration Statistics: Fiscal Year 1988-Advanced Report.*
        Washington, D.C.: U.S. Department of Justice.
Jasso, Guillermina and Mark R. Rosenzweig
1990   *The New Chosen People: Immigrants in the United States.*
        New York: Russell Sage Foundation.
Kraly, Ellen P.
1990   "U.S. Refugee Policies and Refugee Migration Since World
        War II." In *Immigration and U.S. Foreign Policy.* Robert W.
        Tucker, C.B. Keely, and L. Wrigley (eds.), Boulder, CO:
        Westview Press. Pp. 73-98.
Martin, Philip L.
1988   "Immigration Reform and California Agriculture." Davis, CA:
        Unpublished Paper.
Massey, Douglas S.
1991   "Economic Development and International Migration in
        Comparative Perspective." In *Determinants of Emigration from
        Mexico, Central America, and the Caribbean.* Sergio Diaz-Bri-
        quets and Sidney Weintraub (eds.), Boulder: Westview
        Press. Pp. 12-47.
Papademetriou, Demetrios G.
1991   "Migration and Development: The Unsettled Relationship."
        In *Determinants of Emigration from Mexico, Central America, and
        the Caribbean.* Sergio Diaz-Briquets and Sidney Weintraub
        (eds.), Boulder: Westview Press. Pp. 259-294.

Portes, Alejandro and Ruben G. Rumbaut
    1990   *Immigrant America: A Portrait.* Berkeley: University of
               California Press.
Reimers, David M.
    1985   *Still the Gold Door: The Third World Comes to America.*
               New York: Columbia University Press.
Reubens, Edwin P.
    1987   "Benefits and Costs of Migration." In *The Economics of Mass*
               Migration in the Twentieth Century. Sidney Klein(ed.), New
               York: Paragon House Publishers. Pp. 1-40.
Rolph, Elizabeth and Abby Robyn
    1990   *A Window on Immigration Reform: Implementing the*
               Immigration Reform and Control Act in Los Angeles. Santa
               Monica, CA: Rand Corporation.
Scott, William A. and Ruth Scott
    1989   *Adaptation of Immigrants: Individual Differences and Determinants.*
               Oxford: Pergamon Press.

push-pull migration hypothesis

War Brides Act

Immigration and Nationality Act of 1965

Cuban Refugee Program

Indochinese refugees

Refugee Act 1980

Simpson-Mazzoli Immigration Bill

numerical limitations

Immigration Reform and Control Act (IRCA)

Special Agricultural Workers (SAW) program

the Great Depression

McCarran-Walter Act

seven point system

Vietnamese refugees

Soviet refugees

Mariel refugees

family reunification

boat people

population projections

Sample Test Questions

1. Discuss four factors that determine U.S. immigration policies.
2. List five of the preferences allowed under the Immigration and Nationality Act of 1965 and note how each has affected the flow of immigration to America.
3. Discuss four important events that have affected U.S. immigration policies since the passage of the Immigration and Nationality Act of 1965.
4. Discuss four reasons why the flow of immigrants from Asia has increased so dramatically since 1965.

Part II

★ ★ ★

The Asian American Experience

Chapter 5

The Chinese American Experience

Introduction

Of the many immigrants that have set foot on American soil, the Chinese are the first People of Color to emigrate in large numbers and therefore they have the longest history of settlement in America. But in spite of this long period of emigration the actual number of Chinese living in the United States today is small. In 1992 there were just over one million residents of Chinese origin in the United States, which represents about one-half of a percent of the total population. But despite their small numbers they have played a very significant role in the development of American society.

In this chapter we shall consider the forces that first attracted the Chinese to America, to the jobs that they filled, to the prejudice and discrimination that they encountered, to their isolation in Chinatown, and to the very long period of legal restrictions on their immigration. In our consideration of Chinese Americans in modern times we shall focus on their success in American society and the impact of the Immigration Reform Act of 1965. We shall conclude with a demographic profile of Chinese Americans today.

The Push-Pull Factors of Immigration

While recent archaeological finds off the coast of Southern California support the idea that America may have been discovered by Buddhist missionaries from China in the fifth century, it is known that the Spanish employed Chinese shipbuilders in Baja California as early as 1571 (Steiner, 1979:28-35; Tsai, 1986:1). Bancroft records that two men and a woman from China arrived in San Francisco aboard the *Eagle* in February of 1848, and thus became the first Chinese settlers in California (Bancroft, 1890:336). But with the discovery of gold in California their population grew at a phenomenal rate. In 1849 there were only 54 Chinese laborers in California. The following year their population increased to 4,000, and by December of 1851 there were 25,000 Chinese living in California (Tung, 1974:7-8).

During the reign of the emperor the punishment for emigration from China was decapitation. But as a result of political chaos and internal warfare during the nineteenth century, this prohibition was unenforceable. Following the Opium War (1839-1842), the ruling Qing Dynasty (1644-1912) was forced to give Hong Kong to the British and ordered to open trade with Europe. Following the termination of the slave trade the British encouraged the emigration of Chinese laborers to their colonies in the Far East (Kung, 1962:3-29). In the end the Chinese were humiliated by foreigners, faced a heavy tax burden, had to contend with inept and corrupt rulers, and were forced to live under unpredictable social and economic circumstances. These conditions boiled over into the Taiping Rebellion (1850-1864). It is estimated that some 25 million people lost their lives as a result of the warfare that ensued.

To make matters worse China was also hard hit by a series of natural disasters, such as droughts, storms, typhoons, and plagues between 1833 and 1882 that contributed to the social unrest and dislocation. Due to the political turmoil they were unable to maintain their sophisticated flood control systems and the monsoons brought floods, destroying crops and livestock, and producing widespread famine (Walker, 1976:9-13). China was also faced with a serious over population problem. It is estimated that the country's population in 1741 was 143 million, 286 million by 1784, and increased to 430 million by 1850 (Tsai, 1986:2). The over population problem contributed to mass starvation and the wholesale dislocation of people across the land. In view of these tragedies it is not surprising that thousands of Chinese decided to leave their homeland and search for new opportunities abroad (Yen, 1985:32-41).

Without any doubt the most important pull factor for Chinese immigration to America was the discovery of gold at Sutter's mill in January of 1848. But the news of the gold strike did not reach China until the Spring of 1849. The refugees living in Kwangtung (Guangdong) and Fukien (Fujian) provinces were eager to escape the tragedies in their homeland and were among the first to secure passage to Gold Mountain (their name for California) (Mei, 1984a). The American and British shipping companies charged Chinese passengers $40 to $50 for a one-way ticket, and during 1852 alone some 30,000 Chinese traveled to San Francisco and paid $1,300,000 for their passage (i.e., when a good day's wage was a dollar). Overall it is estimated that the shipping companies made more than $11 million in passenger fares alone (Barth, 1964:61- 62).

By custom the Chinese borrowed money for their passage from their families, who usually sold land and property for this purpose. The expectation was that by sending one of their sons to Gold Mountain, they would return wealthy. But before long a credit-ticket system was devised, whereby a group of wealthy Hong Kong merchants sponsored an immigrant's passage to America. In return the immigrant was expected to work for them until his passage was paid (Minnick, 1988:7-9). This arrangement was usually based on a two year labor contract (Barth, 1964:51-57). In their view the voyage to California offered them an opportunity to earn more money in a few years than they could expect to earn in a lifetime at home (Chinn, 1969:16). But unfortunately, many did not return home successful.

To their credit the Chinese were very well organized, for in view of the efficiency of the shipping companies, the credit-ticket system, and the Chinese-Six Companies, they began to arrive in San Francisco at the rate of several hundred a month after 1852 (See Table 5.1). However, it is estimated that over half these immigrants returned home. For this reason some have referred to the Chinese immigrants as sojourners or birds of passage (Ng, 1987:53-58).

Table 5.1
Chinese Immigration to the United States, 1820-1991

Decade	Number	Percent	Decade	Number	Percent
1841-1850*	35	0.004	1931-1940	4,928	0.5
1851-1860	41,397	4.3	1941-1950	16,709	1.7
1861-1870	64,301	6.7	1951-1960	9,657	1.0
1871-1880	123,201	12.9	1961-1970	34,764	3.6
1881-1890	61,711	6.4	1971-1980	124,326	13.0
1891-1900	14,799	1.5	1981-1991	412,686	40.6
1901-1910	20,605	2.1			
1911-1920	21,907	2.3	1820-1991	980,315	100.0
1921-1930	29,907	3.1			

* Only 11 Chinese immigrants between 1820 and 1840
Source: Sandmeyer, 1939:12, 16; Lee, 1960:21; Coolidge, 1968:498; Hoffman, 1993:397; Johnson, 1992:804; U.S. Census, 1950-1988.

The Pioneers in the Labor Market

The Chinese pioneers were predominately young men, as women were prohibited from traveling to foreign lands. Most were peasants, illiterate, did not speak English, and were from rural-agricultural backgrounds. But they were all willing to work hard and eager to learn new skills.

In China every major city had an organization known as the Hui-Guan. The Hui-Guans, also known as benevolent associations, served as reception centers for new arrivals or travelers, and were sponsored by local merchants. The first benevolent association in San Francisco was founded by a restaurateur in December of 1849 (Chen, 1980:28). By 1854, a more formal merchant organization was founded, commonly known as the Chinese Six Companies, representing the nine major districts from which most Chinese immigrants came. The Chinese Six Companies, formally known as the Chinese Consolidated Benevolent Association, sponsored the credit-ticket system and provided immigrants with a variety of social services, such as meeting them at the dock, providing interpreters, giving them temporary housing, putting them in contact with other immigrants from their district, and giving them jobs. Before long the Chinese were organized into work groups and industrial guilds, as new arrivals were given jobs in businesses owned by local merchants. It is estimated that ninety percent of all Chinese immigrants were sponsored and organized by the Chinese Six Company (Commonwealth, 1946:37).

Historically immigrants enter the labor market at the point of least resistance and therefore they usually take the least desirable jobs. This is called the soft spot theory of immigrant employment. Otherwise they create new jobs wherever they perceive a need. Both methods contribute to the development of the local economy. But sometimes immigrants do compete with local labor, that is in terms of wages, quality of work, and quantity of production (Fong and Markham, 1991:472-474).

During the first decade of their arrival the Chinese were welcomed and were considered a godsend, that is in view of the severe labor shortage at the time (Steiner, 1979:108-113). Since only seven percent of California's population was female in 1850, the Chinese found their first jobs as domestic servants, cooks, vegetable peddlers, gardeners, and as laundrymen (Chan, 1991:29- 32). And the laundry business was the most lucrative, for prior to their arrival the elites of San Francisco sent their laundry to Hawaii to be washed by Polynesian women. The first Chinese laundry was established in the spring of 1851, by an immigrant called Wah Lee (Wu, 1928:24-25).

Between 1850 and 1870, most worked in the gold mines, predominately in work gangs of fifty to five hundred men under contract for a wealthy Chinese merchants (Williams, 1930:52). In 1855, the Sacramento *Daily Union* estimated that out of the 36,000 Chinese in California, 20,000 were miners. By 1862, 30,000 were miners, out of a population of 48,000 (Barth, 1964:113). Others found work in the mining camps as laundrymen, cooks, and domestic servants (Minnick, 1988:13-20). Some started their businesses, such as restaurants, bars, general stores, hardware stores, and commercial laundries (McLeod, 1947:46; Williams, 1930).

Besides their creation of the laundry business in San Francisco the Chinese were also involved in cigar manufacturing, where nine out of ten were employed by 1870. Two-thirds of those employed in the woolen industry were Chinese, as were one out of five of those employed in the boot industry (Coolidge, 1909:359). By 1870, there were 1200 Chinese storekeepers and 1500 factory and mill hands in the city (Cather, 1932:51; Ong, 1981). The Chinese were successful because they were hard workers, efficient, and they were willing to work longer hours than their competitors (Mei, 1984b).

Chinese restaurants were also very popular, as everyone knew that they could obtain an excellent meal for a very reasonable price. They also cultivated small gardens to provide a stock of fresh fruits and vegetables for their shops and restaurants. They also operated a small fleet of junks and peddled a variety of fish, clams, shrimp, and crabs (McLeod, 1974:94-98).

The Chinese worked in woolen factories, knitting mills, highway and wharf construction, borax beds, and on farms and dairies. They also worked as wood cutters, brewers, brickmakers, masons, coal heavers, and as sailors and shipbuilders (Nee, 1973). Thousands of others cleared land, reclaimed delta swamp land, developed a salt works, started the garment industry, wagon and cart manufacturing, whip and harness making, and planted the first vineyards in California (Sandmeyer, 1939:20-21; Takaki, 1989:88-99).

But in spite of their contributions to the development of California's economy, the Chinese are best known for their work on the transcontinental railroad. The decision to hire them was made by Charles Crocker in the spring of 1865, following some labor problems that put the Central Pacific behind schedule (Storti, 1991:10-21). For their blood and sweat they were paid $28 a month and were given Sundays off, but they had to supply their food and tents (Chen, 1980:68). When construction was completed in May of 1869 more than 14,000 Chinese were on the payroll (Saxton, 1971:62).

Following their work on the railroad many returned home but others were attracted to the burgeoning agricultural industry of California, where they cleared the land, dug the canals and reservoirs, planted the first orchards and harvested the first crops (Walker, 1976:71-76). As a result of their labor the annual fruit production in California increased from 1.8 to 12 million pounds between 1871 and 1884 (Chen, 1980:88). In addition 3,000 to 4,000 Chinese were contracted to reclaim land in the San Joaquin Delta, where they used hand carts to move mountains of dirt, worked waist deep in water to dam sloughs and cut drainage ditches, and constructed levees three stories high (Chu, 1970). By 1877 they reclaimed more than five million acres of the most fertile land in California, valued at $289,700,000 (Minnick, 1988:63-72; Wu, 1928:26-27).

The Anti-Chinese Movement

As happens with most immigrants, the Chinese were initially welcomed and were considered indispensable for the economic development of California.

However, it did not take long for public opinion to turn against them, as the old racial prejudices that considered them dishonest, crafty, cruel, and lacking in courage and intelligence gained popular acceptance (Miller, 1969:36, 145-150; Spoehr, 1973). The argonauts saw the Chinese as formidable competitors for jobs and for the precious gold nuggets. Therefore it is not surprising that the first act of mob violence against the Chinese occurred in the Sierra gold town of Chinese Camp in 1849 (See Box Reading 5.1).

But in a matter of a few years the city of San Francisco became the hub of popular agitation against Chinese immigration. Essentially there were four primary antagonists involved in this struggle: (1) the unemployed sandlot agitators, (2) the labor unions, (3) the newspapers, and (4) the politicians.

In the fall of 1859 the unemployed of San Francisco organized themselves into Anti-Coolie clubs, with the stated objective of terminating Chinese immigration. They also wanted to make their lives as miserable as possible. These clubs were made up of disgruntled thugs, hoodlums, and racists who took a good deal of pleasure in assaulting the hapless Chinese. The collective mayhem was usually sparked by a sandlot meeting in which the ringleaders galvanized and spurred the agitated mob to acts of violence (Daniels, 1978). By 1867 there was an organized Anti-Coolie club in every ward of the city (Daniels, 1962:16).

Without any doubt labor unions were the harbingers of organized violence against the Chinese, as the anti-Chinese movement was founded by labor leaders in San Francisco (Eaves, 1910:10; Cross, 1935:95-96). The labor leaders educated the white working classes of the city and founded the Workingmen's Party in 1877. Obviously they considered the Chinese as a source of cheap labor and felt that they were taking white men's jobs (Fessler, 1983:95-114; Gardner, 1961:17-22). Within a few years organized labor became synonymous with white labor and the Anti-Coolie movement.

Organized labor had the full support of the newspapers who unflaggingly agitated against Chinese immigration. They supported the sandlot orators and never missed an opportunity to publish their racist views. The *Chronicle* and the *Morning Call* were quick to realize that the publication of racist propaganda and the details of bloody violence against the Chinese was a sure way to increase their circulation and their revenues. The *Chronicle* not only advertised the meetings of the Workingmen's Party, but they also sent their best reporters to write and embellish the speeches given by Denis Kearney, the charismatic leader of the sandlot agitators (Wu, 1928:69).

It did not take long for the politicians to realize that an anti-Chinese position on any issue guaranteed votes on election day. Therefore the politicians made certain to sprinkle their speeches with racists phrases like "the heathen Chinese" and with jingoistic cliches as the "yellow peril" (Gardner, 1961:62-91). Indeed several politicians, such as C.C. O'Donnel,

John Day, and H.L. Knight, built their whole political careers on their anti-Chinese speeches (Cross, 1935:93-129).

In response to the social disruption and political agitation several laws were passed to harass the Chinese and to prevent their immigration. These laws were passed at the (1) local level, (2) state level, and the (3) federal level. At the local level the objective was to harass the Chinese and otherwise make their lives miserable. At the state level the intent was to limit their access to certain types of jobs or to bar them from certain businesses. While the termination of Chinese immigration was the intent of the federal laws (McClain, 1984).

A review of some of the more blatant laws passed by the city of San Francisco provides an interesting insight into the effects of social agitation at the local level (See Figure 5.1 Next Page).

The impact of most of these ordinances are obvious, but others are not so lucid. For example, the Chinese have always carried their goods on long poles across their shoulders, with suspended baskets. Obviously the pole ordinance was intended to tax the Chinese. The Cubic Air Ordinance was passed to prevent them from overcrowding their apartments, but the city jails were in violation of this ordinance. The Queue Ordinance meant that any Chinese who was incarcerated had to have his queue cut, which was a very important cultural symbol of allegiance to their emperor (Chen, 1980; Wu, 1972).

At the state level the laws were more sophisticated, but far more damaging than the local ordinances. A review of some of these state laws provides an insight into the negative impact that these laws had on their civil rights (See Figure 5.1 Next Page).

All the federal laws addressed immigration issues and were devastating to the development of the Chinese American community (See Figure 5.1). Clearly, each of these laws placed more and more restrictions on Chinese immigration. It is noteworthy that the Chinese Exclusion Act was the first law to prohibit the immigration of a specific nationality.

The Social Organization of Chinatown

While the residential concentration of immigrants is not unique to the Chinese American experience, the fact that Chinatown has survived for a 140 years is a mark of distinction. Besides providing many of the basic cultural and material needs of the community, Chinatown also served as the locus of the Chinese family, culture, and religion (Lyman, 1976; Takaki, 1989:239-257).

Figure 5.1
Anti-Chinese Legislation

Year	San Francisco Local Ordinances
1855	Head Tax: a $50 head tax was levied on all aliens not eligible for naturalization,
1860	School Segregation: all Chinese children were barred from attending public schools,
1866	Hospital Ban: all Chinese were refused admission to the city hospital,
1870	Job Discrimination: the city prohibited hiring of Chinese on any public works projects,
1870	Pole Ordinance: the Chinese were prohibited from using poles to transport vegetables or laundry,
1870	Cubic Air Ordinance: required that lodging facilities provide at least 500 cubic feet of air space for each occupant,
1873	Laundry Ordinance: required a $15 per quarter license fee for using poles to carry laundry, but horse drawn vehicles were only charged $2 per quarter,
1873	Firecracker Ordinance: prohibited the use of fire crackers and banned ceremonial gongs,
1876	Queue Ordinance: required all inmates in the county jail to have their hair cut to within one inch of their scalp,
1880	Anti-Ironing Ordinance: was aimed at closing Chinese night time laundries,
1882	New Laundry Licensing Act: required licensing of mostly Chinese businesses.

Year	California State Laws
1850	Foreign Miners Tax: required the payment of $20 per month from all foreign miners (primarily Chinese),
1852	Security Bond Act: required all arriving Chinese to post a $500 security bond,
1854	The California Supreme Court decreed that Chinese cannot testify in court against a white person,
1855	Capitation Tax: required shippers to pay $50 for every Chinese passenger arriving America,
1858	Immigration Ban, prohibited the immigration of any Chinese or Mongolians,
1860	Fishing Tax: required a fee of $4 per month from all Chinese fishermen,

1862	Police Tax: required a tax of $2.50 per month from all Mongolians over the age of 18,
1870	Female Immigration Law: prohibited the immigration of Mongolian females without a special certificate,
1870	Alien Land Law: prohibited Chinese from owning land in the state,
1879	State law prohibited aliens ineligible for citizenship (i.e. Chinese) from obtaining a fishing license,
1879	State law prohibited the hiring of Chinese for municipal work projects,
1879	Residential Segregation Act: state allowed cities to move Chinese residents to specified areas of the city,
1880	Fishing Tax: Chinese required to pay $2.50 a month for a fishing license,
1880	Fishing Act: Chinese prohibited from engaging in any fishing business,
1885	School Segregation Act: state law required all Chinese to attend segregated schools.

Year	United States Federal Laws
1868	The Burlingame Treaty: assured reciprocal rights of voluntary immigration between the United States and China,
1876	The Supreme Court ruled that only the federal government can make laws regulating immigration,
1879	Congressional Act: limited to fifteen the number of Chinese allowed to enter the United States on one ship,
1880	Burlingame Amendment: prohibited the entry of Chinese laborers,
1882	Chinese Exclusion Act: prohibited the entry of Chinese laborers for ten years and denied naturalization rights to all Chinese,
1888	Scott Act: prohibited the reentry of Chinese immigrants after a temporary departure,
1892	Geary Act: extended the ban on Chinese immigration for another ten years and required the Chinese to carry proof of legal residence or face deportation,
1894	U.S.-China Treaty: prohibited Chinese immigration for another ten years,
1898	Chinese Exclusion Act: extended to Hawaii,
1902	Chinese Exclusion Act: extended to the Philippines.

When compared to all the other immigrants who arrived in America, the Chinese were probably the best organized. The primary reason for their efficiency and organization is that they brought existing social organizations with them to insure social harmony and control (Lee, 1965:28-37; Lyman, 1970:79-83; Wong, 1990). The most important of these were:

1. The Hui-Guan—In traditional China it was a district mutual aide society. In America it was an association of fellow provincials away from home.
2. Linguistic Groups—Chinese immigrants organized themselves according to their dialect and formed social, labor, and business ties on this basis.
3. Clan Groups—In an agrarian society people of the same clan often live in the same village.
4. Blood Ties—Individuals with the same surname are related and recognize common ancestors.
5. Guilds—Individuals are organized around specific labor groups, businesses, or craft or trade groups.
6. Ethnic Groups—Representing a larger clustering of clan, linguistic, and regional groups.
7. Secret Societies (Tongs)—Originally established in Chinatown as fraternal organizations for mutual aid, protection, and socializing.
8. Religion—based on a variety of beliefs, such as Taoism, Buddhism, Confucianism, Catholicism, and Protestantism.

The largest and most influential of all the organizations in Chinatown during the nineteenth century was the Hui-Guan (Walker, 1976:31-48). The first was the Kong Chow Company, organized in San Francisco in 1851 (Hoy, 1942). In 1854 a dozen Hui-Guans formed a confederation known as the Chinese Six Company. The Chinese Six Company protected the immigrants from abuse, provided them with assistance, and represented their interest in the greater society (Lai, 1987:14-21).

In the same manner linguistic bonds and regional or clan ties often served as the basis for social organization among the immigrants. Blood ties also served as a strong social bond, as the Chinese believed that individuals with the same surname were related to common ancestors (Pan, 1990:18-20, 111-127). However, having a similar surname also prohibited marriage. This created some serious problems for the Chinese in America, that is in view of the severe shortage of women in their community.

As they arrived in America immigrants from certain districts or linguistic groups organized themselves into guilds, to create a monopoly on a given service, product, or business, and to control the limited number of jobs in certain sectors of the labor market (Wong, 1988:230-236). For example, the Sam Yap guild manufactured and sold clothes, the Yan Wo clan dominated the laundry business, the Tsung Tsin family organized a craft guild of cooks, the Tom clan held a monopoly on hotel work, and the Yeung Wo family controlled the fresh fruit and vegetable markets (Light, 1972:91).

Secret societies were organized around the interest of their members and not on kinship or district ties. The Triad Secret Society established the first lodge in San Francisco in 1853 (Lyman, 1986:134-149). Secret societies often served as a check on the power of the Hui-Guans, for by joining a secret society the individual acquired a sworn fraternity of compatriots who promised to protect his interest. However, some secret societies grew into underground organizations and used intimidation and violence to extract wealth from illegal activities, such as prostitution, narcotics, gambling, and the protection racket. These underground organizations were known as tongs and the battles for illegal markets were called tong wars (Kwong, 1987:107-123). These wars began in 1875, and were headed by highbinders or hatchetmen who enforced the rules of these illegal operations (Dillon, 1962).

Social Problems in Chinatown: 1850-1900

The original Chinese settlers who arrived during the nineteenth century established a community of men, that is a bachelor society without their wives or families. Before long this shortage of women created a serious problem for the cohesiveness and stability of their community.

Initially the Chinese had no strong desire to bring their wives with them and the few women that did emigrate were either prostitutes or the wives of wealthy merchants. For example, it is estimated that by 1870, four out of five of the 1,769 Chinese women living in San Francisco were prostitutes (Chen, 1980:183).

The shortage of women was acute in the Chinese community as there were 33,000 Chinese men in the United States in 1860, but only 1,784 females. The most skewed sex ratio occurred in 1890 when there were over 102,620 males but only 3,868 females (Lyman, 1970:83-84). It took another fifty years for the number of women in Chinatown to reach 25 percent of the population and demographic parity was not obtained until 1980, when there were 102.1 males per 100 females. Unfortunately this drastic shortage of women in the immigrant community had a number of serious long term effects (Lyman, 1974:88):

1. It created a bachelor society.
2. It resulted in the proliferation of prostitution.
3. It encouraged illegal immigration.
4. It delayed the procreation of a second generation of Chinese Americans.
5. And it resulted in the concentration of political and economic power in the hands of a few power brokers.

Their inability to produce a second generation was not only devastating to the life of the Chinese family and community, but it also deprived the immigrants of a generation of American born children who could have bridged the gap between the old immigrant community and the new society. In addition the critical shortage of women contributed to the development of a number of social problems, namely, (1) prostitution, (2) drug abuse, (3) gambling, and (4) organized crime.

One Chinese official who visited California in 1876 estimated that of the 6,000 Chinese women living in the state at the time, approximately 80 to 90 percent were daughters of joy (Hirata, 1979; Tsai, 1986:41). Another serious social problem was the use of opium. It is estimated that there were more than 200 opium dens in San Francisco's Chinatown in 1876, and most of the 3,000 opium addicts were Chinese (Tsai, 1986:39). But the importation of opium, which was legal until 1909, provided thousands of dollars in tax revenue to the U.S. Customs department.

Gambling served as another temptation for the immigrants. For most gambling was a form of recreation and promoted a sense of community and identification with the culture of Chinese male society. But it drove others into a life of poverty and despair. The popular interest in gambling came from the belief that having good luck was a part of being successful, for one bet not only held out the possibility of grasping a fortune, but it also could guarantee a quick trip home to a life of fame and fortune (Lyman, 1974:96-99).

Organized crime evolved in Chinatown as a means of protecting brothel owners, insuring cooperation from the prostitutes, and to insure payoffs to the police (Tang, 1984). The gangsters levied a weekly fee on each prostitute, which the pimp had to pay. Organized gangs also provided protection for the opium dens and insured that customers paid for their drugs and did not cause any trouble. The gambling houses also secured the services of the secret society, to provide security, to insure that debts were paid, and to prevent trouble from the local police. Gang leaders also offered local merchants insurance, so that nothing bad would happen to them or their businesses. Eventually territorial disputes erupted between gangs and resulted in the so-called Tong Wars.

Family and Kinship Patterns

The family in traditional Chinese society served as the foundation of every form of social organization, from the extended family, to the council of elders, to the organization of the clan, to the close identification with linguistic and ethnic groups. Therefore the Chinese community in America was an anomaly, since it was a poor reflection of the Chinese community that flourished in the homeland, as it was a bachelor society, that is a community of men without wives, without children, and without a nuclear or extended family. Such was the life of the Chinese pioneers in America.

Unfortunately they were unable to produce a second generation of native born Americans, who could have served as the bridge between the immigrant community and the new society. Since they were denied naturalization rights, their only means of obtaining American citizenship, that is before 1943, was by birth. But given the drastic shortage of women, it was almost impossible for them to produce a native born population. Fifty years after their arrival in America only ten percent of the Chinese population were native born, and a hundred years after their arrival only half were native born.

The Chinese family in America was shaped by three major forces: (1) the modification of the immigration laws, (2) the decision by some pioneers to remain permanently in America, and (3) changing political conditions in the homeland. In response to these forces the Chinese family evolved into seven historical types: (1) the sojourner family, (2) the immigrant family, (3) the native born family, (4) the separated family, (5) the war bride family, (6) the political refugee family, and (7) the new wave family (Gonzales, 1992:7-17; Lee, 1960:185-251).

The sojourner family was the first to set roots in America. As a result of the extreme shortage of women the number of sojourner families was very limited and most were established by merchants who could afford to send for their wives in China (Hsu, 1948:79-93). Their wives were closely guarded and were rarely seen in public.

The immigrant family evolved between 1870 and 1882. These were the original immigrants who saved sufficient funds to return to China to find a bride. After working for ten or fifteen years they would bring their wives to America and settle permanently. The immigrant family was different from the sojourner family in that these were common working men and not wealthy merchants. But their numbers were very limited.

The native born family was one in which either the husband or the wife was born in America. These families began to appear around the turn of the century, when ten percent of the Chinese population was native born. Given the extreme shortage of women, native born females were in high demand. However, the incest taboos on surname and clan marriages often forced these women to move to another state to marry. According to tradition all marriages were arranged by the parents, who usually hired professional match makers. And it was not unusual to find that couples entered blind marriages, so that neither the man nor the woman had ever seen each other prior to the marriage.

The separated family evolved following the passage of the Immigration Act of 1924, that prohibited the admission of alien born Chinese and/or their unmarried offspring under 21 years of age. This law prevented Chinese alien wives of U.S. citizens from coming to America.

The War Brides Act of December 1943 allowed servicemen and veterans to bring their wives from foreign countries. This allowed Chinese American veterans to travel to China and return with their wives. Many veterans also obtained their American citizenship as a result of their military service. During the first seven years of this Act more than 6,000 Chinese women and over 600 children entered the United States (Lee, 1960:201).

Following the communist takeover in China, the political refugee families were established. The communist revolution left many students and businessmen stranded in the United States, as they were not allowed to return to their homeland when the communist came to power in 1950. Other families who arrived in the United States before World War II could not return home during the war and their children had become accustomed to life in America and had no interest in returning to China (Chen, 1980:202-204).

The new wave families arrived in America following the passage of the Immigration Reform Act of 1965. They came in large numbers and were predominately from Hong Kong. While many came as students, some were professionals in the fields of science, medicine, and engineering. Under the provisions of the family reunification program, and the immigrant preference system, thousands of new families were formed or reconstituted. For example, between 1955 and 1965, three to five thousand Chinese immigrants arrived per year, but between 1965 and 1975 an average of 21,000 arrived each year.

Today the marriage rate for both men and women among Chinese Americans is similar, as 58.4 percent of the men and 60.3 percent of the women are married. Fewer women are single (27.8%), as compared to men (36.9%). It is also interesting to note that twice as many men (22.5%) as women (10.9%) have married outside their group. This is partly related to the historical shortage of women in the Chinese American community and to the higher rate of contact that the new wave immigrants have with members of the dominant society. Their higher levels of education and the greater acceptability of interracial marriages have also contributed to the higher rate of exogamy among Chinese Americans today (Sung, 1987). As a result of their higher levels of education, suburbanization, and increasing rates of intermarriage, the level of assimilation and social acceptability of Chinese Americans is increasing (Wang, 1991).

Chinese American divorce rates are lower than the national average and are the lowest among Asians, and the same holds true for their separation rate. It is important to note that the number of widows is about five times as high as the number of widowers in the Chinese American community. While their life expectancy is lower than the general population, it is still true that the women outlive the men.

Out of a total population of 812,178 in 1980, 97 percent of the Chinese Americans were living in family households. Only two percent of their households were headed by women, with no husband present. This finding supports the prevalence of strong family ties in the Chinese American community today. So does the fact that 93 percent of all children live in a household with both parents present, as compared to only half the children in the greater society.

A Demographic Profile

Historically the Chinese settled on the West Coast and only gradually moved to the East Coast. By 1960 almost two-thirds lived in the West, while only one out of four lived in the Northeast (See Table 5.2 Below). In 1970 the West lost five percent of the population, while the Northeast gained 4.5 percent. By 1990 their dispersion was greater, with only half living in the West, almost three out of ten in the Northeast, and one out of ten in both the South and the Midwest.

Table 5.2
Growth Patterns Of Chinese Population By Regions
And Major States, 1960-1990

Region	1960 Number	%	1970 Number	%	1980 Number	%	1990 Number	%
Northwest	52,846	22.2	115,089	26.7	217,624	26.8	445,000	27.1
Midwest	117,952	7.5	37,811	8.8	74,994	9.2	133,000	8.1
South	16,874	7.1	32,462	7.5	91,415	11.3	204,000	12.4
West	148,412	62.3	246,221	57.1	428,195	52.7	863,000	52.4
Total	238,065	100.0	431,583	100.0	812,178	100.0	1,645,472	100.0

State	1960 Number	%	1970 Number	%	1980 Number	%	1990 Number	%
California	95,600	40.2	170,131	39.4	325,882	40.1	704,850	42.8
New York	37,573	15.8	81,378	18.9	147,250	18.1	284,144	17.2
Hawaii	38,197	16.0	52,039	12.1	55,916	6.9	68,804	4.2
Illinois	7,047	3.0	14,474	3.4	28,847	3.6	49,936	3.0
Massachusetts	6,745	2.8	14,012	3.2	24,882	3.1	53,792	3.3
Percent of Total		77.8		77.0		71.8		70.5
Total		100.0		100.0	806,040	100.0	1,645,472	100.0

Source: U.S. Census, 1960, 1970, 1980, 1990, 1992.

A review of their population growth in the five major states reveals that the number of Chinese living in California remained stable at 41 percent between 1970 and 1990 (See Table 5.2). While New York demonstrated a population loss of 1.7 percent, Hawaii lost one third of its Chinese population, that is based on population distribution. Their representation in Illinois and Massachusetts remained stable over this twenty year period.

In terms of absolute numbers California experienced a growth rate of 1.8 between 1970 and 1980, and almost doubled between 1980 and 1990. Their population increased at a faster rate in New York, where it doubled (2.2) between 1970 and 1980, and almost doubled again (1.8) between 1980 and 1990. Their numbers in Illinois and Massachusetts also doubled between 1980 and 1990. Hawaii experienced the slowest rate of growth of the five major areas of settlement.

Out of a population of 1,645,472, almost two-thirds (63.3) were foreign born in 1990. This represents an increase from 1970, when their foreign population was less than half (47.2). In 1960 it was slightly more than a third (39.3). This increase can be attributed to the liberalization of the U.S. immigration policies in 1965.

If we consider the distribution of Chinese in selected metropolitan areas (known as Standard Metropolitan Statistical Areas or SMSA's), we note that the San Francisco-Oakland area has the largest number of Chinese residents, but a below average number of foreign born residents (See Table 5.3 Next Page). The New York City-New Jersey area is the second largest area of concentration, but they also have the largest percentage of foreign born (75%). Among the ten metropolitan areas with the heaviest concentration of Chinese residents, half are located in California, and except for the Los Angeles-Long Beach area, all have a below average number of foreign born in their populations. By far Honolulu has the smallest number of foreign born in their Chinese American population.

A consideration of the age distribution of Chinese Americans in terms of their level of dependency and their expected level of production, reveals that their productive potential is greater than the general U.S. population. The dependent population is that segment of the population that is either too young or too old to be productive, primarily the children, teenagers, and the elderly. The productive members are those in the middle age categories. The Chinese American population has a dependency ratio of 36.3 percent, compared to the U.S. dependency ratio of 43.3 percent (See Table 5.4 Next Page). Therefore almost two-thirds of the Chinese Americans are active in the labor force, as compared to three out of five in the general U.S. population.

Table 5.3
Chinese Population Distribution
In Ten Major SMSA'S, 1980

SMSA	Number	Percent of Total	Percent Foreign Born
San Francisco-Oakland	143,551	17.7	60.9
N.Y. City-New Jersey	133,074	16.4	75.0
Los Angeles-Long Beach	94,521	11.6	70.3
Honolulu	52,301	6.4	22.6
Chicago	24,980	3.1	61.0
San Jose	22,745	2.8	57.4
Boston	21,442	2.6	68.7
Washington, D.C.	18,250	2.2	67.8
Sacramento	15,440	1.9	49.4
Anaheim-Santa Ana	14,575	1.8	63.2

Source: U.S. Census, 1980.

Table 5.4
Chinese Age Distribution By Selected Categories, 1980

Chinese Age Category	Chinese Number	Chinese Percent	U.S. Percent	Percent Difference
I. Children (1-19 Dependent)	238,208	29.3	32.0	-2.7
II. Young Adults (20-34)	265,954	32.7	25.8	+6.9
III. Middle Aged (35-64)	251,755	31.0	25.7	+5.3
IV. Elderly (65+ Dependent)	56,261	6.9	11.3	-4.4
Total Dependent Population	294,469	36.3	43.3	-7.0
Total population	812,178	100.0	100.0	

Total Chinese Median Age:	29.8
Chinese Male Median Age:	29.7
Chinese Female Median Age:	29.9
Total U.S. Median Age:	30.0

Source: U.S. Census, 1980.

Their labor force characteristics further supports this observation. In 1980 four out of five (82.3%) of the Chinese householders were employed, 16 percent were not in the labor force, and less than two percent reported that they were unemployed. The Chinese American family also had more members in the labor force than the general population, as they had half as many families with no workers (7.1%), as the general population (14.8%), and more families with two and three workers. This very high level of labor force participation, combined with their low dependency ratio means that they are a very productive group.

Their higher levels of labor force participation are reflected in their slightly higher family income, that is when compared to the general population. But these higher incomes are only achieved as a result of the higher than average number of individuals who are active in the labor force and the longer hours of work. In practice the labor force participation rates are actually higher among Chinese Americans as a result of the higher number of unpaid family laborers found in family owed businesses. Their higher than average family income is also affected by the labor production of these unpaid family members (Wong, 1988:192-196).

A survey of the occupational distribution of Chinese Americans reveals some interesting characteristics. It is well known that Chinese Americans have higher than average levels of education and are concentrated in the professional and technical fields. But many fail to realize that Chinese Americans are also concentrated at the bottom of the labor market (Loo, 1991). Most of these Chinese workers are concentrated in the secondary labor market or are totally dependent on jobs in the ethnic labor market (Mar, 1991:11-19). This pattern gives them a bipolar distribution in the labor force. In effect they are over represented in the upper and lower segments of the labor market, with smaller numbers in the middle. This bipolar distribution was already apparent in 1970, when about half (56.6%) were employed in white collar jobs (professional, managerial, technical, sales, and clerical), and about half (43.4%) were employed in blue collar jobs (service, farm, craft, and operatives). Their occupational distribution was very similar in 1960. But a significant change occurred in 1980, when almost two-thirds (62.7%) were in white collar jobs (compared to 52.5% U.S.), and slightly more than one-third (37.3%) held blue collar jobs (47.5% U.S.).

Their concentration in the professional, technical, and managerial categories is not only a reflection of their higher levels of education, but is also affected by the recent influx (i.e., since 1965) of highly educated and professionally trained immigrants from Hong Kong and Taiwan. In 1940 only three percent of the Chinese Americans were in the professional-technical-managerial categories, seven percent in 1950, 15 percent in 1960, 28 percent in 1970, and almost half (45%) in 1980. It is also interesting to note that there is a heavier concentration of men (38.6%) in the managerial-professional ranks, than women (24.9%), but there are almost twice as many women in the technical-sales category (40.2%), as men (22.3%).

Within the managerial-professional ranks, the Chinese are concentrated in executive and administrative positions (39.8%) and in engineering and the natural sciences (24.7%). In the technical-sales area, half hold clerical positions (50.4%), one-third (28.5%) are in sales, and one out of five (16.7%) are in technical positions. Women constitute a majority of clerical and sales workers. In the service occupations the majority (76.1%) of Chinese Americans are found in the food service areas (compared to 35.5% U.S.). Their over representation in the service industry reflects their concentration in the restaurant industry (Fong, 1984; Kinkead, 1991).

The reason for their high concentration in the professional-managerial-technical fields is their high levels of education. While they have always emphasized educational achievements, a college education was difficult to obtain prior to the Second World War. In 1940 the median years of education for Chinese Americans was 5.5 years (compared to 8.6 U.S.), in 1950 it increased to eight years (9.3 U.S.), in 1960 to 9.2 years (10.6 U.S.), in 1970 to 12.6 years (12.1), and in 1980 to 13.7 years (12.5 U.S.).

In this regard it is interesting that there were only 5.5 percent college graduates among Chinese Americans in 1940 (compared to 4.6% U.S.), eight percent in 1950 (6.2%), 16.5 percent in 1960 (7.7%), 25.6 percent in 1970 (10.7%), and 30.8 percent in 1980 (16.2%). Therefore almost one-third (30.8%) of the Chinese Americans were college graduates, twice (16.2%) the national average.

A comparison of the educational achievement between Chinese American men and women reveals that there are as many male college graduates (50.3%) as female college graduates (49.7%). This compares to one out of five (21.3%) of the males and one out of seven (13.3%) of the females in the general population. But almost twice as many Chinese American men (65%) obtain graduate degrees as Chinese American women (35%). This pattern probably reflects their traditional family orientation, that is the belief that men should obtain a higher education than women.

Chapter Summary

With the arrival of the Chinese the economic conditions in California changed rapidly, as their labor power was in great demand. Besides their work in the gold fields, the Chinese also were employed as domestic servants, in restaurants, and in construction. They also created new jobs and started new businesses, primarily in agriculture, in light manufacturing, and in commercial fishing.

Unfortunately their welcome was short lived. With the economic depression that hit California in the 1870's the great mass of unemployed workers searched for a cause of their economic problems and set upon the Chinese as useful scapegoats. The growing prejudice against the Chinese was transformed into public policy with the passage of anti-Chinese laws at the local, state, and federal levels.

In spite of the hard times the Chinese community was sustained by their hard work and their determination to succeed. Their great loss however, was their inability to bring their wives and children to America. Stringent immigration laws prevented them from establishing families in this country.

After the Second World War they were finally allowed to send for their families. With the introduction of families into Chinatown their children were able take advantage of the employment and educational opportunities available in America. As a result their educational achievement has moved dramatically upward since the end of the Second World War.

In general, Chinese Americans are one of the most impressive immigrant groups to establish themselves in America. Following many years of oppression, Chinese Americans are just now making their way into the social and economic foreground of American society.

References

Bancroft, Hubert Howe
1890   *History of California 1860-1890*. San Francisco: The History
            Company Publishers.
Barth, Gunther
1964   *Bitter Strength: A History of the Chinese in the U.S. 1850-
            1870*. Cambridge: Harvard University Press.
Cather, Helen V.
1932   "The History of San Francisco's Chinatown." M.A. Thesis,
            Department of Economics, University of California,
            Berkeley.
Chan, Sucheng
1991   *Asian Californians*. San Francisco: MTL/Boyd & Fraser.
Chen, Jack
1980   *The Chinese of America*. San Francisco: Harper & Row.
            Chinn, Thomas (ed.)
1969   *A History of the Chinese in California, A Syllabus*. San
            Francisco: Chinese Historical Society of America.
Chu, George
1970   "Chinatowns in the Delta: The Chinese in the Sacramento-
            San Joaquin Delta, 1870-1960." *The California Historical
            Society Quarterly* 49:21-38.
Commonwealth Club of California
1946   *The Population of California*. San Francisco: Parker Printing
            Co.
Coolidge, Mary R.
1909   *Chinese Immigration*. Henry Holt & Co. (New York: Arno
            Press, 1969)
Cross, Ira B.
1935   *A History of the Labor Movement in California*. Berkeley:
            The University of California Press.
Daniels, Roger
1962   *The Politics of Prejudice: The Anti-Japanese Movement in
            California and the Struggle for Japanese Exclusion*. Berkeley: The
            University of California Press.
1978   *Anti-Chinese Violence in North America*. New York: Arno
            Press.
Dillon, Richard H.
1962   *The Hatchet Men: The Story of the Tong Wars in San
            Francisco's Chinatown*. New York: Coward-McCann.

Eaves, Lucile
  1910   *A History of California Labor Legislation: With an Intro-
            ductory Sketch of the S.F. Labor Movement.* Berkeley: U.C. Publi-
            cations in Economics, The University of California Press.
Fessler, Lorean W.
  1983   *Chinese in America: Stereotyped Past, Changing Present.*
            New York: Vantage Press.
Fong, Eric and William T. Markham
  1991   "Immigration, Ethnicity, and Conflict: The California
            Chinese, 1849-1882." *Sociological Inquiry* 61(4):471-490.
Fong, Pauline L.
  1984   "The Current Social and Economic Status of Chinese
            American Women." In *The Chinese Americans Experience,*
            Genny Lim (Ed.), The Chinese HistoricalSociety of
            America, San Francisco, CA, pp. 296-299.
Gardner, John B.
  1961   "The Image of the Chinese in the United States, 1885-1915."
            Ph.D. Dissertation, Department of History, University of
            Pennsylvania (University Microfilms, Ann Arbor, MI).
Gonzales, Juan L. Jr.
  1992   *Racial and Ethnic Families in America.* Dubuque, IA: Kendall/Hunt.
Hirata, Lucie Cheng
  1979   "Free, Indentured, Enslaved: Chinese Prostitutes in
            Nineteenth Century America." *Signs* 5(1):3-29.
Hoffman, Mark S.
  1993   *The World Almanac and Book of Facts 1993.* New York:
            Pharos Books.
Hoy, William
  1942   *The Chinese Six Companies.* San Francisco: Chinese Consolidated
            Benevolent Association.
Hsu, Francis L. K.
  1948   *Under the Ancestors' Shadow: Chinese Culture and
            Personality.* New York: Columbia University Press.
Johnson, Otto
  1992   *Information Please Almanac.* Boston: Houghton Mifflin
            Company.
Kinkead, Gwen
  1991   *Chinatown: A Portrait of a Closed Society.* New York: Harper
            Collins.
Kung, Shien Woo
  1962   *Chinese in American Life.* Seattle: The University of
            Washington Press.
Kwong, Peter
  1987   *The New Chinatown.* New York: Hill and Wang.

Lai, Him Mark
1987   "Historical Development of the Chinese Consolidated
        Benevolent Association/Huiguan System." In *Chinese*
        America: History and Perspectives 1987. San Francisco, CA:
        Chinese Historical Society of America. Pp. 13-51.
Lee, Calvin
1965   *Chinatown, U.S.A.* Garden City, NY: Doubleday & Company.
Lee, Rose Hum
1960   *The Chinese in the United States of America.* Hong Kong:
        Hong Kong University Press.
Light, Ivan
1972   *Ethnic Enterprise in America: Business and Welfare Among Chinese,*
        Japanese, and Blacks. Berkeley: The University of California
        Press.
Loo, Chalsa M.
1991   *Chinatown: Most Time, Hard Time.* New York: Praeger.
Lyman, Stanford M.
1970   "Strangers in the Cities: The Chinese on the Urban Frontier."
        In *Ethnic Conflict in California History.* Charles Wollenberg
        (ed.), Los Angeles: Tinnon-Brown, Inc. Pp. 61-100.
1974   *Chinese Americans.* New York: Random House.
1976   "Conflict and the Web of Group Affiliation in San Francisco's
        Chinatown, 1850-1910." In *The Asian American.* Roger
        Daniels (ed.), Santa Barbara: Clio Books. Pp. 26-52.
1986   *Chinatown and Little Tokyo: Power, Conflict, and Com-*
        munity Among Chinese and Japanese Immigrants in American.
        Millwood, N.Y.: Associated Faculty Press.
Mar, Don
1991   "Another Look at the Enclave Economy Thesis: Chinese Im-
        migrants in the Ethnic Labor Market." *Amerasia* 17(3)5-21.
McClain, Charles J. Jr.
1984   "The Chinese Struggle for Civil Rights in Nineteenth Century
        America: The First Phase, 1850-1870." *California Law Review*
        72:529-568.
McLeod, Alexander
1947   *Pigtails and Gold Dust.* Caldwell, ID: The Caxton Printers,
        Ltd.
Mei, June
1984a   "Socioeconomic Origins of Emigration: Guangdong to
        California, 1850-1882." *In Labor Immigration Under Capitalism:*
        Asian Workers in the United States Before World War II. Lucie
        Chen and Edna Bonacich (eds.), Berkeley: University of
        California Press, Pp. 219-247.

1984b   "Socioeconomic Developments Among the Chinese in San Francisco 1848-1906." In *Labor Immigration Under Capitalism: Asian Workers in the United States Before World War II.* Lucie Cheng and Edna Bonacich (eds.), Berkeley: University of California Press, Pp. 370-401.

Miller, Stuart
1969   *The Unwelcome Immigrant: The American Image of the Chinese, 1785-1882.* Berkeley: The University of California Press.

Minnick, Silvia S.
1988   *Samfow: The San Joaquin Chinese Legacy.* Fresno, CA: Panorama West Publishing.

Nee, Victor G. and Brett de Bary Nee
1973   *Longtime Californ: A Documentary Study of an American Chinatown.* New York: Pantheon Books.

Ng, Franklin
1987   "The Sojourner, Return Migration, and Immigration History." In *Chinese America: History and Perspectives.* San Francisco, CA: Chinese Historical Society of America. Pp. 53-71.

Ong, Paul M.
1981   "Chinese Labor in Early San Francisco: Racial Segmentation and Industrial Expansion." *Amerasia 8(1): 69-92.*

Pan, Lynn
1990   *Sons of the Yellow Emperor: A History of the Chinese Diaspora.* Boston: Little, Brown and Company.

Sandmeyer, Elmer C.
1939   *The Anti-Chinese Movement in California.* Urbana: The University of Illinois Press.

Saxton, Alexander P.
1971   *The Indispensable Enemy: Labor and the Anti-Chinese Movement in California.* Berkeley: The University of California Press.

Spoehr, Luther W.
1973   "Sambo and the Heathen Chinese: Californians' Racial Stereotypes in the Late 1870's." *Pacific Historical Review* 42:185-204

Steiner, Stan
1979   *Fusang: The Chinese Who Built America.* New York: Harper & Row.

Storti, Craig
1991   *Incident at Bitter Creek: The Story of the Rock Springs Chinese Massacre.* Ames, IA: Iowa State University Press.

Sung, Betty Lee
    1987   "Intermarriage Among the Chinese in New York City." In *Chinese America: History and Perspectives 1987*. San Francisco, CA: Chinese Historical Society of America. Pp. 101-118.

Takaki, Ronald
    1989   *Strangers from a Different Shore: A History of Asian Americans*. New York: Penguin Books.

Tang, Vincente
    1984   "Chinese Women Immigrants and the Two-Edged Sword of Habeas Corpus." In *The Chinese American Experience*. Genny Lim (ed.), San Francisco, CA: The Chinese Historical Society of America. Pp. 48-54.

Tsai, Henry S.
    1986   *The Chinese Experience in America*. Bloomington: Indiana University Press.

Tung, William L.
    1974   *The Chinese in America 1820-1973: A Chronology & Fact Book*. Dobbs Ferry, NY: Oceana Publications.

U.S. Census
    1991   *Statistical Abstract of the United States, 1991* (111th Edition). Washington, D.C.: USGPO.
    1992   1990 Census of the Population, U.S. Summary. Washington, D.C.: CD-ROM Data.

Walker, Henry T.
    1976   "Gold Mountain Guests: Chinese Migration to the United States, 1848-1882." Ph.D. Dissertation, Department of Economics, Stanford University. (University Microfilms, Ann Arbor, MI).

Wang, L. Ling-chi
    1991   "Roots and Changing Identity of the Chinese in the United States." *Daedalus* Spring:181-206.

Williams, Stephen
    1930   "The Chinese in the California Mines, 1848-1860." M.A. Thesis: Stanford University (San Francisco: R & E Research Associates, 1971).

Wong, Bernard
    1988   *Patronage, Brokerage, Entrepreneurship and the Chinese Community of New York*. New York: AMS Press.

Wong, P., et al.
    1990   "From Despotism to Pluralism: The Evolution of Voluntary Organizations in Chinese American Communities." *Ethnic Groups* 8(4):215-233.

Wu, Cheng-Tsu (ed.)
   1972   *Chink: A Documentary History of Anti-Chinese Prejudice in America.*
               New York: World Publishing
Wu, Ching Chao
   1928   "Chinatowns: A Study of Symbiosis and Assimilation." Ph.D.
               Dissertation, Department of Anthropology,University of
               Chicago. (University Microfilms, Ann Arbor, MI).
Yen, Ching-Hwang
   1985   *Coolies and Mandarins: China's Protection of Overseas
               Chinese During the Late Ch'ing Period (1851-1911).* Kent Ridge,
               Singapore: Singapore University Press.

1849	The first anti-Chinese riot occurred in Chinese Camp, in which sixty Chinese were driven from their mining camp.
1852	400 Chinese expelled by a white mob from Marysville, WA.
1852	300 Chinese were expelled from their diggings on the North Fork of the American River.
1852	In May a Vigilance Committee was organized at Columbia, to keep the Chinese out of the diggings.
1852	Violence erupted at North Forks and Horseshoe Bar when a mob of white miners drove the Chinese out of the diggings.
1858	150 white miners drove 200 Chinese from their quarters in Folsom, California.
1859	Chinese miners were routed out of Vallecito, Douglas Flat, Sacramento Bar, Coyote Flat, Sand Flat, Rock Creek, Spring Creek, and Buckeye.
1866	A mob attacked Chinatown in San Francisco, leaving one dead and fifteen injured.
1871	A mob of several hundred whites shot, hanged, and stabbed 19 Chinese to death on October 24th in Los Angeles.
1877	Several Chinese buildings were razed by arsonists in the city of Los Angeles, the culprits were never found.
1877	For two nights in July a mob of some 10,000 marched on Chinatown in San Francisco. Many Chinese suffered injuries and 25 Chinese laundries were burned and many homes were ransacked. Half a million dollars in damage was sustained.
1880	A mob of 3,000 white men attacked the Chinese quarter in Denver, the mayhem lasted for eight hours and resulted in the death of one Chinese and over $53,000 in property damage.
1885	The entire Chinese population of Humboldt County was expelled as a result of mob violence.
1885	The Chinese community in Seattle was burned down during a night of violence on October 24, 350 Chinese fled the city.
1885	A mob about 300 strong forced 700 Chinese to leave their quarters in Tacoma, and two Chinese died.
1885	A small band of armed masked men raided the Chinese in the coal mining settlement of Coal Creek, Washington. Their quarters and clothing were burned.
1885	A group of white miners drove the Chinese out of Black Diamond, Washington. Nine Chinese were injured.

1885	The Chinese were attacked with dynamite by a mob of unemployed whites in a picked-over gold mine in Alaska.
1885	A band of 150 armed white men attacked a group of Chinese workers at the Rock Springs mines in Wyoming. In the end 28 Chinese were killed (11 were burned alive in their cabins), 15 were wounded, several hundred were driven out of Chinatown, and more than $147,000 in damage was done.
1885	When a merchant was murdered in Pierce, in the Idaho Territory, five Chinese were accused of the crime and were hanged by an angry mob.
1885	The Chinese in Tonapah, Nevada were ordered out of town by a committee of white men and were robbed, beaten, and one Chinese lost his life.
1885	Chinese railroad workers were set upon by a mob of unionized white workers in Virginia City and Gold Hill Nevada.
1885	Atrocities were committed against the Chinese in Eureka
1886	The entire population of Chinese were expelled by force from the cities of Seattle and Tacoma.
1886	All Chinese living and working in the Alaska were arrested and expelled from the territory.
1886	All the Chinese miners at the Treadwell Mines in Alaska were cast adrift in small boats.
1886	The Chinese were attacked and driven out of Juneau.
1886	Thirty-five California communities reported expulsion of Chinese between January and April.
1887	A gang of seven white hooligans attacked the Chinese mining camp at Log Cabin Bar, Oregon and killed ten in a most brutal manner. They took between $5,000 and $10,000 in gold dust from their bodies before dumping them in the Snake River.
1887	Thirty-one Chinese were massacred at a mining camp on the Snake River in eastern Washington.
1893	Mob violence drove the Chinese out of Redlands, California.
1894	Chinese settlers were set upon and driven out of Chico.
1906	When a few Chinese arrived to work in Eureka, they were forcibly removed.
1906	A mob of 15,000 Canadians, lead by union organizers, marched on and destroyed Chinatown in Vancouver.

Important Names		
Charles Crocker	Denis Kearney	Wah Lee

Key Terms

Immigration Reform Act of 1965	Opium War	Qing Dynasty
Taiping Rebellion	Sutter's mill	Kwangtung Province
Fukien Province	Gold Mountain	credit-ticket system
Chinese Six Companies	Chinese pioneers	Hui-Guan
benevolent associations	the Central Pacific	San Joaquin Delta
anti-Coolie Clubs	Workingmen's Party	pole ordinance
cubic air ordinance	queue ordinance	Linguistic Groups
Clan Groups	Guilds	Secret Societies
Tongs	sojourner family	immigrant family
native born family	separated family	war bride family
political refugee family	new wave family	Immigration Act of 1924
War Brides Act 1943	dependent population	secondary labor market
Chinese Consolidated Benevolent Association	ethnic labor market	bipolar distribution

Sample Test Questions

1. Provide a brief discussion of five important historical events that prompted the Chinese to immigrate to America.
2. Discuss five factors that prompted the Chinese to enter certain labor markets in the city of San Francisco.
3. Discuss four groups that worked successfully to terminate Chinese immigration to America.
4. Laws were passed at the local, state, and federal levels to prevent further Chinese immigration. List and describe three of these laws at each of these levels (a total of nine laws).
5. Describe four traditional ways in which the Chinese were organized in Chinatown.
6. Discuss four social problems that plagued the members of the Chinese community in San Francisco during the nineteenth century.
7. Discuss five Chinese family types.
8. What is meant by the "bipolar distribution" of Chinese Americans in the labor market today? Why are they concentrated in certain jobs?

Chapter 6

The Japanese American Experience

Introduction

Our survey of the Japanese American experience will focus on their immigration and settlement in America, the resistance to their immigration, their success in the labor market, their rapid adaptation to the American way of life, and their incarceration in the camps during the Second World War. Following their release from the camps, we shall review their struggle to make up for lost time. Attention will be given to the barriers placed in their path, to the discrimination that still exists in American society, and to the new political consciousness among Japanese Americans.

Japanese Immigration to Hawaii

For centuries Japan was an isolated island nation that prohibited the emigration of its citizens under penalty of death. Commodore Matthew Perry was the first to establish contact with the Japanese in 1853. The rigid restriction on emigration was lifted by the Meiji Emperor in 1868. An action that was taken in response to pressure from the Hawaiian Sugar Cartel (Moriyama, 1984).

The commercial production of sugar in Hawaii began in the early 1840's and this created an insatiable need for agricultural laborers. In 1850 the Royal Hawaiian Agricultural Society was created with the principal goal of developing the industry and of attracting large numbers of tractable laborers. To this end they signed a five year contract with 175 Chinese laborers, who landed in Honolulu in January of 1852 (Glick, 1980:6-7). But the first Japanese laborers did not arrive in Hawaii until 1868. The 148

Japanese laborers were put to work on six plantations under a three year contract that payed them four dollars a month (Yoneda, 1971).

A contract signed in 1886 allowed 29,000 Japanese laborers to emigrate to Hawaii during the following eight year period (Petersen, 1971:11). Soon they became the mainstay of the Hawaiian sugar industry, as two-thirds of the farm workers on the islands in 1894 were Japanese (Okihiro, 1991). By 1900 there were 60,000 living in Hawaii, and by 1910 there were 80,000 (Moriyama, 1985:Table 4). It is estimated that at least 231,000 Japanese immigrants arrived in the Hawaiian Islands between 1868 and 1929 (Kimura, 1988; Moriyama, 1985:xvii).

Japanese Immigration to California

In 1880 there were only 148 Japanese living on the U.S. mainland. Ten years later their population increased to 2,038. By 1900 their population increased to 24,326, and of this number 10,151 were living in California (Naka, 1913:1). Their settlement to America was facilitated by emigration companies. For example, in 1898 nine emigration companies shipped 12,393 laborers abroad, and of the 31,354 emigrants that left Japan the following year, 21,515 were sent by twelve companies (Ichioka, 1988:48).

Although some of these immigrants found work on the railroads, in the fish canneries of Washington and Alaska, and in the mines of Utah and Arizona, the majority were attracted to the California agricultural industry (Boddy, 1921). By 1909 there were 30,000 Japanese farm workers in California (Iwata, 1962). They came to California for the same reasons that they emigrated to Hawaii, they needed the work and they were attracted by the higher wages. The wages in Japan at the time were about 14 cents per day, while they could earn two dollars a day in California (Hale, 1945:3; Moriyama, 1985:18-19).

The first Japanese immigrants found work in the Vaca Valley in 1887. Four years later they were employed in the vineyards of Fresno and in the fruit districts of Newcastle, Marysville, and Suisun (Millis, 1915:109-110). By 1909 Japanese immigrants were picking 87 percent of the berries, 66 percent of the sugar beets, 57 percent of the nursery products, 52 percent of the grapes, 45 percent of the vegetables, 38 percent of the citrus, and 36 percent of the deciduous fruits in California (Millis, 1915:105; Wilson and Hosokawa, 1982:61-66).

To their credit the Japanese not only worked in the fields, but they also brought new crops into commercial production, such as strawberries and rice (Pajus, 1937: 79-83). George Shima, a Japanese immigrant, was the first to reclaim the tule lands of the San Joaquin Delta and produce potatoes on a commercial basis (Bunje, 1937:39-49). Until 1891 they were considered ideal farm workers, when they began to organize themselves into ethnic labor unions (Fuller, 1939:168; Lukes and Okihiro, 1985).

Japanese immigrants were also quick to establish small businesses in the ethnic enclave. Their businesses tended to be small family operations and catered to the needs of the ethnic community (Matsui, 1922; Miyamoto, 1939). A study conducted by the Immigration Commission in 1909 estimated that there were between 3,000 and 3,500 Japanese owned businesses on the West coast, most of them in San Francisco, Seattle, Los Angeles, and Sacramento. This gave them the unusually high ratio of one business for every 22 persons in their population. Most of their businesses were in hotels and boarding houses, restaurants, barbershops, poolrooms, tailor shops, grocery and hardware stores, laundries, and shoe shops (Ichihashi, 1932:116-136; Millis, 1915:62-63; Modell, 1977; Muto, 1991; Strong, 1933:97-129; Takaki, 1989:186).

The Flow of Japanese Immigrants

Japanese immigration can be viewed as occurring in distinct stages or periods. The first period of immigration (1861 to 1890) consisted of sojourners. (See Table 6.1 on the following page.) The pioneers were the second large group of immigrants to arrive in America. The flow of committed settlers occurred during the first decade of the twentieth century, when 127,000 arrived. The fourth period of immigration was affected by the Gentlemen's Agreement and is known for the large influx of wives and children of Japanese settlers. The passage of the Omnibus Act in 1924 greatly reduced the flow of Japanese immigrants, as did the social disruptions of the Great Depression and the Second World War. In retrospect the Gentlemen's Agreement only served to commit the Japanese to a new life in America, as this period is marked by the influx of wives, popularly known as picture brides. This is so since the provisions of the Gentlemen's agreement allowed for family reunification (Daniels, 1988:125-129). The first significant flow of picture brides began in 1912 and continued until 1920 (Ichioka, 1980). The idea of picture brides is based on the Japanese tradition of arranged marriages, whereby the elders of the family act as match makers. This was done to insure a successful marriage. Therefore the use of proxy marriages by Japanese immigrants was a very practical consideration (LaViolette, 1945:13).

The increase in the number of children in the Japanese immigrant community between 1900 and 1940 is a testimonial to the impact of the picture brides (Nakano, 1990:24-29). In 1900 only one percent of the Japanese were native born, by 1910 six percent were, and by 1920 one out of four were native born. By 1930 almost half were native born and by 1940 almost two-thirds (62.7%) were. (See Table 6.2 on the following page.)

Table 6.1
Japanese Immigration to the U.S., 1861-1950

Stage	Dates	Period of Immigration	Number
I.	1861-1890	Sojourners	3,000*
II.	1891-1900	Pioneers	27,000
III.	1901-1908	Settlers	127,000
IV.	1909-1924	Gentlemen's Agreement	118,000
V.	1925-1930	Omnibus Act of 1924	15,000
VI.	1931-1940	The Great Depression	2,000
VII.	1941-1950	World War II Period	1,500
		Total Immigration	293,500

* figures are approximate for each period.
Source: U.S. Census, Historical Statistics, 1980

Table 6.2
Population of Native Born and Foreign Born
Japanese in the United States, 1900-1940

Year	Total Number	Native Born		Foreign Born	
		Number	Percent	Number	Percent
1900	24,326	269	1.1	24,057	98.9
1910	72,157	4,502	6.1	67,655	93.8
1920	111,010	29,672	26.7	81,338	73.3
1930	133,834	63,357	47.3	70,477	52.7
1940	126,947	79,642	62.7	47,305	37.3

Source: Hale 1945:173

Immigration Restrictions: 1900-1924

When the Japanese first arrived they were viewed as an ideal source of labor for a burgeoning agricultural industry. But they were unwilling to work for low wages and were more interested in becoming land owners. Before long they were the competitors of the small farmers in California and the large growers discovered that they could not depend upon the Japanese as a source of cheap labor (Cross, 1935:263).

Therefore the resentment against them began to build, and the racism, once directed at the Chinese, was transferred to the Japanese. Soon the antagonistic forces that were successful in terminating Chinese immigration, namely the unemployed racists, the labor unions, the newspapers, and the politicians, were galvanized into action against the Japanese (Daniels, 1972; Model, 1970:109-114).

The founding of the Asiatic Exclusion League in San Francisco (1905) marked the renewal of racial attacks against all Asians in California. The sole purpose of the League was to direct racial hatred against the Japanese and to promote the passage of anti-Asian legislation (Hata, 1978:131-145). With the help of the newspapers and sympathetic politicians they pressured the San Francisco School Board to pass a measure in October of 1906, that called for the segregation of Japanese, Chinese, and Korean students in a designated Oriental school (Model, 1971). The concern was that Japanese students would compromise the moral values of American students. But of the 25,000 students in the city, only 93 were Japanese, 25 of whom were native born Americans (Petersen, 1971:41). The passage of this law created an international incident between Japan and the United States. In response President Theodore Roosevelt issued Executive Order 589, banning immigration of Japanese laborers from Hawaii, Mexico, and Canada (Chan, 1991a:49-50). Obviously this was an effort by the President to appease the racists in San Francisco.

But the most important law to affect Japanese immigration was the Gentlemen's Agreement of 1908. As a compromise position the United States and Japan agreed to prohibit the immigration of new laborers to America, except for returning laborers, immigrant non-laborers, and the wives and children of resident Japanese aliens. The following year the California legislature passed a law that called for the exclusion of all Japanese immigrants (Ichihashi, 1932).

At the state level the Alien Land Law of 1913 had the most deleterious impact on the lives of the Japanese immigrants. This law held that those individuals who were ineligible for citizenship could not purchase or own agricultural land in California and it prohibited them from leasing agricultural property for more than three years. This law served as a formidable barrier to the Issei farmers, who were just establishing themselves in the agricultural industry.

The Alien Land Law was passed on the basis of the popular belief that the Japanese immigrants were buying up all the valuable agricultural property in the state. But in fact a state study found that they only owned 1.6 percent of the land in agricultural production in 1920. Furthermore most of the land that they owned had never been used for agricultural production and much of it had been considered worthless before it was brought into production by the Japanese (Buell, 1924:285).

In 1920 an amendment to the Alien Land Law was passed to cap a loophole in the law. This new law prohibited the Issei from purchasing land in the name of their native born children, while they served as guardians of the property that they themselves could not legally own. In addition it prohibited them from leasing any agricultural property in the state.

The test case to determine whether the Japanese were eligible for U.S. citizenship was brought before the U.S. Supreme Court by Takao Ozawa. Ozawa had been a resident of the United States for more than twenty years, was a graduate of Berkeley High School, and a former student at the University of California. In 1914 he applied for U.S. citizenship, but his application was opposed by a federal district attorney on the basis that he was not a free white person and therefore was ineligible for American citizenship. In 1922 the Supreme Court ruled that Ozawa was not a free white person and there was ineligible for American citizenship.

The Omnibus Act of 1924 placed severe restrictions on all immigration to the United States. As a result the flow of Japanese immigrants declined significantly. The negative effects of this Act were not rectified until 1952, with the passage of the McCarran-Walters Act, that lifted these restrictions.

Japanese American Culture

In view of the distinct periods of immigration among the Japanese, it is not only possible to delineate specific immigration periods, but it is also possible to distinguish specific generations within the Japanese American community. The first two groups of Japanese immigrants, the sojourners and the pioneers, are called the Issei, as they were born in Japan. The children of the Issei, that is the native born Americans, are called the Nisei. The third generation, the children of the Nisei, are called the Sansei, and in general they were born after the Second World War. The fourth generation are called the Yonsei. Before the Second World War Issei parents would sometimes send their children to Japan for their educations. They were called the Kibei. Following their educations the Kibei often married in Japan before returning to America (Lyman, 1970).

Traditional Japanese society was not only hierarchical and rigid, but it was also elitist, as the figurehead of Japanese society was the emperor. But it was the shogun, with the assistance of the nobility, who actually ruled Japanese society. The samurai or knights served as local chieftains and administrators. While the social elites constituted fifteen percent of the population, most were peasants. Consequently, Japanese culture is affected by conservatism, social hierarchies, deference to those in authority, respect for age, and by the subordination of the individual to the group or the common good.

In their cultural orientation the extended family is collectively recognized as the *ie* and the individual cannot exit without recognition of the dominance and importance of the *ie* or the group. Once settled in America the *ie* became the collective conscious of the Japanese immigrant community and the actions of the individual represented the whole community. Therefore the success or failure of the individual reflects on the whole community, so that the individual can either bring honor or shame on the community. In the end the individual feels a strong sense of identity, commitment, and loyalty to the group and in turn the individual seeks support and approval from the group.

The Japanese philosophy of life is strongly influenced by traditional concepts that place great importance on the family, on loyalty to the group, and on community obligations. For example, some of the more common concepts that guide the individual's daily life are:

1. Ga-man: this means that the individual will work hard to achieve a particular goal, despite any obstacles or suffering that he/she might encounter or have to bear.
2. Enryo: applies to personal relationships and requires that the person practice reserve, deference, and respect others.
3. Oyakoko: refers to filial piety and requires a sense of reciprocal obligation between parents and their children.
4. Giri: requires that the individual maintain a moral and honest relationship with everyone, as their behavior with others will reflect on their family and the community.

In short, the individual shares a communal sense of obligation toward others and any deviation from this norm would result in personal shame and community dishonor (Kitano, 1969:33-39)

During the early period of immigration to America four major religions were practiced in Japan, (1) Buddhism, (2) Shintoism, (3) Confucianism, and (4) Christianity. The oldest and most influential of these was Buddhism, which declined in importance during the Tokugawa regime. In its place the Meiji government adopted Shinto as the state religion. In return Shinto beliefs supported government policies and objectives and even regarded the emperor as a living deity. This resulted in the development of strong feelings of nationalism among the Japanese people at the turn of the century.

Confucianism was introduced from China and is the third major religion of traditional Japanese society. The Confucian classics contributed to a strong sense of morality, duty, and obligation in Japanese society. As a formal religion Christianity played a minor role in the lives of the Issei. Most of the Issei (80% to 90%) were nominally Buddhist and they rarely attended services, as they only did so on formal occasions, such as births, weddings, and deaths (Petersen, 1971:174). For the Issei believed that the primary purpose of any religion was to guide them to a proper life. As such religion encouraged ethical behavior and offered advice on how to relate to one's parents, friends, and strangers.

As a result of their tolerant and eclectic views on religion the Issei were willing to adopt Christian beliefs, as they discovered that Christianity offered many good ideas on how best to conduct oneself and lead a good and moral life. In addition Christianity provided an opportunity to learn the American ways, to learn English, and to integrate themselves into the fabric of American society.

Wartime Evacuation and Relocation

The day after the attack on Pearl Harbor, December 8, 1941, the FBI arrested all enemy aliens whom they deemed suspicious, including hundreds of Issei businessmen, community leaders, Shinto and Buddhist priests, teachers in Japanese language schools, and editors of Japanese language newspapers. But of the 3,600 enemy aliens arrested by the FBI not one was ever found guilty of doing anything to harm the national interest (Petersen, 1971).

On February 19, 1942 President Franklin Roosevelt issued Executive Order 9066. The President's executive order created military zones on the West Coast and ordered the construction of relocation camps. On March 2, General John De Witt, the commander of the Western Defense Area, ordered all persons of Japanese ancestry to evacuate the West Coast. His order affected more than 110,000 Japanese, two out of three of whom were American citizens, including women and children, the elderly, and anyone with as little as one-eighth Japanese blood (Daniels, 1971).

By August all the Japanese on the West Coast were incarcerated in ten permanent camps, with a total capacity of 119,000. These camps were located in California (Manzanar and Tule Lake), Arizona (Poston and Gila River), Idaho (Minidoka), Utah (Topaz), Wyoming (Heart Mountain), Colorado (Granada), and Arkansas (Rohwer and Jerome). The total spent by American tax payers on the construction of these camps was close to $89 million. And it took the Army eleven months to complete the job (Hosokawa, 1969:351). These expenditures do not even cover the day-to-day expenses of maintaining the camps.

The only crime these citizens committed was that they were of Japanese ancestry. The Issei and the Nisei cooperated with the evacuation, as they felt that any resistance would be perceived as a sign of disloyalty (Miyamoto, 1973:23-26). Even the Japanese American Citizens League (JACL) felt that it was best to cooperate with the military authorities during this period. The only groups to protest the mass incarceration were the Quakers and some local chapters of the American Civil Liberties Union.

The first evacuees were moved from Los Angeles to Manzanar during the first week of March 1942. Evacuees were only allowed to take what they could carry. Most were only given a few days to sell their personal belongings, household furniture, and even their homes. Entrepreneurs were forced to sell equipment and businesses for as little as ten cents on the dollar (Armor,

1988). Overall the Japanese lost more than $400 million in personal and real property as a result of the evacuation.

Life in the Relocation Camps

The camps were operated by the United States Army and managed by the War Relocation Authority (WRA). As a result they were operated like army camps, with all the rules and regulations and dehumanizing effects of military regimentation. Scores of families were crowded together in long tar-paper buildings. Privacy was a thing of the past, although bed sheets sometimes provided the semblance of privacy. Meals were taken in a mess hall and the menu did not consider their ethnic pallets. Similarly bathrooms and showers were public. Such living conditions required a radical change in their personal life styles and left long-lasting psychological scars (Emi, 1991).

In their efforts to make the most of a bad situation the Japanese organized themselves into self governing units. Barracks' meetings were held, representatives were elected, grievances were heard, projects were planned, and an inventory of available talent and skills was taken. In addition they established an educational program, including a football team, cheerleaders, and yearbooks. During the harvest season of their first year in the camps, some evacuees were allowed to work on farms outside the restricted military zone. Although most of the adults in the camps were assigned to specific jobs that were required to maintain the facilities. The government payed them between $12 to $19 per month, depending on the type of work and the skill level required. Doctors and dentists were the highest payed persons in the camps, as they earned $19 a month (Bosworth, 1967:141; Thomas, 1946; 1952).

The 100th Infantry and the 442nd

After their first year in the camp the government sent military recruiters into the camps asking for volunteers. The first group of Nisei recruited by the Army offered Japanese language courses for the Military Intelligence Service. By January, 1943 all Nisei were allowed to volunteer for military service.

While some of the Nisei volunteers served in the Pacific as interpreters for the Army Intelligence Service, most of the 30,000 volunteers were organized into two segregated army units, the 100th Infantry Battalion and the 442nd Regimental Combat Team (Murphy, 1955). After two months of training both units were sent to the battle front in Europe, where they served with distinction. For example, the 442nd saw battle in seven major campaigns and received over 18,000 individual decorations, including 52 Service Crosses and one Congressional Medal of Honor. By the end of the war the 442nd was the most decorated unit in the Armed Forces. Unfortunately their exceptional military record was only achieved at the cost of 9,486 casualties (Petersen 1971:87).

Was the Evacuation Necessary?

The camp experience was devastating to the lives of the Japanese, particularly in terms of economic losses, psychological damage, the negative impact on family relations, and in terms of loss time and opportunities. Overall their life chances were severely affected (Drinnon, 1987).

The most unfortunate part of the whole experience is the fact that the whole relocation procedure was unnecessary, as no single Japanese was ever convicted of any act that would have been considered harmful or dangerous to national security. Some experts have pointed out that when the last Japanese evacuees arrived at camp in November of 1942, there was no longer any need, that is based on national security, for incarceration. This does not even address the question as to why the 160,000 Japanese Americans living in Hawaii were never rounded-up, if there was such a concern about national security (Takaki, 1989:385-392).

Following a decision by the Supreme Court in December of 1944 the government was forced to reconsider its policy of mass incarceration. The Court's decision in the Endo case held that the War Relocation Authority had no right to detain loyal American citizens in camps (Chan, 1991b:137-138). On January 2, 1945 the military commander on the West Coast signed papers officially ending the government's incarceration program. But when the War ended in August of 1945, there were still 44,000 persons of Japanese ancestry in the camps (Chan, 1991b:139).

Who Was Responsible for the Mass Incarceration?

In view of these tragic events one has to wonder how the evacuation was possible and who was responsible? In retrospect a number of groups, organizations, and individuals were responsible. But in a general sense the American people were responsible, for it was public pressure, mass hysteria, and racism that prompted the politicians and public officials to conceive of such a malicious plan. The rationalization and the justification for the plan was national security, but it is now clear that the public was suffering from mass hysteria and in their frustration they set upon a convenient scapegoat. The public, particularly in California, was very resentful and prejudiced toward the Japanese and all they needed was a good excuse to vent their hatred.

The politicians supported the evacuation program as they knew from experience that an anti-Asian position would assure strong support from the voters. In the weeks following the attack on Pearl Harbor the California Congressional delegation convinced themselves, and the President, of the imminent danger posed by the Japanese on the West Coast. Their reward was Executive Order 9066. Clearly, if the President had chosen to do so, he could have made a personal appeal to the American people to control their immediate impulses to strike out against Japanese Americans in their fit of anger and frustration. Roosevelt, in his most eloquent and persuasive way, could have convinced the American people that the Japanese were loyal Americans who were not a threat to our national security. But the President chose to take the easy way out, to the detriment of thousands of American citizens.

The American judicial system also must carry the burden of responsibility inasmuch as the system failed the American people. For it is clear that the Supreme Court could have ruled Executive Order 9066 as patently unconstitutional, but the Court did not do so until December of 1944. If the Court had acted in February of 1942, when the Order was issued, this indelible stain on our system of justice never would have taken place and the whole episode would have gone down in history as a silly military proposal (tenBroek, et al., 1970:327-334).

The military must accept a great burden of the responsibility for the incarceration, as it was General DeWitt who proposed and organized the entire evacuation program, under the guise of national security. This action was taken although the military knew, from its own investigation, that the Japanese did not pose any threat to the national security, nor could they have supported a Japanese invasion force. Furthermore, by the fall of 1942 the Japanese Navy had already suffered decisive defeats in the Pacific (Bosworth, 1967:120).

In the final analysis it was racism that supported the incarceration of the Japanese. For public opinion at the time held that all Japanese, regardless of citizenship, were enemy aliens. The designation as enemy aliens was based on a racial definition, as the Germans and Italians never experienced mass incarceration. It was racial hatred that convinced the American public, and the politicians, that something had to be done with the Japanese (Leonard, 1990).

The Post War Years: The Nisei Generation

The post war years are recognized as the Nisei years, since two-thirds of the Japanese living in America in 1950 were Nisei. Therefore most of the

Japanese were not only young but also native born. Following the war the Nisei entered college and ventured into new career fields in record numbers. In college they set new records in academic achievement, as they saw education as a means of making up for lost time, pleasing their parents, and making something out of their lives. By 1960 the Nisei had the highest proportion of college graduates of any group in American society. Most of them were concentrated in the sciences, in engineering, and in the medical fields.

Their specialization in college is reflected in their occupational distribution following the War. In 1950, twenty percent of all Japanese Americans were employed as farm laborers, but this dropped to nine percent in 1960. In 1950, eighteen percent were laborers, but by 1960 only six percent were thus employed. At the other end of the occupational spectrum only four percent were classified as professional-technical workers in 1950, but by 1960 fifteen percent were thus employed. By the early seventies seven out of ten Nisei males held white-collar positions (Levine and Montero, 1973).

While the Nisei have been referred to as the Quiet Americans, because of their unobtrusive manner and their determination to succeed, they were more involved in the new American life-style and many found acceptance in American society (Hosokawa, 1969). Their greater gregariousness is demonstrated in the increase in the number of Caucasian friends, their higher distribution in the public school system, and their integration into the suburbs. In addition the Nisei were far more active in the political arena, as they joined the Japanese American Citizens League (JACL) in greater numbers, they sponsored political candidates, and they elected their candidates to political office (Hosokawa, 1982).

The Sansei: The New Generation

The Sansei are the post-war generation and did not experience the camps or the racism of the post war period. The Sansei were raised in solid middle class families and were given the social and economic advantage of the American middle class life style (Masuda, 1970).

As a group the Sansei are very successful, as they have exceeded the national standards in their educational and occupational achievements, they have entered the mainstream of the professional and business world, and they are well integrated into the greater society (Montero, 1981). Many are established in the professions, such as medicine, engineering, dentistry, architecture, law, and teaching. By this means they have gained social status and recognition.

A most distinctive characteristic of the Sansei is that they have exhibited a high rate of intermarriage (Tinker, 1982). As a result of anti-miscegenation laws and societal racism intermarriage among the Issei was a rarity. For example, one study in Los Angeles found that only two percent of the Issei intermarried between 1924 and 1933. But by 1959 twenty-three percent of the Nisei were intermarried. By 1972 almost half (49%) of the Sansei had intermarried (Kikumura and Kitano, 1973). Similar results were obtained in studies conducted among Japanese Americans living in Fresno and San Francisco. However, a more recent study reveals that intermarriage among the Sansei may have declined to a third of all marriages (Levine and Rhodes, 1981).

The Japanese American Family

Just as the social and cultural life of Japanese Americans is strongly influenced by generational differences, it is the family that serves as the focus of community life. The traditional Japanese family structure is based on respect for rank, position, age, generation, and gender. The family is also imbued with a strong sense of group solidarity, mutual support, filial piety, respect for others, obligation toward parents and elders, strong identity with the family name, and the need and desire to succeed. As a result hard work, duty to the family, and responsibility for personal actions are emphasized.

Traditionally the Japanese shared a strong identification with the ancestral clan, the family name, the home, and the village. The spirits of ancestors are often beseeched, in time of need, when major decisions must be made, and when individuals want to bolster family unity. Within this framework marriage was not the decision of two individuals but rather was considered a commitment between two families, that is a bond between two ancestral groups. Therefore arranged marriages were the customary and expected form of bonding and were managed by family representatives, by go-betweens, and by match-makers who insured that the prospective partners and their families were of the proper social status, proper lineage, impeccable backgrounds, and proper social standing in the community.

Following marriage the couple was expected to have a large family, with an emphasis on male offspring. The family structure was patriarchal, patrilocal, and patrilinial. Consequently the male orientation in the traditional Japanese family was very strong. The son's bride was effectively adopted by his family, and she was expected to work under the supervision of her mother-in-law, whose job it was to show her the role of the good-wife.

As in Japan, the Issei emphasized the importance of the extended family that formed the basis for the solidarity and cohesiveness of the immigrant community. Initially the extended family was modified in America, since the Issei family was without grandparents, as they remained in Japan. Therefore the Nisei extended family experience tended to be more horizontal, than vertical, as their extended family ties centered around relationships with their aunts, uncles, and cousins, rather than with grandparents and tertiary relatives. The introduction of the Picture Brides during the early 1920's insured that the skewed sex-ratio in the Issei immigrant community would stabilize by the time the second generation Nisei were ready for marriage and family (See Table 6.3).

As an adjunct to extended family ties, Issei parents encouraged their children to join clubs and get involved in formal organizations. As a result most Nisei were involved in the Boy Scouts, the YMCA, and a host of school organizations and clubs.

Table 6.3
Japanese Population in the United States
By Sex, 1880-1940

Year	Total	Males	Females	Percent Females	Males Per 100 Females
1880	148	—	—	—	—
1890	2,039	—	—	—	—
1900	24,326	23,341	985	4.0	2,369.6
1910	72,157	63,070	9,097	12.6	694.1
1920	111,010	72,707	38,303	34.5	189.8
1930	138,834	81,771	57,063	41.1	143.3
1940	126,947	71,967	54,980	43.3	130.9

Source: Thomas, 1952:575

The Nisei family was more integrated into American society in that it was more Anglicized than the traditional Issei family. In part the Anglocentric orientation of the Nisei family resulted from the disruption of traditional family patterns during the camp experience. During their incarceration many Nisei matured in a family environment that was no longer traditional, as their father was no longer in charge and their mother no longer played her traditional role. The regimented structure of camp life resulted in a profound alteration in family relationships.

During the fifties and the sixties the Nisei family was more dispersed by region, more urban, and more likely to live in heterogeneous neighborhoods. Their higher level of social integration resulted in a strong middle-class orientation, in the dependence on the two paycheck family, and in higher rates of intermarriage (Connor, 1977).

Today the Sansei have achieved higher levels of social integration and assimilation. When compared to the family patters of their parents, the Sansei are more likely to live in the suburbs and in predominantly Caucasian neighborhoods. And they are less likely to spend time with members of their extended family, less likely to be involved in Japanese cultural events, and less likely to read ethnic newspapers (Connor, 1974). But on the other hand, they are more likely to be Christians or non-religious, more likely to have non-Japanese friends, more likely to belong to non-Japanese social clubs and organizations, and far more likely to have a non-Japanese spouse (Kendis, 1989:35-65; Montero, 1980:79-88).

The Sansei family patterns are strikingly different from their parents as a result of their rapid socio-economic mobility and cultural integration into the mainstream of American society. And these family characteristics are now a part of the lives of their children, the Yonsei. And it is clear that the Yonsei have become more Americanized than their parents (O'Brien and Fugita, 1991:118-136).

A Demographic Profile

One outcome of the forced evacuation of the Japanese was their greater geographical distribution. In 1940, 74 percent were living in California, but in 1950 only 60 percent lived in California. By regions of the country four out of five of the 847,562 Japanese Americans lived in the West in 1990, 8.7 percent lived in the Northeast, 7.4 percent in the Midwest, and 7.9 percent in the South. In terms of their distribution by state most Japanese Americans live in California (36.9%) and Hawaii (29.1%) in 1990. The next most populous states are Washington (4.0%), New York (4.1%), and Illinois (2.6%).

When we consider their geographic distribution by major metropolitan areas their largest concentration occurs in Honolulu, where their population was 190,000 in 1980. This represents one-fourth (26.6%) of the total Japanese population in the United States. In 1990 a total of 45,370 were living in the city of Los Angeles, 12,047 in San Francisco, and 8,673 in San Diego. The cities of New York, San Jose, and Anaheim have populations of approximately 22,000 (Nishi, 1985).

Japanese Americans are a slightly older group, with a median age of 33.5 years, when compared to a median age of 30 years in the general population. Their older age results from the greater proportion of Japanese Americans in the middle age categories and fewer in the younger and older age groups. While one out of four Japanese Americans fall into the youth category (1-19 years), one-third of the U.S. population is in this dependent population group. Three out of ten of the Japanese Americans fall into the young adult category (20-34 years), as compared to one out of four in the general population. A significant difference occurs in the mature adult category (35-64 years) where two out of five are found, but only one fourth of the U.S. population falls into this age category. Only seven percent of the

147

Japanese Americans fall into the elderly category (65 plus), compared to eleven percent for the total population. This simply means that the life expectancy of Japanese Americans is not as great as the general population.

Since Japanese Americans are an older group this means that they have a lower dependency-ratio and therefore more of their members are active in the labor force and are sustaining their economy, as compared to the general population. They also have a much smaller dependent population (that is children and the aged), less than a third (31.5%), when compared to the U. S. population in general (43%).

While most Issei achieved only minimal levels of education, they demonstrated a great respect for education. Indeed, a 1907 study of Issei settlers in California found that almost half (45%) had enrolled in a course of formal education, most often English language schools (Kawakami, 1921:143). Naturally the Issei sought to provide the best education for their children. However, one of the main obstacles was racial hatred. For example in 1930 Asian children attended segregated schools in four districts in California (Pajus, 1937:180).

By 1930 the level of education among the Japanese matched the national average. Unfortunately their educational progress was interrupted by the war time evacuation. By 1970 their median level of education was 12.6 for the males and 12.4 for Japanese American females, compared to the national median of 12.1 years. In 1980 their median educational level was 13.2 years for males and 12.7 years for females, compared to 12.5 years for the national population.

On average Japanese Americans have higher incomes than the general population. In 1970 their median family income was $12,500, compared to $9,600 for all families. By 1980 their incomes had increased to $27,000, compared to $19,900 for all families. Japanese Americans also had the fewest families living below the poverty level (4.2%), when compared to Anglo Americans and all other groups. At the other end of the spectrum, 12 percent had annual family incomes of more than $50,000.

But these higher incomes were only obtained as a result of having more family members in the labor force. For example in 1980, forty-four percent of the Japanese American families had two workers, and one out of five had three or more workers. It is also important to note that they are heavily concentrated in California and Hawaii, where their higher salaries are offset by the higher costs of living.

Several studies have compared the level of educational achievement and occupational distribution among Japanese Americans and have found that they only earn 88 percent of what white men earn for the same type of work and experience (Levine and Montero, 1973). This discrepancy between income and occupation can only be attributed to job segregation and racial discrimination.

In 1980, 28.5 percent were in managerial-professional jobs and 34.2 percent were employed in technical-sales positions. Overall, 63 percent were in white-collar positions, as compared to 52 percent in the general population. The area of highest concentration for men was in managerial-professional positions (33.5%), followed by technical-sales (23.4%) and craft jobs (15.8%). Women were primarily concentrated in technical-sales (46%), followed by managerial-professional (23.1%), and service jobs (17.2%).

Nonetheless a glass ceiling of discrimination bars Asians from the top management positions in American industry (Takaki, 1989). In part, their concentration in professional and white collar positions is a reaction to pass discrimination, since Japanese Americans have historically used education as a means of protecting themselves from prejudice and blatant acts of discrimination. For they realize that they are less likely to be the victims of racism in those occupations that require higher levels of education (Flynn, 1991:92-101).

Japanese American Civil Rights

From their date of arrival the Issei were ineligible for citizenship, a legal position that was affirmed by the Supreme Court in 1922. The only Japanese eligible to vote were the native born Nisei, who were placed in the camps just at the time when they were eligible to vote. Indeed, one of the reasons that the politicians were able to pass racists legislation against the Japanese was that they were not considered a voting threat.

The Japanese American Citizens League (JACL), was founded in 1930 and served as a focal point of Nisei political organization. One of their first projects following the Second World War was to obtain naturalization rights for the Issei and to encourage voter registration among the Nisei. In addition they worked on such practical concerns as citizenship rights, compensation for the camp victims, and efforts to challenge existing discriminatory laws. JACL's first victory came in 1948 when the federal government passed the Japanese American Evacuation Act, which created a process for compensation of camp victims. In 1952, under pressure from the JACL, the federal government repealed the Japanese exclusion provision of the 1924 Omnibus Act and granted the Japanese a token quota (Hosokawa, 1982).

Under pressure from the JACL, and other concerned citizens, Congress finally created the Commission on Wartime Relocation in 1980. Following a close review of the pertinent documents the commission recommended that 66,000 camp survivors receive compensation of one to two billion dollars. In September of 1987 the House passed a bill providing for $1.2 billion in compensation. Even more important the bill recognized that the U.S. government had denied the Japanese their civil rights as a result of racial prejudice. This was the first formal apology given by the federal government, more than forty years late. The Senate approved and passed the bill in April of 1988.

Political Representation and Political Gains

Political gains were particularly significant in Hawaii, as returning Japanese American veterans were determined to cash in on their hard fought battle for freedom. Following years of anti-Asian feelings, Hawaii was finally granted statehood in August of 1959. Daniel Inouye, a war hero, was elected the first U.S. Representative from the state of Hawaii and thus he became the first Japanese American in Congress. In November of 1992 Daniel Inouye was re-elected to the U.S. Senate. When Inouye was elected to the U.S. Senate in 1962, Spark Matsunaga, a veteran of the 442nd and a Harvard law school graduate, became the second Japanese American to serve in the House. The first Japanese American woman to serve in the House, and Hawaii's first Nisei female attorney, was elected in 1964. In 1992 both senators from Hawaii are Japanese Americans.

The Nisei on the mainland worked on political organization and civil rights cases during the fifties and early sixties (Wilson and Hosokawa, 1982:257-285). And it was during the sixties that the first Nisei were elected to the city councils of Los Angeles, Oakland, and San Jose. In 1976 Samuel Hayakawa, a Canadian born scholar, was elected the Republican Senator from California. In the same year Norman Mineta, a camp survivor, became the first Japanese American Representative from the mainland.

In 1992 there were several politicians and judges in California who were Japanese Americans. This list included two congressional representatives (Robert Matsui and Norman Mineta), five mayors, eight city council members, two federal district judges (Robert Takasugi and A. Wallace Tashima), one appellate judge, nine superior court judges, and five municipal court judges.

Chapter Summary

Even though the Japanese arrived in Hawaii in 1868 as contract laborers, only a hundred years have passed since they arrived in California. The Japanese were attracted to California by the employment opportunities. Most found work in the agricultural industry as itinerant farm laborers. By the turn of the century their numbers had increased to the point where they were able to pool their economic resources and began to lease and purchase agricultural property.

The effort to segregate Japanese school children in San Francisco marked a turning point in their immigration experience. In 1908 the

Gentlemen's Agreement placed serious restrictions on their immigration. But they were allowed to send for wives and children, which resulted in the arrival of picture brides in America. The Omnibus Act of 1924 terminated immigration from Japan.

In retrospect it appears that the Japanese may have been a little too successful in California, as they were resented by many people. Following the Japanese attack on Pearl Harbor on December 7, 1941 the public resentment was transformed into law and resulted in the incarceration of over 110,000 Japanese, most of whom were native born American citizens.

As a result of their incarceration in the camps the Japanese lost all their property and personal belongings. Life in the camps was difficult and resulted in a number of long term problems for the Japanese Americans. Over 30,000 Nisei youth volunteered for military duty and compiled a distinguished record of service in several European campaigns.

After the war the Japanese were gradually released from the camps and most moved back to their hometowns to start their lives over again. The Nisei attempted to make up for lost time by applying themselves to their work and studies. Soon the Japanese Americans excelled in education, in occupational mobility, and in average annual income. Today it is the Sansei who have achieved middle class status and have gained new acceptance in American society.

References

Armor, John and Peter Wright
  1988   *Manzanar*. New York: Times Books.
Boddy, E. Manchester
  1921   *Japanese in America*. Los Angeles: E. M. Boddy.
Bosworth, Allan R.
  1967   America's Concentration Camps. New York: Bantam Books.
Buell, Raymond L.
  1924   Japanese Immigration. New York: World Peace Foundation.
Bunje, Emil T. H.
  1937   "The Story of Japanese Farming in California." Ph.D. Dissertation. Berkeley: The University of California.
Chan, Sucheng
  1991a   *Asian Californians*. San Francisco: MTL/Boyd & Fraser.
  1991b   *Asian Americans: An Interpretive History*. Boston: Twayne Publishers.
Connor, John W.
  1974   "Value Continuities and Change in Three Generations of Japanese Americans." *Ethos* 2:232-264.
  1977   *Tradition and Change in Three Generations of Japanese Americans*. Chicago: Nelson-Hall.
Cross, Ira B.
  1935   *A History of the Labor Movement in California*. Berkeley: The University of California Press.
Daniels, Roger
  1971   *Concentration Camps, U.S.A.* New York: Holt, Rinehart & Winston.
  1972   "Japanese Immigrants on the Western Frontier: The Issei in California- 1890-1940." In *East Across the Pacific*. Hilary Conroy and T. Scott Miyakawa (eds.), Santa Barbara: ABC-CLIO. Pp. 82-86
  1988   *Asian America: Chinese and Japanese in the United States Since 1850*. Seattle: University of Washington Press.
Drinnon, Richard
  1987   *Keeper of Concentration Camps*. Berkeley: The University of California Press.
Emi, Frank
  1991   "Resistance: The Heart Mountain Fair Play Committee's Fight for Justice." *Amerasia Journal* 17(1):47-51.
Flynn, James R.
  1991   *Asian Americans: Achievement Beyond IQ*. Hillsdale, NJ: Lawrence Erlbaum Associates, Publishers.

Fuller, Varden Levi
1939   "The Supply of Agricultural Labor as a Factor in the Evolution of Farm Organization in California." Ph.D. Dissertation. Berkeley: The University of California.

Glick, Clarence E.
1980   *Sojourners and Settlers: Chinese Migrants in Hawaii.* Honolulu: The University of Hawaii Press.

Hale, Robert M.
1945   "The United States and Japanese Immigration." Ph.D. Dissertation. Chicago: The University of Chicago.

Hata, Donald T. Jr.
1978   *"Undesirables" Early Immigrants and the Anti-Japanese Movement in San Francisco, Prelude to Exclusion.* New York: Arno Press.

Hosokawa, Bill
1969   *Nisei: The Quiet Americans.* New York: William Morrow and Company.
1982   *JACL in Quest of Justice.* New York: William Morrow and Company.

Ichihashi, Yamato
1932   *Japanese in the United States.* Stanford: Stanford University Press.

Ichioka, Yuji
1980   "Amerika Nadeshiko: Japanese Immigrant Women in the United States, 1900-1924." *Pacific Historical Review* 49(2):339-357.
1988   *The Issei: The World of the First Generation Japanese Immigrants, 1885-1924.* New York: The Free Press.

Iwata, Masakazu
1962   "The Japanese Immigrants in California Agriculture." *Agricultural History* 36:25-37.

Kendis, Kaoru O.
1989   *A Matter of Comfort: Ethnic Maintenance and Ethnic Style among Third-Generation Japanese Americans.* New York: AMS Press.

Kikumura, Akemi, and Harry H. L. Kitano
1973   "Interracial Marriage: A Picture of Japanese Americans." *Journal of Social Issues* 29:67-81.

Kimura, Yukiko
1988   *Issei: Japanese Immigrants in Hawaii.* Honolulu: University of Hawaii Press.

Kitano, Harry H.
1969   *Japanese Americans: The Evolution of a Subculture.* Englewood Cliffs, NJ: Prentice-Hall (Second Edition).

LaViolette, Forrest E.
  1945   *Americans of Japanese Ancestry: A Study of Assimilation in the American Community.* Toronto: The Canadian Institute of International Affairs.
Leonard, Kevin A.
  1990   "Is That What We fought For? Japanese Americans and Racism in California, the Impact of World War II." *Western Historical Quarterly* 21(4):463-482.
Levine, Gene N. and Darrel M. Montero
  1973   "Socioeconomic Mobility Among Three Generations of Japanese Americans." *Journal of Social Issues* 29(2):33-48.
Levine, Gene N. and Colbert Rhodes
  1981   *The Japanese American Community: A Three-Generation Study.* New York: Praeger.
Lukes, Timothy J. and Gary Y. Okihiro
  1985   *Japanese Legacy: Farming and Community Life in California's Santa Clara Valley.* Cupertino, CA: Local History Center.
Lyman, Stanford M.
  1970   "Generation and Character: The Case of the Japanese Americans." In *The Asian in the West.* Stanford M. Lyman, University of Nevada, Reno. Pp. 65-80.
Masuda, Minoru, et al
  1970   "Ethnic Identity in Three Generations of Japanese Americans." *Journal of Social Psychology* 81:199-207.
Millis, Henry A.
  1915   *The Japanese Problem in the United States.* New York: MacMillan Company.
Miyamoto, S. Frank
  1939   "Social Solidarity Among the Japanese in Seattle." *University of Washington Publications in the Social Sciences* 11:57-130.
  1973   "The Forced Evacuation of the Japanese Minority During World War II." *Journal of Social Issues* 29(2):11-29.
Modell, John
  1971   "Tradition and Opportunity: The Japanese Immigrant in America." *Pacific Historical Review* 40:163-182.
  1977   *The Economics and Politics of Racial Accommodation: The Japanese of Los Angeles, 1900-1942.* Urbana: University of Illinois Press.
Montero, Darrel
  1980   *Japanese Americans: Changing Patterns of Ethnic Affiliation Over Three Generations.* Boulder, CO: Westview Press.
  1981   "The Japanese Americans: Changing Patterns of Assimilation Over Three Generations." *American Sociological Review* 46:829-839.

Moriyama, Alan T.

1984   "The Causes of Emigration: The Background of Japanese Emigration to Hawaii, 1885 to 1894." In *Labor Immigration Under Capitalism: Asian Workers in theUnited States Before World War II,* Lucie Cheng and Edna Bonacich (eds.), University of California Press, Berkeley. Pp. 248-276.

1985   *Imingaisha: Japanese Emigration Companies and Hawaii, 1894-1908.* Honolulu: University of Hawaii Press.

Murphy, Thomas D.

1955   *Ambassadors in Arms: The Story of Hawaii's 100th Battalion.* Honolulu: University of Hawaii Press.

Muto, Sheila

1991   "Three Generations of S.F. Japantown." *Asian Week* March 8, Pp. 14-18.

Naka, Kaizo

1913   "Social and Economic Conditions Among Japanese Farmers in California." M.A. Thesis. University of California: Berkeley.

Nakano, Mei T.

1990   *Japanese American Women: Three Generations 1890-1990.* Berkeley: Mina Press. O'Brien, David J. and Stephen S. Fugita

1991   *The Japanese American Experience.* Bloomington: Indiana University Press.

Okihiro, Gary Y.

1991   *Cane Fires: The Anti-Japanese Movement in Hawaii, 1865-1945.* Philadelphia, PA: Temple University Press.

Pajus, Jean

1937   *The Real Japanese California.* Berkeley: James J. Gillick.

Petersen, William

1971   *Japanese Americans.* New York: Random House.

Strong, Edward K. Jr.

1933   *Japanese in California.* Stanford, CA: Stanford University Press.

Takaki, Ronald

1989   *Strangers from a Different Shore: A History of Asian Americans.* New York: Penguin Books.

tenBroek, Jacobus, E.N. Barnhart, and F.W. Matson

1970   *Prejudice, War and the Constitution.* Berkeley: The University of California Press.

Thomas, Dorothy S.

1946   *The Spoilage.* Berkeley: University of California Press.

1952   *The Salvage.* Berkeley: University of California Press.

Tinker, John N.
  1982   "Intermarriage and Assimilation in a Plural Society:
              Japanese Americans in the United States." In *Intermarriage in
              the United States*, Gary A. Crester and Joseph J. Leon (eds.),
              The Haworth Press, New York. Pp. 61-74.
Wilson, Robert A. and Bill Hosokawa
  1982   *East to America: A History of the Japanese in the United
              States*. New York: Quill.
Yoneda, Karl
  1971   "100 Years of Japanese Labor History in the USA." In *Roots:
              An Asian American Reader*. Amy Tachiki, E. Wong, F. Odo,
              and B. Wong (eds.), Los Angeles: Asian American Studies
              Center, University of California. Pp. 150-158.

1868	The first contingent of Japanese contract laborers arrived in Honolulu.
1869	The Wakamatsu Colony of Japanese immigrants was established in California.
1906	The San Francisco Board of Education ordered all Asian students to attend a segregated Asian school.
1908	The Gentlemen's Agreement was signed.
1913	The Alien Land Law was passed in California.
1920	A more rigid Alien Land Law was passed in California.
1922	The Ozawa case restricted American citizenship to "free white persons".
1924	Omnibus Act passed by Congress prohibited all Asian immigration into the United States.
1930	The Japanese American Citizenship League (JACL) was founded.
1941	Japan attached Pearl Harbor on December 7.
1942	President Roosevelt issued Executive Order 9066 on February 19, authorizing the internment of 110,000 Japanese.
1943	The 100th Infantry Battalion and the 442nd Regimental Combat Team, composed of Nisei volunteers, were organized.
1946	The 442nd was recognized as the most decorated unit in the Armed Forces. The last Japanese internment camp was closed.
1948	President Truman signed the Japanese American Evacuation Claims Act, providing some compensation for financial losses.
1952	The McCarran-Walter Immigration Act was passed by Congress, it ended the exclusion of Asian immigrants and granted Asian Americans naturalization rights.
1959	Daniel Inouye was elected the first U.S. Representative from Hawaii and became the first Japanese American in Congress.
1962	Daniel Inouye elected to the U.S. Senate.
1964	The first Japanese American woman (from Hawaii) was elected to the House of Representatives.
1976	Samuel Hayakawa was elected Senator from California. Norman Mineta became the first Japanese American Representative from the mainland.
1988	Congress passed a bill to provide $20,000 compensation to camp survivors.

1989	Government compensation payments to camp victims are delayed as a result of government red tape.

Important Names

General John De Witt	Meiji Emperor	Samuel Hayakawa
Daniel Inouye	Robert Matsui	Spark Matsunaga
Norman Mineta	Takao Ozawa	Franklin Roosevelt
George Shima		

Key Terms

emigration companies	sojourners	pioneers
Gentlemen's Agreement 1908	Omnibus Act 1924	picture brides
Asiatic Exclusion League	Alien Land Law 1913	sojourners
Alien Land Law 1920	The Ozawa Case 1922	Issei
Omnibus Act 1924	Nisei	Sansei
McCarran-Walters Act 1952	Yonsei	Kibei
the *ie*	Ga-man	Enryo
Oyakoko	Giri	Buddhism
Shintoism	Confucianism	relocation camps
Executive Order 9066	Poston	Gila River
Western Defense Area	Manzanar	Tule Lake
Minidoka	Topaz	Heart Mountain
Granada	Rohwer	Jerome
the Quakers	the Endo Case	dependency-ratio
Japanese American- Citizens League (JACL)	American Civil Liberties Union (ACLU)	the Quiet Americans
War Relocation Authority (WRA)	100th Infantry Battalion	glass ceiling
442nd Regimental Combat Team		Evacuation Act 1980
Commission on Wartime Relocation		

1. Discuss five push factors and five pull factors that affected Japanese immigration to America.
2. Japanese immigrants arrived in distinct stages. Name and provide a brief description of four of these stages.
3. What was the picture bride program and what were the long term effects of this program?
4. List and discuss the impact of four laws passed against Japanese immigrants in an attempt to terminate their settlement in America.
5. Discuss five unique cultural characteristics found in the traditional Japanese immigrant community in America during the early twentieth century.
6. Discuss five ways in which the wartime evacuation and the camp experience of the Japanese had a negative impact on their lives in America.
7. Provide five good reasons why the wartime evacuation of Japanese Americans was unnecessary.
8. List the four generations of Japanese Americans and indicate why they are unique or different from one another (provide three characteristics or reasons for each).

Chapter 7

The Korean American Experience

Introduction

Until the end of the Second World War there were only a few thousand Koreans living in the United States and most of these were concentrated in Los Angeles and New York City. But following the liberalization of the immigration laws in 1965, thousands of Koreans began arriving each year, making them the third fastest growing ethnic group in American society today. From a few thousand immigrants in the early 1960's, they now number 798,849. It is estimated that there will be 1,321,000 Koreans in the United States by the year 2000 (Bouvier and Agresta, 1987: Table 12.2). Today most Koreans are foreign born (82%), many arrive with professional degrees and technical skills, and most intend to remain permanently in the United States.

Korean immigration to the United States is not a new phenomenon but rather the size of the Korean community and the flow of immigrants from Korea is new and different. Like other Asian groups Koreans were attracted to the United States at the turn of the century in search of jobs and new opportunities. In addition to the opportunities they sought in America, the Korean pioneers left their homeland in order to avoid the harsh economic conditions and political turmoil that plagued their nation at the turn of the century.

The Background to Korean Immigration

As a geographically small nation Korea was historically surrounded by more powerful neighbors, such as the Chinese, the Japanese, and the Russians. But for hundreds of years the Koreans nonetheless managed to maintain a distinct national identification and culture. However, toward the close of the nineteenth century China, Japan, and the United States took an interest in the vast natural wealth of Korea and became aware of its strategic location in the modern world of global politics (Hurh and Kim, 1984:43).

Like other Asian nations, Korea was primarily a society of peasants and farmers who were oppressed by a few hundred war lords and social elites. At the top of Korean society were the members of the royal family and the nobility, known as the yangban. The nobility represented about three percent of the nation's population. Below the nobility was a small group of literati and civil servants, who served as scholars and local administrators. The largest social class in Korean society was the sangmin class, composed of farmers, merchants, fishermen, and common laborers. They constituted about seventy-five percent of the population. At the lowest level of this preindustrial society were the social outcasts, the slaves, monks, entertainers, and butchers (Chang, 1974; Hoare, 1988).

In addition to a series of political problems, Korean society was also plagued by inflation and high taxes. The traditional system of tax farming, imposed by the Yi Dynasty (1392-1910), allowed noblemen and high government officials to collect taxes from private land and agricultural holdings. As a result the small farmers were faced with a never ending tax burden, as more and more demands were made on their labor and on their ability to pay. The inordinate tax burden on the farmers and peasants and the political corruption and instability at the top left the country open to foreign exploitation (Kim and Kim, 1967).

Though China was a very powerful neighbor, it was the Japanese that the Koreans feared the most. With the rise to power of the Meiji Dynasty (1868), the Japanese began to search the Far East for new sources of raw materials. By the early 1870's the Japanese initiated a trading policy whereby they purchased rice directly from Korean farmers at inflated prices. Within ten years the Korean farmers and the Korean national economy were totally dependent on the Japanese rice merchants for survival. Tragically by selling their rice to foreigners the farmers were contributing to the mass starvation of the Korean peasants in the countryside (Kim and Kim, 1967).

During this period of economic dependency Japanese investors arrived in Korea in large numbers and bought thousands of acres of agricultural land at a fraction of its true value. In a matter of only a few years the Japanese became the new ruling class in Korean society. Feeling the power of their economic domination and their political clout in Asia the Japanese established a protectorate over Korea in 1905. This was the same year that they defeated the Russians on the battlefield. In 1910 the Japanese secured their economic and political position in Korea with the formal annexation of the country. From this point forward the Korean people were under the dictatorial control of the Japanese until their defeat in the Second World War.

Korean Immigration to Hawaii

Even though the date of arrival of the first Koreans in the United States is still open to debate, the best evidence indicates that the first Koreans to arrive were graduates of Protestant mission schools. The top students in the Korean missionary schools were encouraged to continue their educations in the United States. Between 1890 and 1900 a total of 64 students arrived in America (Melendy, 1977:121). However, the first two official Korean immigrants who reported to the American immigration authorities arrived in Honolulu on January 15, 1900 (H. Kim, 1977:110).

Two years later the first Korean laborers arrived in Hawaii. In the fall of 1902 the Hawaiian Sugar Planters Association (HSPA) entered into formal negotiations for Korean laborers. On November 16, the Emperor Konjong established a department of immigration, and he authorized the HSPA to recruit Korean laborers (Pomerantz, 1984:294-295). The labor contractors and the representatives of the Hawaiian Sugar Planters Association described Hawaii as having a mild climate, free education, and plantation jobs that guaranteed a salary of $16 per month. On average Korean men earned between sixty-five to seventy cents a day and Korean women earned between fifty to sixty-five cents a day (Choy, 1979:94- 95).

The first group of 121 Korean immigrants boarded the *S.S. Gaelic* on December 22, 1902 and arrived in Honolulu on January 13, 1903 (Kim and Patterson, 1974:2-3). The second group of 90 Korean contract laborers arrived in Honolulu on March 2, 1903. In 1903 a total of 1,133 Koreans sailed for Hawaii, and in 1904 3,434 arrived, and the following year 2,659 settled in the islands. By November of 1905, when the Korean government terminated all emigration to America, a total of 7,226 immigrants had settled in Hawaii. This first wave of Korean immigrants consisted of 6,048 men, 637 women, and 541 children (Chai, 1981; Patterson, 1977).

Most of these early Korean immigrants were young men, between the ages of twenty to thirty, and were single or traveling without their wives or families. Some were farmers from North Korea and others were from the Seoul-Inchon region. The immigrants from Seoul were primarily army veterans, miners, house servants, or woodcutters. Six out of ten of these pioneers were illiterate (Harvey, 1980; Patterson, 1979, 1988).

Second Wave Korean Immigrants

The Second Wave Korean immigrants began to arrive in 1906, that is following the formal termination of Korean immigration, and ended with the passage of the Omnibus Act in 1924 (Yun, 1977). The Omnibus Act prohibited emigration from Japan and the Koreans were subject to the provisions of this Act since they were under the political domination of the

Japanese. The Second Wave saw the immigration of picture brides, the arrival of political refugees, and the introduction of Korean immigrants to the mainland.

Just as the Japanese immigrants in the United States had sent for and married their picture brides by proxy, so the Koreans took advantage of this last opportunity to establish their families in America. Between 1910 and 1924 approximately one thousand Korean picture brides joined their new husbands in Hawaii, when the sex ratio was ten men for every woman (B. Kim, 1937).

Almost all the picture brides were recruited by relatives or friends of the Koreans working in Hawaii. In a matter of weeks professional match-makers appeared and made it their business to recruit picture brides. Their fee for securing a new bride for a contract laborer working in Hawaii was between $300 to $400. Most of these women were young, between 18 and 24, and were primarily recruited from impoverished families in Northwestern Korea (Lyu, 1977:26-28). Sometimes they reluctantly volunteered to became picture brides as a last desperate effort to escape from the poverty and starvation in their homeland (Yang, 1987). The arrival of these picture brides encouraged many Korean farm workers to leave the plantations and settle in Honolulu.

The second largest group of Korean immigrants to arrive during this period were students and intellectuals, as the immigration records reveal that 541 arrived between 1910 and 1918. Most of these immigrants had no choice but to leave their homeland as they were political activists who were fleeing Japanese oppression (McCune, 1956:4). In order to allow their entry into the United States the government granted these political refugees the status of students, as most arrived without proper documents, passports, or visas. During their stay in the United States most carried on their fight against the Japanese occupation of their homeland and some became the future leaders of the Korean American community (Mangiafico, 1988:79).

The first Korean immigrants arrived on the West Coast in 1904, as American railroad companies sent labor agents to Honolulu to recruit Korean workers. By the time immigration from Hawaii was terminated in 1907, approximately 2,000 Koreans were living in San Francisco. They were attracted to the mainland where jobs were more plentiful than in Hawaii and the hourly wages were higher. A railroad construction worker could earn from $1.20 to $1.50 a day, as opposed to 70 cents a day for plantation work in Hawaii. Before long most of these immigrants abandoned railroad con-struction and service work in order to follow the crops in California. Their attraction to and concentration in the California agricultural industry was not surprising as most had worked on farms in Korea.

By 1910 there were only 461 Koreans living on the mainland and by 1920 their numbers had increased to 1,677. While most Koreans lived in the rural areas of California, their heaviest concentration was in the central city area of Los Angeles (Givens, 1939). Their population did not increase significantly over the years as there were only 1,800 Koreans living in the mainland in 1930, and only 1,700 in 1940 (W. Kim, 1971:26).

The New Wave Immigrants

The most obvious characteristics of the New Wave Korean immigrants is that they are urban, educated, and very likely to come from a professional or technical background. In effect they have the skills, education, and experience that are most needed by American employers (Takaki, 1989:436-445). The social and economic characteristics of the New Wave immigrants reflect the changes that were brought about by the Immigration Reform Act of 1965 (Hurh, 1974; Ryu, 1977).

The most dramatic impact of the Immigration Reform Act on the flow of Korean immigrants to America was that it allowed for family reunification. This provision of the Act simply meant that immediate relatives of permanent legal resident aliens, and naturalized citizens, would be given a higher preference for immigration on the seven point rating scale for all immigration (See Appendix A). However, it is also important to note that a significant proportion, as high as 50 percent, of the immigrant visas issued to immediate relatives in Korea, are given to Korean children who are adopted by American families (Mangiafico, 1988: Table 8.3).

The multiplier effect of the family reunification provision in the new immigration law is clear when we consider the flow of Korean immigrants between 1950 and 1987. For example, between 1950 and 1964 a total of 15,049 Koreans arrived in the United States, but between 1970 and 1979 a total of 240,398 were admitted (Koo and Yu, 1981). In effect this ten year period accounts for almost four out of ten (36.7%) of all Korean immigrants admitted between 1965 and 1991 (See Table 7.1).

According to the U.S. Census Bureau there were 798,849 Koreans living in the United States in 1990. Although in 1985 the Korean Ministry of Foreign Affairs estimated that there were at least 920,000 Koreans living in the United States (I. Kim, 1987:22). In 1990 most Korean Americans were concentrated on the West Coast, as 44 percent lived in Western states, 23 percent in the Northeast, 14 percent in the Midwest, and 19 percent in the South (U.S. Census, 1992:Table 26) (See Table 7.2).

In view of their recent immigration, four out of five (81.9%) Koreans are foreign born. As a group Koreans have a low rate of naturalization, that is when compared to other groups of immigrants, as only one out of three (34.6%) were naturalized citizens in 1980. But when we control for length of residence it is clear that six out of ten (62%) of the Koreans who arrived before 1975 were naturalized by 1980, that is allowing for the mandatory five year waiting period for naturalization. This finding reveals that Koreans will apply for U.S. citizenship once they are eligible. The expectation is that the rate of naturalization among Korean immigrants will continue to increase as they meet the mandatory five year waiting period.

The highest level of concentration of Korean Americans occurs in California, as 259,941 lived there in 1990. This means that California is the home of one-third (32.5%) of all Koreans living in the United States. New York had the second highest population of Koreans with 95,648 (12%), Illinois had 41,506 (5.2%), Hawaii had 17,500, and Maryland had 15,000. Since Hawaii is the oldest area of Korean settlement it has the lowest percentage of foreign born Koreans (54%). The other top ten states of Korean residence have a minimum of 82 percent foreign born in their populations (U.S. Census, 1992:Table 26).

Table 7.1
Korean Immigration to the United States, 1965-1991

Years	Total Number	Percent of Total	Cummulative Rate	Rate Per Year
1965-1969	18,469	2.8	—	3,694
1970-1974	93,445	14.3	111,914	18,689
1975-1979	146,953	22.5	258,867	29,391
1980-1984	163,088	24.9	421,955	32,618
1985-1987	106,878	16.3	528,833	35,626
1988-1991	125,300	19.1	654,133	31,325

Source: Hoffman, 1993:397; INS, 1988; U.S. Census, 1991:7.

With a population of 72,970 in 1990, the Los Angeles area has the largest population of Koreans outside Korea. Their high concentration in one area means that they can maintain a healthy cultural support system. In the vicinity of Olympic boulevard in downtown Los Angeles there are dozens of Korean shops, grocery stores, liquor stores, appliance stores, book stores, and restaurants that support the Korean culture (Light, 1985). The same social and cultural environment can be found in New York City, which has a large Korean population (28,000), as does Chicago (21,000), Washington D.C. (18,000), and Honolulu (17,000). Their concentration in metropolitan areas and settlement in ethnic neighborhoods is a reflection of their higher levels of education, occupational segregation, and entrepreneurial ambitions (Schifrin, 1988).

Table 7.2
Korean Immigration to the United States
and Metropolitan Area of Intended Residence: 1990

	Metropolitan Settlement Area	Number	Percent
1.	Los Angeles-Long Beach, CA	6,059	18.8
2.	New York, NY	3,586	11.1
3.	Washington, D.C.	1,940	6.0
4.	Chicago, IL	1,238	3.8
5.	Anaheim-Santa Ana, CA	1,219	3.8
6.	Philadelphia, PA	909	2.8
7.	Bergen-Passaic, NJ	727	2.3
8.	San Jose, CA	516	1.6
9.	Oakland, CA	401	1.2
10.	Nassau-Suffolk, NY	389	1.2
11.	Riverside-San Bernardino, CA	373	1.2
12.	San Francisco, CA	358	1.1
13.	Houston, TX	263	0.8
14.	San Diego, CA	205	0.6
15.	Newark, NJ	195	0.6
	Total	18,378	56.9
	All Korean Immigrants	32,301	100.0

Source: U.S. Census, Statistical Abstract 1992:Table 11.

When compared to the general population Korean Americans had a higher labor force participation rate, as three out of four of the men and half the women were active in the labor force (Chu, 1988). And it is important to note that their labor force participation rate increases with length of residence (See Table 7.3). Nonetheless the unemployment rate in the Korean American community is similar to the general U.S. population. But their unemployment rate does decrease significantly with length of residence. A comparison between men and women reveals that Korean women have higher unemployment rates (Bonacich, et al, 1987).

According to the U.S. Census the occupational distribution of Korean Americans is very similar to the national population. In 1980, 29 percent were in professional-technical jobs (compared to 26% U.S.), 27 percent in clerical-sales positions (24% U.S.), and 31 percent in blue collar jobs (33% U.S.) (Ishi, 1988:Table 1, Table 2). One significant difference in their occupation distribution is that Koreans have a higher rate of self-employment. On average Korean Americans are twice as likely to be self-employed, as compared to members of the general population (12.2% compared to 6.3% U.S.). Those Korean Americans who are self employed are usually involved in the operation of a small family business (H. Kim, 1976; I. Kim, 1987; Ming, 1984). For example, in Los Angeles, mom and pop stores are very popular in the Korean American community (Bonacich, et al, 1980; Bonacich and Light, 1988; Light 1981). (See Figure 7.1 (1990).)

Table 7.3
Occupational Distribution of Korean Immigrants
Admitted to the United States, 1969 and 1979

	1969		1979	
Occupation	Number	Percent	Number	Percent
Total	6,045	100.0	29,248	100.0
Housewives and Children	4,405	72.9	22,076	75.5
Professional-Technical	1,081	65.9	1,832	25.5
Managerial-Administrative	83	5.1	1,380	19.2
Sales Workers	14	0.9	151	2.1
Clerical	125	7.6	834	11.6
Craftsmen	52	3.2	727	10.1
Operatives	48	2.9	1,374	19.2
Laborers	14	0.9	148	2.1
Service Workers	93	5.7	415	5.8
Private Household	125	7.5	59	0.8
Sub-Total	1,640	100.0	7,172	100.0

Source: INS Annual Report 1969, 1979.

One of the most formidable barriers to the integration of Koreans into the labor force and economic market place is their inability to speak English. Most Korean immigrants have a language problem when they arrive in America, as only one out of four are fluent in English (U.S. Census, 1984). When compared to other Asian immigrants, the English speaking ability of Korean immigrants is only slightly above that of the more recent settlers, the Vietnamese (Jiobu, 1988:103). Naturally their fluency in English often improves with length of residence and degree of contact with members of the greater society.

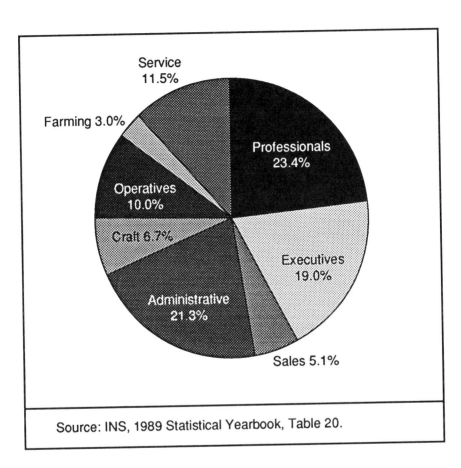

Figure 7.1
Occupational Distribution of Korean Immigrants
Admitted to the United States, 1989

Service 11.5%

Farming 3.0%

Professionals 23.4%

Operatives 10.0%

Craft 6.7%

Executives 19.0%

Administrative 21.3%

Sales 5.1%

Source: INS, 1989 Statistical Yearbook, Table 20.

As a result of the language barrier and discrimination, it is not unusual to find highly educated Koreans working at jobs that are far below their level of preparation (Hurh, et al, 1978; 1980). The extent of incongruent job placement among Koreans was made abundantly clear by the results of one study conducted in Los Angeles that found that half the Korean immigrants who were doctors, pharmacists, and nurses in their homeland were now working as operatives, craftsmen, or salespersons (Kim and Wong 1977:231; Shin and Chang, 1988). The result of this misappropriation of talents and skills is frustration, underemployment, and poverty (Takaki, 1989:439-440). Therefore despite the fact that both the husband and wife work outside the home in the typical Korean family, they often find it very difficult to establish themselves and make their way in American society (Yu, et al, 1982).

Chapter Summary

Like other Asian groups, the flow of Korean immigrants to the United States increased dramatically following the passage of the Immigration Reform Act of 1965. The majority of recent Korean immigrants have come from the more educated and professional classes of Korean society and have established themselves in the major metropolitan areas of American society, particularly in California and New York. The largest and best known area of Korean American settlement is in Los Angeles and in recent times has served as the focus of Korean American life.

The first Korean immigrants were recruited by the representatives of the Hawaiian plantations who were in search of a new source of Asian labor. In view of the poverty and political oppression in their homeland many Koreans decided to emigrate to Hawaii in an effort to improve their lives. Hundreds of Korean immigrants were also encouraged to emigrate to Hawaii by the leadership of their Christian churches, who felt that they would be able to establish a stronger and more cohesive Korean Christian community in Hawaii.

During the early 1920's some Korean settlers in Hawaii were encouraged to migrate to California, where they were offered jobs in the agricultural industry. Many of these early Korean immigrants to California were disappointed with conditions that they found in the rural areas of the state and quickly established themselves in the major urban areas, primarily in Los Angeles and San Francisco. Some of these early immigrants started small family owned and operated businesses. The Korean community in Los Angeles quickly became the center of Korean American life, as the community was able to support the social and cultural needed of Korean immigrants.

The new wave Korean immigrants who began to arrive in the late sixties are highly educated and have settled in diverse urban centers on the East and West coasts. Though many of these new wave immigrants are highly educated, many find that they are unable to obtain employment in their professions. In part this is due to the language barrier, but it is also the result of job discrimination and the difficulty that Korean immigrants have in meeting state licensing requirements in certain professions. As a result, many highly educated Korean immigrants are disappointed with the limited opportunities available to them in America and are often forced to take jobs that fall far below their qualifications and experiences.

The children of new wave Korean immigrants are taking advantage of the educational opportunities and are creating a new force in the Korean

American community. While many of their parents were unable to fulfill their dreams as immigrants, many of these second generation Korean Americans are determined to reach the goals that they have set for themselves.

References

Bonacich, Edna, Ivan Light, and Charles C. Wong
1980   "Korean Immigrants: Small Business in Los Angeles." In Roy
        S. Bryce-Laporte (ed.), *Sourcebook on the New Immigration.*
        New Brunswick, NJ: Transaction Books.
Bonacich, Edna, Mokerrom Hossain, and Jae-hong Park
1987   "Korean Immigrant Working Women in the Early 1980s."
        In Eui-Young Yu and Earl H. Phillips (eds.), *Korean Women
        in Transition: At Home and Abroad.* Los Angeles:Center for
        Korean-American and Korean Studies, California State
        University, Pp. 15-27.
Bonacich, Edna and Ivan Light
1988   *Immigrant Entrepreneurs: Koreans in Los Angeles.*
        Berkeley: University of California Press.
Bouvier, Leon F. and Anthony J. Agresta
1987   "The Future Asian Population of the United States." In
        James T. Fawcett and Benjamin V. Carino (eds.), *Pacific
        Bridges: The New Immigration From Asia and the Pacific Islands.*
        Staten Island: Center for Migration Studies. Pp. 285-301.
Chai, Alice
1981   "Korean Women in Hawaii, 1903-1945." In Hilar F. Thomas
        and Rosemary Skinner Keller (eds.), *Women in New Worlds,*
        Nashville, TN.
Chang, Dae-hong
1974   "A Study of Korean Cultural Minority: The Paekchong." In
        Andrew C. Nahm (ed.), *Traditional Korea: Theory and Practice.*
        Kalamazoo: Center for Korean Studies, WesternMichigan
        University. Pp. 55-88
Choy, Bong-youn
1979   *Koreans in America.* Chicago: Nelson-Hall.
Chu, Judy
1988   "Social and Economic Profile of Asian Pacific Women:
        Los Angeles County." In Gary Okihiro, et al, (eds.), *Reflec-
        tions on Shattered Windows.* Seattle: Washington State Univer-
        sity Press. Pp. 193-205
Givens, Helen Lewis
1939   "The Korean Community in Los Angeles County." M.A.
        Thesis, University of Southern California.
Harvey, Young S.
1980   "The Koreans." In John McDermott, Jr., et al (eds.), *People
        and Cultures of Hawaii,* Honolulu: University of Hawaii Press.
Hoare, James and Susan Pares
1988   *Korea: An Introduction.* London: Kegan Paul International

Hoffman, Mark S.
1993   *The World Almanac and Book of Facts 1993.* New York:
            Pharos Books.
Hurh, Won Moo
1974   "Comparative Study of Korean Immigrants in the United
            States: A Typology." *Korean Christian Scholars Journal* Spring:
            60-69.
1980   "Towards a Korean-American Ethnicity: Some Theoretical
            Models." *Ethnic and Racial Studies* 3(4):444-464.
Hurh, Won Moo, Hei Chu Kim, and Kwang C. Kim
1978   *Assimilation Patterns of Immigrants in the United States: A
            Case Study of Korean Immigrants in the Chicago Area.*
            Washington, D.C.: University Press of America.
1980   "Cultural And Social Adjustment Patterns of Korean
            Immigrants in the Chicago Area." In Roy S. Bryce-Laporte
            (ed.), *Sourcebook on the New Immigration,* New Brunswick, NJ:
            Transaction Books, Pp. 295-302.
Hurh, Won Moo and Kwang Chung Kim
1984   *Korean Immigrants in America.* Rutherford: NJ: Fairleigh
            Dickinson University Press.
Immigration and Naturalization Service (INS)
1969   *Annual Report of the Immigration and Naturalization
            Service.* Washington, D.C.: U.S. Department of Justice.
1979   *Annual Report of the Immigration and Naturalization
            Service.* Washington, D.C.: U.S. Department of Justice.
1981   *1980 Statistical Yearbook of the Immigration and Naturaliza-
            tion Service.* Washington, D.C.: U.S. Department of Justice.
1988   *1987 Statistical Yearbook of the Immigration and Naturaliza-
            tion Service.* Washington, D.C.: U.S. Department of Justice.
1990   *1989 Statistical Yearbook of the Immigration and Naturaliza-
            tion Service.* Washington, D.C.: U.S. Department of Justice.
Ishi, Tomoji
1988   "International Linkage and National Class Conflict: The
            Migration of Korean Nurses to the United States." *Amerasia
            Journal* 14(1):23-50.
Jiobu, Robert M.
1988   *Ethnicity and Assimilation.* Albany: State University of New
            York Press.
Kim, Bernice B.
1934   "The Koreans in Hawaii." *Social Science* 9(4):409-413.
1937   "The Koreans in Hawaii." M.A. Thesis, University of Hawaii.
Kim, C. I. Eugene, and Han-kyo Kim
1967   *Korea and the Politics of Imperialism, 1876-1910.* Berkeley:
            The University of California Press.

Kim, David S. and Charles Choy Wong
1977   "Business Development in Koreatown, Los Angeles." In
            Hyung- chan Kim (ed.), *The Korean Diaspora*, Santa Barbara:
            ABC Clio Press. Pp. 229-245.
Kim, Hyung-chan
1976   "Ethnic Enterprises Among Korean Emigrants in America."
            Journal of Korean Affairs July: 40-58.
1977   "Some Aspects of Social Demography of Korean Americans."
            In Hyung-chan Kim (ed.), *The Korean Diaspora*, Santa Bar-
            bara: ABC Clio Press, Pp. 109-126.
Kim, Hyung-chan and Wayne Patterson (eds.)
1974   *The Koreans in America 1882-1974: A Chronology & Fact
            Book.* Dobbs Ferry, NY: Oceana Publications.
Kim, Illso
1987   "The Koreans: Small Business in an Urban Frontier." In
            Nancy Foner (ed.), *New Immigrants in New York*. New York:
            Columbia University Press. Pp. 219-242.
Kim, Warren Y.
1971   *Koreans in America.* Seoul: Po Chin Chai Printing Co.
Koo, Hagen and Eui-Young Yu
1981   *Korean Immigration to the United States: Its Demographic
            Pattern and Social Implications for Both Societies.* Honolulu:
            East-West Population Institute.
Light, Ivan
1981   "Immigrant Entrepreneurs in America: Koreans in Los
            Angeles.170 In Nathan Glazer (ed.), *Clamor at the Gates.*
            San Francisco: Institute for Contemporary Studies.
1985   "Immigrant Entrepreneurs in America: Koreans in Los
            Angeles." In Nathan Glazer (ed.), *Clamor at the Gates.* San
            Francisco: Institute for Contemporary Studies.
Lyu, Kingsley K.
1977   "Korean Nationalist Activities in Hawaii and the Continental
            United States, 1900-1945 Part I: 1900-1919." *Amerasia Journal*
            4:23-90.
McCune, Shannon
1956   *Korea's Heritage: A Regional and Social Geography.* Rutland:
            Charles E. Tuttle Co.
Mangiafico, Luciano
1988   *Contemporary American Immigrants: Patterns of Filipino, Korean,
            and Chinese Settlement in the United States.* New York: Praeger.
Melendy, H. Brett
1977   *Asians in America: Filipinos, Korean, and East Indians.*
            Boston: Twayne Publishers.

Ming, Pyong G.
1984 "From White-Collar Occupations to Small Business: Korean Immigrants' Occupational Adjustment." *Sociological Quarterly* 25:333-352.

Patterson, Wayne
1977 "The First Attempt to Obtain Korean Laborers for Hawaii, 1896-1897." In Hyung-chan Kim (ed.), *The Korean Diaspora*, Santa Barbara:ABC Clio Press, Pp. 9-31.
1979 "Upward Social Mobility of the Koreans in Hawaii." *Korean Studies* 3:81-92.
1988 *The Korean Frontier in America: Immigration to Hawaii, 1896-1910.* Honolulu: University of Hawaii Press.

Pomerantz, Linda
1984 "The Background of Korean Emigration." In Lucie Cheng and Edna Bonacich (eds.), *Labor Immigration Under Capitalism: Asian Workers in the United States Before World War II.* Berkeley: The University of California Press. Pp. 277-315.

Ryu, Jai P.
1977 "Koreans in America: A Demographic Analysis." In Hyung-chan Kim (ed.), *The Korean Diaspora*, Santa Barbara: ABC Clio Press, Pp. 205-228.

Shin, Eui Hang and Kyung-Sup Chang
1988 "Peripherization of Immigrant Professionals: Korean Physicians in the United States." *International Migration Review* 22(4):609-626.

Takaki, Ronald
1989 *Strangers from a Different Shore: A History of Asian Americans.* New York: Penguin Books.

U.S. Census
1981 *1980 Census of the Population, U.S. Summary.* Washington, D.C.: USGPO.
1984 *Foreign Born Immigrants: Koreans-Tabulations from the 1980 U.S. Census of the Population and Housing.* Washington, D.C.: USGPO. October.
1991 *Statistical Abstract of the United States, 1991* (111th Edition). Washington, D.C.: USGPO.
1992 *1990 Census of the Population, U.S. Summary.* Washington, D.C.: CD-ROM Data.

Yang, Eun Sik
1987 "Korean Women in America: 1903-1930." In Eui-Young Yu and Earl H. Phillips (eds.), *Korean Women in Transition: At Home and Abroad.* Los Angeles: Center for Korean-American and Korean Studies, California State University. Pp. 167-181.

Yu, Eui-Young, E. H. Phillips, and E. S. Yang
  1982   *Koreans in Los Angeles: Prospects and Promises.* Los
            Angeles: Center for Korean American and Korean Studies,
            California State University.
Yun, Yo-jun
  1977   "Early History of Korean Immigration to America." In
            Hyung-chan Kim (ed.), *The Korean Diaspora*, SantaBarbara:
            ABC Clio Press, Pp. 33-46.

1882   The Treaty of Amity and Commerce was signed by the United States and Korea on May 22.
1884   Suh Jae-pil came to America and was naturalized as Philip Jaisohn.
1901   The Bureau of Immigration recorded Peter Ryu as the first Korean immigrant to arrive in Hawaii, on January 9.
1902   The emperor of Korea gave D.W. Deshler permission to hire contract laborers for employment in Hawaii.
1903   On January 13, the first group of 102 Korean immigrants arrived in Honolulu harbor aboard the S.S. Gaelic. The group consisted of 56 men, 20 women, and 25 children. During March and April a total of 215 Korean immigrants arrived in Honolulu. Most of these were assinged to the Waialua plantation on Oahu.
1904   Between February and September a total of 702 Korean immigrants arrived in Hawaii as contract laborers.
1905   Pak Yong-man, a famous Korean nationalist, arrived in San Francisco.
        The first Korean church was dedicated at the Ewa plantation on Oahu.
        The Mutual Cooperation Federation was founded in San Francisco and published one of the first Korean newspapers on the mainland.
1907   The U.S. Congress passed the Anti-Oriental Immigration Law.
1908   Syngman Rhee received a Master's degree from Harvard University.
1910   Korea was annexed by Japan.
        Syngman Rhee received a Ph.D. from Princeton University.
        Sarah Choi was the first picture bride to arrive in Hawaii (November 28). A total of 951 picture brides arrived in Hawaii from Korea.
1913   On April 19 the Korean Women's Association was organized in Honolulu. California's Alien Land Law affected all Koreans living in the state.
        Syngman Rhee founded the Korean Girls' Seminary in Honolulu.
1916   A group of 60 Koreans living in Manteca, California leased 1,300 acres of farm land and planted sugar beets. Another group leased 640 acres outside of Woodland, California.

1917	Koreans living in Stockton and Manteca leased 3,920 acres for the cultivation of sugar beets. Kim Chong-nim leased 2,815 acres of rice land.
1919	A group of Korean women founded the Women's Friendship Association in Los Angeles.
	The First Korean Congress was held in Philadelphia.
1920	It is estimated that Koreans living in California had almost 8,000 acres of land under rice cultivation.
	The U.S. Census reported 1,224 Koreans living in the continental U.S.
1923	A group of Koreans raised funds and founded the Methodist Mission in New York City.
1924	The Oriental Exclusion Law terminated all immigration from Korea.
1928	Koreans living in Stockton, California organized a Mutual Relief Society.
1930	A Korean Methodist church was founded in Los Angeles.
1934	Syngman Rhee married an Austrian woman. This went against his own position on intermarriage and racial purity.
1936	A Korean Christian church was founded in Los Angeles.
1941	Haan Kil-soo warned the U.S. that Japan was planning an attack.
	December 7, Koreans in Los Angeles announced their support for the U.S. against Japan and later sponsored a war bonds drive and some volunteered for military service.
1943	On December 4, Military Order No. 45 was issued, exempting Koreans from enemy alien status.
1948	The Republic of Korea was founded and Syngman Rhee was its first president.
1949	On June 25, the Korean War started.
1952	The Alien Land Law of 1913 was finally ruled unconstitutional.
	The McCarran Walter Immigration Act was passed.
1953	On July 27, the armistice ending the Korean War was signed.
1955	Mr. and Mrs. Chong Sung-gu became the first Korean immigrants to arrive in the United States as war refugees.
1957	The Korean Foundation was founded by Kim Ho.
1961	The Korean Chamber of Commerce of California was founded in Los Angeles.
1964	Alfred Song became the first Korean American ever elected to a state legislature.
1967	The Korean American Chamber of Commerce was founded in San Francisco.

| 1972 | The Korean American Political Association of Southern California was founded in Los Angeles on July 1. |
| 1992 | The riot following the Rodney King decision resulted in the destruction of dozens of Korean owned businesses in central Los Angeles. In the November elections Jay Kim became the first Korean American to win a seat in Congress. |

Source: Kim and Patterson, 1974:1-83.

Key Terms

yangban	tax farming
Omnibus Act	picture brides
Immigration Reform Act	family reunification

Sample Test Questions

1. Discuss three characteristics of each of the three waves of Korean immigration to America.
2. List and discuss four sociological characteristics of the new wave Korean immigrants.
3. Discuss four significant problems facing members of the Korean American community today.

Chapter 8

The Filipino American Experience

Introduction

One reason that Filipinos are one of the fastest growing ethnic groups in the country is that they have registered the second highest rate of immigration since the late seventies. According to the Census there were 774,652 Filipinos living in the United States in 1980, and in 1990 their population increased to 1,406,770. Seventy percent of Filipino Americans live in the West and half (52%) live in California.

Similar to the experiences of other new Asian immigrants, Filipinos only achieved numerical significance as a result of the liberal provisions in the Immigration Reform Act of 1965. Prior to the immigration reforms of 1965 Filipinos were restricted to specific immigration periods that fluctuated with the needs of the agricultural labor markets in Hawaii and California.

Today most Americans are still ignorant of the Filipino culture and are totally unaware of the important contributions that Filipinos have made to the economic development of American society. In the following review we shall examine the historical background to Filipino immigration, their contribution to the American agricultural industry, and their more recent contribution of skills and talent needed by post industrial American society.

Background to Filipino Immigration

In this day of advanced educational achievement and world wide communication systems it is still the case that Americans are likely to confuse Filipinos with other Asians, but it is never the case that anyone ever refers to someone as a Filipino by mistake. This observation simply reflects the fact that Americans know very little about Filipino culture or history.

The Philippines consist of a cluster of 7,100 tropical islands, located in the South China Sea. The total land mass of the Philippine islands make them about the size of the state of Arizona. Although eleven islands contain 95 percent of the total land mass. The largest island is Luzon and is about the size of the state of Kentucky. Manila, the nation's capital, is located on Luzon and is home to 1,598,918 Filipinos. Quezon City, the nation's second largest city, is also on Luzon and is home to 1,666,766 Filipinos. The second largest island is Mindanao, and is about the size of Indiana (Wright, 1993:446).

The population of the Philippines in 1991 was 65,758,788. Eight out of ten Filipinos are Catholics and one out of ten are Protestants. Tagalog is the national language, but English is widely spoken in the urban areas and is used by the educated classes and in business and commerce.

Ferdinand Magellan discovered the Malay Archipelago in 1521 and claimed the territory for Spain. The islands were named for Prince Philip, who encouraged Spanish exploration and settlement. One lasting effect of almost four hundred years of Spanish domination was the conversion of most Filipinos to Catholicism. The Spanish also imparted their culture, language, and political system. To their credit the Spanish unified the Filipinos into one nation of people.

The victory of the United States Navy over the Spanish in the battle of Manila Bay brought the Spanish American War to an end in 1898. The Treaty of Paris (1899) formally ended the war and transferred control of the Philippines to the United States. President McKinley announced that the islands would be an American protectorate until the Filipinos could establish a stable constitutional government. In September of 1900 the President appointed William Howard Taft as the first provisional governor of the Philippines (Melendy, 1977:17-24). In 1916 the U.S. Congress passed the Jones Act that allowed for the creation of the Philippine Legislature. The Tydings-McDuffie Act of 1934 insured that the Filipinos would have a smooth political transition. In 1935 the Commonwealth of the Philippines was established and Manuel Quezon became the new nation's first president. On July 4, 1946 the United States granted the Filipino people full political independence.

The Origins of Filipino Immigration

The *pensionados* (the students) were the first organized group of Filipino emigrants. They constitute the first wave in a four stage immigration process. The flow of *pensionados* continued from 1903 to 1924. The second wave of Filipino immigration consisted of farm workers who emigrated to Hawaii and California between 1906 and 1934. The third wave was composed of Filipino veterans, who arrived in the United States between 1946 and 1964.

The fourth wave consist of the so-called brain drain immigrants, who arrived in the United States after the immigration reforms of 1965 (See Table 8.1).

Table 8.1
Filipino Immigration to the United States: 1903-1991

Immigration Period	Inclusive Years	Total Number	Cummulative Rate	Rate Per Year
I. *Pensionados* (Students)	1903-1924	400	—	19
II. The Pinoys (Farm Workers)	1906-1934	120,036	120,436	4,301
III. WWII Veterans	1946-1964	35,700	156,136	1,983
IV. The New Wave (Brain Drain)	1965-1991	1,039,966	1,196,102	39,999

Source: Arnold, et al, 1987: Table 3; Hoffman, 1993:387; INS, 1988.

In August of 1903 the United States Congress authorized a program whereby selected Filipino students were given scholarships to pursue college educations in America. The idea was that these elite Filipino students (*pensionados*) would absorb the principles of democracy and return to their homeland as representatives of the American way of life. The provisions of the *Pensionado* Act allowed one hundred Filipino students to attend American universities and live with American families.

In addition to the government sponsored Filipino students, approximately 14,000 so-called self supporting students entered the United States between 1910 and 1930. However, only about ten percent of these students actually enrolled in American colleges and universities (Catapusan, 1941). Most of these Filipino students obtained their visas with the idea of finding jobs in the United States and did not have any intentions of enrolling in college. Upon their return to their homeland the pensionados were often greeted with jealousy by other Filipinos and with hostility and disdain from the American colonials.

Filipinos in Hawaii

As a result of their protectorate status Filipinos were made U.S. Nationals. As U.S. Nationals, Filipinos were allowed to travel freely, and without immigration restrictions, to any state or territory of the United States. Immediately the growers in Hawaii realized that Filipinos would not only serve as an inexhaustible source of low cost labor, but unlike other Asian immigrants the flow of Filipinos could not be affected by U.S. immigration restrictions (Lasker, 1931).

The first organized recruitment of Filipinos by the labor agents of the Hawaiian Sugar Planters Association (HSPA) occurred in the spring of 1906. By December of 1906 the first group of fifteen Filipino laborers arrived in Honolulu. These pioneers were from Ilocanos, a province on the island of Luzon, where unemployment was high, wages were low, and poverty and disease were a way of life. During this first year Filipinos were also actively recruited in Manila-Cebu and on the Visayan Islands (Clifford, 1967; Teodoro, 1981).

While only a few hundred Filipinos arrived in Hawaii during the two year period between 1907 and 1909, the significant flow of immigrants began in 1910, when 3,000 laborers arrived. Between 1909 and 1920 a total of 33,273 Filipinos arrived in Hawaii, for an annual average flow of 2,800. Between 1921 and 1932 a total of 85,163 arrived, for an annual average flow of 7,100. During this entire period of active labor recruitment in the Philippines (1909-1932) a grand total of 118,436 Filipino laborers arrived in Hawaii (Sharma, 1984a:339). However, by 1935 it is estimated that 58,000 Filipinos had returned home and another 18,500 had migrated to the mainland (Sharma, 1980:96).

In 1910 there were only 2,300 Filipinos living in Hawaii, but over the next ten years their population increased ten fold. By 1930 there were 63,000 Filipinos working on plantations throughout the islands. Overall they represented about one out of five (17%) of Hawaii's population, but they constituted seven out of ten of the plantation labor force (Anderson, 1984:2-3). This high level of representation on the plantations gave the Filipinos a virtual monopoly on the plantation labor force in the Hawaiian islands (Takaki, 1983).

Understandably work on the Hawaiian sugar and pineapple plantations was long and arduous. For their labor the Filipinos were only paid $18 to $20 a month, that is for a ten to twelve hour day. They were required to work six days a week, since their Christian bosses recognized Sunday as a day of rest. Plantation laborers were usually awakened at three in the morning to prepare their breakfast and lunch for the day. At five o'clock they boarded buses or loaded onto cane trains. By six in the morning they were cutting cane. At 7:45 they were allowed a 15 minute break for breakfast and at 11 A.M. they were given a half hour for lunch. The work day usually ended at four and they arrived back at their huts by five. When they arrived at their barracks they had to prepare their meals over an open flame and usually had dinner at six. By eight o'clock most of the men were in bed (Sharma, 1984b:589).

Filipinos in California

In 1910 there were only 160 Filipinos living on the mainland. By 1920 there were 5,600, including 2,674 in California. In 1923, 2,426 Filipinos arrived in California, over half (56%) came from Hawaii, one third (35%) from the Philippines, and the others from various Asian ports (Rabaya, 1971:190). Filipino immigration to California increased dramatically between 1923 to 1929, as an average of 4,200 Filipinos arrived each year (Anonymous, 1965; Crouchett, 1982).

Most of the Filipino farm workers were young men, that is between the ages of 16 to 29, and single. The sex ratio in the Filipino community at this time was fourteen males to one female. Most of these farm workers were illiterate and did not speak either English or Spanish, but spoke one of the many dialects from the islands (Alba, 1967; Melendy, 1976:104). And as a result of the language barrier, racism, and their general lack of skills, most Filipinos were relegated to agricultural work (Anthony, 1931; Bogardus, 1929a; Catapusan, 1934; Vallangca, 1977).

A study conducted in 1930 found that of the 27,000 Filipinos working in California, sixty percent were involved in agriculture. Most of these worked as stoop laborers in the asparagus and lettuce fields of the San Joaquin and Salinas valleys. One out of four were employed in domestic service—primarily in San Francisco and Los Angeles–as bus boys, cooks, dishwashers, kitchen helpers, door boys, bell boys, janitors, and house cleaners. A handful were employed in manufacturing (5.8%) and in transportation (3.2%) (Almirol, 1985:52-59; Bloch, 1930; Catapusan, 1938).

While agricultural work in California was plentiful during this early period of settlement, the wages were low and the work was physically exhausting and dangerous. For example, one pinoy (the name given to Filipino farm workers) Manuel Buaken spent the best years of his life harvesting onions, carrots, and potatoes. For this stoop labor Buaken was payed $2.50 a day, plus room and board for a six day week (Buaken, 1948). This was less than half the hourly wage of $5.52 per day paid to factory workers in 1927 (Schwartz, 1945:154).

The Great Depression not only brought a reduction in wages and an increase in labor production, but it also marked the end of Filipino immigration and a dramatic increase in racial violence (Anonymous, 1930). In response to the economic hard times and the pervasive anti-immigrant feelings in the United States, the U.S. Congress passed the Tydings-McDuffie Act in 1934. This act deprived the Filipinos of their status as U.S. Nationals and limited Filipino immigration to fifty per year. The following year Congress passed the Repatriation Act, that offered to pay the passage of any Filipino desiring to return home during the Depression, with the proviso that they would promise never to return to the United States (Bogardus, 1936; Coloma, 1939). Obviously this was an effort by some racists to remove all Filipinos from California. However only 2,200 Filipinos, out of a population of more than 45,000, took advantage of the government's offer (Catapusan, 1936; McWilliams, 1964:244).

The high unemployment rates and the depressed economic conditions in California resulted in a dramatic increase in racial violence against Filipinos (Bogardus, 1929b). During the apple harvest of 1928 in the Yakima Valley of Oregon, a mob of 150 whites attacked two bus loads of Filipino farm workers and ran them out of the valley. They feared that the pinoys were taking jobs away from local white workers. The following year Filipinos harvesting figs in Exeter, California were attacked by a group of whites who smashed their cars, as they saw the pinoys as a threat to their jobs.

In January of 1930 a white mob attacked the Filipino club in Watsonville, California and set off a week of violence. At times the white mob number more than 700. On the fourth night of terror a mob of whites drove to a nearby farm where they began firing random shots into bunkhouses and outbuildings. When the violence was over several pinoys were seriously injured and Fermin Tober lay dead with a bullet in his heart (DeWitt, 1979:96). A few days later the Filipino Federation of America Hall in Stockton (California) was fire bombed. And these were not isolated incidents, as racial violence broke out wherever Filipinos worked (Melendy, 1967).

Third Wave Immigration

Third wave immigrants (1946-1964) were primarily Filipino veterans who were granted U.S. citizenship and allowed to bring their families to live in America. Prior to this time Filipinos were considered U.S. Nationals and therefore were ineligible for citizenship. However, Congress passed a law in 1925 that allowed Filipinos to become U.S. citizens, but only after serving three years in the U.S. military.

Early in the Second World War thousands of Filipinos from California and Hawaii volunteered for military service and, like the African Americans, they were organized into special racially segregated military units. Most of these volunteers served in the Philippine Scouts or in the First and Second Regiments of the U.S. Army (Santos, 1942). Their primary assignment was to fight the bloody guerrilla war in the Philippines, which was bombed by the Japanese on December 8, 1941 and was occupied by the Japanese military forces for the duration of the war. At the end of the war these Filipino commando units were among the most highly decorated Army units in the war (Buaken, 1943).

In recognition of their service to the United States these Filipino veterans were granted U.S. citizenship and allowed to settle their families in the United States (Feria, 1946). And of equal importance on July 2, 1946,

186

just two days prior to the granting of independence to the Philippines, Congress approved legislation that made all resident Filipinos eligible for U.S. citizenship. For the first time all Filipinos were eligible for naturalization, either as veterans or as legal resident aliens (Vallangca, 1987:34-76).

During the next two decades following the Second World War (1946 to 1965) some 35,700 Filipinos immigrants arrived in the United States. The third wave Filipino immigrants were different from the farm workers of the second wave, as they were veterans and could use their veterans benefits to obtain technical training or a college education. In addition, many third wave immigrants could read, write, and speak English, and were familiar with the American way of life. As veterans many found work at military installations and in the industrial sector.

In 1950, sixty percent of the Filipinos living in California resided in urban areas. Ten years later eighty percent lived in urban areas. This urban relocation also meant that Filipinos abandoned agricultural work and moved into industrial jobs, as two out of three (62%) were farm workers in 1940, but only one out of ten (11%) were farm workers by 1960 (Smith, 1976:322-325). Their blue collar jobs and the strong Filipino family unit also meant that their American born children could take full advantage of the new educational opportunities that became available after the war. Overall, third wave Filipinos were in a much better position to improve their lot in American society, that is when compared to the difficulties and resistance encountered by the second wave agricultural workers.

The New Wave Generation

The most recent Filipino immigrants to settle in the United States are sometimes referred to as the New Wave or brain drain generation, as they arrived following the immigration reforms of 1965. The brain drain phenomena derives from the emphasis on the needs of the U.S. national economy and the American labor market (Keely, 1973; Medina, 1984). Based on a seven point immigration preference scale established by the Immigration Reform Act of 1965 (See Appendix A), immediate family members of legal resident aliens or naturalized citizens are given first preference under the family reunification policy. But of primary importance, those immigrants with professional and technical skills that are needed by the United States are given special consideration in all immigration decisions (Pido, 1980).

The Immigration Reform Act of 1965 set a quota of 20,000 immigrants per year from all countries and a total of 170,000 immigrants per year from Asia. The impact of this law was three fold as it: (1) resulted in a very significant increase in Filipino immigration, (2) attracted highly skilled and technical personnel, and (3) allowed legal resident aliens and naturalized citizens to sponsor relatives for immigration. It is important to note that the last provision of the Immigration Reform Act instituted a multiplier effect in the immigration process, in that once new immigrants established themselves in the United States, they were allowed to sponsor their relatives for immigration (DeJong, et al, 1986; Portes, 1976).

One of the most tangible results of the Immigration Reform Act was the exponential growth rate of immigration after 1965. For purposes of comparison during the five year period between 1960-1964 the average annual flow of Filipino immigrants was only 3,151, resulting in a five year total of 15,753. But during the first five year period under the new Immigration Reform Act (1965-1969) the average annual flow increased to 11,513, that is by a factor of three (See Table 8.2). Since then the annual flow of Filipinos has increased progressively and the Philippines has become the second largest source of new immigrants for the United States. In addition more than 100,000 Filipinos apply for tourist visas each year and between 40,000 to 50,000 apply for permanent immigration on the basis of family ties in the United States (Mangiafico, 1988:42).

Table 8.2
Filipino Immigration to the United States, 1960-1991

Years	Total Number	Percent of Total	Cummulative Rate	Rate Per Year
1960-1964	15,753	1.5	—	3,151
1965-1969	57,563	5.4	73,316	11,513
1970-1974	152,706	14.5	226,022	30,541
1975-1979	196,397	18.6	422,419	39,279
1980-1984	215,504	20.4	637,923	43,100
1985-1991	417,796	39.6	1,055,719	69,633

Source: Arnold, et al, 1987: Table 3; Hoffman, 1993: 397; INS, 1988; U.S. Census, 1991:Table 7.

Fourth wave immigrants are strikingly different from all the other previous waves of Filipino immigrants, as they (1) have higher levels of education, (2) come from professional or technical backgrounds, (3) speak English, and (4) arrive in nuclear family units. For example, of those Filipino immigrants who arrived in 1989, three out of ten were professionals, one out of eight were executives, and one out of six were administrators (Gardner, 1992:79). In the managerial and professional ranks Filipino men are most often employed as accountants or as engineers, and Filipino women work as registered nurses, elementary school teachers, or as accountants. Only a few Filipinos were employed as physicians, attorneys, architects, or as social workers (Cabezas, 1986:7). But on the other hand, only one-third of these more recent immigrants could be classified as blue collar workers (See Figure 8.1).

Figure 8.1
Occupational Distribution of Filipino Immigrants
Admitted to the United States, 1989

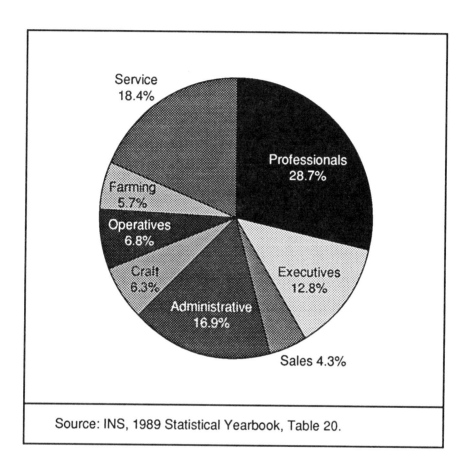

Service 18.4%
Professionals 28.7%
Farming 5.7%
Operatives 6.8%
Craft 6.3%
Executives 12.8%
Administrative 16.9%
Sales 4.3%

Source: INS, 1989 Statistical Yearbook, Table 20.

Of the Filipino professionals admitted in 1965 only 66 were physicians, but by 1969, 785 were physicians. Overall Filipinos accounted for one-fourth of all physicians arriving in the United States in 1969 (Pernia, 1976). Today the Philippines is still the largest supplier of physicians and nurses, that is among all immigrants arriving in America (Joyce and Hunt, 1982). It is estimated that there are 50,000 Filipino nurses in the United States today. Of this number some 20,000 are working in New York City. The major attraction for Filipino nurses is the rate of pay, as they can earn $2,000 per month as a starting salary, whereas they could only expect to earn from $60 to $105 per month in the Philippines, where jobs in the medical field are difficult to obtain (Mangiafico, 1988:42).

The massive influx of fourth wave immigrants since the late sixties has resulted in some very dramatic demographic changes in the Filipino American community. For example, in 1940 only one percent of the Filipinos were native born, but forty years later 35 percent were native born. In 1940, 61 percent were living in urban areas, but by 1970, 93 percent were urban residents. Over the past decade the more recent Filipino immigrants tend to settle in those areas that have historically served as Filipino reception areas, primarily in California and Hawaii, but also in the urban centers of the north-east, like Chicago and New York City (See Table 8.3).

Table 8.3
Filipino Immigration to the United States
and Metropolitan Area of Intended Residence: 1990

Metropolitan Settlement Area	Number	Percent of Total
1. Los Angeles-Long Beach, CA	11,644	18.3
2. New York, NY	4,750	7.4
3. San Francisco, CA	3,574	5.6
4. San Diego, CA	3,539	5.6
5. Honolulu, HI	3,051	4.8
6. Oakland, CA	2,678	4.2
7. Chicago, IL	2,655	4.2
8. San Jose, CA	2,440	3.8
9. Anaheim-Santa Ana, CA	1,407	2.2
10. Washington, D.C.	1,228	1.9
11. Riverside-San Bernardino, CA	1,224	1.9
12. Seattle, WA	1,025	1.6
13. Vallejo-Fairfield-Napa, CA	983	1.5
14. Jersey City, NJ	889	1.4
15. Newark, NJ	883	1.4
Total	41,970	65.8
All Filipino Immigrants	63,756	100.0

Source: U.S. Census, Statistical Abstract 1992:Table 11.

The median years of schooling for Filipinos in 1940 was 7.4 years, but by 1970 it was 13.5 years, well above the national average. Similarly in 1940 only eight percent of Filipinos had any college, while 43 percent had some college in 1970. Occupational changes were also significant as only 1.2 percent were professionals in 1940, but one out of four (24.3%) were professionals in 1970. And in 1940, half the Filipinos (48%) were farm workers, but this dropped to only ten percent in 1970.

In an attempt to understand why the flow of Filipino immigrants has increased so dramatically over the past 25 years it is clear that certain push factors have contributed to the brain drain from the Philippines (Carino, 1987:313-314; Gupta, 1973:181-184). Some of the most important factors are:

1. Filipino professionals were attracted by the higher wages offered in the U.S.
2. They were attracted by the employment opportunities.
3. They were attracted by the research facilities and specialized training available in the United States.
4. The Philippines is overstaffed in the medical field, in engineering, and in teaching.
5. Often a person needs more than professional qualifications and a degree to get a position in the Philippines.
6. The creation of martial law in 1972 prompted many Filipino professionals to emigrate.
7. Many fourth wave Filipinos moved to the United States for the benefit of their children.
8. Others moved as part of a family reunification plan.

Filipino Americans Today

Today the 1,406,770 Filipino Americans are concentrated on the West Coast, as two out of three (70%) live there, eleven percent are in the South, ten percent in the Midwest, and ten percent in the Northeast. According to the U.S. Census half (52%) of the Filipinos live in California (731,685), and the second largest concentration occurs in Hawaii (168,682), while others live in Illinois (64,224), New York (62,259), New Jersey (53,146), Virginia (35,067), and Texas, (34,350) (U.S. Census, 1992).

The more recent areas of Filipino settlement are Chicago (41,000) and New York City (32,000). However, the largest number of Filipinos live in Honolulu (96,000), followed by Los Angeles (87,625), San Diego (63,381), San Francisco (42,652), and San Jose (38,169) (U.S. Census, 1992). While Honolulu has one of the largest Filipino populations, it also has the lowest number of foreign born Filipinos (47.1%) of any major area of Filipino settlement. In contrast Eastern cities are most likely to attract new arrivals from the Philippines (as these cities have 71 to 79 percent foreign born populations).

All social indicators reveal that Filipino Americans have very stable families. The marriage rate among Filipinos is higher than in the general population (68% compared to 58%) and their divorce rate is half the national average. Filipinos are also less likely to be separated (Almirol, 1982). The high level of family stability among Filipino Americans today can be attributed to the fact that, (1) nine out of ten are Catholics, (2) divorce is not legally possible in the Philippines, and (3) strong family bonds among Filipinos work against the possibility of divorce. However, it is interesting to observe that divorce rates are higher among those Filipinos who marry exogamously and as their length of residence in the United States increases (Posadas, 1981).

Household size among Filipinos today reveals a strong traditional orientation, as their households are significantly larger than the general population. But this larger household size results from the common pattern among immigrants of sharing their home with recent arrivals and close relatives. In addition, the strong kinship network and close family relations among Filipinos results in larger households (3.63 compared to 2.74 per household U.S.). Therefore it is not unusual to find two or three attenuated families living in the same house. These clustered families allow the Filipinos to distribute their household expenses and child care responsibilities among a larger group of relatives (Almirol, 1985:162-173). This is clearly an adaptive mechanism for families living in the Filipino community.

Some are quick to attribute this larger household size to higher fertility rates, which is true in the Philippines, but this is definitely not the case among recent Filipino immigrants in the United States. In the Philippines religion and family traditions encourage high fertility rates. But in view of the higher educational levels of recent Filipino immigrants, and their strong desire for upward mobility, Filipino women actually have a lower fertility rate than the general U.S. population (Card, et al, 1978). Filipino Americans also tend to have their children early in their marriages, and they consciously confine their child bearing years to this early period (Del Rosario, 1987:36- 37).

One of the interesting characteristics of the fourth wave Filipino immigrants is that more females have emigrated than males. For example, in 1965, two-thirds of all Filipino immigrants admitted were females. In 1980 the sex ratio among foreign born Filipinos was 86.4 males for every 100 females, compared with 94.5 percent in the U.S. population. However, this imbalance in the sex-ratio is offset by the large number of Filipino women who marry American men, both in the Philippines and in the United States. For this and other reasons, the Filipino mail-order bride system has become the focus of considerable criticism in recent years.

Perhaps the most distinguishing characteristic of fourth wave immigrants is their level of educational achievement. Of all Filipinos over the age of twenty-five (in 1980), 87 percent were high school graduates and 47 percent had four or more years of college. This compares with 66.5 percent and 16.2 percent respectively for the general U.S. population. It is also interesting to note that more Filipino women graduate from college (43%)

than men (34%). This high level of educational achievement among Filipinos can, in great part, be attributed to the fact that most Filipino immigrants arrive with college degrees (58% in 1980), as opposed to obtaining their educations in the United States (Card, et al, 1984).

Their level of educational achievement is an indication of their desire for social improvement in the American labor market. The rate of labor force participation among Filipinos is higher (73%) than the national average (62%). There are also more Filipino women in the labor force (69%) than is true for white women (49%) in America. This also explains why the unemployment rate among Filipinos is well below the national average. And it is also true that when Filipinos are out of work they record the shortest period of unemployment. This in part reflects the fact that they are more likely to accept a position that might not necessarily be in their particular field of expertise.

Chapter Summary

Filipino Americans are the fastest growing Asian ethnic group in American society today. Their rapid rate of growth can be attributed to the dramatic increase in the flow of Filipino immigrants since the liberalization of U.S. immigration policies in 1965. The preference for immigrants with skills and educations and the family reunification provisions in the immigration laws have resulted in the creation of a chain migration process from the Philippines.

The first Filipinos to settle in the United States in significant numbers were the *pensionados,* that is Filipino students who received government support to study in the United States at the turn of the century. In addition thousands of Filipino farm workers were encouraged to emigrate to the Hawaiian islands at the turn of the century to work on the sugar cane plantations. In just a few years Filipinos became the primary labor force in Hawaii.

Following the First World War Filipino laborers began to arrive in California, where they were encouraged to take jobs in the agricultural industry. Filipinos were used as stoop laborers in the San Joaquin and Salinas Valleys where they planted and harvest row crops. The shortage of Filipino women and the ban on intermarriage with Anglo women prevented most Filipino farm workers from establishing families in California. The onset of the Great Depression not only made life much more difficult for the Filipino farm workers but it also resulted in a dramatic increase in the incidents of racial attacks and random violence in the Filipino community.

Following the Second World War Filipino veterans were allowed to send for their families and start new lives in America. The Filipino veterans were able to use their families as the basis for the creation of a new Filipino community in America. Most of these veterans found jobs in the industrial sector and were able to improve the living conditions for their families.

The New Wave Filipino immigrants began to arrive following the passage of the Immigration Reform Act of 1965. These immigrants were very different from the previous waves of Filipino immigrants as they were drawn from the highly educated and professional classes in Filipino society. For this reason these New Wave immigrants are sometimes referred to as the brain drain immigrants.

Filipino Americans today are not only the fastest growing Asian American group but also have one of the most impressive records of adaptation to American society. As a group they have high levels of educational achievement and have integrated themselves into the upper levels of the labor force. The second generation, native born Americans, are taking advantage of the educational opportunities and are meeting or exceeding the social mobility of their parents.

References

Alba, Jose C.
1967 "Filipinos in California." *Pacific Historian* 11:39-41.
Almirol, Edwin B.
1982 "Rights and Obligations in Filipino American Families." *Journal of Comparative Family Studies* 13:291-306.
1985 *Ethnic Identity and Social Negotiation: A Study of a Filipino Community in California.* New York: AMS Press.
Anderson, Robert
1984 *Filipinos in Rural Hawaii.* Honolulu: University of Hawaii Press.
Anonymous
1930 "Filipino Problems in California." *Monthly Labor Review* 30:1270-1272.
1965 *Californians of Japanese, Chinese, and Filipino Ancestry.* San Francisco: California Department of Industrial Relations.
Anthony, Donald E.
1931 "Filipino Labor in Central California." *Sociology and Social Research* 16:149-156.
Arnold, Fred, U. Minocha, and J.T. Fawcett
1987 "The Changing Face of Asian Immigration to the United States." In James T. Fawcett and Benjamin V. Carino (eds.), *Pacific Bridges: The New Immigration from Asia and the Pacific Islands.* Staten Island: Center for Migration Studies. Pp. 105-152.
Bloch, Louis
1930 *Facts About Filipino Immigration into California.* Sacramento: California Department of Industrial Relations.
Bogardus, Emory S.
1929a "The Filipino Immigration Problem." *Sociology and Social Research* 13:472-479.
1929b "American Attitudes Toward Filipinos." *Sociology and Social Research* 14:59-69.
1936 "Filipino Repatriation." *Sociology and Social Research* 21:67-72.
Buaken, Manuel
1943 "Life in the Armed Forces." *New Republic* 109:279-280
1948 *I Have Lived with the American People.* Caldwell, Idaho: Caxton Printers.
Cabezas, Amado, L.H. Shinagawa, and G. Kawaguchi
1986 "New Inquiries into the Socioeconomic Status of Filipino Americans in California." *Amerasia* 13(1):1-21.

Card, Josefina J., W. J. Wood, and E. B. Jayme
1978   "The Malleability of Fertility-Related Attitudes and Behavior in a Filipino Migrant Sample." *Demography* 15:459-476.
1984   "Assimilation and Adaptation: Filipino Migrants in San Francisco." *Philippine Sociological Review* 32:55-67.
Carino, Benjamin V.
1987   "The Philippines and Southeast Asia: Historical Roots and Contemporary Linkages." In James T. Fawcett and Benjamin V. Carino (eds.), *Pacific Bridges: The New Immigration From Asia and the Pacific Islands*. Staten Island: Center for Migration Studies. Pp. 305-325
Catapusan, Benicio T.
1934   "The Filipino Occupational and Recreational Activities in Los Angeles." M.A. Thesis Los Angeles: University of Southern California.
1936   "Filipino Repatriates in the Philippines." *Sociology and Social Research* 21:72-77.
1938   "The Filipino Labor Cycle in the United States." *Sociology and Social Research* 19:61-63.
1941   "Problems of Filipino Students in America." *Sociology and Social Research* 26:146-153.
Clifford, Mary D.
1967   "The Hawaiian Sugar Planters Association and Filipino Exclusion." In J.M. Saniel (ed.), *The Filipino Exclusion Movement, 1927-1935*. Quezon City: University of the Philippines, Institute of Asian Studies. Pp. 11-29
Coloma, Casiano P.
1939   "A Study of the Filipino Repatriation Movement." Los Angeles: M.A. Thesis, The University of Southern California (R and E Research Associates, S.F. 1974).
Crouchett, Lorraine J.
1982   *Filipinos in California: From the Days of the Galleons to the Present*. El Cerrito: Downey Place Publishing.
DeJong, Gordon F., B.D. Root and R.G. Abad
1986   "Family Reunification and Philippine Migration to the United States: The Immigrants' Perspective." *International Migration Review* 20:598-611.
Del Rosario, Carolina A.
1987   "The Filipinos in San Leandro, California." Hayward: M.A. Thesis, Department of Sociology, California State University.
De Witt, Howard A.
1976   *Anti-Filipino Movements in California*. San Francisco: R and E Research Associates.

1979   "The Watsonville Anti-Filipino Riot of 1930: A Case Study of
            the Great Depression and Ethnic Conflict in California."
            Southern California Quarterly 61:291-302.
Feria, R. T.
1946   "War and Status of Filipino Immigrants." *Sociology and Social
            Research* 31:48-53.
Gardner, Robert W.
1992   "Asian Immigration: The View from the United States."
            Asian and Pacific Migration Journal 1 (1):64-99.
Gupta, M. L.
1973   "Outflow of High-level Manpower From the Philippines:
            With Special Reference to the Period 1965-1971." *Internation-
            al Labour Review* 107:167-191.
Hoffman, Mark S.
1993   *The World Almanac and Book of Facts 1993.* New York:
            Pharos Books.
Immigration and Naturalization Service (INS)
1988   *1987 Statistical Yearbook of the Immigration and Naturalization
            Service.* Washington, D.C.: U.S. Department of Justice. (Oc-
            tober)
1989   *Immigration Statistics: Fiscal Year 1988 Advanced Report.*
            Washington, D.C.: U.S. Department of Justice. (April)
Joyce, Richard E. and Chester L. Hunt
1982   "Philippine Nurses and the Brain Drain." *Social Science and
            Medicine* 16:1223-1233.
Keely, Charles B.
1973   "Philippine Migration: Internal Movements and Emigration
            to the United States." *International Migration Review* 7:177-
            187.
Lasker, Bruno
1931   *Filipino Immigration.* Chicago: University of Chicago.
Mangiafico, Luciano
1988   *Contemporary American Immigrants: Patterns of Filipino, Korean, and
            Chinese Settlement in the United States.* New York: Praeger.
McWilliams, Carey
1964   *Factories in the Field.* Santa Barbara: Peregrine Publishers,
            Inc.
Medina, Belen T.
1984   "The New Wave: Latest Findings on Filipino Immigration to
            the United States." *Philippine Sociological Review* 32:135-143.
Melendy, H. Brett
1967   "California's Discrimination Against Filipinos, 1927-1935." In
            J.M. Saniel (ed.), *The Filipino Exclusion Movement, 1927-1935.*

Quezon City: University of the Philippines, Institute of Asian Studies. Pp. 3-10

1976   "Filipinos in the United States." In Norris Hudley, Jr. (ed.), *The Asian American: The Historical Experience.* Santa Barbara: Cleo Books. Pp. 101-128

1977   *Asians in America: Filipinos, Korean, and East Indians.* Boston: Twayne Publishers.

Pernia, Ernesto M.

1976   "The Question of the Brain Drain from the Philippines." *International Migration Review* 10:63-72.

Pido, Antonio J.A.

1980   "New Structures, New Immigrants: The Case of the Pilipinos." In Roy S. Bryce-Laporte (ed.), *Sourcebook on the New Immigration.* NJ: Transaction Books. Pp. 347-356

Portes, Alejandro

1976   "Determinants of the Brain Drain." *International Migration Review* 10:489-508.

Posadas, Barbara M.

1981   "Crossed Boundaries in Interracial Chicago: Pilipino American Families Since 1925." *Amerasia* 8:31-52.

Rabaya, Violet

1971   "Filipino Immigration: The Creation of a New Social Problem." In Amy Tachiki, et al (eds.), *Roots: An Asian American Reader.* Los Angeles: UCLA Asian American Studies Center. Pp. 188-200

Santos, Bienvenido

1942   "Filipinos in War." *Far Eastern Survey* 11:249-250.

Schwartz, Harry

1945   *Seasonal Farm Labor in the United States.* New York: Columbia University Press.

Sharma, Miriam

1980   "Pinoy in Paradise: Environment and Adaptation of Pilipinos in Hawaii, 1906-1946." *Amerasia* 7:91-117.

1984a   "The Philippines: A Case of Migration to Hawaii, 1906 to 1946." In Lucie Cheng and Edna Bonacich (eds.), *Labor Immigration Under Capitalism: Asian Workers in the United States Before World War II.* Berkeley: The University of California Press. Pp. 337-358

1984b   "Labor Migration and Class Formation Among the Filipinos in Hawaii, 1906-1946." In Lucie Cheng and Edna Bonacich (eds.), *Labor Immigration Under Capitalism: Asian Workers in the United States Before World War II.* Berkeley: The University of California Press. Pp. 579-615

Smith, Peter C.
1976   "The Social Demography of Filipino Migrations Abroad."
        International Migration Review 10:307-353.
Takaki, Ronald T.
1983   *Pau Hana: Plantation Life and Labor in Hawaii.* Honolulu:
        University of Hawaii Press.
Teodoro, Luis V. Jr.
1981   *Out of This Struggle: The Filipinos in Hawaii.* Honolulu:
        University of Hawaii Press.
U.S. Census
1982   *Foreign Born Immigrants: Filipino-Tabulations From the
        1980 U.S. Census of the Population and Housing.* Washington,
        D.C.: USGPO (October).
1991   *Statistical Abstract of the United States, 1991* (111th Edition).
        Washington, D.C.: USGPO. 1992 1990 Census of the
        Population, U.S. Summary. Washington, D.C.: CD-ROM
        Data.
Vallangca, Caridad C.
1987   *The Second Wave: Pinay & Pinoy* (1945-1960). San Francisco:
        Strawberry Hill Press.
Vallangca, Roberto V.
1977   *Pinoy: The First Wave* (1898-1941). San Francisco: Strawberry
        Hill Press.
Wallovits, Sonia E.
1966   "The Filipinos in California." M.A. Thesis, University of
        Southern California (R and E Research 1972).
Wright, John W.
1993   *The Universal Almanac 1993.* Kansas City, KS: Andrews and
        McMeel.

Ferdinand Magellan   William McKinley
William Howard Taft   Manuel Buaken
Fermin Tober

Treaty of Paris   Jones Act
Tydings-McDuffie Act   *pensionados*
brain drain   U.S. Nationals
Repatriation Act   pinoys
Philippine Scouts   Filipino Veterans
New Wave Generation   Immigration Reform Act

1. Discuss four important events in Filipino immigration.
2. Describe four characteristics of each of the four waves of Filipino immigration to America.
3. Discuss five important sociological characteristics of Filipino Americans today.

Chapter 9

The Asian Indian Experience

Introduction

In 1980 the U.S. census recorded 361,544 Asian Indians living in the United States. By 1990 their population more than doubled to approximately 815,447 (Hoffman, 1993:388). Most Asian Indians living in the United States today are Hindus, as they constitute 93 percent of the population of India. Since 1965 they have represented the largest ethno-religious group of immigrants arriving from India. And like the Korean and the Filipino immigrants of the new wave generation, the Asian Indians who have arrived since 1965 are also highly educated, concentrated in the professions, are fluent in English, have emigrated as nuclear families, and have settled in the major metropolitan areas of the United States.

Basis for Asian Indian Immigration

Asian Indians are not unaccustomed to emigration and settlement in new lands as they have a long history of migration since the time of Christ (Kondapi, 1951:1). However, the modern period of emigration from India is marked by the introduction of the indentured labor system by the British. Since the British formally abolished slavery in 1834, they simply introduced the indentured labor system as a practical substitute for slavery.

In practice and application the indentured labor system devised by the British was similar to slavery, with the exception that after working out their contracts the indentured servants were simply released and then re-employed under a new labor contract (Gangulee, 1947:21). Therefore the indentured labor system could hold these servants in perpetual bondage, just as if they were operating under a traditional system of slavery. The development of the indentured labor system resulted in an Asian diaspora that supplied the necessary labor for the extraction of raw materials that were essential to the maintenance and expansion of the British empire.

Asian Indians in Canada

The first Asian Indians to arrive in North America were the Sikhs, who began their immigration and settlement in Canada in 1905. During this first year of settlement only 45 Asian Indians arrived in Canada. The following year (1906) a total of 387 Asian Indian immigrants were admitted. Most of the early settlers arrived in 1907 (2,124) and 1908 (2,623), and most of these pioneer immigrants settled in British Columbia (Chadney, 1984:25- 43; Das, 1923:4-5).

The Sikhs were attracted by the employment and economic opportunities available in Vancouver. Unfortunately their welcome was short-lived, as the public resisted their introduction and the Canadian government was forced to ban further immigration from India in 1908. The immigration ban had an immediate effect on the number of Asian Indians allowed to settle in Canada, as only 118 immigrants were allowed to settle in Canada between 1909 and 1920 (Das, 1923:4-5). Naturally this ban on immigration from India met with strong resistance and political action from Asian Indians living in British Columbia (Buchignani, et al, 1985:32- 47).

In view of the immigration restrictions, racial problems, and violence encountered in British Columbia, the Asian Indians gradually moved south into Washington, Oregon, and California. Many Sikh immigrants who were forced out of British Columbia settled in California. To their surprise they found that the topography, soil, and weather of Northern California was very similar to the living and working conditions in their homeland (Millis, 1911).

Settlement in California

Few Americans are aware that the first Asian Indians arrived in the United States in the early 1820's. But these Asian Indians were primarily students, sailors, and diplomats (Jacoby, 1979:160). However the first significant flow of Asian Indian immigrants occurred between 1904 and 1911. During this early period of immigration approximately 6,100 Asian Indian pioneers arrived in the United States.

Like those Asian Indians who settled in Canada, the first Asian Indians to arrive in the United States were unskilled, uneducated, non-English speaking agriculturalists from the Punjab. And like the other Asian immigrants who arrived before them, the Asian Indians were primarily single men or married men who came without their wives and children. Like thousands of other immigrants they were also attracted to America by the employment and investment opportunities, higher wages, and the possibility of owning agricultural land (Jensen, 1988:24-41).

The first Asian Indians arrived in northern California in 1907 and they found employment in the fruit growing sections on the outskirts of Sacramento, primarily in the cities of Folsom, Orangeville, Loomis, and Newcastle (Das, 1923:19; Gonzales, 1986b; 1990; LaBrack, 1988). Most of these early Asian Indian settlers were unskilled and illiterate farmers and peasants from the Punjab. Almost all of them were young, single men, or married men who had immigrated without their families (G. Singh, 1946:214).

In the beginning they hired themselves out as itinerant farm workers, but they quickly formed labor gangs. They also resided in common living quarters, where they could eat and sleep. These living arrangements offered them companionship, cultural support, and common leadership (Das, 1923:29-31). Before long they organized themselves into agricultural and economic cooperatives, similar to the practice among Japanese immigrants. These labor cooperatives allowed them to pool their economic resources for long-term capital investments in land and farm equipment. Initially their farm holdings were modest and they worked their land in common and pooled their profits. The profits from their labor were quickly reinvested in more agricultural property and farm equipment (Das, 1923:66-67).

The Sikhs and Sikhism

The original Asian Indian settlers in California were from Northwestern India, primarily from the state of Punjab. The Punjab is the homeland of the Sikhs, who constituted 85 to 90 percent of the original Asian Indian immigrants to America (Jacoby, 1956:7; Latif, 1974; Millis, 1911:75). The Sikhs are a distinct social group in India and are considered an ethno-religious minority, for they are different in a number of ways. They are physically distinct from other Indians, as they are larger in body build, they are taller, and their religion requires that they wear turbans and keep their beards (McGregor, 1970).

Much of their distinctive appearance and cultural uniqueness can be attributed to their religious beliefs that require them to observe the tradition of the "Five K's," which means that they have to (1) wear their hair and their beard unshorn (*Kesh*), (2) carry a comb (*Kanga*), (3) wear a pair of shorts (*Kuchha*), (4) wear a steel bracelet (*Karah*), and (5) they must always carry a saber (*Kirpan*) (K. Singh, 1964:10, 1966). The reason that they were required to observe these religious requirements is that they were supposed to strive for the ideal of ascetic saintliness and were expected to be prepared to defend their families and their religion as soldier-saints (Cole and Sambhi, 1978:122-129; K. Singh, 1963).

As a religion Sikhism dates back to the fifteenth century when their leader Guru Nanek first gathered his followers near Lahore, in the Punjab. Guru Nanek's teachings held that there is only one God, that this world is an illusion, and that all ritual is a distraction (Wenzel, 1968:247). Much of the religious theology of Sikhism is derived from the teachings of Hinduism and Islam. As a result the Sikh holy book, the *Granth Sahib*, contains the writings of various Gurus and the teachings of Hindu and Muslim saints of all castes and creeds (Cole and Sambhi, 1978; K. Singh, 1964). In addition to observing all of their religious and cultural beliefs, Sikhs are required to be courageous and militant, to avoid the use of tobacco, and to take the common name of "Singh" (literally lion) (Singh and Singh, 1950:62, Wenzel, 1966:10).

Immigration Restrictions

Similar to the experiences of other Asians in California, Asian Indians were also the victims of racism and random acts of violence. The most boisterous of the anti-Asian groups at the time of their arrival in California was the Asiatic Exclusion League. In a matter of months the League effectively turned public opinion against further immigration from Asia (Hess, 1974:580-582; Hill, 1973).

The Asiatic Exclusion League was assisted in its efforts by the newspapers of the day, who not only encouraged racial agitation but also promoted and supported racists ideologies. The newspapers use of such headlines as the "Hindu Invasion" and "the Tide of Turbans" were particularly offensive to the Asian Indian community and were very effective in turning public opinion against the Asian Indians living in California at the time (Anonymous, 1910:15; Das, 1923:17). These inflammatory banners served to promote the idea that Asian Indians were somewhat less than human. As a result, the American public viewed Asian Indians as outsiders or aliens who could never be accepted or fully integrated into the fabric of American society (Brown, 1948; Scheffauer, 1910:617).

But the most important element in the racial conspiracy to terminate Asian Indian immigration were the efforts of local and state politicians. These demagogues used this racial agitation as an opportunity to secure more votes and insure their re-elections. Indeed several state legislators advanced their political careers by making racist statements and speeches against Asian Indians (Hess, 1969:62-64; 1974:581-583; Jensen, 1969).

From the historical perspective it is important to understand the inter-connection between negative public opinion against Asian Indians, and the indefatigable efforts of political pressure groups to prevent further immigration, the profit motives of the newspapers, and the political ambitions of legislators that resulted in the passage of anti-Asian laws (Jacoby, 1982). The most important anti-Asian law passed in California during this period was the Alien Land Law of 1913.

While the provisions of the Alien Land Law of 1913 were originally directed at the Japanese immigrants living in California, it had a direct impact on the entrepreneurial ambitions of Asian Indians (Leonard, 1984:75-76). This was true since the Alien Land Law prohibited aliens, who were ineligible for American citizenship, from owning or leasing land in California (Chandrasekhar, 1982b). Those Asian Indians who did own land prior to the passage of this law lived in constant fear of having their property confiscated by the state. By 1920 the Asian Indians owned or leased approximately 85,000 acres of farm land in the Sacramento and San Joaquin Valleys, and they had another 30,000 acres under cultivation in the Imperial Valley (Bose, 1919; Das, 1923:22-26, 31-32, 49-50; 93-95; Chandrasekhar, 1945).

Without any doubt the two most important anti-Asian actions at the federal level were the Immigration Act of 1917 and the Supreme Court's decision in the Thind Case. The Immigration Act of 1917 created the so-called Pacific Barred Zone that held that immigrants from certain parts of Asia (including India, most of the Arab nations, Burma, Indonesia, and Siam), would no longer be allowed to immigrate to the United States. For all practical purposes this law put an end to all immigration from India (Chandrasekhar, 1982b:18; Hess, 1969; 1982:18; Jacoby, 1958; LaBrack, 1982; Millis, 1911:75; 1912).

However, the most devastating blow to civil rights in America was delivered by the U.S. Supreme Court in February of 1923, in its ruling in the *United States v. Bhaghat Singh Thind*. In this landmark decision (commonly referred to as the Thind Case) the High Court ruled that Bhaghat Singh Thind, an Asian Indian attorney who had been granted American citizenship by a federal court in Oregon was not really a free white person and therefore ruled that he was ineligible for American citizenship, that is in view of the fact that citizenship was limited to free white persons (Das, 1927; Ireland, 1966; Scott, 1923; G. Singh, 1946). Therefore the High Court held that all Asian Indians were ineligible for American citizenship. Even more disastrous was the provision in the Court's ruling that all Asian Indians naturalized prior to the Court's decision had received their documents fraudulently and therefore were not really American citizens after all (Garner, 1927; Hess, 1969:63-64; 1974:589; Ireland, 1966; Jacoby, 1958:2). It is estimated that the federal government secured and revoked the citizenship papers of 50 to 70 Asian Indians between 1923 and 1926 (Chandrasekhar, 1982a:20; Hess, 1969:69; Jensen, 1980:299; G. Singh, 1946:211). The most serious ramifications of the Court's ruling was that since these Asian Indians lost their

American citizenship, they were then considered stateless persons (Garner, 1927).

The overall impact of these various discriminatory laws on the lives of Asian Indians was that they, (1) were not allowed to purchase or lease property, (2) could not send for their wives or children, (3) were prohibited from traveling outside of the United States (as they would not be allowed to return), (4) were segregated in certain occupations, (5) could not legally marry Caucasians, and (6) were completely isolated from the mainstream of American society. In brief they were stigmatized as outsiders and were considered undesirables by the American public.

The Termination of Immigration: 1915-1944

In view of the rampant racial hostility in California and the legal barriers to immigration, the flow of Asian Indians was drastically reduced. For example, between 1915 and 1929 only 1,646 Asian Indian immigrants were admitted into the United States. Their immigration was also severely limited by the economic crisis of the Great Depression and the social crisis brought on by the Second World War, when only 183 Asian Indians arrived in America (See Table 9.1).

The point also should be made that approximately 2,000 Asian Indians were deported between 1900 and 1950. Furthermore an additional 4,750 returned to India voluntarily during this period (Gonzales, 1986a; Jacoby, 1979:164). In total the Asian Indian community lost about 7,000 members during this fifty year period (LaBrack, 1979). However, one authority on Asian Indian immigration has reported that some 3,000 Asian Indians entered this country illegally, mostly via Mexico, between 1920 and 1930 (Jacoby, 1956:8).

Second Wave Immigrants: 1945-1965

As a demonstration of their gratitude for the role of the Indian government in assisting the United States in the defeat of Japan during the Second World War, and the indefatigable lobbying efforts of prominent Asian Indians living in the United States, the federal government proposed some major changes in the immigration laws. In the long term the modification of the restrictive immigration laws was very important for the development of the Asian Indian community in America.

In July of 1946, the U.S. Congress passed the Luce-Celler Bill and freed the Asian Indians from the Pacific Barred Zone immigration restrictions. In addition this bill granted India an annual immigration quota of 100 per year. But of greater significant the Luce-Celler Bill finally granted Asian Indians naturalization rights, which in the long term was critical to the development of a permanent Asian Indian community in America.

Table 9.1

Asian Indian Immigration to the United States, 1900-1991

Period	Years	Total	Cumulative Rate	Rate Per Year
I. Sojourners	1900-1906	870	—	124
II. First Wave	1907-1914	5,943	6,813	743
III. WWI and the Recession	1915-1929	1,646	8,459	110
IV. Great Depression and WWII	1930-1944	183	8,642	12
V. Second Wave	1945-1965	6,371	15,013	303
VI. Third Wave	1966-1985	317,416	323,787	15,871
	1986-1991	182,067	505,854	36,413
Key Immigration Periods	1820-1940	9,873	9,873	82
	1941-1960	3,734	13,607	187
	1961-1970	27,189	40,796	2,719
	1971-1991	468,675	509,471	23,434
Total Immigration	1820-1991	509,471		2,979

Source: INS, 1987; U.S. Census, 1991:Table 7; Hoffman, 1993:397.

As a result of these dramatic changes in the immigration laws a total of 6,371 Asian Indians were admitted into the United States between 1945 and 1965 (See Table 9.1 Above). In retrospect the immigration restrictions of the Pacific Barred Zone were in effect for 25 years and almost succeeded in bringing about the demise of the Asian Indian community in America. But the real victory for Asian Indians was the legal right, after 30 years, to send for their wives and children. For the first time Asian Indians were allowed to establish their families and bring the second generation of Asian Indian Americans into being.

Third Wave Immigrants: 1966-1993

In contrast to the second wave immigrants, the third wave Asian Indians were young, well educated, and heavily concentrated in the professions. The third wave immigrants were also more likely to arrive as family units, come directly from an urban or metropolitan area, and be fluent in English (Dworkin, 1980; Saran, 1977; 1987).

A study conducted by the Immigration and Naturalization Service found that of those Asian Indians who were naturalized in 1987, half (49.3%) held professional or technical positions (INS, 1987). Another study revealed that since 1965 India has served as America's major source of scientists and engineers. In 1965 only 94 scientists or engineers arrived from Indian as permanent legal resident aliens, but five years later almost three thousand arrived (Pernia, 1976:65). This heavy concentration in the professions reflects the high proportion of well educated and highly skilled immigrants among the third wave population. However, this occupational pattern conforms to the typical brain drain phenomena found among all the new Asian immigrants.

In real numbers this means that approximately half to two-thirds of all Asian Indians who have settled in the United States over the past two decades were professionals. For example, between 1977 and 1981 a total of 98,748 Asian Indians arrived, for an annual average of almost 20,000 per year. In view of their concentration in the professions, this means that approximately 10,000 to 15,000 professionals arrive from India each year.

Table 9.2
Asian Indian Immigration to the United States, 1960-1991

Selected Years	Total Number	Percent of Total	Cummulative Rate	Rate Per Year
1966-1970	25,289	5.1	—	5,172
1971-1975	70,294	14.2	96,153	14,059
1976-1980	98,732	20.0	194,885	19,746
1981-1985	119,701	24.2	314,586	23,940
1986-1991	179,430	36.3	494,016	35,886

Source: INS, 1987; U.S. Census, 1991:Table 7; Hoffman, 1993:397.

Asian Indians Today

As a result of the immigration reforms of 1965, it is clear that India has experienced a brain drain of its own. As demonstrated above, the flow of Asian Indian immigrants before 1965 was insignificant, but since 1965 their flow has become very significant. For example, between 1966 and 1970 a total of 26,000 Asian Indians arrived, resulting in an average flow of 5,000 per year (See Table 9.2 Above). This marked the initial flow of immigrants following the immigration reforms of 1965. For the five year period between 1971 to 1975, their annual average flow increased to 14,000. And for each successive period from 1976 to 1992 the number of Asian Indians admitted to the United States has increased dramatically. In 1988 a total of 26,268 Asian Indian immigrants arrived and this increased to 31,175 in 1989, 28,800 in 1990, and climbed dramatically to 42,700 in 1991.

Table 9.3
Asian Indian Immigration to the United States
and Metropolitan Area of Intended Residence: 1990

Metropolitan Settlement Area	Number	Percent
1. New York, NY	3,530	11.5
2. Chicago, IL	3,024	9.9
3. Washington, D.C.	1,465	4.8
4. Los Angeles-Long Beach, CA	1,440	4.7
5. Middlesex, NJ	1,093	3.6
6. Philadelphia, PA	931	3.0
7. Houston, TX	854	2.8
8. San Jose, CA	816	2.7
9. Newark, NJ	813	2.7
10. Nassau-Suffolk, NY	807	2.6
11. Bergen-Passaic, NJ	790	2.6
12. Oakland, CA	769	2.5
13. Anaheim-Santa Ana, CA	667	2.2
14. Jersey City, NJ	612	2.0
15. Detroit, MI	552	1.8
Total	18,163	59.2
All Asian Indian Immigrants	30,667	100.0

Source: U.S. Census, 1992:Table 11.

While Asian Indian Americans were predominately rural settlers prior to 1960, today they are 92 percent urban. Most have settled in large metropolitan areas, primarily in the Northeast, where one-third (35%) have settled. One out of five have settled in the Midwest (17.9%) and the West (23.1%), and one out of four (24%) have settled in the South. California claims the largest population of Asian Indians (159,973), followed by New York (140,985), New Jersey (79,440), Illinois (64,200), Texas (55,795), Florida (31,457), Pennsylvania (28,396), and Maryland (28,330). Most Asian Indians call New York City their home (56,000), followed by Chicago

(34,000), Los Angeles (17,227), Washington, D.C. (16,000), and San Jose (10,672) (U.S. Census, 1992:Table 26). Their concentration in the large metropolitan areas of the country reflects their professional and technical backgrounds (See Table 9.3).

Figure 9.1
Occupational Distribution of Asian Indian Immigrants
Admitted to the United States, 1989

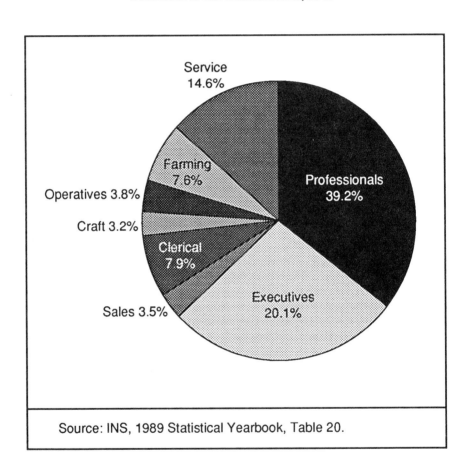

Source: INS, 1989 Statistical Yearbook, Table 20.

One survey conducted among Asian Indian immigrants found that 80 percent of the adult males were professional or technical workers. Two out of three (63.1%) of the adults (25 years and older) in the Asian Indian community are college graduates and almost half of them (46.1%) have graduate training. Overall, only ten percent were blue collar workers and one out of four were house-wives (with no occupations reported) (Gibson, 1988:43). Obviously Asian Indians are heavily concentrated in the professions and white collar positions (See Figure 9.1).

Chapter Summary

Asian Indians were encouraged to emigrate following the abolition of slavery by the British in 1834. The interest of the British in maintaining a system of labor exploitation resulted in the active recruitment and dispersion of Asian Indians throughout the British empire. As a result, Asian Indians were attracted to British Columbia, where they took advantage of employment and investment opportunities. Unfortunately their welcome was short-lived, as the Canadian government banned their immigration in 1908.

In 1905 Asian Indians began to settle in California, where they found the land and conditions very similar to those in their homeland. Most of the original Asian Indian settlers in America were Sikhs, from the Punjab. The Sikh pioneers settled in the Sacramento valley, where they worked in cooperative groups and pooled their capital and resources to lease and purchase farm land.

As a result of immigration restrictions the Asian Indians in California were not permitted to bring their families to the United States and those who traveled to India were not allowed to return to the United States. In view of the stringent immigration restrictions and the prejudice and discrimination that they experienced in America, Asian Indians were forced to live and work in a community of isolated men without their wives or families.

The government's prohibition on immigration from India was not lifted until the end of the Second World War, when India was granted a quota of 50 immigrants per year. Fortunately the new immigration law allowed the pioneer Sikh settlers to return to India to bring their wives back with them. For the first time the Asian Indian community was given the opportunity to establish cohesive family units in America.

The recent flow of Asian Indians is not only significant for the large number of immigrants that have settled in the United States but is also noteworthy for the high proportion of educated professionals who have immigrated following the passage of the Immigration Reform Act of 1965. Some have viewed this dramatic flow of Asian Indians into the United States as a brain drain phenomenon.

Asian Indian immigrants today are highly educated and have taken their place in the economic and occupational structure of the United States. Most Asian Indians have settled in the large metropolitan areas of the East coast, Texas, and California. Despite the fact that they have settled in large urban areas they have nonetheless managed to maintain their cohesive family structures and their culture and traditions. Some have even described the Asian Indians as one of the new bicultural communities in American society.

References

Anonymous
　1910　"Hindu Invasion." *Collier's* Vol. 45, March 26.

Bose, Subhindra
　1919　"Asian Immigration in the United States." *Modern Review*
　　　　25:521-526 (May).

Brown, Giles T.
　1948　"The Hindu Conspiracy, 1914-1917." *Pacific Historical Review*
　　　　42(3):299-310.

Buchignani, Norman and Doreen M. Indra
　1985　*Continuous Journey: A Social History of South Asians in
　　　　Canada.* Toronto: McClelland and Steward Ltd.

Chadney, James G.
　1984　*The Sikhs of Vancouver.* New York: AMS Press.

Chan, Sucheng
　1979　"Overseas Sikhs in the Context of International Migrations."
　　　　In Mark Juergensmeyer and N. Gerald Barrier (eds.), *Sikh
　　　　Studies: Comparative Perspectives on Changing Tradition.*
　　　　Berkeley, CA: Graduate Theological Union, Lancaster-
　　　　Miller Publishers. Pp. 191-206.

Chandrasekhar, Sripati
　1945　"The Indian Community in the United States." *Far Eastern
　　　　Survey* 14:147-149.

　1982a　"Some Statistics on Asian Indian Americans in the United
　　　　States." In Sripati Chandrasekhar (ed.), *From India to
　　　　America.* La Jolla, CA: Population Review Press. Pp. 86-92.

　1982b　"A History of United States Legislation With Respect to
　　　　Immigration From India." In Sripati Chandrasekhar (ed.),
　　　　From India to America. La Jolla, CA: Population Review Publi-
　　　　cations. Pp. 1-28

Cole, Owen W. and Piara Singh Sambhi
　1978　*The Sikhs: Their Religion, Beliefs and Practices.* London:
　　　　Routledge and Kegan Paul.

Das, Mary
　1927　"True Status of Hindus Regarding American Citizenship."
　　　　Modern Review 41:461-465.

Das, Rajani Kanta
　1923　*Hindustani Workers on the Pacific Coast.* Berlin and Leipzig:
　　　　Walter De Bruyter & Co.

Dworkin, Roslyn J.
　1980　"Differential Processes in Acculturation: The Case of the
　　　　Asiatic Indians."

Gangulee, N.
1947   *Indians in the Empire Overseas.* Bombay: The New India
        Publishing House, Ltd.
Garner, James W.
1927   "Denationalization of American Citizens." *American Journal
        of International Law* 21:106-107.
Gibson, Margaret A.
1988   *Accommodation Without Assimilation: Sikh Immigrants in
        an American High School.* Ithaca: Cornell University Press.
Gonzales, Juan L. Jr.
1986a   "Asian Indian Immigration Patterns: The Origins of the Sikh
        Community in California." *International Migration Review*
        20(1):46-57.
1986b   "The Sikhs of Northern California: Settlement and
        Acculturation in Two Communities." *Human Mosaic*
        20(1&2):28-38.
1990   "The Settlement of Sikh Farmers in the Sacramento Valley of
        California." In Mahin Gosine (ed.) *Dothead Americans: The
        Silent Minority in the United States.* New York: Windsor Press.
        Pp. 32- 47.
1992   *Racial and Ethnic Families in America.* Dubuque, IA:
        Kendall/Hunt Publishing.
Hess, Gary R.
1969   "The 'Hindu' in America: Immigration and Naturalization
        Policies and India." *Pacific Historical Review* 38:59-79.
1974   "The Forgotten Asian Americans: The East Indian
        Community in the United States." *Pacific Historical Review*
        43:576-596.
1982   "The Asian Indian Immigrants in the United States, 1900-
        1965." In Sripati Chandrasekhar (ed.), *From India to America.*
        La Jolla, CA: Population Review Press. Pp. 29-34.
Hill, Herbert
1973   "Anti-Oriental Agitation and the Rise of Working Class
        Racism." *Society* 10:43-54.
Hoffman, Mark S.
1993   *The World Almanac and Book of Facts 1993.* New York: Pharos
        Books.
Immigration and Naturalization Service (INS)
1987   *1987 Statistical Yearbook of the Immigration and Naturalization
        Service.* Washington, D.C.: U.S.Department of Justice.
1989   *Immigration Statistics: Fiscal Year 1988 Advanced Report.*
        Washington, D.C.: U.S. Department of Justice.

Ireland, Ralph R.
1966   "Indian Immigration in the United States, 1901-1964."
            Indian Journal of Economics 46(183):465-476.
Jacoby, Harold S.
1956   "A Half Century of Appraisal of East Indians in the United
            States." Stockton, CA: Sixth Annual College of the Pacific
            Faculty Research Lecture, University of the Pacific.
1958   "More Thind Against Than Sinning." *The Pacific Historian*
            2(4):1-2, 8.
1979   "Some Demographic and Social Aspects of Early East Indian
            Life in the United States." In Mark Juergensmeyer and N.
            Gerald Barrier (eds.), *Sikh Studies*. Berkeley: Graduate
            Theological Union, Lancaster-Miller Publishers. Pp. 159-
            171.
1982   "Administrative Restriction of Asian Indian Immigration into
            the United States, 1907-1917." In Sripati Chandrasekhar
            (ed.), *From India to America*. La Jolla, CA: Population Review
            Press. Pp. 35-40.
Jensen, Joan M.
1969   "Apartheid: Pacific Coast Style." *Pacific Historical Review*
            39:335-340.
1980   "East Indians." In Stephan Ternstrom (ed.), *Harvard
            Encyclopedia of American Ethnic Groups*. Cambridge, MA: Har-
            vard University Press. Pp. 296-301.
1988   *Passage From India: Asian Indian Immigrants in North
            America*. New Haven: Yale University Press.
Kondapi, C.
1951   *Indians Overseas*. New Delhi: Indian Council of World
            Affairs.
LaBrack, Bruce
1979   "Sikhs Real and Ideal: A Discussion of Text and Context in
            the Description of Overseas Sikh Communities." In Mark
            Juergensmeyer and N. Gerald Barrier (eds.), *Sikh Studies*.
            Berkeley: Lancaster-Miller Publishers. Pp. 127-142.
1982   "Immigration Law and the Revitalization Process: The Case
            of the California Sikhs." In Sripati Chandrasekhar (ed.),
            From India to America. La Jolla, CA: Population Review Press.
            Pp. 59-66.
1988   *The Sikhs of Northern California 1904-1975: A Socio-
            Historical Study*. New York: AMS Press.
Latif, Syad Muhammed
1974   *History of the Punjab from the Remotest Antiquity to the Present
            Time*. New Delhi: Eurasia Press.

Leonard, Karen
1984   "The Pahkar Singh Murders: A Punjabi Response to California's Alien Land Law." *Amerasia* 11(1):75-87.
McGregor, William L.
1970   *A History of the Sikhs.* Punjab, India: Patiala Press.
Millis, H. A.
1911   "East Indian Immigration to British Columbia and the Pacific Coast States." *American Economic Review* 1:72-76.
1912   "East Indian Immigration to the Pacific Coast." *Survey* 28:379-386.
Saran, Parmatma
1977   "Cosmopolitans from India." Society 14(6):65-69.
1987   "Pains and Pleasures: Consequences of Migration for Asian Indians in the United States." *Journal of Ethnic Studies* 15:23-46.
Scheffauer,
1910   "The Tide of Turbans." *Forum* 43:616-618.
Scott, James Brown
1923   "Japanese and Hindus Naturalized in the United States." *American Journal of International Law* 17:328-330.
Singh, Gurdial
1946   "East Indians in the United States." *Sociology and Social Research* 30(3):208-216.
Singh, Khushwant
1963   *A History of the Sikhs: Volume 1, 1469-1839.* Princeton, NJ: Princeton University Press.
1964   *The Sikhs Today.* Bombay: Orient Longmans.
1966   *A History of the Sikhs: Volume 2.* Princeton, NJ: Princeton University Press.
Singh, Teja and Ganada Singh
1950   *A Short History of the Sikhs: Volume One, 1469-1765.* Bombay: Longman Green and Co.
U.S. Census
1991   *Statistical Abstract of the United States, 1991* (111th Edition). Washington, D.C.: USGPO.
1992   *1990 Census of the Population, U.S. Summary.* Washington, D.C.: CD-ROM Data.
Wenzel, Lawrence A.
1966   "The Identification and Analysis of Certain Value Orientation of Two Generations of East Indians in California." Ed.D. Dissertation, University of the Pacific, Stockton, CA.
1968   "The Rural Punjabis of California: A Religio-Ethnic Group." *Phylon* 29:245-256.

Box Reading 9.1
A Brief Chronology of Asian Indian American History

1820	The entry of the first Indian immigrant is officially recorded.
1901	Arrival of Sikh immigrants in Canada.
1906	First Asian Indians arrive in the United States.
1907	Sikh settlers become the victims of various acts of random violence in Washington state.
1910	Asian Indians are declared eligible for U.S. citizenship in the case of *United States v. Balsara*.
1917	The U.S. Congress passed a law barring Asian Indians, and all other Asians, from become U.S. citizens.
1923	The U.S. Supreme Court rules in *United States v. Bhaghat Singh Thind* that Asian Indians are not eligible for citizenship since they were not considered white persons according to the naturalization law of 1790 that restricted citizenship to "free white" persons.
1926	Sakaram Ganesh Pandit, an Asian Indian lawyer, successfully argued the case that Asian Indians are Aryans, and therefore are whites. As a result of this court ruling Pandit was allowed to retain his American citizenship.
1946	The U.S. Congress passed the Luce-Celler bill allowing Asian Indians to become U.S. citizens. An immigration law was passed that granted India an immigration quota of 100 persons per year.
1956	Dalip Singh Saud became the first Asian Indian to be elected to a seat in the U.S. Congress.
1965	Immigration Reform Act grants India an annual immigration quota of 20,000 persons per year and creates a new immigration preference ranking system.
1986	The Asian Indian community supports the passage of new immigration laws allowing for family reunification.
1990	Asian Indian becomes an official U.S. Census category.
1992	Asian Indians play an active role in the presidential elections.

Guru Nanek   Bhaghat Singh Thind

Key Terms

indentured labor   Sikhs
Sikhism   Punjab
ethno-religious group   the Five K's
Granth Sahib   Asiatic Exclusion League
Alien Land Law of 1913   Immigration Act of 1917
Thind Case   Pacific Barred Zone
free white person   Luce-Celler Bill
brain drain phenomenon

Sample Test Questions

1. Discuss four important cultural characteristics of the Sikhs who arrived in America at the turn of the century.
2. Discuss four of the immigration restrictions placed against the Asian Indians.
3. List and describe three important characteristics of three waves of Asian Indian immigration.

Part III

★ ★ ★

The Latino American Experience

Chapter 10

The Mexican American Experience

Introduction

Today Mexican Americans are the fastest growing ethnic group in American Society. In 1993 there were approximately 14 million Mexican Americans in the United States, which gave this country the largest population of Mexicans outside of Mexico and the fifth largest concentration of Latinos in the world. With an average immigration rate of 155,419 per year (since 1970) the flow of Mexican immigrants is the highest of any group. Since their fertility rate is also among the highest of any group, their numbers will certainly increase.

For example, between 1970 and 1980 the Mexican origin population experienced a 93 percent increase. From a population of 8.7 million in 1980, their population increased to 12.6 million by 1990. Over the decade this represents a growth rate of 44.8 percent, compared to a national growth rate of only 9.5 percent, over the same period. The population projections predict that the Mexican American population will exceed 17 million by the year 2000. Eight out of ten (79.3%) Mexican Americans live in either California (6,119,000 or 48.4%) or Texas (3,891,000 or 30.9%). Today (1993) one out of five (20.6%) of the residents of California are of Mexican origin and it is estimated that by the year 2000 they will represent three out of ten of the state's population.

This chapter will present an overview of Mexican American history and will recognize the many contributions that they have made to the social, cultural, and economic development of American society. Since their initial settlement was in the Southwest attention will be given to their work in the agricultural industry, construction, and service. This chapter will conclude with an examination of some contemporary social issues that have affected the Mexican American community, such as immigration issues, labor market conditions, economic survival, and needed educational reforms.

Mexicans in the Southwest: 1821-1920

The year 1519 not only marked the arrival of Hernando Cortez in Mexico and the onset of the conquest of Native Americans, but also resulted in the extension of Spanish domination throughout the Southwest. Three hundred years later (1821), Mexico gained its independence from Spain.

When compared to the United States, Mexico was not a strong military force and public opinion in the United States was very supportive of expansionism, and the philosophy of Manifest Destiny supplied the needed justification for America's expansionist goals. In a few short years Texas became the focal point of America's expansionist ambitions.

In 1821 Mexico granted Stephen F. Austin permission to establish a permanent settlement in Texas. By the late 1830's there were 20,000 settlers in Texas. Soon the American and European settlers in Texas viewed the Mexicans as intruders. The Texas revolt (1835) concluded with the defeat of the Mexicans at the Battle of San Jacinto (1836). Texas became a republic (1836-1845) and gained admission into the Union in 1845. This resulted in the declaration of war with Mexico, in May of 1846 (Acuña, 1988:5-15).

The Treaty of Guadalupe Hidalgo (1848) ended the war between the United States and Mexico, and gave the United States (what is now), California, New Mexico, Nevada, and parts of Colorado, Arizona, and Utah. In return Mexico received $15 million and promised to recognize Texas as part of the United States. The treaty also granted all the rights of American citizenship to those Mexican nationals living in the American Southwest at the time (Sanders, 1950:2). As a result, some 75,000 Mexicans were granted (1) American citizenship, (2) the right to religious freedom, (3) all property rights, and (4) the right to maintain their culture and traditions (Moquin and Van Doren, 1971:241- 249).

Unfortunately these treaty provisions were quickly forgotten, as all Mexicans were treated as a conquered and defeated people. In short order their constitutional rights were ignored, their land was taken, and they were relegated to the lowest level of social existence. But with the construction of railroads and the development of the cattle and agricultural industries in the Southwest, all Mexicans were considered an ideal source of cheap labor. Mexicans living in Los Angeles and Santa Barbara were hired by cattle barons to maintain their herds and move their cattle to market (Pitt, 1971:244-276). And the demand for Mexican labor increased significantly following the completion of the transcontinental railroad (1869), since crops grown in California could now be transported to the lucrative Eastern markets (McWilliams, 1971:61,63).

The combination of the development of a rail system and the expansion of agricultural production in the Southwest resulted in an ever increasing need for cheap, tractable labor. Consequently Mexicans were eagerly sought by the railroads and by growers throughout the Southwest. By the mid-1880's Mexican laborers constituted 70 percent of the section crews and 90 percent of the extra gangs on the railroads (McWilliams, 1968:168). And by the turn of the century, the railroad companies were sending labor contractors into the interior of Mexico (Cardoso, 1980:58).

The development of the agricultural industry in the Southwest was supported by the federal government, since the Federal Reclamation Act (1902) provided funds for the construction of massive irrigation projects. Besides the thousands of Mexican laborers recruited for the construction of canals, dykes, and reservoirs, thousands of other Mexicans cleared the deserts and prepared the soil for cultivation (Fernandez, 1977:97; Gann and Duignan, 1986:36-41).

The *Mejicanos* were not only attracted by the promises of labor recruiters, the availability of jobs, higher rates of pay, and the ease of transportation between the U.S. and Mexico, but they were also escaping a life of poverty in their homeland. After 1910 they were also escaping the ravages of the Mexican Revolution (1910-1924), when almost half a million fled the violence and bloodshed. Between 1900 and 1929, over 715,000 Mexicans crossed the border into the United States (See Table 10.1 Next page).

In terms of the number of Mexicans living permanently in the United States, there were 42,435 in 1870, 68,399 in 1880, 77,853 in 1890, 103,393 in 1900, and 221,915 in 1910. By 1920 the Mexican origin population in the United States was almost half a million (486,418) (Dept. of Industrial Relations, 1930:Table 8). At the turn of the century seven out of ten (68.7%) of all Mexicans lived in Texas and less than one out of ten (7.8%) lived in California. By 1920 only half (51.8%) lived in Texas and one out of five (18.2%) lived in California (Dept. of Industrial Relations, 1930:Table 9). Three out of four (73.5%) of the Mexicans living in California in 1920 were concentrated in southern California (Dept. of Industrial Relations, 1930:49).

The Great Depression

According to the census there were 1.5 million Mexicans living in the United States in 1930. Although there were more Mexicans living in the United States at the time, that is given the census undercount and the fact that thousands of Mexicans crossed the border without inspection until the Border Patrol was established in 1924 (Reisler, 1976:12-13). But with the failure of thousands of businesses and the loss of millions of jobs in the

United States during the Depression, a very critical look was given to all Mexicans.

Table 10.1
Mexican Immigration To The United States: 1900-1991

Years	Total Number	Percent of Total	Cumulative Rate	Rate Per Year
1900-1904	2,830	0.06	—	566
1905-1909	28,358	0.6	31,188	5,672
1910-1914	88,358	1.8	119,546	17,671
1915-1919	96,976	2.0	216,522	19,395
1920-1924	255,774	5.3	472,296	51,155
1925-1929	243,171	5.1	715,467	48,634
1930-1934	21,944	0.5	737,411	4,389
1935-1939	10,765	0.3	748,176	2,153
1940-1944	18,258	0.5	766,434	3,652
1945-1949	37,873	0.8	804,307	7,575
1950-1954	69,804	1.5	874,111	13,961
1955-1959	204,061	4.3	1,078,172	40,812
1960-1964	220,423	4.6	1,298,595	44,085
1965-1969	213,689	4.5	1,512,284	42,738
1970-1974	300,339	6.3	1,812,623	60,068
1975-1979	308,610	6.5	2,121,233	61,722
1980-1984	327,690	6.8	2,448,923	65,538
1985-1988	295,000	6.1	2,743,923	73,750
1989-1991	2,032,168	42.5	4,776,091	677,389

Source: Grebler, et al, 1970:64; INS, 1988; Johnson, 1992:804; U.S. Census, 1992:Table 7,11.

With an unemployment rate of 25 to 30 percent it was not long before Anglo Americans were willing to pick crops in the field. In addition, the dust bowl conditions in Arkansas, Oklahoma, and Texas attracted thousands of Anglo migrants to California. Before long farmers established a policy of hiring their own, rather than the *Mejicanos*, who they said should return to Mexico. In a short time Mexicans were perceived as the competition by white labor (Majka and Majka, 1982:105-108).

In response to the dire economic conditions during the Great Depression the government created a Repatriation Program. The objective of this program was to encourage Mexicans, many of whom were American citizens, to return voluntarily to Mexico. As a result of this program half a million Mexicans and Mexican Americans, primarily from Texas and California, were deported (Meier and Rivera, 1972:164). The Repatriation Program sent a clear message, that is Mexican laborers could be called upon when needed and deported when they were no longer needed. In effect Mexico was considered a reservoir of surplus labor for the American economy.

In 1931, as a cost saving measure, the city of Los Angeles instituted a Repatriation Program of its own. The mayor of Los Angeles estimated that the cost of $14.70 to ship one person by rail to Mexico City was less than a week's board and lodging offered by the city's social services department to the indigent. During the first three months of the program it is estimated that the city saved $350,000 (McWilliams, 1933). From 1931 to 1934, the city of Los Angeles ordered the deportation of more than 13,000 Mexicans. Most unfortunately, many of these deportees were children born in the United States (Hoffman, 1974).

The Bracero Program

When the United States entered the Second World War labor needs were critical, particularly since thousands of laborers were drafted into the military forces. Laborers were needed in the industrial plants, shipyards, bomber factories, automobile and truck assembly lines, weapons factories, and in agricultural production. And, as in the past, America looked south of the border in time of need. The expectation was that Mexico would supply a continuous source of cheap labor during the war.

To this end the Bracero Program was ratified and allowed for the importation of Mexican laborers. The objective of the program was to offset the shortage created by the draft and wartime industries. This bilateral agreement between the United States and Mexico was approved in July of 1942. During the first year of the program, more than 80,000 Mexican laborers harvested crops in the Southwest.

Although the Bracero Program was initially adopted as a temporary wartime emergency, Congress approved annual extensions of the program since American farmers became totally dependent on cheap Mexican labor (Cockcroft, 1986: 67-75). The post-war Bracero Program was given formal approval in 1951, with the passage of Public Law 78. When the program was finally abolished in December 1964, an estimated five million Mexicans had participated in this international labor exchange (See Table 10.2 Next page).

An unanticipated aspect of the Bracero Program was that it stimulated the flow of undocumented aliens into the United States. Since the program placed restrictions on where Braceros were allowed to work and stipulated their rate of pay, the advantage for the *campesinos* (Mexican farm workers) was that they could undercut the wages offered to the Braceros and they could work in non-agricultural jobs, from which Braceros were legally barred. In addition the *campesinos* could cut all the red tape, inconvenience, and personal expenses involved in registering for the Bracero Program. Likewise, farmers could eliminate the red tape and save the $25 bond and the $15 registration fee required for each Bracero, (Grebler, 1966:32).

Table 10.2
Number of Braceros Contracted: 1942-1968

Years	Total Number	Percent of Total	Cumulative Rate	Rate Per Year
1942-1944	118,471	2.3	—	39,490
1945-1949	277,872	5.5	396,343	55,574
1950-1954	984,411	19.5	1,380,754	196,882
1955-1959	2,152,269	42.6	3,533,023	430,453
1960-1964	1,381,133	27.3	4,914,156	276,227
1965-1968*	135,937	2.7	5,050,093	33,984

Source: Samora, 1975:72 (Statistics Added)
* Aliens admitted between 1966-1968 arrived as temporary contract laborers.

Operation Wetback

The fact that the Bracero Program encouraged illegal entry into the United States is substantiated by the records of the Immigration and Naturalization Service (INS). During the first year of the Bracero Program, 8,000 undocumented Mexican aliens were apprehended by the INS. By 1951 half a million undocumented aliens were apprehended and deported. In 1954 the INS responded with Operation Wetback. This was an all out effort to return the wetbacks (the derisive term for undocumented aliens who swam the Rio Grande river) to Mexico. During the five year period of this program, an estimated 3.8 million *mojados* (wetbacks) were apprehended and deported (Garcia, 1980).

It is also important to point out that the Bracero Program caused irreparable harm to Mexican American farm workers. Since the Bracero Program guaranteed growers a continuous source of cheap labor they had no incentive or reason to pay local Mexican Americans a living wage. As a result Mexican Americans had to live under a substandard regional economy based on subsistence wages paid to Braceros and *mojados*. The *mojados* applied a continuous downward pressure on wages, so that Mexican Americans could only expect to receive Mexican wages for their labor. The presence of this large surplus labor force also forestalled unionization efforts in the agricultural industry, as growers could always hire *mojados* as scabs

226

(Copp, 1971). As a result it took Caesar Chavez, and other labor organizers, many years to establish an agricultural union.

The Sleepy Lagoon Case

California history is not only interlaced with accounts of racial attacks against Asians, but it is also a chronicle of racial violence against hapless Mexicans. The racial hatred and hostility toward Mexicans was made abundantly clear during the repatriation movement, when thousands of Mexicans were sent back to Mexico. In the summer of 1942, war time tensions were high and Mexican Americans served as a convenient lightning rod for pent up racial tensions in the city of Los Angeles.

Sleepy Lagoon was the name of an old gravel pit where Mexican American youth congregated during the hot summer evenings. On the night of August 1, 1942 a young man was slain near the gravel pit. The next morning the newspapers sensationalized the story and portrayed the killing as gang related. The police followed suit and arrested 24 juveniles, all reputed members of the 38th Street gang, on suspicion of murder. Following a mass trial, seventeen teen-agers were convicted and sent to prison for the murder of Jose Diaz (McWilliams, 1968:228-229).

The Sleepy Lagoon case was important because it highlights the relationship between racial prejudice, the racially biased motives of the police, and the conspiracy by the press to sway public opinion against Mexican Americans. What followed was a long period of police brutality, acts that were sanctioned and condoned by the press and the public. During the War it was not uncommon for the police to set up road blocks, stop and search all vehicles with occupants who looked Mexican, and incarcerate them. Clearly this was a case of officially sanctioned harassment. During one of these police operations, 600 Mexicans were taken into custody and 175 were booked on a variety of charges (McWilliams, 1968:236).

The Zoot Suit Riots

The police actions in the barrios of Los Angeles culminated in the Zoot Suit Riots. The zoot suit, popularized by Mexican American youth, was known for its baggy trousers, long draped jacket, and wide-brimmed hat. The zoot-suiters (or pachucos) were known for their tattoos and duck-tail haircuts, and spoke in their patois (Dieppa, 1973). The zoot suiters belonged to *palomillas* (neighborhood clubs), but the newspapers portrayed the zoot suit as a badge of crime and gang membership.

The Zoot Suit riots began in Los Angeles during the summer of 1943, as tensions increased between off duty sailors and the zoot suiters. As a result of negative press and police actions, the sailors considered the pachucos fair game. On the evening of June third, about 200 sailors piled into taxi cabs and arrived in the barrio to teach the Mexicans a lesson. The sailors assaulted any Mexicans they could find and stripped them of their zoot suits. The next day, the newspapers portrayed the sailors as heroes and the police ignored the whole incident (McWilliams, 1943). These racial attacks continued for a whole week, that is until the State Department placed Los Angeles off limits to all military personnel (Fogelson, 1969).

The negative image that emerged from these incidents not only reinforced a racial stereotype of Mexicans as prone to violence and as a social problem in the community, but it also set the stage for the development of harsh feelings in the barrio against Anglos. These incidents made it very difficult for Mexican Americans to receive equal treatment under the law, whether in the courts or on the streets (Morales, 1972:20-46).

The Post War Period

It is ironic that public opinion toward Mexican Americans was so negative during the war, when more than 400,000 Mexican Americans had served their country. On the positive side, military service offered them an opportunity to travel, live among Anglos, and experience life on a different level. In addition the new skills and educational opportunities obtained in the military were transferred to civilian life. And as veterans many were eligible for educational benefits, home mortgages, and preference in government jobs (Morin, 1963).

The war also opened up new opportunities for Mexican Americans in the civilian labor force, since jobs that had been closed to them were made available during the war. For the first time Mexican Americans were hired by automobile plants, shipyards, steel mills, aircraft assembly plants, and by the construction industry. The result was a general upgrading of the job skills in the barrio and an increase in their standard of living (Acuña, 1988:260-261).

To their dismay many veterans returned from the war to discover that in many ways America had not changed, since they encountered prejudice and racial hostility at every level. The most blatant cases of racism occurred when decorated veterans in uniform were refused service in restaurants, were segregated in theaters, buses, and trains, encountered signs that read "NO MEXICANS ALLOWED" at public swimming pools and parks, were denied lodging in hotels, and were harassed by the local police (McWilliams, 1968: 261-263).

In one incident a mortuary in Three Rivers, Texas refused to bury Felix Longoria, a Mexican American war hero, because the cemetery was an all-white cemetery. This blatant act of racism is historic since it planted the seed for organized political protest, as Mexican Americans stood up for their rights and transformed their frustration into political action.

Political Participation

The fact that Mexican Americans have a long history of political participation is often ignored. The popular stereotype would have us believe that they are not interested in politics, are apathetic, are ignorant of political issues, and are guided by traditionalism. However, a review of American political history reveals that Mexican Americans have a long history of political involvement.

At the turn of the century, the general attitude was that *Mejicanos* were simply here to serve as a source of cheap labor, and were therefore considered apolitical. That is, they were viewed as apolitical until their votes were needed to insure the election of a local Anglo *patron* (political boss). The most blatant examples of this Southwestern version of the Yankee political machine occurred in New Mexico (Valdes y Tapia, 1976:53-80).

When it was not to the benefit of Anglo politicians to vote their Mexicans in mass, the common practice was to deny them the vote. This was achieved in several ways. In Texas, Mexican Americans were required to pass a literacy test and had to pay a poll tax before casting a vote. They were also required to register to vote once a year, usually at a time and place when most of them were at work (Foley, 1978).

Even when they were successful in overcoming these barriers, Mexican Americans found their political power diluted by such duplicitous practices as gerrymandering and at-large elections. Gerrymandering insured that no barrio would ever have enough eligible voters in it to insure victory for any aspiring Mexican American politician. At-large elections made it difficult for any Mexican American who secured a majority of the votes in his/her district in the primary election, to be successful in the run-off election (De La Garza, 1974).

Consequently, these political maneuvers either served to neutralize the Mexican American vote, or insured that their votes would not count on election day. In response Mexican Americans formed their own political organizations, since the establishment was unresponsive to their needs.

Mexican American political history can be divided into four periods from:

1. the signing of the Treaty of Guadalupe Hidalgo to the turn of the century (1848-1909),
2. from the Mexican Revolution to the Second World War (1910-1940),
3. from the Second World War to the mid-sixties (1941-1964),
4. from the Chicano Movement to the present (1965-1993).

Each of these periods is noted for the development of a particular type of political organization. The first period is recognized for the development of *mutualistas*, that is mutual benefit associations. The migrant generation (1910-1940) is known for its founding of melting pot organizations. The G.I. Generation (1941-1965) promoted the ideals of democracy and fought against racism and discrimination, while the Chicano generation relied on the politics of nationalism.

One of the first expressions of Mexican American political activity took the form of mutual benefit societies. These organizations served as burial societies, insurance companies, and lending institutions. In effect, they provided the community with basic social services that were otherwise unavailable to Mexican Americans. The earliest *mutualistas* were founded in El Paso, Brownsville, Tucson, and Los Angeles (De Leon, 1982).

The first assimilationist organization was founded in San Antonio, in 1918 and was known as *La Orden de Los Hijos de America* (The Order of the Sons of America), or simply as OSA (Navarro, 1974:62). The OSA encouraged the complete Americanization of all Mexicans and limited its political activities to voter registration drives, citizenship classes, and struggled to get qualified Mexican Americans to serve on juries. Politically the organization considered itself nonpartisan.

Following a split with the OSA in 1928, a group of Mexican Americans founded the League of United Latin American Citizens (LULAC) in Corpus Christi, Texas in the spring of 1929 (Marquez, 1988:13). Like the OSA, LULAC also had a strong assimilationist orientation and drew its membership from the Mexican American middle class. LULAC is still active today and has offices across the country.

Following the Second World War, the G.I. Generation founded several political organizations (Camarillo, 1971). The best known of these were the Community Service Organization (CSO), the American G.I. Forum, the Council of Mexican-American Affairs (CMAA), the Mexican American Political Association (MAPA), and the Political Association of Spanish Speaking Organizations (PASSO).

The Community Service Organization evolved as part of a city-wide effort by Mexican Americans to elect Edward Roybal to the Los Angeles city council in 1947. In the process, the CSO registered over 40,000 citizens, most of whom lived in the barrios of Los Angeles (Navarro, 1974). The G.I. Forum was founded by Dr. Hector Garcia, a physician and Army veteran, in 1948 following an act of discrimination in which a funeral home in Texas refused to bury a Mexican American veteran (Ramos, 1982:11-12, 17-26).

In 1953, the Council of Mexican American Affairs was founded in Los Angeles, with the stated goal of uniting all Mexican American organizations into one unified group. Three years later a more activist group was founded in California, the Mexican American Political Association. Their goal was to encourage and assist Mexican Americans who sought political office (Dvorin

230

and Misner, 1966). The Political Association of Spanish Speaking Organizations was founded in Texas in the early 1960's, primarily as an outgrowth of the Viva Kennedy Movement. Its primary goal was to form a coalition of Mexican American political organizations throughout the Southwest.

The Chicano Movement evolved during the sixties and initiated the politics of confrontation. *El Movimiento* relied on group demonstrations, boycotts, strikes, sit-ins, and civil disobedience to achieve its goals. Members adopted the name Chicano, to show their allegiance to the new political activism. The term Chicano was used by the activists to denote their ethnicity, militancy, rejection of assimilation, and their goal of self-determination (Meier and Rivera, 1981:83).

Political Representation

Today Mexican American politics has moved into a period of adjustment and accommodation. The political arena is dominated by professional politicians who regularly court the Latino vote, since they recognize its potential. This was made clear in the recent Presidential election. However, a significant representational gap remains, since Mexican Americans are not represented at a level commensurate with their proportion in the population.

For example, in California Mexican Americans constitute 21 percent of the population, but there are only seven Latino representatives in the State Legislature, out of a House of 120 members (6% representation). Of the 47 members of the 1992 California Congressional Delegation only three (Martinez, Roybal, and Torres) are Mexican Americans. Proportional representation would require three times this number. At the Congressional level only nine members of the 535 voting members of the 102nd Congress are Latinos, far less than the 44 members needed for proportional representation. Congress has more than 20,000 staff members, but only 70 are Latinos, or 0.3 percent of the total (Pachon, 1983).

Clearly, Mexican Americans are severely underrepresented at all levels of government and the reason is that the American political system has only reluctantly considered the political rights of Mexican Americans. The American political system has never completely welcomed their participation. Any progress that has been made in the political arena has been made in spite of the political system, rather than because of it.

The Mexican American Family

The origins of the Mexican American family can be traced to the Spanish conquest, when the Spanish infused their political system, their religion, and their military ambitions into Aztec society. From the beginning the Catholic missionaries not only set out to convert the heathens, but also to insure that they would marry in the church and follow all Catholic religious teachings (Gonzales, 1986).

Following Mexico's independence from Spain, the Mexican government relieved the Catholic church of much of its secular power, guaranteed freedom of religion, and allowed for divorce. Nonetheless, the family maintained many of the traditions acquired during the Spanish period. When Mexicans began to settle in the Southwest, they often migrated as families (Griswold del Castillo, 1984:10-24). By the turn of the century family migration was encouraged by Texas growers, as they realized that families working in the harvest were a more stable work force than single men. The farmers also discovered that women and children picked almost as much fruit and cotton as the men (Gonzales, 1985a; Taylor, 1930).

As Mexican families settled in the larger cities of the Southwest, they evolved into extended family units. Naturally, these larger families were able to share in the child care and household expenses. This also meant that the adults could work longer hours and even remain away from home when required, since other relatives were always available to tend to their children.

By the seventies, Mexican Americans were predominantly urban. Life in the city not only encouraged the maintenance of nuclear families, but also promoted, out of necessity, smaller families. Therefore, while Mexican American families are larger than the general population, their overall family size is gradually declining.

The role that women play in the family has changed in the eighties. As with most women, the Mexican American woman has been affected by the Women's Movement and the Civil Rights Movement. As a result the Mexican American woman is no longer the subservient-submissive female of the mythical past (Baca-Zinn, 1975). While it is true that Mexican American women have always played a central role in the family, today they have carried their role beyond the family. Today Chicanas are independent, are active in the labor force, and play a more significant role in the family. In part, the decline in fertility rates can be attributed to the ambitions of upwardly mobile women in the Mexican American family today.

Given the gradual increase in the levels of education and the occupational mobility that Mexican Americans are experiencing, it is anticipated that their basic socio-economic conditions will improve. Additionally, as economic well-being improves, there will be an improvement in family life style.

A Demographic Profile

In 1980, the Mexican American population was estimated at 8,700,000, and it increased to 12,565,000 by 1990. However, the actual number of Mexican origin people is certainly larger, as these are conservative government estimates and do not include undocumented aliens, nor do they consider the traditional undercount of ethnic minorities.

In 1990 the total Mexican American population was 12,565,000. By 1995 it will be 13,755,000, and by the year 2000 it will reach 15,386,000, that is almost twice what it was in 1980 (8,740,000). The Census Bureau has estimated that the Mexican American population will reach 19 million by the year 2010 (Garwood, 1991:Table 105; U.S. Census, 1991:Table 15). This rate of growth can be attributed to, (1) the high rate of immigration from Mexico, (2) the youth of the population, and (3) the high fertility rate among Mexican Americans. As a result the annual Latino growth rate is three times as great (3.1%) as the national average (0.9%).

Mexican Americans represent 62.6 percent (12.6 million) of the total Latino population and are concentrated in California (48.4%) and in Texas (30.9%). In 1993, Mexican Americans represented 20.6 percent (6,119,000) of the population of California. By the year 2000 they will constitute 30 percent of the state's population (8,931,000) (Fay, et al, 1987:7). In Texas, they represent 22.9 percent of the population (3,891,000) and are heavily concentrated in south Texas and along the U.S.-Mexico border. New Mexico has the largest proportion of Mexican Americans of any state (35%), but only represents 2.6 percent of the total Mexican American population (329,000) (Saenz and Vinas, 1990:472-474).

The city of Los Angeles has the largest population of Mexicans outside of Mexico, with an estimated population of 2.8 million (1992). But the total number of Latinos living in Los Angeles metropolitan area is 4,781,000. San Antonio has the second largest area of concentration of Mexican Americans (448,000), followed by Houston (373,000), El Paso (282,000), Riverside-San Bernardino (252,500), Anaheim-Santa Ana (232,000), San Diego (228,000), Dallas-Fort Worth (225,000), McAllen-Pharr (221,000), San Jose (177,000), Phoenix (177,000), and Albuquerque, (112,000). Historically each of these cities attracted Mexican agriculture and railroad workers. In view of the growth rate of the Mexican American population it is expected that the Mexican origin population in each of these cities will double by the year 2000.

Population Growth and Fertility Rates

Aside from immigration, the rapid growth of the Mexican American population can be attributed to their overall youth and to their high fertility rates

(Stephen and Bean, 1992:74-83). In 1992, their median age was 23.9 years, compared to the national average of 32.9 years. By the year 2000, their median age will be 25, compared to a national average of 36 years. In 1990 two out of five (39%) were 18 or younger, but only four percent were over 65 (Schick and Schick, 1991:17, 18). This means that almost half the population is dependent upon the other for survival, which gives Mexican Americans one of the highest dependency ratios of any group. It also means that a very small proportion of Mexican Americans live to retirement age (4% compared to 14% Anglo), although the elderly population is growing nationwide. The lower life expectancy among Mexican Americans can be attributed to the difficulty of their working lives, to their exposure to unsafe and dangerous working environments, and to the lack of appropriate medical care.

Mexican American women have one of the highest fertility rates of any group in the nation. For example, the birth rate among Mexican Americans is 26.6 live births per 1,000 in the population, compared to only 14.2 among Anglos, 22.9 among African Americans, and 23.5 among all Latinos.

Another indication of their higher fertility rates are the larger family size found among Mexican Americans. The average family size among Latinos in general was 4.28, compared to 3.52 among Anglo Americans in 1970. In 1980 the Latino family size decreased to 3.90, compared to 3.23 among Anglos. By 1990 the average family size among Latinos was 3.76, compared to 3.11 among Anglos (U.S. Census, 1991:Table 67). In 1988 the average family size among Mexican Americans was 4.06, slightly higher than the 3.76 among all Latinos (U.S. Census, 1988:Table 1). In effect this means that on average the Mexican American family in 1993, is about one person larger than the typical Anglo American family.

The larger family size among Mexican Americans can be attributed to three factors, (1) higher fertility rates, (2) recent immigrants sharing accommodations, and (3) the general overcrowding that occurs among the low income families living in America's barrios today (Saenz and Vinas, 1990:Table 1). Much of this overcrowding in the barrios can be attributed to high rents and the effects of residential segregation.

For many years it was assumed that the teachings of the Catholic church were responsible for the high fertility rates among Mexican Americans, but several studies have found that the impact of religion is negligible (Gonzales, 1992b; Sabagh, 1984). And as is true among other groups, the availability of birth control information and contraceptive services reduces the fertility rate among Mexican American women. Overall, the strongest predictor of lower fertility rates among Mexican American women is their level of education, for as education increases fertility rates and family size decreases (Abma and Krivo, 1991:154-159; Bean and Swicegood, 1985).

Income and Occupational Distribution

The larger family size among Latinos in general also means that their annual per capita income is much less than the general population. In 1989 Latino households earned 72 percent ($21,921) of what Anglos earned ($30,406). This means that on average Anglo households earn an average of $707 more a month than Latino households. But in constant dollars Latino household income has only increased by $1,489, in the past fifteen years (U.S. Census, 1991:Table 721 and 722). More than half (55.6%) of the Latino households earned less than $25,000 a year, compared to only two out of five Anglo households (U.S. Census, 1991:Table 723). Among Mexican American men and women, 86.9 percent earn less than $25,000 a year (81.6% of the men and 92.3% of the women) (Schick and Schick, 1991:186).

Even more telling is the fact that the income-gap increases with years of education and job experience. For example, in 1985 Latinos with less than eight years of education earned $13,600, while Anglos earned $14,000, a difference of only $400. But among college graduates Latinos earned $40,000, compared to $47,000; an income gap of $7,000. Furthermore, since Latino households tend to be larger, their per capita annual income is much less (Tienda and Wilson, 1992:673-676).

When annual family income is examined, only one out of three (31.6%) Anglo families earned less than $25,000 in 1989, compared to more than half (53.3%) the Latino families and two out of three of the Mexican American families. Two and a half times as many Mexican American families (28.5%) were living below the poverty level (1989) as compared to Anglo families (10.1%) (Schick and Schick, 1991:186). Four out of ten (39.3%) Latino children lived below the poverty level, compared to only one out of seven (15%) of Anglo children (Melendez, et al, 1991:7-8; Schick and Schick, 1991:218). At the other end of the economic spectrum, five times as many Anglo wage earners (5.5%) made over $50,000 a year (1989), as compared to Mexican American wage earners (1%) (Schick and Schick, 1991:186).

Mexican Americans are underrepresented in white-collar positions and over represented in blue-collar jobs (Stolzenberg, 1990). In 1989, only 10.5 percent were in managerial-professional positions, compared to 26.4 percent in the general population. There were 21.5 percent in technical-sales positions, compared to 31.8 percent in the general population, and 26.3 percent worked as operators and laborers, compared to only 15 percent in the general population (Schick and Schick, 1991:186; U.S. Census, 1991:Table 633).

Overall only one-third (32%) of the Mexican Americans hold white collar positions, compared to about two-thirds of the Anglo Americans in the labor market. The remaining two-thirds (68%) are employed in blue-collar jobs and are concentrated in service jobs (19.3%), craft positions (14.4%), operators and laborers (26.3%), and farm work (8%). This compares to about one-third of the general population who hold blue collar positions (U.S. Census, 1991:Table 633).

When Mexican American men and women were compared there were more women in the professions (12.8% compared to 8.7% men) in technical, sales, and clerical positions (36.8% to 12%) and in service jobs (24.6% to 17.7%). Men were overrepresented in craft positions (19.8% compared to 3% women), operators and laborers (30.7% to 20.9%), and farm laborers (11.1% to 1.9%) (Schick and Schick, 1991:186). Overall, two and a half times more Mexican American women hold white collar positions (49.6%) as compared to Mexican American men (20.7%). Conversely, half the women are employed in blue-collar jobs (50.4%), compared to four out of five of the men (79.3%) (Schick and Schick, 1991:186). This heavy concentration of Mexican Americans in blue-collar jobs means that most are still relegated to the secondary and tertiary sectors of the labor market, with all the disadvantages associated with the lower segment of the labor market.

A Case of Educational Neglect

Even a cursory review of Mexican American history reveals that Mexican Americans have suffered from years of discrimination and neglect, particularly at the hands of the educational establishment. Until recently, it was a common practice for school districts in both Texas and California to maintain separate Mexican schools, which were always underfunded and staffed by the most unqualified and ill prepared teachers (Carter, 1970:9-13).

Texas has a long tradition of maintaining three separate school systems, one for Anglos, one for African Americans, and one for Mexican Americans. Even as late as 1981 a U.S. District Court found that the Texas educational system was guilty of pervasive and invidious discrimination against Mexican Americans (Moore and Pachon, 1985:146). In practice *Brown vs. the Board of Education* (1954) has had little effect on school segregation in Texas. When the High Court ordered Texas to desegregate its public schools Mexican Americans were classified as whites, consequently Mexican Americans and African Americans were mixed at all grade levels to provide the semblance of integration.

One of the reasons the drop-out rate among Mexican Americans is about 55 percent is their long history of educational neglect. Many studies have found that Mexican American children receive less praise and attention from their teachers than Anglo children. The perception among many teachers is that Mexican American children will never complete high school, so why bother (Velez, 1989). This general attitude promotes a self-fulfilling prophecy. Educational neglect is also reflected in the allocation of funds and resources in school districts that have a high concentration of Mexican Americans, since Mexican schools always receive fewer dollars, resources, books, and inferior equipment. Mexican American students are often used for the daily attendance records, so that school districts can be assured of funding, which is rarely distributed equitably.

Figure 10.1
Mexican Americans with Less than 12 Years of Education
By Decade and Age Categories

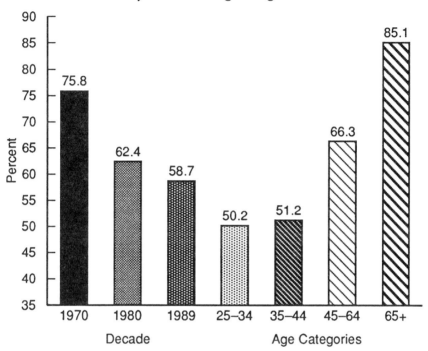

Source: U.S. Census, 1992: Table 226

Another example of educational neglect is the gross underrepresentation of Mexican Americans in the educational system. According to the Census Bureau only 3.7 percent of the nation's teachers are Latinos, and of this small number only about half are Mexican Americans. In Texas and California (where 22.9% and 20.6% of the population are Mexican Americans respectively), only four to seven percent of the teachers, administrators, and counselors are Mexican Americans. This woefully low level of teacher-administrator representation occurs in school districts where 80 to 90 percent of the students are Mexican Americans (Fay, et al, 1987:72; U.S. Census, 1991:Table 26, 652). Likewise a study of Mexican American representation among the faculty of the nine campuses of the University of California system found that of the 7,485 faculty positions, only 152 (i.e., 2%)

were filled by Mexican Americans (Gonzales, 1992a). This situation exists in a state with a population of more than six million Mexican Americans.

The product of educational neglect is educational failure. The statistics on educational achievement among Mexican Americans support this contention (See Figure 10.1). The median years of education for Mexican Americans (25 years and over) today is 10.8 years, compared to 12.7 among Anglo Americans. Four out of ten (40.3%) had eight years of education or less, compared to only one out of ten (10.7%) among the Anglo population. Less than half (44.6%) of the Mexican Americans today graduate from high school, compared to eight out of ten (78.4%) of the Anglo Americans. And three times as many Anglo Americans (21.8%) graduate from college, as Mexican Americans (7.1%) (Schick and Schick, 1991:94; U.S. Census, 1991:Table 225).

However, when Latinos do attend college they will most likely enroll in a community college (80% across the nation do so), and less than seven percent transfer to four year institutions (Cal SCHA, 1985) (See Figure 10.2).

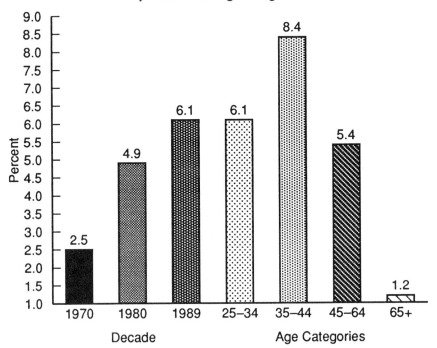

Figure 10.2
Mexican Americans with Four Years of College or More
By Decade and Age Categories

Source: U.S. Census, 1992: Table 226

238

The community college is primarily used by Mexican Americans for vocational training and is often a terminal educational experience. And it is still true that more Mexican American males attend college (19.5%) and graduate from college (8.1%), than Mexican American females (16.6% and 6% respectively)

Undocumented Immigration

It should be obvious to everyone that the flow of illegal aliens across the border will continue so long as there is a demand by American employers for cheap labor and so long as the depressed economic conditions in Mexico force workers to seek better opportunities in the United States. Although thousands of illegals are apprehended and deported annually, thousands more find employment in the tertiary labor market (Gonzales, 1984).

Despite the passage of the Immigration Reform Act of 1986, that imposed sanctions on employers who hire undocumented aliens, the number of Mexican undocumented aliens living in the United States remains at approximately two to four million (Bean, et al, 1986:24). Though the actual number of undocumented aliens living in the United States today is still the source of much debate (Garcia, 1991:29; Heer, 1990:34-53). Illegals continue to cross the border for the same reasons that all immigrants come to America, that is to find work and to improve their lives. What the public fails to understand is that American employers depend on their labor. Contrary to the popular opinion that undocumented workers are taking jobs away from American citizens, they are in fact making a significant contribution to the American economy (Massey, 1987).

One of their most obvious contributions to the American economy is their support of the wage differential, which represents the difference between what employers would normally pay an American employee and the wages that are commonly offered to undocumented aliens (Portes and Rumbaut, 1990:79-83). For example, one study found that undocumented workers only received 60 percent of the average hourly wage paid to similarly employed American workers (North and Houstoun, 1976:124). In practical terms, this means that if an employer normally payed an American worker $10 an hour, then he/she would only pay an undocumented alien $6 an hour. When projected over a year this means that an employer could save $8,000 in wages per undocumented worker. Based on labor costs alone, an employer would save $800,000 a year by hiring one hundred undocumented aliens (Chiswick, 1988: 98-102; Gonzales, 1985b).

Unfortunately the presence of undocumented aliens in the labor market has contributed to the creation of an underclass of workers in American society. This results when illegals are paid less than the minimum wage. In the long term wages are depressed in those industries and regions where undocumented aliens are concentrated. Therefore this has a direct effect on the wages paid to Mexican Americans in the Southwest. For example, one study found that, after controlling for various socio-economic factors, an annual income difference of $1,680 (or 20%) existed between the border regions of Texas and comparable non-border regions (Smith and Newman, 1977). In a real sense, these areas of heavy concentration of undocumented aliens are viewed as labor reservations (Portes and Rumbaut, 1990:222-226).

Undocumented aliens also serve as economic shock absorbers for the American economy. The shock absorber effect is brought into play when our economy is expanding and there is a need for an abundance of laborers. But during a recession, the illegals are expelled at the bottom. The most noteworthy examples of this expulsion of surplus labor occurred during the Great Depression (the Repatriation Program), during the recessions following the Korean War (Operation Wetback) and the Vietnam War, and during the recession of 1992. Undocumented aliens also serve as convenient scapegoats for the economic woes and are often blamed for a whole host of social and economic problems.

The availability of Mexican undocumented workers is particularly important to those businesses where labor costs represent the major portion of an entrepreneur's expenditures. Statistically most illegals are employed in large urban areas by employers who hire fifty workers or less (Cornelius, et al, 1982:34). These tend to be businesses such as restaurants; garment factories, hotel and motels, hospitals and convalescent homes, small fabricating shops, assembly line work (e.g., electronic components), gardening and landscape work, and light construction. These are all businesses where the work is unskilled or low-skilled, physically demanding, requires long hours, pays low wages, and is often hazardous to the health and safety of the workers (Chavez, 1992:101-106). Obviously, these are the characteristics of the tertiary labor market.

In the long term, it is not only American employers who benefit from the labor of undocumented workers, but the American consumer also benefits. American consumers benefit because they can pay less for a whole host of products that would normally sell at much higher prices, if it were not for the availability of cheap Mexican labor.

Chapter Summary

When Mexico gained its independence from Spain in 1821 thousands of Mexicans were already settled throughout the American Southwest. While the signing of the Treaty of Guadalupe Hidalgo (1848) ended the war between Mexico and the United States, it also marked a new period in the social and economic history of the Mexican population in the Southwest.

During the latter part of the nineteenth century, and the early part of the twentieth century, Mexican laborers were encouraged to migrate north across the border to provide the labor needed for the construction of railroads, highways, and irrigation systems. They also formed the backbone of the labor force in the agricultural and mining industry in the Southwest.

With the onset of the Great Depression the welcome mat was no longer set out for Mexican laborers. As a result of the economic hard times and the scarcity of jobs, racial tensions ran high. One solution to the unemployment problem, was to send the Mexicans back to Mexico. Under their Repatriation Program thousands of Mexicans, many of whom were American citizens, were shipped back to Mexico on chartered trains.

Following the Second World War Mexican Americans took advantage of their veterans benefits and obtained higher educations and learned new skills. In their efforts to improve their social and economic conditions they organized themselves and became active participants in the political arena. During the Civil Rights Movement young Chicanos throughout the Southwest marched and protested in an effort to secure their rights and improve their opportunities for success in American society.

References

Abma, Joyce C. and Lauren J. Krivo
1991   "The Ethnic Context of Mexican American Fertility."
        Sociological Perspectives 34(2):145-164.

Acuña, Rodolfo
1988   *Occupied America: A History of Chicanos.* New York:
        Harper & Row (3rd Edition).

Baca-Zinn, Maxine
1975   "Political Familism: Toward Sex Role Equality in Chicano
        Families." *Aztlan* 6:13-26.

Bean, Frank D. and Gray Swicegood
1985   *Mexican American Fertility Patterns.* Austin: University
        of Texas Press.

Bean, Frank, and Alan King, Jeffrey Passel
1986   "Estimates of the Size of the Illegal Migrant Population of
        Mexican Origin in the United States: An Assessment, Review
        and Proposal." In *Mexican Immigrants and Mexican Americans:
        An Evolving Relation.* Harley L. Browning and Rodolfo De La
        Garza (eds.), Austin: Center for Mexican American Studies,
        The University of Texas, Pp. 13-36.

Cal-SCHA
1985   *Education Reform in California: An Hispanic Community
        Appraisal, First Term Report to Superintendent of Public Instruc-
        tion Bill Honig.* Sacramento: California Superintendent's
        Council on Hispanic Affairs, April.

Camarillo, Albert M.
1971   "The G.I. Generation." *Aztlan* 2:145-150.

Cardoso, Lawrence A.
1980   Mexican Emigration to the United States, 1897-1931: Socio-
        Economic Patterns. Tucson: University of Arizona Press.

Carter, Thomas P.
1970   *Mexican Americans in School: A History of Educational
        Neglect.* New York: College Entrance Examination Board.

Chavez, Leo R.
1992   *Shadowed Lives: Undocumented Immigrants in American Society.*
        NY: Harcourt Brace Javanovich.

Chiswick, Barry R.
1988   *Illegal Aliens: Their Employment and Employers.*
        Kalamazoo, MI: W. E. Upjohn Institute.

Cockcroft, James D.
1986   *Outlaws in the Promised Land: Mexican Immigrant
        Workers and America's Future.* New York: Grove Press, Inc.

Copp, Nelson G.

1971   'Wetbacks' and Braceros: Mexican Migrant Laborers and American Immigration Policy, 1930-1960. San Francisco: R. and E. Research Associates, (1963).

Cornelius, Wayne A., et al

1982   "Mexican Immigrants and Southern California: A Summary of Current Knowledge." La Jolla, CA: Working Paper in U.S.-Mexican Studies, No. 36, University of California San Diego.

De La Garza, Rudolph O.

1974   "Voting Patterns in 'Bi-Cultural El Paso': A Contextual Analysis of Chicano Voting Behavior." Aztlan 5:235- 260.

De Leon, Arnoldo

1982   The Tejano Community, 1836-1900. Albuquerque, NM: University of New Mexico Press.

Department of Industrial Relations

1930   Mexicans in California: Report of Governor C.C. Young's Mexican Fact-Finding Committee. San Francisco: State Printing Office.

Dieppa, Ismael

1973   The Zoot Suit Riots Revisited: The Role of Private Philanthropy in Youth Problems of Mexican-Americans. Los Angeles: University of Southern California Press.

Dvorin, Eugene P. and Arthur J. Misner

1966   California Politics and Policies. Palo Alto: Addison Wesley.

Fay, James S., and S.W. Fay, R.J. Boehm

1987   California Almanac (3rd Edition). Santa Barbara, CA: Pacific Data Resources.

Fernandez, Raul

1977   The United States-Mexico Border: A Political Economic Profile. Notre Dame, IN: The University of Notre Dame.

Fogelson, Robert M.

1969   The Los Angeles Riots. NY: New York Times Books.

Foley, Douglas E.

1978   From Peones to Politicos: Ethnic Relations in a South Texas Town, 1900-1977 (Monograph No. 5). Austin: University of Texas Press.

Gann, L. H. and Peter J. Duignan

1986   The Hispanics in the United States: A History. Boulder, CO: Westview Press.

Garcia, Alejandro

1991   "The Changing Demographic Face of Hispanics in the United States." In Empowering Hispanic Families: A Critical Issue for the '90s. Marta Sotomayor (ed.), Milwaukee, WI: Family Service America. Pp. 21-38.

Garcia, Juan R.
1980   *Operation Wetback: The Mass Deportation of Mexican Undocumented Workers in 1954.* Westport, CT: Greenwood Press.

Garwood, Alfred N.
1991   *Hispanic Americans: A Statistical Sourcebook.* Boulder, CO: Numbers and Concepts.

Gonzales, Juan L. Jr.
1984   *The Tertiary Labor Force and the Role of Undocumented Mexican Laborers in the American Economy.* El Paso: The Center for Inter-American and Border Studies, University of Texas.

1985a   *Mexican and Mexican American Farm Workers: The California Agricultural Industry.* New York: Praeger Press.

1985b   "The Contributions of Undocumented Mexican Laborers to the American Economy." *Free Inquiry in Creative Sociology* Vol. 13 (May)

1986   "The Origins of the Chicano Family in Mexico and the American Southwest." *The International Journal of Sociology of the Family* 16:181-196.

1992a   "Survey of Chicano Faculty at the University of California." San Francisco: Research report prepared for Latino Issues Forum. August 20.

1992b   "Fertility Rates Among Mexican Americans: An Analysis of the Causal Factors." Paper presented at the Annual Meetings of the California Sociological Association, San Diego, CA. October 16-18.

Grebler, Leo
1966   *Mexican Immigration to the United States.* Los Angeles: Graduate School of Business Administration, University of California Advanced Report #2.

Griswold Del Castillo, Richard
1984   *La Familia: Chicano Families in the Urban Southwest, 1848 to the Present.* Notre Dame: University of Notre Dame Press.

Heer, David M.
1990   *Undocumented Mexicans in the United States.* Cambridge: Cambridge University Press.

Hoffman, Abraham
1974   *Unwanted Mexican-Americans in the Great Depression: Repatriation Pressures 1929-1939.* Tucson: University of Arizona Press.

Hoffman, Mark S.
1993   *The World Almanac and Book of Facts 1993.* New York: Pharos Books.

Johnson, Otto
1992   *Information Please Almanac.* Boston: Houghton Mifflin.
Majka, Linda C. and Theo J. Majka
1982   *Farm Workers, Agribusiness, and the State.* Philadelphia: Temple University Press.
Marquez, Benjamin
1988   "The League of United Latin American Citizens and the Politics of Ethnicity." In *Latino Empowerment: Progress, Problems, and Prospects.* Roberto E. Villarreal, N. G. Hernandez and H. D. Neighbor (eds.), Westport, CT: Greenwood Press, Pp. 11- 24.
Massey, Douglas S.
1987   "Understanding Mexican Migration to the United States." *American Journal of Sociology* 92:1372-1403.
McWilliams, Carey
1933   "Getting Rid of the Mexicans." *The American Mercury* 28:322-324 (March).
1943   "Zoot Suit Riots." *New Republic* 108(25):818-820 (June 21).
1968   *North From Mexico: The Spanish-Speaking People of the United States.* New York: Greenwood Press.
1971   *Factories in the Field: The Story of Migratory Farm Labor in California.* Santa Barbara: Peregrine Publishers.
Meier, Matt and Feliciano Rivera
1972   *The Chicanos.* NY: Hill and Wang.
1981   *Dictionary of Mexican American History.* Westport: CT Greenwood Press.
Melendez, Edwin and C. E. Rodriguez, J. B. Figueroa
1991   "Hispanics in the Labor Force: An Introduction to Issues and Approaches." In *Hispanics in the Labor Force: Issues and Policies.* Edwin Melendez, C. E. Rodriguez, and J. B. Figueroa (eds.), NY: Plenum. Pp. 1-21.
Moore, Joan and Harry Pachon
1985   *Hispanics in the United States.* Englewood Cliffs, NJ: Prentice-Hall, Inc.
Moquin, Wayne and Charles Van Doren
1971   *A Documentary History of the Mexican Americans.* New York: Bantam Books.
Morales, Armando
1972   *Ando Sangrando (I Am Bleeding): A Study of Mexican American-Police Conflict.* Fair Lawn, N.J.: R. E. Burdick.
Morin, Raul
1963   *Among the Valiant.* Los Angeles: Borden Publishing Co.
Navarro, Armando
1974   "The Evolution of Chicano Politics." *Aztlan* 5:57-84.

North, David and Marion F. Houstoun
1976   *The Characteristics and Role of Illegal Aliens in the U.S. Labor Market: An Exploratory Study.* Washington, D.C.: Linton & Co., Inc.

Pachon, Harry
1983   "Hispanic Underrepresentation in the Federal Bureaucracy: The Missing Link in Policy Process." In *The State of Chicano Research on Family, Labor, and Migration.* Armando Valdez, et al (eds.), Stanford: Stanford Center for Chicano Research, Pp. 209-218.

Pitt, Leonard
1971   *The Decline of the Californios: A Social History of the Spanish-Speaking Californians, 1846-1890.* Berkeley: University of California Press.

Portes, Alejandro and Ruben G. Rumbaut
1990   *Immigrant America: A Portrait.* Berkeley: University of California Press.

Ramos, Henry A.
1982   *A People Forgotten, A Dream Pursued: The History of the American G.I. Forum 1948-1972.* Corpus Christi, TX: American G.I. Forum's National Historical Foundation and Archives.

Reisler, Mark
1976   *By the Sweat of Their Brow: Mexican Immigrant Labor in the United States, 1900-1940.* Westport, CT: Greenwood.

Sabagh, Georges
1984   "Fertility Expectations and Behavior Among Mexican Americans in Los Angeles, 1973-1982." *Social Science Quarterly* 65:594-608.

Saenz, Rogelio and Jaime Vinas
1990   "Chicano Geographic Segregation: A Human Ecological Approach." *Sociological Perspectives* 33(4):465-481.

Schick, Frank L. and Renee Schick (eds.)
1991   *Statistical Handbook on U.S. Hispanics.* Phoenix, AZ: Oryx Press.

Smith, Barton and Robert Newman
1977   "Depressed Wages Along the U.S.-Mexico Border: An Empirical Analysis." *Economic Inquiry* 15:51-66.

Stephen, Elizabeth H. and Frank D. Bean
1992   "Assimilation, Disruption and the Fertility of Mexican-Origin Women in the United States." *International Migration Review* 26(1):67-88.

Stolzenberg, Ross M.
1990   "Ethnicity, Geography and Occupational Achievement of
          Hispanic Men." *American Sociological Review* 55:143-154.
Taylor, Paul S.
1930   *Mexican Labor in the United States: Dimit County, Winter
          Garden District, South Texas.* Berkeley: University of California
          Publications in Economics, Vol. 6, No. 5.
Tienda, Marta and Franklin D. Wilson
1992   "Migration and the Earnings of Hispanic Men." *American
          Sociological Review* 57(5):661-678.
U.S. Census
1985a   *Projections of the Hispanic Population:* 1983-2080.
          Washington, D.C.: USGPO Current Population Reports,
          Series P-25, No. 995.
1985b   *Persons of Spanish Origin in the United States: March
          1985 (Advance Report).* Washington, D.C.:USGPO Current
          Population Reports, Series P-2O, No. 403, December.
1988   *The Hispanic Population in the United States: March 1988
          (Advance Report).* Washington, D.C.:USGPO Current Popula-
          tion Reports, Series P-2O, No. 431, August.
1991   *Statistical Abstract of the United States, 1991* (111th
          Edition). Washington, D.C.:USGPO. U.S. Civil Rights
1974   *Toward Quality Education for Mexican Americans.*
          Washington, D.C.: U.S. Commission on Civil Rights,
          Mexican American Study Report No. 4 (February).
Valdes y Tapia, Daniel
1976   *Hispanos and American Politics.* NY: Arno Press.
Velez, William
1989   "High School Attrition Among Hispanic and Non-Hispanic
          Youths." *Sociology of Education* 62:119-133.
Wright, John W.
1993   *The Universal Almanac 1993.* Kansas City, KS: Andrews
          and McMeel.

1519	Hernan Cortes landed in Mexico.
1821	Cortes defeated the Aztecs at Tenochtitlan.
1598	Juan de Oñate founded the first Spanish settlement in New Mexico, which he named San Gabriel.
1769	Father Junipero Serra founded the mission at San Diego.
1810	Father Miguel Hidalgo gave the battle cry of *El Grito de Dolores*, on September 16 and started the Mexican Revolution.
1821	Mexico gained its independence from Spain.
1836	General Santa Anna was defeated at the Battle of San Jacinto and forced to sign the Treat of Velasco, that created the Lone Star Republic.
1845	The United States Annexed Texas.
1846	The United States declared war on Mexico on May 13.
1848	The Treaty of Guadalupe Hidalgo was signed.
1859	The Gadsden Purchase was signed.
1862	French forces were defeated by Mexican troops at Puebla on May 5 (*Cinco de Mayo*).
1880	Bureau of the Census estimates a Mexican population of 230,000 in the U.S.
1910	Start of the Mexican Revolution.
1916	Ezequiel Cabeza de Vaca was elected the first Mexican American governor (New Mexico) in U.S. history.
1917	Thousands of Mexican Americans fought for their country during World War I.
1921	*La Orden de Hijos de Americas* was founded in San Antonio.
1924	The Border Patrol was founded.
1927	*La Confederacion de Uniones Obreras Mexicanas* (CUOM) was organized in southern California.
1928	The League of United Latin American Citizens (LULAC) was founded in Corpus Christi, Texas.
1929	Thousands of Mexicans, many of whom were American citizens, were repatriated to Mexico during the Great Depression.
1933	El Monte (California) Berry Strike resulted in the organization of a Mexican American farm labor union.
1942	The Bracero Program was established by the U.S. government to supply Mexican labor during the war.
1943	The Zoot-Suit riots of Los Angeles.
1946	Seventeen Mexican Americans were awarded the Congressional Medal of Honor for their acts of valor during World War Two.

1948	The American G.I. Forum was founded in Corpus Christi, Texas.
1953	The Council of Mexican American Affairs was found in Los Angeles.
1954	Operation Wetback deported more than a million Mexicans.
1959	The Mexican American Political Association (MAPA) was founded in southern California.
1963	Cesar Chavez began organizing farm laborers in the central valley of California.
1964	The Bracero Program was officially terminated.
1965	Joseph M. Montoya was elected to the U.S. Senate from New Mexico.
1965	The Delano grape strike was called by Cesar Chavez.
1966	Rodolfo Corky Gonzales formed the Crusade for Justice in Denver.
1966	Starr County (Texas) melon strike was called.
1967	Jose Angel Gutierrez founded the Mexican American Youth Organization (MAYO) in San Antonio.
1967	David Sanchez organized the Brown berets in Los Angeles.
1967	The Mexican American Legal Defense Education Fund (MALDEF) was organized in Texas.
1968	*El Plan de Santa Barbara* resulted from a conference held by Chicano activists.
1969	Corky Gonzales founded La Raza Unida Party in Colorado.
1969	*El Movimiento Estudiantil Chicano de Aztlan* (MECHA) was organized by Chicano college students.
1970	Jose Angel Gutierrez formed *La Raza Unida* Party in Crystal City, Texas.
1972	Ramona Acosta Bañuelos became the first Mexican American treasurer of the United States.
1974	Raul H. Castro was elected the first Mexican American governor of Arizona.
1974	Jerry Apodaca was elected governor of New Mexico.
1978	Cesar Chavez and the UFW ended their strike against lettuce growers, table grapes, and Gallo.
1980	Professor Julian Nava appointed the first Mexican American ambassador to Mexico.
1988	Lauro F. Cavazos appointed U.S. Secretary of Education.
1989	Manuel Lujan Jr. appointed U.S. Secretary of the Interior.
1992	Cesar Chavez died in April.

Stephen F. Austin Hernando Cortez Edward Roybal
Hector Garcia Felix Longoria Cesar Chavez

Key Terms

at-large elections
Bracero Program
Chicano Movement
Community Service Organization (CSO)
Federal Reclamation Act (1902)
Immigration Reform Act of 1986
League of United Latin American Citizens
Mexican American Political Association
Operation Wetback
patron
Repatriation Program
Sleepy Lagoon Case
tractable labor
Zoot Suit Riots

Battle of San Jacinto
campesinos
Mejicanos
gerrymandering
Mexican Revolution (1910)
Manifest Destiny
mojados
mutualistas
palomillas
Public Law 78
shock absorber effect
surplus labor
Treaty of Guadalupe Hidalgo

Sample Test Questions

1. List and discuss four important historical events in the history of Mexican Americans in the Southwest between 1836 and 1930.
2. Discuss the contributions made by Mexican labor to the development of four major industries in the Southwest.
3. List and discuss five of the most important push-pull factors that attracted Mexican labor to the Southwest at the turn of the century.
4. Provide a brief discussion of the following historical events: the Bracero Program, Operation Wetback, sleepy lagoon, and the zoot suit riots.
5. Provide four examples of effective political participation among Mexican Americans. Be prepared to discuss and provide specific information for each example.
6. Discuss four major problems facing Mexican Americans today.

Chapter 11

The Puerto Rican Experience

Latinos vs. Hispanics

The official Bureau of the Census designation of any person who is of Spanish origin or descent is Hispanic. The word Hispanic derives from the Latin word *Hispania*, designating residents of the Iberian Peninsula. In 1980, the U.S. Census adopted the term to designate all those who are of Spanish/Hispanic origin or descent, and includes, (1) Mexicans, Mexican Americans, Chicanos, (2) Puerto Ricans, (3) Cubans, (4) Central and South Americans, and (5) Other Hispanics. However, some in the Spanish Speaking community prefer the term Latino or Latina (from *Latino Americano/a*), as it is a cultural-linguistic term encompassing all groups in the Americas who share the Spanish language, culture, and traditions (Padilla, 1985:60-83).

In 1990 there were 20,505,000 Latinos in the United States, representing 8.2 percent of the population. This estimate does not include the 3.4 million Puerto Ricans living in Puerto Rico, but does include an estimated 1.3 million undocumented aliens. In 1993 the population of Latinos in the United States was approximately 22 million. By the year 2000, the Latino population in the United States is expected to reach 25.2 million (Garcia, 1991:Table 6).

The Latino population is recognized for its rapid rate of growth. In 1950 there were only four million Latinos in the population, which increased to 6.9 million in 1960. By 1970 there were 10.5 million and their numbers increased (by 60 percent) to 14.6 million in 1980. In 1990 their total population increased to 20.5 million. By the year 2000, Latinos will become the largest minority group in the United States, at 25.2 million (U.S. Census, 1991:Table 15). Their average growth rate of 60 percent is well above the 9.5

percent growth rate of the general U.S. population, and is still higher than the 18 percent growth rate among African Americans.

Most of the 20.5 million Latinos in the United States (1990) are of Mexican origin, followed by the Puerto Ricans, Cubans, Central and South Americans, and Other Hispanics (See Figure 11.1). The 3.5 million Puerto Ricans living in Puerto Rico were not included in this estimate, but if they were included they would account for 28 percent of the total.

Figure 11.1
Composition of U.S. Latino Population, 1990

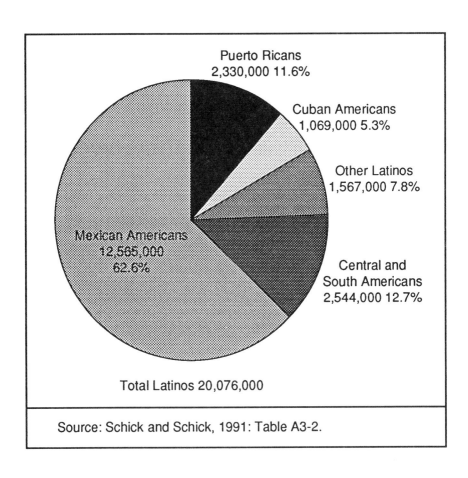

Puerto Ricans
2,330,000 11.6%

Cuban Americans
1,069,000 5.3%

Other Latinos
1,567,000 7.8%

Central and
South Americans
2,544,000 12.7%

Mexican Americans
12,565,000
62.6%

Total Latinos 20,076,000

Source: Schick and Schick, 1991: Table A3-2.

In 1990 seven out of ten of all Latinos lived in four states, California (7,688,000 or 34%), Texas (4,340,000 or 19%), New York (2,214,000 or 10%), and Florida (1,574,000 or 7%). Most Latinos living in California (85%) and Texas (90%) are of Mexican origin, while most Latinos living in

New York (60%) are Puerto Ricans, and most of those living in Florida are Cubans (70%). Of these areas, California experienced the most dramatic rate of growth between 1980 and 1990 (166.3%), followed by Florida (151.3%), Texas (122.1%), and New York (102.8%). According to the 1990 Census the largest concentration of Latinos in the major metropolitan areas occurred in Los Angeles (4.8 million), New York (2.8 million), Miami (1.6 million), San Francisco (969,215), Chicago (895,326 million), Houston (771,888), and San Antonio (620,000).

Introduction

In view of the availability of bargain flights between San Juan and New York City following the Second World War, the Puerto Rican population on the mainland has increased dramatically. In 1940 there were 70,000 Puerto Ricans living on the mainland, and by 1950 there were 300,000, a better than fourfold increase. By 1960 there were 855,000 Puerto Ricans living on the mainland and by 1970 there were 1.4 million. Their population reached 2,013,943 in 1980. In 1990 there were 2,330,000 Puerto Ricans living in the U.S. mainland. Today (1993) their mainland population is estimated at 2,727,754 (Hoffman, 1993:388).

For historic reasons, mainland Puerto Ricans are concentrated in New York City, and live primarily in East Harlem, the Bronx, and Brooklyn (Chenault, 1970; Sanchez, 1983). In 1990 half (45%) were living in New York state. Altogether almost two-thirds live in either New York or New Jersey. More recent settlement patterns reveal that they have settled in other areas, such as Chicago, Philadelphia, Los Angeles, Miami, San Francisco, and Boston.

Though many people refer to the Puerto Rican immigration to the United States, they are not really immigrants, but rather they are migrants to the mainland. But in a historical sense they were immigrants, since they, (1) entered an alien English speaking environment, (2) experienced social resistance to their entry, and (3) they have suffered from discrimination, segregation, and economic exploitation (Miranda, 1974). Much like the Mexicans and the Filipinos, Puerto Ricans also were also the victims of U.S. military conquest and historically have been treated as a conquered people.

The Conquest of Puerto Rico

The island of Puerto Rico was discovered by Columbus during his second voyage to the New World on November 19, 1493. When Columbus landed on the island it was inhabited by 50,000 Tainos Indians. Ponce de Leon founded the first settlement in Caparra in 1510 and quickly pressed the

Indians into forced labor (Hauberg, 1974:13). De Leon forced the Tainos to work in the mines, in agriculture, and on cattle ranches established by the Spanish. The Indians were forcefully pressed into the labor intensive needs of commercial production and were subjected to the relentless indoctrination of the Spanish missionaries (Cruz-Monclova, 1958:20-56; Golding, 1973).

By 1530 most of Indians had died of a combination of smallpox and exhaustion, and their rapidly dwindling population was soon replaced by slave labor (Moscoso, 1980:22-23). By the mid-nineteenth century (1846) there were 51,000 slaves in Puerto Rico, out of a population of 440,000 (Cordasco, 1973:4). Most of the slaves were required to work on tobacco and sugar plantations. The island was beset with slave revolts and a host of social and health problems. The Spanish finally abolished slavery in 1873.

Following years of social unrest and political agitation Spain granted Puerto Rico its independence on November 25, 1897. Three months later the American battleship *U.S.S. Maine* was blown-up in Havana Harbor. On April 21, 1898, Congress declared war on Spain (Golding, 1973:94). American troops landed on the south coast of Puerto Rico on July 25. On October 18, 1898 the Spanish flag was lowered for the last time in Old San Juan and was replaced with the Stars and Stripes.

The Treaty of Paris, ending the war between the United States and Spain, was signed on April 11, 1899. As a result of the Treaty, Puerto Rico became a colony of the United States and served as a base for U.S. naval operations in the Caribbean. As in the Philippines, the President appointed a military governor in Puerto Rico to administer the government and manage internal affairs.

The American Influence

Following the military conquest of Puerto Rico the American way of life became the law of the land. The American governor of the island was advised by a two-chamber legislative body. All decisions of the Puerto Rican legislature required the approval of the U.S. governor and any actions of these representatives could be nullified by the U.S. Congress (Golding, 1973:109-110). Without any doubt the people of Puerto Rico realized that they were now a colony of the United States.

From the onset English was designated the official language of government and commerce. In March of 1903, the U. S. government established the University of Puerto Rico. The idea was that the children of the elite families of the island would be educated to accept the American way of life and American values. In response to a critical labor shortage in the United States during the First World War, Puerto Ricans were granted American citizenship under the provisions of the Jones Act (1917). But this also made all Puerto Rican men eligible for the draft.

On the positive side, the first thirty years of American domination of Puerto Rico brought about much needed improvements in education, health care, transportation, and the development of commerce. But these improvements in the infrastructure also meant that these healthy and literate Puerto Ricans would make better factory workers and farm laborers (Falcon, 1991:147-150).

With the development of manufacturing, the agricultural industry was transformed into an export industry with heavy capital investment in sugar and coffee production. The value of Puerto Rican exports in 1901 was only $8.5 million but increased to $103.5 million in 1928, with sugar exports representing about half the total (Christopulos, 1980:136).

Following years of internal political turmoil and external conflict with the United States, Puerto Rico became a Commonwealth in 1948, and elected its first governor, Luis Muñoz Marin (1948-1964). Puerto Rico's new political standing, know as *Estado Libre Asociado* (Associated Free State), meant that while Puerto Ricans are U.S. citizens and can elect their governor, they cannot vote in Presidential elections and do not have representatives in Congress. But they are subject to all federal laws and their judicial system derives from the U.S. legal system (Cripps, 1984). While Puerto Ricans pay local taxes, they do not pay federal income taxes. Of course all Puerto Ricans born on or living in the mainland enjoy all the rights and duties of citizenship granted to all U.S. citizens.

Background to Migration

Though some Puerto Ricans migrated to the U.S. mainland shortly after their colonization, their numbers did not become significant until after 1930. By one account there were no more than 1,600 Puerto Ricans living in the mainland in 1910 (Chenault, 1970:53). A decade later their population increased to 12,000. In 1930 there were more than 53,000 Puerto Ricans on the mainland. By 1940 their population increased to more than 70,000.

As with thousands of other immigrants to America, the Puerto Ricans also had their reasons for leaving their homeland, but in addition to the common push-pull factors of poverty, unemployment, overpopulation, and the wage differential, there were also planned structural factors that prompted their migration (Davis, 1953; Senior, 1953). When the U.S. government colonized Puerto Rico, it instituted a policy of modernization (Lopez, 1980).

The most important of these new policies was the land closure movement, whereby American investors were allowed to purchase thousands of acres of land below market value, prepare it for commercial production (primarily in sugar and tobacco), and mechanized the production process (Mintz, 1960). As a result of this policy, thousands of farm workers were displaced and forced into a life of poverty. Out of desperation thousands of peasants moved to the urban centers, primarily to San Juan and Ponce, where most of them sank into a life of squalor and despair (LaRuffa, 1971). For many the only way to escape a life of poverty was to travel to the mainland (Davis, 1953). Most of these displaced migrants found work in the garment industry of New York, and others followed the agricultural harvest in New Jersey (Falcon, 1991:150-154).

Puerto Rican migration can be viewed as having occurred in three distinct stages:

1. The Pioneer Migration (1900-1945): consisting primarily of landless peasants and unskilled laborers.
2. The Great Migration (1946-1964): primarily based in New York City and concentrated in blue collar jobs.
3. The Revolving Door Migration (1965-Present): based on the movement of families between Puerto Rico and the mainland.

The Pioneer Migration: 1900-1945

Like thousands of other immigrants, the first Puerto Rican migrants were drawn to the mainland by their search for new opportunities. While most were unskilled and poorly educated, many found jobs in the labor intensive industrial sectors of New York City (Sanchez, 1983). Others found work as farm laborers and followed the crops from the heartland of New Jersey to the humid orange groves of southern Florida (Maldonado-Denis, 1980:83-88).

But the early movement of Puerto Ricans to the mainland was not significant, as their average flow was about 2,000 per year between 1909 and 1930. This minimal flow was further reduced to 900 a year during the Great Depression (Senior, 1965:39). By 1930, 53,000 Puerto Ricans were dispersed across the 48 states. In 1939 there were 63,000 Puerto Ricans living in New York, and only 1,900 in California, 780 in New Jersey, and 607 in Pennsylvania (Senior, 1953:130). Those who lived in New York settled in East Harlem, between 96th and 130th streets (Alers, 1985; Sanchez, 1988; Sexton, 1965:6-7).

While most migrants perceived their move to the mainland as an opportunity to improve their lives, some were disappointed by the life they found in the big city (Sanchez, 1988). In their homeland Puerto Ricans did not make sharp distinctions between racial groups, rather they related to people in terms of their social and economic position. But on the mainland Puerto Rican migrants were confronted with discrimination and residential segregation, based on their ethnicity and race (Morales, 1986:45-58). For example, in Manhattan (during the 1920's) they discovered that light skinned Puerto Ricans were accepted in the working class neighborhoods on the west side and around the Navy yard in Brooklyn. But the dark skinned Puerto Ricans were only accepted in upper Manhattan, where they served as a buffer group between Black Harlem on the west and the Italians to the east (Rodriguez, 1980).

The Great Migration: 1946-1964

Following the Second World War the flow of Puerto Ricans to the mainland exceeded all previous records. Between 1946 and 1964 a total of 615,000 migrants arrived in the mainland, for an average annual flow of 34,000. The high point in the migration was reached in 1953, when 74,600 Puerto Rican migrants arrived (See Table 11.1).

Several factors serve to explain this very rapid rate of migration. An important factor was the introduction of commercial air service between San Juan and New York City, following the Second World War. Before the War, the journey could only be made by boat, which took five days and cost around $150. Following the War, Puerto Ricans could purchase an airline ticket for $64 and land in New York City seven hours later (Levine, 1987:95-98; Senior, 1953:131). This became the first airborne migration in history.

The push-pull factors in the Great Migration were similar to those affecting other immigrants, mainly to escape from poverty and to find work. In addition some viewed the Great Migration as an escape valve, as it relieved the pressure of population growth in Puerto Rico (Davis, 1953; Maldonado, 1976). The basic human resources and the capacity of the infrastructure of the Puerto Rican economy could no longer support the growing population of the island. If the children born to these migrants are considered, it is estimated that almost two million Puerto Ricans were displaced by the Great Migration (Hernandez, 1967:13-28). Without this escape value it is very likely that the people of Puerto Rico would have, at some point, resorted to open rebellion (Maldonado-Denis, 1980:47).

On the pull side of the equation, the Puerto Ricans that arrived during this period were better educated, had a variety of job experiences, and were more motivated, that is when compared to the general population of the island (Sandis, 1973). This dramatic flow of migrants supplied American capitalists with an ideal source of unskilled labor for their factories, assembly plants, and farms (Hernandez, 1968).

The introduction of television into Puerto Rico also encouraged many to migrate, as they wanted to partake of the American lifestyle. Returning migrants, most of whom made it a point to display their new found success, also did their part to stimulate the flow of migrants. Before long friends and relatives living in New York City did their part to encourage migration, as having family and friends ready to assist new arrivals went a long way in encouraging the Great Migration (Doyle, 1982; Macisco, 1968).

Table 11.1
Migration Between Puerto Rico And
The U.S. Mainland, 1946-1974

Fiscal Year	Traveled to U.S. Mainland	Traveled to Puerto Rico	Net Migration to U.S. Mainland
1946	70,618	45,997	24,621
1947	136,259	101,115	35,144
1948	132,523	104,492	28,031
1949	157,338	124,252	33,086
1950	170,727	136,572	34,155
1951	188,898	146,978	41,920
1952	258,884	197,226	61,658
1953	304,910	230,307	74,603
1954	303,007	258,798	44,209
1955	315,491	284,309	31,182
1956	380,950	319,303	61,647
1957	439,656	391,372	48,284
1958	467,987	442,031	25,956
1959	557,701	520,489	37,212
1960	666,756	643,014	23,742
1961	681,982	668,182	13,800
1962	807,549	796,186	11,363
1963	930,666	925,868	4,798
1964	1,076,403	1,072,037	4,366
1965	1,265,096	1,254,338	10,758
1966	1,475,228	1,445,139	30,089
1967	1,628,909	1,594,735	34,174
1968	1,858,151	1,839,470	18,681
1969	2,105,217	2,112,264	-7,047
1970	1,495,587	1,479,447	16,140
1971	1,566,723	1,605,414	-38,691
1972	—	—	- 19,462
1973	1,780,192	1,799,071	-18,879
1974	1,622,001	1,630,525	-8,524

Source: U.S. Commission on Civil Rights, 1976: Table 8.

While some migrants (12,500) were farm workers in 1952, most were employed in the industrial or service sectors of the economy (Senior,

1953:132). But like other immigrants in New York City, the Puerto Ricans were forced to take those jobs that were routinely rejected by most Americans. In 1950, two-thirds of the Puerto Rican men in New York City were employed as operatives (37.4%) or as service workers (29.3%). Eighty percent of the Puerto Rican women worked in the garment industry (Fitzpatrick, 1971:61). The occupational distribution of the Puerto Ricans living in New York City did not change significantly until after 1960. Obviously, Puerto Rican migrants were relegated to the secondary labor market (Delgado, 1974).

The Revolving Door Migration: 1965-1993

In view of the continuous movement of Puerto Ricans between the island and the mainland, the most recent period of migration is referred to as the revolving door migration. For example, between 1965 and 1974 a total of 109,800 Puerto Ricans migrated to the mainland, for an average annual flow of almost 22,000. But during the same period a total of 92,600 returned to Puerto Rico, for an annual average flow of 18,500 (Boswell, 1985) (See Table 11.1). Therefore the overall annual net increase in arrivals was only 3,500 (U.S. Civil Rights, 1976:19-21; Stockton, 1978).

The primary reason for the revolving door phenomena was the evolution of the trans-national family. This means that Puerto Rican families have members who live on the mainland and others who live in Puerto Rico (Lucca and Pacheco, 1992). As a result, parents, children, and extended family members are constantly traveling between the island and the mainland (Levine, 1987:98-102). This has resulted in the development of the trans-national family, particularly as retired parents return to the homeland and as younger Puerto Ricans set firm roots in the mainland (Mascisco, 1968).

A new settlement pattern has evolved among the more recent migrants, as they are more likely to settle in other areas besides New York and New Jersey. In part this is an effort to avoid the hustle and bustle of urban life, but it also represents an effort to escape the racism, crime, and drug problems that are so often associated with life in the big city (Chenault, 1970). Apparently these more recent Puerto Rican migrants believe that their smaller numbers and greater dispersion will make it easier for them to blend into the core of American society.

The Puerto Rican Family

Like the Mexican American family, the Puerto Rican family and culture was most profoundly affected by the Spanish conquest. Historically five factors have contributed to the form and structure of the Puerto Rican family today:

1. The influence of the Tainos Indians
2. The infusion of the Spanish culture
3. The indoctrination to Catholicism
4. The impact of slave culture and society
5. The evolution of a *mestizo* Puerto Rican culture.

Unfortunately, very little is known about the family life of the Tainos, but it is known that they were a peaceful group of settlers who arrived in Boriquen (Puerto Rico) in 1270 from Venezuela (Golding, 1973:20). But we do know that their society was based on domestic agricultural production and was ruled by a chief and guided by a medicine man. As such the Tainos family was patriarchial and patrilinial in structure and organization.

When the Spanish arrived Boriquen society was destroyed, as most of the population died of various diseases and forced labor. As in Mexico, the Spanish missionaries destroyed all symbols of the indigenous religion and replaced their beliefs with the teachings of Catholicism. Furthermore, they organized the natives into productive villages, they paired couples and insisted on early marriages, they required early baptism, and they demanded unequivocal allegiance to the Spanish Crown.

The Spanish introduced slaves into Puerto Rico in the 1520's, in order to replace the rapidly dwindling Indian population. Within the first generation the Spanish sexually exploited Indian and slave women. This resulted in a very diverse racial mixture on the island. To this day, family members draw clear distinctions between their racial features and their social standing in the community. This genetic intrusion is often referred to as the great *mestizaje*, or racial blending of *Latino America* (Rogler, 1946).

Following their migration to the mainland, the Puerto Rican family underwent some important modifications in terms of primary relationships and family structure. These fundamental changes in the family occurred in response to (1) the influence of American culture, (2) the labor needs of an urban-industrial society, and (3) the economic and social problems that have plagued the Puerto Rican community on the mainland. When reduced to its most basic form there are four family types among mainland Puerto Ricans today (Gonzales, 1992:219-241):

1. The Nuclear Family—characterized by a two generational structure of parents and their children. The independent nuclear family is becoming more common today, specifically in response to the needs of urban society. These families are often confronted with a host of problems, such

as cramped apartments, the demanding schedule of urban life, crime and drug problems, and limited economic resources and employment opportunities. Within a brief period of time this structural pattern has contributed to a loss of community cohesiveness and cultural identity among the more recent Puerto Rican migrants (Gurak, 1988:60-64).

2. The Extended Family—found among the long term migrants in the central city. The extended family consist of three generations, the parents, their children, and their grandchildren. The extended family structure has traditionally provided social, emotional, and economic support to its members. As such it evolved in response to the harsh and demanding conditions of life in the barrio. This family structure promotes traditional cultural values and demands family loyalty, family interdependence, and mutual support.

3. The Attenuated Nuclear Family—is sometimes referred to as a blended family structure. While the blended family is viewed as a new phenomena among middle class Anglo Americans, it has existed for years among Puerto Ricans living in urban America. The attenuated nuclear family consists of two or more altered nuclear families who share a common household. Following divorce or separation a man who has children from a former marriage may marry a woman who also has children from a former marriage. This merging of nuclear families is further complicated by the introduction of step-children, that is children who are born to the husband and wife in the attenuated family. To the outsider these family relationships appear complicated.

4. The Female Headed Family—is becoming more common in the Puerto Rican community. Female headed families are supported by women who are separated, divorced, abandoned, widowed, or have had children out of wedlock. The high proportion of female headed families in the Puerto Rican community can also be attributed to their high levels of premarital cohabitation and the general acceptance of informal unions (Landale and Fennelly, 1992; Landale and Forste, 1991). Today, almost half (44%) of Puerto Rican families are headed by women, with no man present in the household.

Occupational Distribution

Much like the thousands of European immigrants who arrived at the turn of the century, the Puerto Ricans who arrived during the 1950's were forced to take jobs that most Anglo Americans would not consider. This is an example of the soft spot theory of occupational distribution, as immigrants have historically taken the least desirable jobs and usually work for the lowest level of remuneration (Melendez, 1991; Rodriguez, 1991).

Slightly more than seven out of ten of the Puerto Rican men held blue collar positions (primarily as laborers, operatives, and service workers) during the 1950's and 1960's. And their position in the industrial labor force did not change significantly until the early eighties. Their concentration in the secondary labor market (specifically in the lower level blue collar positions) increased to 76.2 percent in 1970 and stabilized at 75 percent in 1980, but dropped to 65.2 percent in 1990.

Only one-third (32.9%) of the Puerto Rican men held white collar positions in 1990 and of these only one out of ten (10.6%) were in managerial or professional positions. In contrast, twice as many (63.3%) Puerto Rican women held white collar positions and twice as many (20%) of these were in professional or managerial positions. However, within the white collar stratum half (44.7%) of the Puerto Rican women held low status, low paying clerical (file clerks and typists) and sales positions (store clerks and cashiers).

The two out of three Puerto Rican men who held blue collar positions were in service jobs (21.2%), craft positions (20.2%), or were operators and laborers (25.4%). Only one-third (36.7%) of the Puerto Rican women were blue collar workers and they were either in service positions (18.1%) or worked as operators or laborers (15.7%) (Schick and Schick, 1991:187). Within the blue collar positions most Puerto Rican women were employed in the garment industry, or in restaurants and hotels. Whether they were white collar or blue collar workers, Puerto Rican women consistently held the least desirable jobs and the lowest payed positions (Ortiz, 1986:622-624)

Despite the prosperity experienced by middle America during the 1980's, Puerto Ricans still experienced high unemployment rates and suffered from underemployment. In view of their concentration in the secondary labor market it is easy to understand why Puerto Ricans have the highest unemployment rates of any ethnic group in the nation. While their official unemployment rate was twice as high (10.5 %) as non-Latinos (5.4%), it is certain that their actual rate was much higher, as the official rate does not include those discouraged workers who have given up looking for work (Wagenheim, 1975:27-29).

Poverty and Economic Conditions

Their heavy concentration in the secondary labor market and their high unemployment rates are in great part responsible for the prevalence of poverty among Puerto Ricans. With the exception of Native Americans, Puerto Ricans are the poorest minority group in American society today (Tienda and Wilson, 1992:673-676).

In 1990 the median annual income of Puerto Rican men and women was only $13,681, compared to a median annual income of $21,268 among

Anglo American men and women. More than four out of five (85.5%) of the employed Puerto Rican women and three out of four (75.4%) of the Puerto Rican men earn less than $25,000 a year. Overall, Puerto Rican families earn less than half ($15,185) of what Anglo American families earn ($33,852). This is a statistical relationship that has not changed in the past 25 years (Schick and Schick, 1991:187; U.S. Census, 1991:Table 678, 679). Seven out of ten (68.3%) Puerto Rican families earned less than $25,000 a year, compared to only four out of ten (38.1%) of the non- Latino families. Four out of ten (37.9%) Puerto Rican families live below the poverty level, compared to only one out of ten (9.7%) of non-Latino families (See Figure 11.2). Half the Puerto Rican children (50.3%) under the age of 18 live below the poverty level.

Figure 11.2
All Families Below the Poverty Level, 1987

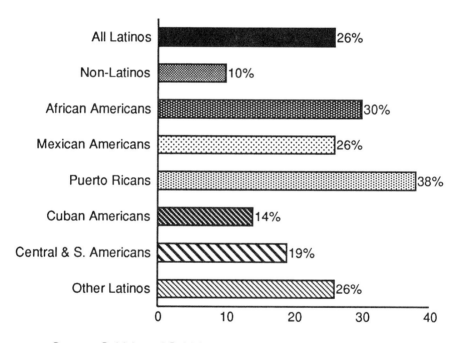

Source: Schick and Schick, 1991: 221.

While there are several ways to explain the wage gap that exists between Puerto Ricans and Anglo Americans, clearly racism and segregation have played a very important role in the abnormally high concentration of Puerto Ricans in the secondary labor market. This is a segment of the labor market that offers the lowest wages and the worst working conditions. The pervasive poverty that plagues the Puerto Rican community is also explained by their very high rate of unemployment and underemployment (DeFreitas, 1991:60-65, 95-166).

It is now an accepted fact that there is a direct relationship between high unemployment rates and high divorce rates. This is true among Puerto Ricans, as two-thirds (65.3%) of the Puerto Rican families living below the poverty level are supported by women (See Figure 11.3). The relationship-between economic deprivation and family disruption is also reflected in the fact that almost half (45%) the Puerto Rican families are supported by women, with no husband present (Schick and Schick, 1991:221). The message should be obvious, that is, if the husband cannot support his family, the economic disruption often results in the destruction of the nuclear family.

Figure 11.3
Female-Headed Families Below the Poverty Level, 1987

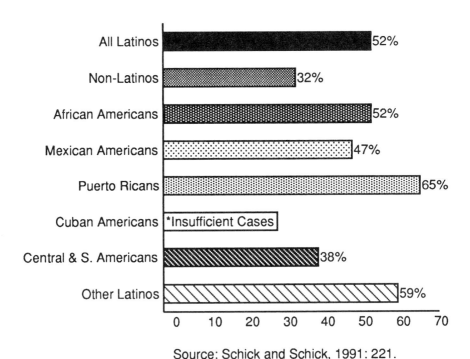

Source: Schick and Schick, 1991: 221.

The Failure of Education

As a group Puerto Ricans are confronted with many of the same educational issues and obstacles that face Mexican Americans today. The primary obstacles to educational achievement among Puerto Ricans are school segregation, substandard facilities, ill prepared and insensitive teachers, a negative educational environment, a disregard for linguistic and cultural differences, and the plague of poverty. These educational issues and social problems are particularly difficult to address in the large central city schools, which are often unresponsive to the needs of Puerto Rican students.

The median school years completed by Puerto Ricans (25 years and older) is 12.0 years, about one year less than Anglo Americans. But only one out of six (59%) of the Puerto Ricans (25 years and older) graduated from high school in 1990 and two out of five (40.1%) have an eighth grade education or less (Schick and Schick, 1991:93). Once Puerto Rican youth reach the age of 18, only half as many (18%) remain in school as is true in the general population (37%). Therefore, of those who graduate from high school, their 12th year is often their terminal year of formal education. At the other end of the educational spectrum only one out of ten (9.6%) graduate from college, compared to one out of five (21%) among Anglo Americans (U.S. Census, 1988:Table 1).

Puerto Rican youth drop out (or are pushed out) of school because they are bored with school, do not understand or see the relevance of the materials, or they feel a need to contribute to the support of their families. The unfortunate aspect of the drop out rate is that most drop out of high school during their last two years of school. And it should be pointed out that there are some key structural, administrative, and policy reasons why the drop out rate is so high among Puerto Rican youth:

1. Pronounced language and cultural differences between Puerto Rican students and their teachers.
2. The high levels of racial and ethnic segregation in large central city schools.
3. Ill prepared and uninterested teachers.
4. Insensitive and unconcerned administrators.
5. Inferior and substandard school facilities.
6. High proportion of Puerto Rican students and a very low representation of Puerto Rican teachers, counselors, and administrators.
7. Educational tests that have a strong middle class bias.
8. Institutions that are not culturally sensitive to Puerto Ricans and other minority students.
9. And a racial tracking system that insures that Puerto Rican students will eventually fail.

Chapter Summary

Hispanic is the term that is used by the U.S. Bureau of the Census to categorize the Spanish speaking population in the United States. But the preferred term for these groups is Latino. Puerto Ricans are the second largest Latino group in the United States today. The largest group of Latinos are the Mexican Americans and the third largest are the Cuban Americans.

According to the provisions of the Treaty of Paris, ending the Spanish American War, the island nation of Puerto Rico became a colony of the United States. American manufacturers took advantage of the natural resources of the island and the available pool of unskilled laborers to produce products with a high profit margin.

During the Second World War Puerto Rican labor was needed to support the war effort and thousands of Puerto Rican men were drafted into the U.S. military. Commercial air service between San Juan and New York City was introduced following the Second World War and before long this produced the Great Migration, as thousands of Puerto Ricans left their homeland in search of new opportunities. Most of these Puerto Ricans settled in the low income areas of New York City, where they found work in the service and manufacturing industries. To this day the largest concentration of Puerto Ricans are still found in New York City.

Partly as a result of their concentration in a large metropolitan area plagued by a host of social problems, Puerto Ricans have had to struggle against the high unemployment rates, the pain of poverty, dilapidated and overcrowded housing, inadequate schools, crime, and drug problems. But in spite of these obstacles, Puerto Ricans have managed to increase their overall standard of living, have experienced a certain level of social mobility, and have increased their level of education.

As a group Puerto Ricans have also been very effective in making their voice heard in the political arena, as they have created a very effective organizational structure for political representation in New York City. Over the years they have elected representatives of their community to high positions in city government, the judiciary, and in state political offices. In November of 1970 Herman Badillo, an attorney from the Bronx, became the first Puerto Rican to win a seat in the U.S. Congress (Gonzales, 1991:171-174). The Puerto Rican community's most recent political success came in November of 1992, with the election of Nydia Velazquez to a seat in Congress. Ms. Velazquez became the first Puerto Rican woman to be elected to a seat in Congress.

References

Alers-Montalvo, Manuel
1985   *The Puerto Rican Migrants of New York City: A Study of Anomie.* NY: AMS Press.
Boswell, Thomas D.
1985   "Puerto Ricans Living in the United States." In Jesse O. McKee (ed.), *Ethnicity in Contemporary America: A Geographical Appraisal,* Dubuque, IA: Kendall/Hunt. Pp. 117-144.
Chenault, Lawrence R.
1970   *The Puerto Rican Migrant in New York City.* New York: Russell & Russell.
Christopulos, Diana
1980   "The Politics of Colonialism: Puerto Rico From 1898 to 1972." In *The Puerto Ricans: Their History, Culture and Society.* Adalberto Lopez (ed.), Cambridge: Schenkman Publishing Company, Inc. Pp. 129-169.
Cordasco, Francesco
1973   *The Puerto Ricans 1493-1973: A Chronology & Fact Book.* Dobbs Ferry, NY: Oceana Publications, Inc.
Cripps-Samoiloff, Louise
1984   *Portrait of Puerto Rico.* New York: Cornwall Books.
Cruz-Monclova, L.
1958   *Historia de Puerto Rico, 1808-1895* (Vols. 1 & 2). San Juan, PR: Universidad de Puerto Rico.
Davis, Kingsley
1953   "Puerto Rico: A Crowded Island." *Annals of the American Academy of Political and Social Science* 285:95-103.
DeFreitas, Gregory
1991   *Inequality at Work: Hispanics in the U.S. Labor Force.* NY: Oxford University Press.
Delgado, Melvin
1974   "Social Work and the Puerto Rican Community." *Social Casework* 55:117-124.
Doyle, Ruth
1982   *Hispanics in New York: Religious, Cultural and Social Experiences. Vol. 1.* New York: The Office of Pastoral Research, Archdiocese of New York.
Falcon, Luis M.
1991   "Migration and Development: The Case of Puerto Rico". In *Determinants of Emigration from Mexico, CentralAmerica, and the Caribbean.* Sergio Diaz-Briquets and Sidney Weintraub (eds.), Boulder, CO: Westview Press. Pp. 145-187.

Fitzpatrick, Joseph P.
1971   *Puerto Rican Americans: The Meaning of Migration to the Mainland.* Englewood Cliffs, NJ: Prentice-Hall.

Garcia, Alejandro
1991   "The Changing Demographic Face of Hispanics in the United States." In *Empowering Hispanic Families: A Critical Issue for the '90s.* Marta Sotomayor (ed.), Milwaukee, WI: Family Service America. Pp. 21-38.

Golding, Morton J.
1973   *A Short History of Puerto Rico.* NY: New American Library.

Gonzales, Juan L. Jr.
1991   *The Lives of Ethnic Americans.* Dubuque, IA: Kendall/Hunt.
1992   *Racial and Ethnic Families in America.* Dubuque, IA: Kendall/Hunt.

Gurak, Douglas T.
1988   "New York Hispanics: A Demographic Overview." In *The Hispanic Experience in the United States.* Edna Acosta-Belen and Barbara R. Sjostrom (eds.), NY: Praeger, Pp. 57- 78.

Hauberg, Clifford A.
1974   *Puerto Rico and the Puerto Ricans.* NY: Twayne Publishers, Inc.

Hernandez-Alvarez, Jose
1967   *Return Migration to Puerto Rico.* Berkeley: Institute of International Studies, University of California.
1968   "The Movement and Settlement of Puerto Rican Migrants Within the United States, 1950-1960". *International Migration Review* 1:40-52.

Hoffman, Mark S.
1993   *The World Almanac and Book of Facts 1993.* New York: Pharos Books.

Landale, Nancy S. and R. Forste
1991   "Patterns of Entry into Cohabitation and Marriage Among Mainland Puerto Rican Women." *Demography* 28:587-607.

Landale, Nancy S. and Katherine Fennelly
1992   "Informal Unions Among Mainland Puerto Ricans: Cohabitation or an Alternative to Legal Marriage?" *Journal of Marriage and the Family* 54:269-280.

LaRuffa, Anthony
1971   *San Cipriano: Life in a Puerto Rican Community.* New York: Gordon and Breach Science Publishers.

Levine, Barry B.
1987   "The Puerto Rican Exodus: Development of the Puerto Rican Circuit." In *The Caribbean Exodus.* Barry B. Levine (ed.), NY: Praeger, Pp. 93-105.

Lopez, Adalberto (ed.)
1980   *The Puerto Ricans: Their History, Culture, and Society.* Cambridge: Schenkman.

Lucca-Irizarry, Nydia and Angel M. Pacheco
1992   "Intercultural Encounters of Puerto Rican Migrants." *Environment and Behavior* 24(2):226-238.

Macisco, John J. Jr.
1968   "Assimilation of the Puerto Ricans on the Mainland: A Socio-Demographic Approach." *International Migration Review* 1:21- 39.

Maldonado, Rita M.
1976   "Why Puerto Ricans Migrated to the United States in 1947-73." *Monthly Labor Review* 9:7-18.

Maldonado-Denis, Manuel
1980   *The Emigration Dialectic: Puerto Rico and the USA.* NY: International Publishers.

Mascisco, John J.
1968   "Assimilation of Puerto Ricans on the Mainland: A Socio-demographic Approach." *International Migration Review* 2:21-37.

Melendez, Edwin
1991   "Labor Market Structure and Wage Differences in New York City: A Comparative Analysis of Hispanics and Non-Hispanic Blacks and Whites." In *Hispanics in the Labor Force: Issues and Policies.* Edwin Melendez, C. Rodriguez and J. B. Figueroa (eds.), NY: Plenum Press, Pp. 101-118.

Mintz, Sidney
1960   *Workers in the Cane.* New Haven, CT: Yale University Press.

Miranda-King, Lourdes
1974   "Puertorriquenas in the United States: The Impact of Double Discrimination." *Civil Rights Digest* 6:20-27.

Morales, Julio
1986   *Puerto Rican Poverty and Migration.* NY: Praeger.

Moscoso, Francisco
1980   "Chiefdom and Encomienda in Puerto Rico: The Development of Tribal Society and The Spanish Colonization to 1530." In *The Puerto Ricans: Their History, Culture and Society.* Adalberto Lopez (ed.), Cambridge: Schenkman Publishing Company. Pp. 3-24

Ortiz, Vilma
1986   "Changes in the Characteristics of Puerto Rican Migrants From 1955-1980." *International Migration Review* 20(3): 612-628.

Padilla, Felix M.
1985   *Latino Ethnic Consciousness: The Case of Mexican Americans and Puerto Ricans in Chicago.* Notre Dame, IN: University of Notre Dame Press.

Rodriguez, Clara E.
1980   "Puerto Ricans: Between Black and White." In *The Puerto Rican Struggle: Essays on Survival in the U.S.* Clara E. Rodriguez, Virginia Sanchez-Korrol, and Jose Oscar Alers (eds.), NY: Puerto Rican Migration Research Consortium. Pp. 20-30.

1991   "The Effect of Race on Puerto Rican Wages." In *Hispanics in the Labor Force: Issues and Policies.* Edwin Melendez, C. Rodriguez and J. B. Figueroa (eds.),NY: Plenum Press. Pp. 77-98.

Rogler, Charles C.
1946   "The Morality of Race Mixing in Puerto Rico." *Social Forces* 25:77-81.

Sandis, Eva
1973   "Characteristics of Puerto Rican Migrants to, and from, the United States." In *The Puerto Rican Experience.* Francesco Cordasco and E. Bucchoni (eds.), Totowa, NJ: Littlefield & Adams. Pp. 127-149

Sanchez-Korrol, Virginia
1983   *From Colonia to Community: The History of Puerto Ricans in New York City, 1917-1948.* Westport, CN: Greenwood Press.

1988   "Latinismo Among Early Puerto Rican Migrants in New York City: A Sociohistoric Interpretation." *In The Hispanic Experience in the United States.* Edna Acosta-Belen and Barbara R. Sjostrom (eds.), NY: Praeger Press. Pp. 151-161.

Santana-Cooney, Rosemary and Alice Colon
1980   "Work and Family: The Recent Struggle of Puerto Rican Females." In *The Puerto Rican Struggle: Essays on Survival in the U.S.* Clara E. Rodriguez, Virginia Sanchez-Korrol, and Jose Oscar Alers (eds.), NY: Puerto Rican Migration Research Consortium. Pp. 58-73.

Schick, Frank L. and Renee Schick (eds.)
1991   *Statistical Handbook on U.S. Hispanics.* Phoenix, AZ: Oryx Press.

Senior, Clarence
1953   "Migration and Puerto Rico's Population Problem." *The Annals of the American Academy of Political and Social Science* 285:95-103.

1965   *The Puerto Ricans: Strangers-Then Neighbors.* Chicago: Quadrangle Books.

Sexton, Patricia Cayo
1965   *Spanish Harlem.* NY: Harper & Row.

Steward, Julian
1957   *The People of Puerto Rico: A Study of Social Anthropology.*
        Urbana, IL: University of Illinois Press.

Stockton, William
1978   "Going Home: The Puerto Ricans' New Migration." *New*
        York Times Magazine. November 12, Page 20.

Tienda, Marta and Franklin D. Wilson
1992   "Migration and the Earnings of Hispanic Men." *American*
        Sociological Review 57(5):661-678.

U.S. Census
1985   *Projections of the Hispanic Population:* 1983-2080.
        Washington, D.C. USGPO Current Population Reports,
        Series P-25, No. 995.

1988   *The Hispanic Population in the United States: March 1988*
        (Advance Report). Washington, D.C.:USGPO Current Popula-
        tion Reports, Series P-20, No. 431, August.

1991   *Statistical Abstract of the United States, 1991* (111th Edition).
        Washington, D.C.:USGPO.

U.S. Civil Rights
1976   *Puerto Ricans in the Continental United States: An*
        Uncertain Future. Washington, D.C. USGPO.

Wagenheim, Kal
1975   *A Survey of Puerto Ricans on the U.S. Mainland in the 1970's.*
        NY: Praeger.

Wright, John W.
1993   *The Universal Almanac 1993.* Kansas City, KS: Andrews
        and McMeel.

800-1492	The evolution of Taino Indian culture and society on the island of Boriquen (Puerto Rico).
1493	Columbus discovered Puerto Rico on November 19, 1493.
1508	Juan Ponce de Leon begins the Spanish occupation.
1509	Arrival of the first slaves.
1530	Thousands of slaves introduced to replace the loss of Indian labor.
1726	Coffee trees are introduced to the island.
1775	The population of Puerto Rico is 70,250, including 6,467 Black slaves.
1848	Slave rebellions occur in Ponce and Vega Baja.
1873	Slavery is abolished in Puerto Rico.
1897	Spain grants Puerto Rico an Autonomous Charter.
1898	The United States declares war on Spain.
1899	The Treaty of Paris, ending the war, was signed in September in which Spain ceded Puerto Rico to the U.S.
1900	The Foraker Act creates a civil government and Charles H. Allen becomes the first U.S. colonial governor.
1903	The University of Puerto Rico is established.
1917	The Jones Act makes Puerto Ricans American citizens and also makes them eligible for the draft.
1935	Nationalist militants are killed by the police at the University of Puerto Rico.
1937	Twenty Nationalists were killed by police on Palm Sunday in the Ponce Massacre.
1947	President Truman signs the Crawford-Butler Act, allowing Puerto Ricans to elect their own governor. Operation Bootstrap goes into effect.
1948	Luis Muñoz Marin became the first elected governor of Puerto Rico and remained in office until 1964.
1950	Puerto Rican Nationalists try to kill President Truman.
1952	On March 3, the Commonwealth of Puerto Rico (or Associated Free State) was established.
1954	On March 1, four Puerto Rican Nationalists open fire in the House of Representatives wounding five congressmen.
1965	The Civil Rights Act of 1965 held that Puerto Ricans no longer had to pass a literacy test to vote in New York.
1970	Herman Badillo becomes the first Puerto Rican American elected to Congress.
1976	President Ford issues a declaration supporting statehood for Puerto Rico.

1980	The U.S. mainland Puerto Rican population reached two million.
1981	U.N. Decolonization Committee recommends a hearing in the case of Puerto Rico. This move was defeated by the members of the U.S. delegation.
1990	The U.S. Puerto Rican population reached 2,330,000.
1992	Nydia Velazquez became the first Puerto Rican woman to win a seat in Congress.

Important Names

Ponce De Leon
Herman Badillo

Luis Muñoz Marin
Nydia Velazquez

Key Terms

attenuated nuclear family
escape valve
extended family
The Great Depression
The Great Migration
Latino
nuclear family
The Revolving Door Migration
Spanish American War (1898)
Treaty of Paris (1899)

Boriquen
Estado Libre Asociado
female headed family
the great *mestizaje*
Jones Act (1917)
mestizo
Pioneer Migration
Tainos Indians
U.S.S. Maine

Sample Test Questions

1. Discuss four important events in Puerto Rican history.
2. Provide three specific characteristics of each of the three stages of Puerto Rican migration.
3. Discuss four major problems facing Puerto Ricans today.

Chapter 12

The Cuban American Experience

Introduction

Among Latinos, Cubans are the third largest group. Since the Revolution (1959) the number of Cubans living in the United States has increased dramatically and today Cubans represent the fifth largest flow of immigrants. When they first arrived most Cubans settled in south Florida and as a result half (50.7%) of all Cuban Americans still live in the Miami area today. Consequently, the state of Florida has the largest concentration of Cuban Americans (58.5%), followed by New Jersey (10.1%), New York (9.6%), and California (7.6%).

The census reported 803,226 Cubans living in the United States in 1980, which represents a growth rate of 47 percent over the previous decade. This is a much higher growth rate than the general population and can be attributed to the large number of political refugees that arrived during this period. In 1990 the Cuban American population reached the one million mark (1,069,000), representing a growth rate of 33.8 percent for the decade. This is considerably higher than the 9.5 percent growth rate for the nation as a whole during this period. Today (1993) there are approximately 1,120,000 Cubans in the United States.

Although Cuban Americans represent only a small proportion of the total number of Latinos in the United States (5.3%), it is their historical and political ties to Cuba and their concentration in south Florida that has drawn national attention to their cause. Furthermore, Cubans are well known for their social and economic achievements.

When compared to other Latinos, Cubans are recognized for their higher levels of education, higher income, greater representation in professions and white collar positions, entrepreneurial skills and business success, high rates of naturalization, and active participation in politics. In August of 1989, Ileana Ros-Lehtinen was elected to Congress and became the first Cuban American to win a seat in Congress. Representative Ros-Lehtinen can attribute her successful bid for Congress to the strong support provided by the Latino community in Miami (Gonzales 1991:149-151).

In short, Cubans have followed the model of immigrant success in American society. But the degree of their success can only be appreciated against the backdrop of their history and their flight to freedom.

Cuba: An Historical Sketch

Cuba was ruled by the Spanish for four hundred years (1492-1898), as it was one of the first Spanish colonial possessions in the New World, and one of its last. Its name derives from the Indian name, Cubanacan. On his first voyage of discovery Columbus landed in Cuba to secure provisions for his ships. But the Spanish did not colonize the island until 1511, when they surveyed the island for the presence of natural resources. In 1515 they established the ports of Havana and Santiago (Suchlicki, 1975).

It is estimated that there were 100,000 Indians living on the island of Cuba when the conquistadors landed, but within thirty years there were only about 3,000 left alive (Boswell and Curtis, 1983:12). As in all areas of European settlement in the New World, the Indians in Cuba died or were exterminated as a result of war, forced labor, and diseases. During this initial period of settlement cattle husbandry and the production of tobacco and various food crops constituted the basis for the colonial economy. In an effort to replace the dwindling Indian labor the Spanish began importing slaves in 1517. With the full scale production of coffee and sugar cane in the mid-nineteenth century, the slave trade became an indispensable aspect of Cuba's economy. By 1846 there were 660,000 slaves in Cuba, 220,000 free Blacks and mulattoes, and 565,000 whites (Blutstein, 1971:32).

In 1898, Spanish domination on the island came to an abrupt end when the United States defeated Spain in the Spanish American war. When the Treaty of Paris was signed in 1899 (ending the war) the United States not only gained the territories of Puerto Rico and the Philippines, but also took possession of Cuba. Between 1898 and 1902, U.S. military forces occupied and administered Cuba as a colonial possession. In 1902 Cuba gained its political independence from the United States and remained a quasi-democratic capitalist state until January of 1959.

During this quasi-democratic period (1902-1959) Cuba experienced the political corruption of one regime after another and became economically dependent on the United States. American investors were involved in every aspect of the economy. Within a few years American capitalists monopolized the sugar industry (which accounted for 80% of Cuba's exports), the tobacco industry, the mines, the railroads, and all public utilities. In total, the United States purchased 75 percent of Cuba's exports and provided 65 percent of their imports (Boswell and Curtis, 1983:18). Unfortunately, America's strangle hold on Cuba's economy was only possible because of the support of corrupt political leaders, who sold favors to American investors and left office as multi- millionaires. Perhaps the most corrupt of these was Fugencio Batista, who entered Cuban politics in 1933 and ruled with dictatorial power until his overthrow in 1959.

As a young attorney, Fidel Castro was one of the leaders of several popular opposition groups that opposed Batista's dictatorship. Following a bloody confrontation with Batista's troops in July of 1953 Castro was sentenced to 15 years in prison. In celebration of his re-election as president in 1955, Batista freed all political prisoners. His newly obtained freedom gave Castro the opportunity he needed to travel and gather support in Mexico and the United States. And in January of 1959 Fidel Castro assumed power in Cuba (Chaffee, 1989:6-12).

An Overview of Cuban Immigration

A close review of the immigration data reveals that the real immigration of Cubans to the United States did not start until 1959, when Castro came to power. Before the Revolution the flow of Cuban immigrants to the United States was insignificant. For example, the 1870 census only counted 5,000 Cubans in the United States. And due to the political instability in Cuba during the 1880's, a wave of political refugees moved to Key West, Tampa, and New York City. This was also the period when the Cuban cigar manufactures established themselves in south Florida, as the first Cuban cigar workers arrived in Tampa in 1886, aboard the side-wheeler *S.S. Hutchinson* (Mormino and Pozzetta, 1987:66).

By 1900 there were 11,000 Cubans in the United States, and this increased to 15,000 in 1910. In 1930, when Miami first became a center for Cuban settlement, their population in America was still only 35,500. On the eve of the Revolution (1958) their population was estimated at only 40,000, with the majority residing in south Florida (Bach, 1985:79).

As with other immigration experiences the segmentation of Cuban immigration is rather clear, as their influx responded to the changing political conditions in Cuba. For example, the first wave of so-called anticipatory refugees began late in 1958, when it was clear that Castro would assume power (Kunz, 1973:131-135). This period of immigration ended with the onset of the Cuban missile crisis in October of 1962. The next period of immigration is marked by high levels of political tension between the United States and Cuba (See Table 12.1).

Table 12.1
Cuban Immigration to the U.S., 1959-1991:
By Selected Periods

Wave	Period	Total Number	Percent of Total	Cumulative Rate
1. Golden Exiles	January 1959-October 1962	215,000	22.4	—
2. Cuban Missile Crisis	November 1962-November 1965	74,000	7.7	289,000
3. Freedom Flights	December 1965-April 1973	340,000	35.4	629,000
4. Political Closure	May 1973-April 1980	38,000	4.0	667,000
5. Marielitos	May 1980-September 1980	125,000	13.0	792,000
6. Modern Refugees	1981-1991	167,500	17.5	959,500

Source: Portes and Bach, 1985:84-87; U.S. Census, 1992:Table 7; Hoffman, 1993:397.

From late 1965 until April of 1973, Fidel Castro reluctantly allowed his people to emigrate. It was during this period that the U.S. government organized the Cuban freedom flights, that brought more than 340,000 refugees to our shores. Unfortunately, Cold War tensions reduced the flow of refugees between May 1973 to April 1980. The most recent mass movement of Cuban refugees occurred during the summer of 1980, when more than 125,000 Marielitos arrived in south Florida (Hernandez, 1985).

It is estimated that more than 800,000 Cuban refugees arrived in the United States between 1959 and 1980. This represents about one-tenth of the island's population (Portes and Bach, 1985:84). However, according to the Immigration and Naturalization Service a total of 533,600 Cuban refugees arrived between 1961 and 1980. And between 1981 and 1989, an additional 148,600 Cuban refugees were admitted. Therefore the official government data reveals that a total of 682,200 Cuban refugees were admitted to the United States between 1961 and 1989 (U.S. Census, 1991:Table 7). The point should also be made that these immigration figures do not include the 40,000 to 50,000 Cubans who settled in Puerto Rico, or the 61,000 to 126,000 who settled in Spain, Mexico, Canada, Venezuela, Costa Rica, and Peru (Boswell, 1985:101; Duany, 1992:Table 1)

The first wave immigrants were predominately Batista supporters, who lost their freedom and investments to Castro's communist regime. Most of these early refugees were political elites who supported Batista (Pedraza-Bailey, 1985a:18-23). But before long wealthy landowners and businessmen joined the exodus, as the communist government expropriated all the farm land and American owned factories and businesses were seized, that is collectivised, by the government (July of 1960).

This first wave of Cuban refugees are popularly referred to as the Golden Exiles, as they were the social, political, and economic elites of Cuban society (Bach, 1987:113). Most were investors, businessmen, and professionals, whose businesses were adversely affected by Castro's economic policies. One study found that two-thirds (64%) of these refugees held white collar positions in Cuba (31% professional-managerial and 33% clerical-sales), compared to only one-fourth (23%) of the general Cuban population (Fagen, et al, 1968:115). For Cuba, the departure of the Golden Exiles represented an immediate brain drain.

The flow of refugees was greatly reduced as a result of the political fallout following the Cuban missile crisis. Most of the refugees from this period (1962-1965) were forced to rely on various clandestine methods to escape from Castro's Cuba. While others had to immigrate to another country first, usually Mexico or Spain, before obtaining a visa to come to the United States.

In December of 1965, the United States and Cuba signed an agreement allowing refugees to be airlifted to Miami. The two daily freedom flights, operated from December 1965 to April 1973, brought more than 340,000 refugees to the United States. Most of these refugees were from the working classes of Cuban society, although a few were small merchants and independent craftsmen (Pedraza-Bailey, 1985b:16). In May of 1973, for no apparent reason, Castro abruptly terminated the freedom flights to America. Consequently the flow of refugees was greatly reduced for the next seven years, that is through April 1980.

The last significant flow of Cuban refugees arrived during the Mariel boat lift (May to September 1980), which captured the nation's attention. During this five month period more than 125,000 refugees arrived in south Florida. The Marielitos were different from previous waves of Cuban refugees in several important respects, as most were men (85%), most were single (65.6%), most were blue collar workers (86.2%), and a disproportionate number were Black (40%) (compared to only 4% of U.S. Cubans). Though some Marielitos were detained in government camps, as they were suspected of being convicts or mental patients (Portes and Bach, 1985:87), only a small proportion (16%) were actually released from Castro's prisons (Bach, et al, 1981; Bach, 1987:114-127). And of these, only four percent were hard-core criminals (Boswell, 1985:100).

Unfortunately riots in some U.S. government camps and malicious propaganda issued by the Cuban government—that described the Marielitos as misfits, delinquents, and antisocials—resulted in negative press coverage in the United States. In response, many Americans disapproved of the boat lift and some Cuban-Americans avoided the Marielitos (McCoy and Gonzalez, 1985:26-35).

The Cuban Community in Miami

Historically Cubans have had a natural attraction for south Florida, as some 40,000 lived in Miami before the revolution. Many pioneer refugees settled in Miami as they considered their stay temporary and they were only waiting for the inevitable overthrow of Castro's regime (Azieri, 1981:58-60). Furthermore, the dynamic density and cultural support system available to the recent arrivals in Miami naturally attracted other Cuban refugees.

Most Cuban refugees were attracted to south Florida by the availability of government assistance programs. Early in 1959 President Eisenhower allocated $1 million for refugee assistance, while the Kennedy administration provided millions more for education, job training, welfare benefits, and housing programs (Pedraza-Bailey, 1985a:40-42).

In 1970, four out of ten Cuban Americans lived in Miami. Today it is estimated that six out of ten live in the Miami area. Two of the most important reasons for their concentration in Miami is the absence of a language barrier and the general availability of jobs. Little Havana is an area where Cubans can live and work in a totally Spanish speaking environment (Fradd, 1983). It is also a customary practice for Cuban businessmen to hire their compatriots, as the refugees offer their loyalty and the Cuban entrepreneurs guarantee them a job (Butler and Herring, 1991:80-83). Unfortunately these ethnic loyalties sometimes result in wage and labor abuses (Model, 1992:67-70; Wilson and Portes, 1980).

One reason for the success of those living in Little Havana is the financial and business support provided by Cuban Americans. Besides the high proportion of professionals in the first wave immigration, there were also many businessmen and investors. In 1967 there were less than a thousand (919) Cuban owned businesses in the Miami area, but by 1976 there were 8,000 (Portes and Bach, 1985:89). By 1990 there were more than 28,000 Cuban owned businesses in the greater Miami area (Portes and Rumbaut, 1990:20-21). In Dade County there are over 18,000 Cuban owned firms, most in construction, finance, textiles, leather, furniture, and cigar making. In addition sixteen Cuban Americans are presidents of banks, 250 are vice presidents, 3,500 are doctors, 500 are lawyers, and they own 500 supermarkets, 250 drug stores, and over 60 auto dealerships (Boswell, 1985:112).

Income, Occupation, and Education

When the socio-economic characteristics of Cuban Americans are compared to other Latinos, it is obvious that they are economically advanced. Briefly, there are three reasons why Cuban Americans have been so successful in American society, (1) the selective nature of their immigration, (2) the advantages they received from government assistance and training programs, and (3) their strong economic base in Miami.

The very fact that Cuban Americans are, as a group, an older population (38.7 years compared to 32.2 years U.S.) also means that their human capital is more highly developed. In effect they have more skills and experience upon which they can draw. Their higher market skills in part derive from the knowledge that they probably will never return to Cuba, hence they invest in education to increase their human potential (Borjas, 1982). (See Table 12.2)

Table 12.2

Selected Demographic Characteristics of Non-Latinos,
Cuban Americans, and Mexican Americans, 1988

	Non-Latinos	Cuban Americans	Mexican Americans
AGE			
Median Age (Years)	32.9	38.7	23.9
Under 5 (Percent)	7.3	4.7	11.8
Under 21	29.9	22.2	43.9
65 and Over	12.4	12.8	4.0
SEX (Percent)			
Male	48.5	50.9	52.5
Female	51.5	49.1	48.5
EDUCATION			
(Total 25 years and over)			
Less than 5 years	1.7	5.5	15.9
4 years of high school	77.9	60.5	44.6
4 or more years of college	21.0	17.2	7.1
Median school years	12.7	12.4	10.8
FAMILY INCOME (Percent)			
Less than $25,000	38.1	46.2	60.4
$25,000 or more	62.1	53.9	39.5
Mean Income	$37,388	$36,572	$25,010

Source: U.S. Census, 1988:Table 1, 2.

When compared to the annual income of other Latinos, Cubans had the highest average family income of $27,294 in 1987 (compared to $30,853 U.S.). But this level of income is only achieved by combining individual family members' incomes (Perez, 1985:9-11). Nonetheless this still leaves an income gap of $3,559, when compared to all Americans. Almost half (46.2%) of the Cuban families earned less than $25,000 per year and 13.8 percent live below the poverty level (compared to 10.6% U.S.) (U.S. Census, 1988: Table 2).

The rapid rate of economic success of Cuban Americans can be attributed to (1) their higher positions in the labor force, (2) the higher proportion of women who are employed full-time (47.1% compared to 40.1% U.S.), and (3) more workers per family (18.6% had three or more workers per family, compared to 12.5% U.S.) (Perez, 1985:Table 5). The fact that half the Cuban American women are employed outside the home is in sharp contrast to the role of women in pre-revolutionary Cuba, where only 9.8 percent of the women were employed outside the home (i.e. in 1958). From their perspective having a wife at home was considered an indication of a man's wealth and enhanced his social standing in the community (Keremitsis, 1989:102).

According to the 1990 census, one out of four (23.7%) of the Cuban Americans held professional or managerial positions and one out of three (33.5%) were in technical or sales positions. Therefore almost three out of five (57.2%) were working in white collar positions, and only four out of ten (42.8%) were working in blue collar jobs (U.S. Census, 1991:Table 633).

In 1988, 23.7 percent of the Cuban men were professionals and managers, and 27.8 percent were in technical, sales and clerical positions. Overall half (51.5%) were employed in white collar positions, compared to 46.1 percent of the general population. But more Cuban American women (69.1%) were white collar workers, as compared to Cuban men (51.5%). However, most of the Cuban American women holding white collar positions were relegated to low status, low paying, clerical-sales positions (44.7%). On the other hand, more Cuban American women (27.3%), than Cuban American men (23.7%), held professional-managerial positions (U.S. Census, 1988: Table 2) (See Figure 12.1).

Four out of ten (39.7%) Cuban Americans were blue collar workers in 1988. Of these blue collar workers, 9.1 percent were in craft positions, 17.9 percent were operatives and laborers, and 11.8 percent were in service positions. Their representation in these positions is only slightly different from the general population. Within the blue collar category, both Cuban men (21.1%) and Cuban women (14.7%) were concentrated in the operative-labor positions, compared to 20.9 percent and 8.8 percent respectively in the general population (U.S. Census, 1988: Table 2).

Their higher levels of education and technical training can account for the higher representation of Cuban Americans in white collar positions.

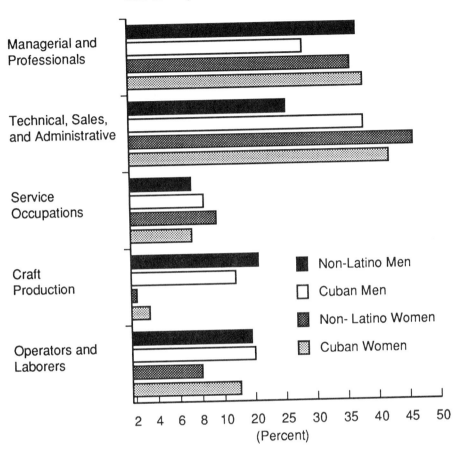

Figure 12.1
Occupational Distribution of Non-Latino
and Cuban, Men and Women, 1988

Managerial and
Professionals

Technical, Sales,
and Administrative

Service
Occupations

Craft
Production

Operators and
Laborers

■ Non-Latino Men

□ Cuban Men

▨ Non- Latino Women

▧ Cuban Women

2 4 6 8 10 20 25 30 35 40 45 50
(Percent)

Source: U.S. Census. 1988: Table 2

And among Latinos, they have achieved the highest level of education. Part of the reason for their success is the higher social status of the pioneer refugees who encouraged their children to take advantage of every educational opportunity. Furthermore, as refugees they were eager to take advantage of a college education. Therefore, they were highly motivated in their pursuit of a higher education (Portes, et al, 1982:6-7).

According to the 1990 census, almost two-thirds (63%) of all Cuban Americans were high school graduates and one out of five (19.8%) were college graduates. This compares to eight out of ten (78.4%) Anglo American high school graduates and one out of five (21.8%) Anglo

American college graduates (U.S. Census, 1991:Table 226). Their median years of education was 12.4, compared to 12.7 among all Americans, 12.0 among Puerto Ricans, and 10.8 among Mexican Americans (Schick and Schick, 1991:35). As with other Latinos, Cuban Americans still confront such problems as the language barrier, segregated schools, the racial tracking system, and insensitive teachers, counselors, and administrators.

The Family Today

Like other Latinos, Cubans place great importance on family relationships. And in view of their refugee experience, Cuban Americans place an emphasis on the role of the family in their community. Over the years they have worked assiduously at family reunification refugee assistance programs (Richmond, 1980).

When compared to other Latino families, the Cuban family is the smallest. In 1988 the average Cuban family size was 3.16, compared to 3.17 in the general population, 3.79 among Latinos, and 4.06 among Mexican Americans (U.S. Census, 1988:Table 1). This small family size obtained despite the fact that Cubans were more likely to have other relatives living in their households (9%), as compared to other Latinos (6%) and Americans in general (4%). The smaller family size among Cuban Americans can be attributed to (1) the older age of their population (38.7 years), (2) to their low fertility rate (16 per 1,000, compared to 17 U.S.) (Boswell, 1985:107), and (3) to their higher socio-economic positions. Their smaller family size is also related to the higher labor force participation rate among Cuban women (53.6%), which is the highest among Latinos. This is important since there is a direct relationship between the proportion of women in the labor force and lower fertility rates (See Table 12.3).

It is interesting to discover that while Cubans have the highest proportion of married couples (58.5%) and the lowest percentage of singles (24.8%) among Latino (57.1% and 32.1% respectively), they also have the highest divorce rate (9.1%) among Latinos (6.9% Latinos and 7.4% U.S.) (Schick and Schick, 1991:35). This is related to several factors, such as their immigration experience, refugee status, the greater number of women in the labor force (giving them greater independence), their lower fertility rate, and the greater acceptance of divorce in the Cuban-American community (Aguirre, 1981). However, Cuban men are not only more likely to remarry following divorce, but they also remarry sooner. In contrast, Cuban women are not as likely to remarry following divorce and are more likely to be the primary parent following divorce. As a result, three times as many single parent households were headed by Cuban women (16.1%), as compared to Cuban men (5.8%) (Schick and Schick, 1991:35). The proportion of female headed households in the Cuban American community is similar to the number found in the general population.

Table 12.3
Family Characteristics of Non-Latinos,
Cuban Americans, and Mexican Americans, 1988

	Non-Latinos	Cuban Americans	Mexican Americans
MARITAL STATUS			
Never Married (Percent)	25.8	24.8	31.9
Married	59.3	58.5	58.0
Widowed	7.4	7.6	3.5
Divorced	7.5	9.1	6.6
TYPE OF FAMILY			
Married Couples	80.3	78.1	74.4
Female Headed	15.8	16.1	18.5
Male Headed	4.0	5.8	7.1
SIZE OF FAMILY			
Two persons	42.4	32.8	21.9
Three persons	23.6	32.8	21.7
Four persons	20.8	24.1	24.7
Seven or more persons	1.6	*	7.9
Mean number of persons	3.13	3.16	4.06
FAMILIES BELOW POVERTY LEVEL			
Percent below poverty level	9.7	13.8	25.5
Female, husband absent	32.3	*	47.1

* Insufficient Numbers
Source: U.S. Census, 1988:Table 1, 2.

The higher rate of divorce among Cuban Americans may be related to their higher rate of exogamy (outmarriage). This is true since divorce rates tend to be slightly higher among those who marry outside their group. One study found that among second generation (i.e. American born) Cuban women the rate of exogamy was 46 percent, compared to 33 percent for Puerto Rican women and 16 percent of Mexican American women (Jaffe, et al, 1980:63-68).

More recently, the 1990 census found that 14.6 percent of Cuban American men married a non-Latino wife, as compared to 14.9 percent of Cuban American women who married a non-Latino husband (about 1,000 more marriages). But the same proportion of Cuban American men and women (10.9%) married another Latino (U.S. Census, 1991:Table 55).

Therefore, Cuban American women have a slightly greater propensity to marry someone outside their ethnic group (primarily Anglo American men). Overall, this high rate of exogamy indicates a higher rate of acceptance of intermarriage between Cubans and non-Latinos.

Recently the Cuban American family has undergone some important changes, primarily in response to changing social and economic conditions. As with other immigrant groups, a common point of conflict within the family is the difference in values between traditional parents and their Americanized children. Even within the Cuban enclave, it is not unusual to find that children are torn between the demands and expectations of their parents and those of the youth culture in American society.

Another important area of change is the greater equality that exists today in the Cuban American family. While the first generation was strongly attached to the patriarchial orientation of the Latin culture, with its emphasis on machismo, the second generation is moving toward greater social equality and greater independence for women (Richmond, 1980:33-39). This in part is due to the higher number of Cuban American women in the labor force and the higher levels of education achieved by Cuban Americans (Boswell, 1985:108-109).

Chapter Summary

Like Mexico and Puerto Rico, Cuba was also conquered by the Spanish in the early part of the Fifteenth century and was transformed into a vast plantation system that depended on slave labor. As a result of disease and the harsh treatment they received at the hands of their Spanish landlords, the Indians on the island died off by the thousands.

Following the Spanish American War, and the signing of the Treaty of Paris (1899), the United States assumed control of the island nation. In 1902 the United States granted the Cuban people their independence. For the next fifty years Cuba was ruled by a series of corrupt political leaders who became wealthy at the expense of the people. In January of 1959 Fidel Castro assumed control of the government.

In order to insure total control of the government and economic structure of Cuban society, Fidel Castro ordered the expulsion of thousands of entrepreneurs, professionals, and scholars. For this reason the first wave of Cuban refugees are often referred to as the Golden Exiles. With the help of federal government programs the Golden Exiles established themselves in south Florida and quickly created a robust Cuban American community in Miami. Thousands of Cuban refugees have entered the United States since the arrival of the first refugees in the early 1960's. The most recent mass movement of Cuban refugees occurred in 1980, during the Mariel boat lift.

Today, Cuban Americans are very successful and have adapted to the needs and expectations of American society. As a group Cuban Americans are not only recognized for their educational achievements, high standard of living, and occupational mobility, but also for their success in the political arena and in the market place. Today Cuban Americans living in south Florida are represented at every level of government. In addition some Cuban Americans have become nationally recognized leaders in business and industry.

References

Aguirre, Benigno E.
1981   "The Marital Stability of Cubans in the United States."
            Ethnicity 8(4):387-405

Azieri, Max
1981   "The Politics of Exile: Trends and Dynamics of Political
            Change Among Cuba-Americans." *Cuban Studies* 11:55-73.

Bach, Robert L.
1985   "Cubans." In *Refugees in the United States.* David W. Haines (ed.),
            Westport, CT: Greenwood Press, Pp. 77-93.

1987   "The Cuban Exodus: Political and Economic Motivations."
            In *The Caribbean Exodus.* Barry B. Levine (ed.), NY: Praeger,
            Pp. 106-130.

Bach, Robert L., and J. B. Bach, T. Triplett
1981   "The Flotilla 'Entrants': Latest and Most Controversial."
            Cuban Studies 11:29-48 (July).

Blutstein, Howard K., et al
1971   *Area Handbook for Cuba.* Washington, D.C.:USGPO.

Borjas, George J.
1982   "The Earnings of Male Hispanic Immigrants in the United
            States." *Industrial and Labor Relations Review* 35:343-353.

Boswell, Thomas D.
1985   "The Cuban-Americans." *In Ethnicity in Contemporary
            America: A Geographical Appraisal.* Jesse O. McKee (ed.),
            Dubuque, IA: Kendall/Hunt, Pp. 95-116.

Boswell, Thomas D. and James R. Curtis
1983   *The Cuban-American Experience: Culture, Images, and
            Perspectives.* Totowa, NJ: Rowman & Allanheld.

Butler, John S. and Cedric Herring
1991   "Ethnicity and Entrepreneurship in America: Toward an
            Explanation of Racial and Ethnic Group Variations in Self-
            Employment." *Sociological Perspectives* 34(1):79-94.

Chaffee, Wilber A., Jr.
1989   "Cuba: A Background." In *Cuba: A Different America.*
            Wilber A. Caffee, Jr. and Gary Prevost (eds.), Totowa, NJ:
            Rowman & Littlefield, Pp. 1-18.

Duany, Jorge
1992   "Caribbean Migration to Puerto Rico: A Comparison of
            Cubans and Dominicans." *International Migration Review*
            26(1):46- 66.

Fagen, Richard R., and R. A. Brody, T. J. O'Leary
1968   *Cubans in Exile: Disaffection and the Revolution.* Stanford,
            CA Stanford University Press.

Fradd, Sandra
    1983   "Cubans to Cuban Americans: Assimilation in the United
                States." *Migration Today* 11:34-42.
Gonzales, Juan L. Jr.
    1991   *The Lives of Ethnic Americans.* Dubuque, IA: Kendall/Hunt.
Hernandez, Roberto E.
    1985   "The Origins of the Mariel Boatlift." In *Coping With
                Adolescent Refugees: The Mariel Boatlift.* Jose Szapocznik, R. E.
                Cohen, and R. E. Hernandez (eds.), NY: Praeger, Pp. 3-21
Hoffman, Mark S.
    1993   *The World Almanac and Book of Facts 1993.* New York:
                Pharos Books.
Jaffe, A. J., and Ruth M. Cullen, Thomas D. Boswell
    1980   *The Changing Demography of Spanish Americans.* NY:
                Academic Press.
Kremitsis, Dawn
    1989   "Women in the Workplace." *In Cuba: A Different America.*
                Wilber A. Caffee, Jr. and Gary Prevost (eds.) Totowa, NJ:
                Rowman & Littlefield, Pp. 102-115.
Kunz, E. F.
    1973   "The Refugee in Flight: Kinetic Models and Forms of
                Displacement." *International Migration Review* 7:125-146.
MacCoy, Clyde B. and Diana H. Gonzalez
    1985   "Cuban Immigration and Mariel Immigrants." In *Coping
                With Adolescent Refugees: The Mariel Boatlift.* Jose Szapocznik,
                R. E. Cohen, and R. E. Hernandez (eds.), NY: Praeger, Pp.
                22-38.
Model, Suzanne
    1992   "The Ethnic Economy: Cubans and Chinese Reconsidered."
                The Sociological Quarterly 33(1):63-82.
Mormino, Gary R. and George E. Pozzetta
    1987   *The Immigrant World of Ybor City: Italians and Their Latin
                Neighbors in Tampa, 1885-1985.* Urbana: University of Illinois
                Press.
Pedraza-Bailey, Silvia
    1985a   *Political and Economic Migrants in America: Cubans and Mexicans.*
                Austin: University of Texas Press.
    1985b   "Cuba's Exiles: Portrait of a Refugee Migration."
                International Migration Review 19(1):4-34.
Perez, Lisandro
    1985   "The Cuban Population of the United States: the Results of
                the 1980 U.S. Census of Population." *Cuban Studies* 15(2):1-
                18.

1986   "Immigrant Economic Adjustment and Family Organization: The Cuban Success Story Re-examined." *International Migration Review* 20:4-20.

Portes, Alejandro, and J. M. Clark, M. M. Lopez
1982   "Six Years Later, the Process of Incorporation of Cuban Exiles in the United States: 1973-1979." *Cuban Studies* 11:1-24.

Portes, Alejandro and Robert L. Bach
1985   *Latin Journey: Cuban and Mexican Immigrants in the United States.* Berkeley: University of California Press.

Portes, Alejandro and Ruben G. Rumbaut
1990   *Immigrant America: A Portrait.* Berkeley: University of California Press.

Richmond, Marie L.
1980   *Immigrant Adaptation and Family Structure Among Cubans in Miami, Florida.* NY: Arno Press.

Schick, Frank L. and Renee Schick (eds.)
1991   *Statistical Handbook on U.S. Hispanics.* Phoenix, AZ: Oryx Press.

Suchlicki, Jaime
1975   *Cuba: From Columbus to Castro.* NY: Scribner's.

Tienda, Marta and Franklin D. Wilson
1992   "Migration and the Earnings of Hispanic Men." *American Sociological Review* 57(5):661-678.

U.S. Census
1985   *Projections of the Hispanic Population: 1983-2080.* Washington, D.C.:USGPO Current Population Reports, Series P-25, No. 995.

1988   *The Hispanic Population in the United States: March 1988 (Advance Report).* Washington, D.C.:USGPO Current Population Reports, Series P-20, No. 431, August.

1991   *Statistical Abstract of the United States, 1991* (111th Edition). Washington, D.C.:USGPO.

Wilson, Kenneth L. and Alejandro Portes
1980   "Immigrant Cubans in Miami." *American Journal of Sociology* 86:295-319.

Wright, John W.
1993   *The Universal Almanac 1993.* Kansas City, KS: Andrews and McMeel.

1492	Columbus discovered the island of *Cubanacan*, the original Indian name for Cuba.
1511	The Spanish began to colonize the island.
1515	Seven cities were founded, including Havana and Santiago.
1517	The Spanish introduced the slave trade to Cuba.
1519	Out of an original population of 100,000 Indians, only 3,000 survived the Spanish conquest.
1762	The British captured Havana and held it for ten months.
1819	Steam powered mills were introduced into Cuban agriculture and stimulated sugar production.
1830	The production of tobacco reached a new peak.
1886	Slavery was finally abolished in Cuba.
1895	Cuba experienced an economic depression, with a fall in sugar, coffee, and tobacco production and prices.
1898	The battleship Maine was blown up, killing 260 U.S. sailors. This sparked a war between the U.S. and Spain.
1899	The Treaty of Paris is signed in April ending the war.
1901	The Platt Amendment allowed the U.S. to maintain a naval base at Guantanomo Bay.
1902	Cuba receives its independence from the United States.
1934	Fulgencio Batista became chief of staff of the army and served until 1940.
1940	Batista was elected president and served until 1944.
1952	Following a coup d'etat Batista assumed the presidency.
1953	On July 26, Fidel Castro led an attack on an army post in the city of Santiago. For his role Castro was sentenced to 15 years in prison.
1954	As the only candidate for the office, Batista was legally elected president.
1955	Following his reelection to office Batista granted amnesty to all his former enemies, including Fidel Castro.
1956	Castro and 83 rebels landed in Cuba and established a guerrilla camp in the Sierra Maestra Mountains.
1959	Batista fled Cuba on January 1, and Castro and his army marched into Havana on January 8th to assume power.
1960	Diplomatic relations between the U.S. and Cuba were severed.
1961	In April the Cuban exile brigade landed at the Bay of Pigs.
1962	Commercial flights were terminated between the U.S. and Cuba. The Russian missile crisis occurred in October.
1965	Beginning of the U.S. freedom flights in December.

1973	The freedom flights were terminated and few refugees were allowed to leave Cuba.
1980	The Mariel boatlift occurred between May and September.
1992	The U.S. Cuban American population reached one million.

Important Names

Illeana Ros-Lehtinen   Fugencio Batista   Fidel Castro

Key Terms

Cubanacan	Treaty of Paris	freedom flights
golden exiles	brain drain	Cuban missile crisis
Marial boat lift	Marielitos	Little Havana

Sample Test Questions

1. Discuss the characteristics of four distinct groups of Cuban immigrants.
2. Provide four sound sociological reasons for the success of Cuban Americans today.
3. Provide a brief discussion of four important events in Cuban history.
4. Outline and discuss five socio-economic or demographic characteristics of Cuban Americans today.

Part IV
★ ★ ★
The African American Experience

Chapter 13

The African American Experience

The Slave Trade

It is important to understand that the European slave trade was not only profitable in terms of the value of the Black cargo, but also in terms of the exchange of products. By the eighteenth century the English had established a very lucrative triangular trade system that allowed them to exchange commodities produced in Britain such as textiles, guns, and spirits, for slaves captured on the West Coast of Africa. The British established trading posts in Africa where they exchanged their products for slaves. Local African chiefs were commissioned to capture members of rival tribes, who were then incarcerated and sold to British slave traders.

Almost half the slaves died during the middle passage, due to the crowded quarters and the unhealthy conditions on board the slave ships. Their voyage ended in the Caribbean, where they were exchanged for sugar, tobacco, cotton, and rum. Once settled on the islands their spirits were broken before they were put on the auction block in the United States. Their sojourn in the islands was referred to as the seasoning in the islands. The triangular trade pattern was completed when the British ships returned to the motherland with their Caribbean goods (Williams, 1966:51-84). While the profits from the slave trade launched Europe into the industrial age, millions of Africans were forcibly removed from their native lands and lost their lives to the slave trade.

Africans in the New World

Contrary to popular conceptions, the first Blacks did not arrive in the New

World as slaves, rather they were explorers, laborers, and servants. While some historians believe that one of Columbus' sailors was an African, it is known that there were thirty African sailors with Balboa when he discovered the Pacific Ocean in 1513. Six years later when Hernando Cortez landed in Mexico, several of his men were Africans (Franklin, 1967:46).The best known African (Spanish) explorer in the New World was Estevanico, who discovered and explored the states of Texas, New Mexico, and Arizona.

The twenty Africans who arrived on a Dutch frigate in Jamestown in 1619 were not slaves, but were indentured servants. The acute labor shortage in the colonies prompted the British to institute a system of indentured servitude, whereby those individuals without any resources could sign a labor contract (usually for seven years) and have their passage and upkeep paid by their master. When they completed their contracts they were given their freedom and a plot of land. Unfortunately the Africans found that their contracts were arbitrarily extended and eventually they were given the legal standing of perpetual servants.

In 1661 the colony of Virginia earned the historic distinction of being the first to recognize slavery as a legal institution. Two years later Maryland and the Carolina's legalized slavery. These slave laws also stipulated that any children born to an African woman, would be given the status of a slave, thus guaranteeing the proliferation of slavery in America.

The Institution of Slavery

Slavery was justified on two points, first that Africans were a separate species and second that they were heathens who had to be Christianized (Jordan, 1968:179-265). The popular belief was that slaves were like children who had to be watched, could not be trusted, and were potentially dangerous. Christian beliefs held that Africans were the lost tribe of the children of Ham, who's skin color was black due to God's punishment. As such, their lot in life was to work as servants. While their souls could be saved, they could not be freed, for their role in life was to be good slaves (Gossett, 1965:28-53).

By the turn of the nineteenth century the slave population had reached a million, with the heaviest concentration in the South. Most of the emancipated slaves lived in the North. When the Civil War broke out, the African American population reached 4.5 million (See Table 13.1).

It is interesting to note that very few Southern whites actually owned slaves, as three out of four did not. And it was rare for anyone to own more than a hundred slaves (Stamp, 1956). On the eve of the Civil War (i.e. in 1860) only one out of eight (12%) slave masters owned twenty or more slaves (Meier and Rudwick, 1966:56).

Table 13.1
The African American Population of the
United States, 1790-2000

Year	Total African American Population	African American Percentage of Total Population	Percentage of African Americans Enslaved
1790	757,000	19.3	92.1
1800	1,002,000	18.9	89.2
1810	1,378,000	19.0	86.5
1820	1,772,000	18.4	87.4
1830	2,329,000	18.1	86.9
1840	2,874,000	16.8	87.0
1850	3,639,000	15.7	88.5
1860	4,442,000	14.1	89.5
1870	4,880,000	12.7	——
1880	6,581,000	13.1	——
1890	7,489,000	11.9	——
1900	8,834,000	11.6	——
1910	9,828,000	10.7	——
1920	10,463,000	9.9	——
1930	11,891,000	9.7	——
1940	12,866,000	9.8	——
1950	15,042,000	10.0	——
1960	18,872,000	10.5	——
1970	22,581,000	11.1	——
1980	26,683,000	11.8	——
1988	30,287,000	12.3	——
1990	30,788,000	12.4	——
1995*	33,199,000	12.7	——
2000*	35,129,000	13.1	——

*Projections
Source: U.S. Census, 1991:Table 12, Table 16.

Most slaves worked on large family farms or plantations, where they were engaged in the planting and harvesting of commercial crops such as cotton, tobacco, rice, and sugar cane. Besides working in the fields, slaves were required to clear land, haul water, cut and split wood, and maintain the livestock. By all historical accounts slaves typically worked from sunrise to sunset, and sometimes into the night.

On large plantations a clear distinction was made between house servants and field hands. The house servants, who were the cooks, maids, gardeners, and drivers, were usually given special privileges and felt superior to the field hands. It was also customary for slave masters to assign their slave children to the staff of household servants. Consequently it was not uncommon for house servants to exhibit distinct Caucasian features.

Slaves were closely supervised and the use of corporal punishment was common. While most slaves were whipped for even minor transgressions, cases of mutilation and even branding were not unknown. In addition, a system of slave codes were devised to insure that all slaves conformed to their master's expectations. The slave codes impressed upon them that, slavery was for life, they were chattel, they had no rights, and that intimidation and coercion would be used to maintain the system.

The slave family lacked legal standing, as husbands, wives, and children could be separated and sold at any time. Slave breeding was common and slave women were encouraged to produce as many children as possible. Technically southern laws held that the father of a slave was unknown, as the law did not recognize slave marriages. In practice, the white slave master was the father of all the slave families, as he made all the decisions for the slave family.

While the slave family was almost destroyed, religion played an important role in their lives, since the teachings of Christianity were used by slave masters to insure docility and compliance with the oppressive conditions of slavery. For its part Christianity offered the slaves eternal salvation. Nonetheless, religion did make life on the plantation bearable and over time provided the leadership that was once lacking in the slave community.

The Abolitionist Movement

The Massachusetts Constitution that was adopted in 1780 stated that "all men are born free and equal," thus signaling the beginning of the end of slavery. By the turn of the century New York and New Jersey passed manumission acts.

But the ardent fervor of the abolitionist's movement did not take hold until the early 1830's. The publication of *David Walker's Appeal*, a strong anti-slavery narrative written by a former slave from North Carolina, set the abolitionist movement ablaze. Similarly the publication of William Lloyd Garrison's *The Liberator* (1831) focused national attention on the slavery question. But it took the impact of Nat Turner's rebellion in Southampton County, Virginia (1831), to bring the nation to the brink of panic. This act of open rebellion struck terror into the hearts of all Southerners (Litwack, 1961:230-246).

The abolitionists argued against slavery on three basic principles, namely that slavery was (1) inconsistent with the teachings of Christianity, (2) contrary to the Constitution and the American way of life, and (3) was a menace to the peace and safety of all citizens. Some former slaves, such as

Frederick Douglass, Theodore Wright, William Jones, and Charles Gardner, were full time propagandists for the abolitionists. It is also interesting to note that all African American newspapers founded before the Civil War were abolitionists sheets.

The Compromise of 1850 was the first serious blow to national harmony, as it held that fugitive slave laws could be enforced in all states. The Supreme Court exacerbated the situation when it ruled, in the Dred Scott case (1857), that slaves were private property and could not, under any circumstances, be taken away from their owners. The Court's decision was a clear-cut victory for the South, as the highest court in the land upheld the legitimacy of the institution of slavery.

The Civil War and Reconstruction

John Brown's raid at Harpers Ferry (1859) and the Republican victory in the presidential election of 1860 were the two events that set the stage for the Civil War. When Lincoln arrived in Washington to take office in February of 1861, seven states had already seceded from the Union. The final act of defiance came on April 13, 1861, when Confederate forces attacked Fort Sumter.

President Lincoln issued the Emancipation Proclamation on January 1, 1863, freeing all the slaves held in the rebellious Southern states. But this was strictly a military strategy on his part and not a humanitarian gesture, as he only wanted to strip the South of its slave power.

By the end of the war more than 186,000 African Americans had served in the Union Army (Franklin, 1967:293). This was the second great war in the history of this young nation in which African Americans were asked to sacrifice their lives for the preservation of freedom and democracy.

In 1865 the Thirteenth Amendment abolished slavery. And in an attempt to protect the civil rights of the former slaves the Reconstruction Act of 1867 established martial law in the South. For the first time African American and white children attended the same schools and integration was the rule on trains and streetcars. In addition, the Black Codes were abolished and the passage of the Fifteenth Amendment guaranteed every person the right to vote, regardless of their race, color, or previous condition of servitude. In less than a dozen years African Americans elected several hundred local officials, six lieutenant governors, sixteen state representatives, twenty congressmen, and two senators (Stamp, 1965).

Jim Crow Segregation

The institutionalized segregation patterns that evolved in the South following the Civil War are known as Jim Crow laws. These laws affected all public facilities, including public transportation, schools, libraries, housing, restaurants, lodging facilities, public bathrooms, public water fountains, public beaches, and a host of other facilities (Johnson, 1970; Woodward, 1974). In 1896, the Supreme Court supported Jim Crow segregation in its decision in *Plessy vs. Ferguson*. In this historic case the High Court held that separate but equal accommodations for African Americans was a reasonable use of the power of state governments.

In 1898, the Supreme Court ruled that the use of poll taxes, literacy tests, and residential requirements, all of which deprived African Americans of their right to vote, were constitutional. In addition, the understanding clause, the grandfather clause, and the good character clause were also used to prevent African Americans from voting (Woodward, 1966).

Life in the Northern Cities

Approximately nine out of ten of all African Americans were still living in the South at the turn of the century, that is in spite of the harsh economic conditions and the heavy mantle of racism. In 1860, only 16 percent lived in cities, but by 1900, 28 percent lived in urban areas. By 1920, six cities had African American populations of more than 100,000. In response to the demand for labor during the First World War and the termination of European immigration, it is estimated that between half a million to a million African Americans left the South to work in the Northern industries between 1914 to 1920 (Meier and Rudwick, 1966:189-192).

While life in the South was fraught with poverty and racism, African Americans soon discovered that life in the Northern cities also posed certain dangers, for it was not long before they became the victims of racial violence. The first large scale urban riot took place in Springfield, Illinois, in August of 1908. The mob violence resulted in the lynching of two African American men, the destruction of numerous homes and businesses, and the death of four white men. It took a force of five thousand militiamen to restore order.

A more serious riot in East St. Louis in 1917 resulted in the death of 39 African Americans and nine whites. The Red Summer of 1919, marked the high point in mob violence, as more than 26 riots broke out across the country. The most serious riot occurred in Chicago, where 38 were killed, 23 of them African Americans (Grimshaw, 1969).

The irony of course, was that during this period of urban violence some 400,000 African Americans were serving in the Armed Forces (in segregated units), to protect freedom and democracy in the world. By the end of the First World War, African Americans were disillusioned with the American dream. They realized that the level of racism in the North was not much different from that which they experienced in the South.

The Great Depression and World War II

With the onset of the Great Depression in the 1930's African Americans were among the hardest hit. Life before the Depression was onerous, but life during the Depression was oppressive. As a rule African Americans have always suffered from higher unemployment rates than the general population, but during the Depression employers became very selective in their hiring practices and many refused to hire African Americans. Many labor unions enforced a whites only policy. African Americans also faced discrimination from the relief agencies established during the Depression, since many agencies screened out African American applicants.

While many New Deal programs were effective in providing relief to millions of Americans, by 1940 it was clear that these relief efforts were not enough to bring the country out of the Depression. In the end, it took the tragedy at Pearl Harbor (1941) to turn the American economy around. As in all wars, African Americans were given an equal opportunity to serve their country. During the first year of the war over 370,000 African Americans joined the armed services and at the peak of the war (1944), 700,000 African Americans were in uniform (Franklin, 1966:75). Overall a total of one million African Americans served their country during World War II.

Post War Race Relations

In response to the racial disorders that occurred during the Second World War, African Americans reacted by organizing themselves. The best known civil rights organization of this period was the Congress of Racial Equality (CORE), founded in 1942, in Chicago. CORE's objective was to fight racial discrimination in a nonviolent direct fashion, that is in the Gandhian tradition. CORE was a biracial nonreligious organization, and was effective in using sit-ins to open restaurants to African Americans in Chicago, Baltimore, and Los Angeles. They also initiated the freedom rides into the South (1947) to test a court ruling that prohibited segregated seating on interstate buses.

With the death of President Franklin Roosevelt in April of 1945, Harry S. Truman took office and continued many of the racial reform policies initiated during the Roosevelt administration. Late in 1946 Truman created a Presidential Committee on Civil Rights and convened an interracial committee to investigate problems in higher education. Two years later he issued Executive Order 9981, that called for the desegregation of the Armed Forces. Truman also created a permanent Civil Rights Commission and a Fair Employment Practices Committee.

The Supreme Court was also active during this period. Early in 1944, the Court decided in *Smith vs. Allwright* that the white primary was unconstitutional inasmuch as it deprived African Americans of their voting rights. Two years later the Court ruled in *Morgan vs. Virginia* that interstate bus passengers could not be segregated. In the historic case of *Shelley vs. Kraemer* (1948) the Court ruled that racially restrictive covenants in the conveyance of real estate could not be enforced in the courts. In 1950 the Court held that African Americans could not be segregated in railway dining cars.

School Desegregation

The new era for civil rights is marked by the Supreme Court decision in *Brown vs. The Board of Education* (1954). In this case Linda Brown, a seven year old, was not allowed to enroll in a white school four blocks from her home, but was directed by the Topeka, Kansas School Board to attend an all Black school two miles from her home. The NAACP took her case to the Supreme Court and argued that the Fourteenth Amendment ruled out segregation in public schools. The Court ruled in their favor and held that "separate educational facilities are inherently unequal" (Blaustein and Zangrando, 1968:414-467). Unfortunately it took violence to initiate the integration of public schools across the country.

When the school year opened in September of 1956 mob violence prevented African American students from enrolling in public high schools in Texas, Tennessee, and Kentucky. The most publicized incident occurred the following year at Central High School in Little Rock, Arkansas, when an African American student was met by a jeering crowd of whites, who prevented her from entering the school. Finally the President ordered 10,000 National Guardsmen to the campus, to ensure that the nine African American students were enrolled. The federal troops remained on campus for the remainder of the school year to discourage further acts of violence.

During the fall semester of 1962, James Meredith attempted to enroll at the University of Mississippi. The ensuing violence resulted in the loss of two lives and over one hundred injuries. In addition 12,000 federal troops were stationed on campus so that Meredith could attend classes. In January of 1963, Governor George Wallace literally stood in the schoolhouse door to prevent two African American students from enrolling at the University of Alabama. President Kennedy was forced to federalize the Alabama National Guard to allow these students to enroll in the University.

The Civil Rights Movement

The modern Civil Rights Movement was launched in Montgomery, Alabama on December 1, 1955, by Rosa Parks. Ms. Parks, an African American seamstress, refused to give up her seat to a white man on a crowded bus. The

Jim Crow laws of the day required any African American person to give up their seat to any white person on a crowded bus. Mrs. Parks was promptly arrested and the Montgomery Bus Boycott was underway (Gonzales, 1991:213-219). The boycott ended a year later when the Supreme Court ruled in *Gayle vs. Browder* that racial segregation on buses was unconstitutional. Similar boycotts were organized in Tallahassee and Birmingham.

The Montgomery Bus Boycott resulted in the organization of the Montgomery Improvement Association, lead by Martin Luther King, Jr. The involvement of Dr. King resulted in the first successful boycott based on the philosophy of nonviolence, based on six key elements: (1) active resistance to evil, (2) attempts to win one's opponent through understanding, (3) directing one's attack against forces of evil, rather than against people, (4) willingness to accept suffering without retaliation, (5) refusal to hate one's opponent, and (6) the conviction that the universe is on the side of justice (King, 1958:102-107).

During a short period several civil rights organizations were founded and committed themselves to direct nonviolent action, such as the Southern Christian Leadership Conference (SCLC) (founded by Dr. King) and the Student Non-Violent Coordinating Committee (SNCC). These organizations were assisted in their work by the NAACP, the National Urban League, and dozens of religious, civic, and labor organizations across the country.

On February 1, 1960, four African American college students from North Carolina A & T State University were refused service at a lunch counter in Greensboro. State law did not allow African Americans to eat at lunch counters or at restaurants that served whites. The students remained in their seats until the store closed. This marked the beginning of the sit-in movements. By the summer thousands of students, both African American and white, sat at lunch counters throughout the South in nonviolent protest against institutional discrimination. They also used white water fountains and white bathrooms, sat in white libraries, swam at white beaches and pools, and slept in white hotel lobbies. Over a period of a year and a half some 70,000 African American and white protestors participated in the sit-ins and more than 3,600 were arrested (Bennett, 1966:407).

The following spring CORE sent freedom riders into the South to protest the segregation laws on the interstate bus system. The freedom riders were attacked by mobs in Montgomery, and were hosed, clubbed, and cattle-prodded in both Birmingham and Selma. They were also harassed and victimized by local officials, night riders, and by angry crowds throughout the South. By the summer of 1961 Southern jails were jammed with freedom riders, as the demonstration involved more than 1,000 persons and their legal expenses exceeded $300,000 (Lomax, 1962:132-146).

In April of 1963, Dr. King began a series of marches in Birmingham to demand the immediate desegregation of all public facilities, fair employment opportunities, and the integration of public schools. The following month the police chief of Birmingham, Eugene "Bull" Connor, used dogs and water cannons on the marchers. Television and newspaper coverage of the police violence against the demonstrators sparked nationwide support for the marchers. The following month Medgar Evers, the secretary of the Mississippi NAACP, was shot to death outside his Jackson, Mississippi home. His cold blooded murder touched off nationwide sitins, mass demonstrations, school strikes, and marches.

In September of 1963, the 16th Street Baptist Church in Birmingham was fire-bombed and four African American children were killed. Only one of the killers of the four Sunday school girls was found and convicted (Motley, 1966:516). These senseless murders were in response to the civil rights demonstrations that occurred throughout the South during the summer of 1963.

In sum, these demonstrations claimed ten lives, saw the bombing or burning of 35 homes and churches, and resulted in the incarceration of more than 20,000 demonstrators (Pinkney, 1975:184). The year ended with a nationwide march on Washington, which is now immortalized for Dr. King's "I Have a Dream" speech, delivered on August 28, 1963. Without any doubt the most tragic event of the year was the assassination of President Kennedy on November 22, 1963. His passing left some doubt about the future of the Civil Rights movement.

Urban Unrest and Racial Violence

Collective violence against African Americans has always taken the form of communal violence. This is true since whites have historically used violence to either keep African Americans out of, or to remove them from, their territory. For example, this occurs when African Americans move into all white neighborhoods or when they use white beaches or other recreational areas (Janowitz, 1968:9-17). In his study Grimshaw (1969) found that thirty-three major racial disturbances occurred in the United States between 1900 and 1949.

However, the urban violence that took place in the sixties was different, as these were commodity riots, since the objective of these disturbances was to obtain merchandise from white owned stores and businesses, which African Americans recognized as symbols of white oppression. The sentiment was that the African American community was an internal colony controlled from the outside by white landlords and businessmen. The urban violence represented African American reaction to years of frustration and disappointment with the system.

The new urban violence was also confined to the African American community and tended to pit local police and the militia against ghetto residents. Therefore few white civilians were involved in the urban violence and the ultimate result was the destruction of ghetto property, principally owned by white outsiders.

The riot that captured the nation's attention occurred in Los Angeles, in August of 1965. The Watts Riot lasted five days and resulted in the destruction of $40 million in property, the loss of thirty-four lives, more than 1,000 injuries, and over 4,000 arrests. At the peak of the riot 10,000 people were in the streets, and were confronted by 15,500 policemen and National Guardsmen (Pinkney, 1975:198). The Watts Riot was the worse incident of civil disorder in this country since the Detroit riot of 1943.

On April 29, 1992 racial violence and destruction struck south- central Los Angeles again, following the announcement of the innocent verdicts in the Rodney King case. To date this is now the worse riot in American history.

The Newark riot of 1967 resulted in 26 deaths, 1,100 injuries, and more than 1,600 arrest. Property damage was estimated at $15 million. It took a force of 3,000 National Guardsmen, 1,400 local police, and 500 state troopers several days to restore order. Shortly after the Newark riot, Detroit exploded into violence and claimed forty-three lives, 2,000 injuries and more than 5,000 arrests. Property damage exceeded $500 million.

One study estimated that 257 disorders occurred in 173 cities in 1967 alone. These disturbances resulted in the loss of 87 lives, over 2,500 injuries, and 29,200 arrests (Baskin, et al, 1971).

The Rise of Black Nationalism

During a march in Mississippi in 1966, Stokely Carmichael proclaimed to a crowd, "what we need is Black Power." He defined Black Power as "the ability of Black people to . . . organize themselves so that they can speak from a position of strength rather than a position of weakness" (Ladner, 1967:14).

One faction of the Black Power movement took a strong socialist route and viewed capitalism as the evil force in the African American community, while another faction viewed whites as holding the real power in society and held them responsible for African American oppression. A more radical segment of the movement took a separatist route, as they wanted to work for the total independence of African Americans from white society and en-visioned a Black nation.

The most radical of the Black nationalist movements was the Nation of Islam and under the leadership of Malcolm X they became known as the Black Muslims. They believed that whites were devils who were created to be the enemy of African Americans for six thousand years, a period that ended in 1914 (Draper, 1970: 78). They wanted to free all African Americans from the evil influence of whites, with the goal that they would eventually establish a separate Black nation within the United States.

Without any doubt the most militant direct-action group to adopt the theme of Black Power was the Black Panther party, founded in 1966 by Huey Newton and Bobby Seale in Oakland, California. The Panther's were first organized as a self-defense group, but soon adopted a radical ideology that promoted the overthrow of capitalism. Their policy of armed self-defense resulted in several shoot-outs with the police. As a result, between 1968 and 1970 dozens of Panthers were killed and thousands were arrested. By 1973 Newton admitted that the Panther's had alienated the Black community and had become too radical (Woodward, 1974:205). On the morning of August 22, 1989, Huey Newton was found shot to death on the streets of West Oakland.

The African American Family

Contrary to the popular image of the African American family as plagued by a host of social dysfunctions, the reality belies this stereotype. In fact, several studies have found that the African American family has a strong traditional and conservative orientation, is highly religious, encourages hard work, and the family and children provide ultimate satisfaction (Farley and Allen, 1987:60-187).

The stereotype of the African American family holds that it consists of a single mother, who is the head of the household and is on welfare. While the proportion of female headed households are greater among African Americans, this is simply a reflection of the lack of jobs and educational opportunities. The primary distinction between African American and white families is the pervasiveness of poverty among African Americans. Therefore it is poverty based on the lack of jobs that has given the African American family its distinction (Swinton, 1987).

In 1990, half (50.2%) of African American families had both spouses present, compared to four out of five (83%) of white families. Two out of five (43.5%) African Americans lived in a female headed household, compared to only one out of eight (13%) white families. Eleven percent of African Americans were separated, compared to four percent of all families and 10.2 percent were divorced, compared with 12.2 percent of white families. One-third (34.6%) of all African Americans were single, compared to only one out of five (20.5%) Anglo Americans (U.S. Census, 1991:Table 43, Table 50).

These statistics reflect the impact of racial discrimination and the lack of opportunity for social improvement in the African American community. Sociologists have long recognized that family stability is dependent on economic stability. Consequently, the high rate of unemployment among African Americans has a direct impact on family stability. This also accounts for the higher divorce rates and separation rates among African Americans today. In addition, substandard housing, inferior schools, low wages, dead-end jobs, and a life of poverty have adversely affected family stability.

While female-headed households are three times more likely to occur in the African American community and the number of unwed mothers is higher, it is misleading to focus on such comparative statistics. For to focus on female-headed households and the number of unmarried mothers in the African American community is to ignore the social and economic pressures that are placed on the African American family today. Therefore if white families were confronted with similar living conditions and life chances the statistical reports on such social indicators as divorce, separation, poverty rates, and unemployment would be similar.

The historical roots of the African American family are in Africa and as such the African American family has its origins in a distinct culture and society, as is true of most immigrant groups in American society today. Since African Americans came from Africa they came from (1) a society with different norms and values, (2) a society with many different tribes (each with their language, customs, and traditions), and (3) they arrived with few women and (4) came as slaves.

The basis for the African American family was the African kinship group that held the village as its focus, but placed a strong emphasis on family and kinship ties. The life of the community depended upon cooperation, mutual aid and assistance, and the maintenance of social order. When a woman married she remained a member of her family, but was considered the wife of the family and not just the wife of a husband (Franklin, 1967:28-31).

In pre-Colonial African society the family was patriarchal, as the male was viewed as the protector of the family and children were considered the future of the family and tribe. Obviously, the slave experience devastated the African family system, as slaves were sold without regard to tribal origins or family ties.

Marriage among slaves in America was an informal affair that carried no legal weight or consideration. Slave masters viewed conjugal ties between slaves as a breeding opportunity that would serve to build their stock of slaves. While the slave experience devastated the African family structure, it also resulted in the genesis of a new slave family and slave community that became the source of strength for all African Americans held in bondage.

In his book, *Black Families in White America* Andrew Billingsley (1968) provides a detailed description of the structure of African American families and notes that there are three major types of family structures in the African American community:

1. The Nuclear Family: husband and wife, and their children, with no other relatives present
2. The Extended Family: includes other relatives or in-laws who share the same household
3. The Augmented Family: includes individuals who are not related to the family head, but who share the same household.

According to Billingsley, fifteen percent of African American families have one or more minor relatives living with them. This figure is even higher among the urban poor. In his analysis of the African American family Billingsley identifies four classes of relatives, (1) minor relatives: cousins, nieces, nephews, grandchildren, (2) peers of the primary parents: siblings, cousins, and other adult relatives, (3) elders of primary parents: aunts and uncles, and (4) parents of the primary heads.

The universal reliance on the extended family is a reaction to the need for mutual aid and support in a hostile environment. Therefore in time of need family members know that they can count on relatives for support. For this reason the African American family is a very functional unit, as kinsmen can always count on one another for financial assistance, labor sharing, child care, advice, and moral and emotional support (Hunter and Ensminger, 1992:424-425; Stack, 1974; Staples and Johnson, 1992).

Educational Neglect

Since the 1954 Court order to integrate all public schools, the focus in educational circles has been on African American educational achievement and the quality of African American education. While some progress has been made in both areas, a good deal of work remains to be done. For example, in 1950, almost nine out of ten (87%) of the African Americans had not graduated from high school. By 1990, four out of ten (36%) African Americans had not, compared to only one out of five (22%) Anglo Americans (U.S. Census, 1991:Figure 4.2).

In 1960, the median level of education for whites was 10.9 years and for African Americans it was only eight years. Thirty years later their median levels of education are 12.7 and 12.4 years, respectively (U.S. Census, 1991:Table 224). Obviously the educational gap between African Americans and Anglo Americans is closing rapidly. But the quality of education must be considered, for it is a well known fact that most African American students are relegated to highly segregated central city schools, where they are summarily passed from one grade to the next. These are the very school districts that are confronted with the most serious problems in the nation's educational system (Meier, et al, 1989:40-57).

In 1990, one-third (35.4%) of African Americans 25 years and older had less than a high school education, while only one out of five (21.6%) whites fell into this category. At the other end of the educational spectrum almost twice as many whites (21.8%) were college graduates, as African Americans (11.8%). In this regard it is interesting to note that African American women are more likely to have a college degree than African American men and are also more likely to have earned a master's degree or a doctorate than African American men (See Table 13.2).

Table 13.2
Degrees Earned by African Americans, 1988-1989

	Associate	Bachelor's	Master's	Doctorate	Professional
Men	12,826	22,365	5,200	497	1,608
Women	21,585	35,651	8,876	574	1,493
Total	34,411	58,016	14,076	1,071	3,101

Source: The Chronicle of Higher Education Almanac, August 28, 1991.

African American students often face obstacles that make it particularly difficult for them to complete high school, or to qualify for college. For example, they are more likely to experience financial difficulties, are not encouraged to go on to college, and receive poor counseling. They also find that their teachers are insensitive and tend to be the lowest paid and the least experienced (Blackwell, 1990:38-46; Table 4).

Within the educational system itself, the teacher-student ratio in predominately African American schools is usually higher than in other schools, school facilities and programs are inferior, adjustments are not made for racial and cultural differences of the student body, and the course offerings are usually irrelevant to the African American experience. Particularly discouraging is the fact that their schools usually have higher crime rates, drug abuse rates, and absentee rates. Clearly, drop-out rates and test scores do not tell the whole story of educational neglect among African American students.

The Income Gap

For African Americans the persistence of the income gap is one of the most important issues today. The income gap refers to the differences between what the average white worker earns at a given job, compared to what the average African American worker earns at the same job. For example, in 1989 the median household income of white Americans was $30,406, while it was only $18,083 for African Americans.

In terms of the income gap, this means that African Americans only earned 59 percent of what whites earn, or a thousand dollars less a month than whites. The income gap not only reflects the impact of discrimination, but it also supports the observation that many African Americans are employed in the secondary labor market, which offers minimal pay and few benefits (Bonacich, 1990:189-197).

Another way to demonstrate the economic impact of the income gap on the African American community is to compare the median family income for African Americans and Anglo Americans. (See Table 13.3). Despite the common perception of social progress in American society it is clear that the median family income of African American families has increased by less than $300 since 1970, while the income gap between African Americans and white Americans has increased by more than $2,000 over the past twenty years.

Table 13.3
Black-White Median Family Income for
Selected Years, 1970-1990
(in 1990 dollars)

Year	Median Family Income		Percent Black Income of White	Income Gap
	Black	White		
1970	21,151	34,481	61.3	13,330
1972	21,462	34,757	61.7	13,295
1974	21,225	35,546	59.7	14,321
1976	21,229	35,689	59.5	14,460
1978	21,808	36,821	59.2	15,013
1980	20,103	34,743	57.9	14,640
1982	18,417	33,322	55.3	14,905
1984	19,411	34,827	55.7	15,416
1986	20,993	36,740	57.1	15,747
1988	21,355	37,470	57.0	16,115
1990	21,423	36,915	58.0	15,492

Source: Swinton, 1992:Table 8

Political Participation

The Civil Rights Movement was a milestone in African American political participation inasmuch as it moved a significant number of African Americans into the political process. In brief, the Civil Rights Movement,

1. encouraged voter registration,
2. fostered block voting patterns,
3. stimulated the formation of grass-roots political organizations,
4. provided concrete examples of the effectiveness of political participation,
5. encouraged community leaders to play a more activist role,
6. stimulated pride and political consciousness in the community,

7. encouraged others to support minority issues, and
8. resulted in the more equitable representation of African Americans at all levels of government.

The effectiveness of the Civil Rights Movement in stimulating political participation among African Americans can be determined from the ever increasing levels of political involvement. For example, in 1970 there were only 1,479 African American elected officials across the country. But twenty years later their level of representation was five times as great, as it increased to 7,370. Of these elected officials, 447 were federal and state legislators and 4,499 were city and county officials (U.S. Census, 1988:Table 415).

As a result of the national elections in November of 1992, the size of the Congressional Black Caucus increased from 26 to 40 members. Overall, 17 new African American representatives were added to Congress, but three members of the Caucus retired. Of particular significance is the fact that Carol Moseley Braun of Illinois became the first Black woman ever elected to the United States senate.

Although the number of African American politicians has increased over the years, some would say that these figures are deceptive, that is in view of the fact that political power in the African American community has not witnessed any significant change. This observation is based on several valid points. For example, African American politicians often hold insignificant positions in the overall power structure of the school board, city, or county. Second, the actual number of African American politicians on any given school board, city council, or county board of supervisors is often not enough to make any significant difference, as their vote on any issue may only represent one vote out of a dozen. In the past this level of representation was referred to as tokenism or window dressing. Some critics also point out that there is little difference between an African American politician and a white politician, so it makes no difference who the mayor is, as they will continue to make the same political decisions.

Some have also made the point that the increase in the number of African American mayors, is really an indication that whites have abandoned the cities and taken refuge in the suburbs. In the short term African American mayors are blamed for all the social problems that confront big cities today. In smaller cities they are usually ceremonial mayors and have very little power to effect real social change. These mayors often serve as good will ambassadors to the African American community and are supported by white liberals as a symbol of racial progress.

Some observers have made the point that at-large elections and gerrymandering have nullified the African American vote in many cities. Both practices prevent block voting. For example, the at-large election requires African American candidates for political office to attract votes from across the city and not just from the local African American constituency. The policy of gerrymandering dissects areas of heavy African American concentration in the city into smaller political districts. This practice insures that African Americans will always constitute a minority of the eligible voters.

The Question of Social Progress

When we consider the very broad question whether African Americans have made any real progress over the past twenty years, we almost have to say that the progress that they have made is not as real as it may seem. For example, in 1970, 33.5 percent of African Americans were living below the poverty level, and in 1992, 31.1 percent were still living in poverty. The poverty rate among African American families remains three times higher than it is among white families. In 1967 the average annual per capita income of an African American family was 58 percent of white family income, and in 1992 it was still 58 percent.

If annual income is controlled for inflation (i.e., held in constant 1990 dollars), the average annual income of African American men was $14,003 in 1970, but decreased to $12,868 in 1990, representing a real loss in annual income of $1,135. In contrast, the average annual income for Anglo American males in 1990 was $21,170, representing a difference of $8,302 (i.e. an income gap of almost $700 a month). In 1970 the averal annual income of African American men was only 59.3 percent of Anglo American men's income, but by 1990 African American men only earned 60.8 percent of what Anglo American men earned. It is also interesting to note that the combined average annual income of an African American man and woman is $21,196, which is only $26 more than the average annual income of one Anglo American male. (Swinton, 1992:Table 7).

Most demographers accept the fact that the official government unemployment rates are conservative and consistently undercount African Americans, but for purposes of comparison the official white unemployment rate in 1972 was 5.1 percent, while the African American unemployment rate was twice as high (10.4 %). By 1992 the unemployment rate was 5.8 percent for whites and 13.3 percent for African Americans. Twenty years later the unemployment rate is still twice as high for African Americans.

Furthermore, African Americans suffer from under-employment, which means that they cannot find full-time employment and must rely on part-time and temporary work (Cherry, 1989:93-107; Sigelman and Welch, 1991:24-30). Discouraged workers also contribute to a higher unemployment rate among African Americans, as they are not counted in the official unemployment rates. One study has clearly demonstrated that the inclusion of discouraged and involuntary part-time workers in the monthly unemployment rates would increase the official annual unemployment rate among African Americans from 11.3 percent (in 1990) to the hidden unemployment rate of 21.5 percent. The official unemployment rate among African

American teenagers in 1990 was 31.1 percent, but the actual hidden unemployment rate was 53.1 percent (Tidwell, 1992:Table 18, Table 19).

Most African Americans are blue collar workers. In 1990 they were concentrated in the service occupations (17.6%), and in the operators and laborers (15.1%). Within the service occupations they were employed as cleaners and servants (36.5%), maids (26.7%), cleaning and building services (22.9%), and nurses aides and orderlies (31.4%). Since African Americans represent 12 percent of the population, it is clear that there are more than twice as many African Americans in these jobs as one would expect statistically. In contrast they only represent 10.2 percent of all managers and professionals and only 9.3 percent of the technical and sales force.

In 1960 the infant mortality rate among whites was 22.9 percent, but for African Americans it was twice as high (44.3%). Twenty-eight years later the rate for whites was 8.5 percent, and the rate for African Americans was still twice as high (17.6%) (U.S. Census, 1991:Table 111). It is obvious that the benefits of modern health care are not equally distributed in the population. In certain cities infant mortality rates among African Americans are dreadfully high, particularly crib deaths. Most infant deaths are the result of non-existent or poor prenatal care, inadequate medical facilities, and the lack of post-natal health care.

In 1990 the life expectancy for whites was 75.8 years, and for African Americans it was 69.4 years, that is six years less. The death rate for young African American men (35-44) is almost three times as high (2.7 times) as it is for white men. In 1989 African American men had a death rate of 701 per 100,000 in the population, as compared with 260 for white men. African Americans are also much more likely to be the victims of homicide, as their homicide rate was 48.4 (per 100,000) in 1985, as compared with a rate of only 8.2 for whites.

Chapter Summary

Contrary to popular conception, the first African Americans did not arrive in America as slaves, but they came as explorers, sailors, and soldiers. The first African American settlers arrived in Jamestown in 1619 as indentured servants. Some forty years later the Colony of Virginia was the first to recognize the institution of slavery.

By the turn of the nineteenth century a very active abolitionist movement was firmly established. The final move toward abolition came with John Brown's raid and the election of Abraham Lincoln in 1860. Following the Civil War the Reconstruction Act was passed to insure that the rights of the newly freed slaves would be protected.

Due to the labor shortage during the First World War many African Americans migrated into Northern industrial centers. Unfortunately, they quickly discovered that they were unwelcome in the North, as the period between 1917 and 1920 was marked by numerous outbreaks of racial violence.

The onset of the Second World War saw the introduction of African Americans into industrial jobs that had historically been closed to them. Following the war, new federal policies and the decisions handed down by the Supreme Court encouraged a change in race relations.

The Civil Rights Movement started in Montgomery, Alabama on December 1, 1955, when Rosa Parks refused to give up her seat to a white man on a crowded bus. By the mid-1960's the Black Power Movement was underway and marked a more radical approach to social change.

A critical review of the social and economic conditions of African Americans today demonstrates that they have made little progress over the past 30 years. For example, no significant change has occurred in their poverty rate, unemployment rate, or the income gap. Therefore, conditions for African Americans have not changed significantly since the arrest of Rosa Parks.

References

Baskin, Jane A., et al
    1971   *Race Related Civil Disorders: 1967-1969.* Waltham, MA: Lemberg Center for the Study of Violence, Brandeis University.

Bennett, Lerone, Jr.
    1966   *Before the Mayflower.* Baltimore: Penguin.

Billingsley, Andrew
    1968   *Black Families in White America.* Englewood Cliffs, NJ: Prentice-Hall.

Blackwell, James E.
    1990   "Current Issues Affecting Blacks and Hispanics in the Educational Pipeline." In *U.S. Race Relations in the 1980s and 1990s: Challenges and Alternatives.* Gail E. Thomas (ed.), New York: Hemisphere Publishing Corporation. Pp. 35-52.

Blaustein, Albert P. and Robert L. Zangrando
    1968   *Civil Rights and the American Negro: A Documentary History.* NY: Washington Square Press.

Bonacich, Edna
    1990   "Inequality in America: The Failure of the American System for People of Color." In *U.S. Race Relations in the 1980s and 1990s: Challenges and Alternatives.* Gail E. Thomas (ed.), New York: Hemisphere Publishing Corporation. Pp. 187-208.

Cherry, Robert
    1989   *Discrimination: Its Economic Impact on Blacks, Women, and Jews.* Lexington, MA: Lexington Books.

Draper, Theodore
    1970   *The Rediscovery of Black Nationalism.* New York: Viking Press.

Farley, Reynolds and Walter R. Allen
    1987   *The Color Line and the Quality of Life in America.* New York: Russell Sage Foundation.

Franklin, John Hope
    1966   "A Brief History of the Negro in the United States." In *The American Negro Reference Book.* John P. Davis (ed.), Englewood Cliffs, NJ: Prentice-Hall, Pp. 1-95.
    1967   *From Slavery to Freedom.* New York: Vintage Books.

Gonzales, Juan L., Jr.
    1983   "The Growth of the Anti-Nuclear Movement and the Demise
            of Civil Rights and Minority Issues in the 1980's" Logan,
            Utah: Paper presented at the Annual Meetings of The
            American Association for the Advancement of Science.
    1991   *The Lives of Ethnic Americans.* Dubuque, IA: Kendall/Hunt.
Gossett, Thomas F.
    1965   *Race: The History of an Idea in America.* New York:
            Schocken Books.
Grimshaw, Allen D. (ed.)
    1969   *Racial Violence in the United States.* Chicago: Aldine.
Hunter, Andrea G. and Margaret E. Ensminger
    1992   "Diversity and Fluidity in Children's Living Arrangements:
            Family Transitions in an Urban Afro-American Com-
            munity." *Journal of Marriage and the Family* 54:418-426.
Janowitz, Morris
    1968   *Social Control of Escalated Riots.* Chicago: University of
            Chicago Center for Policy Study.
Johnson, Charles S.
    1970   *Backgrounds to Patterns of Negro Segregation.* New York: Thomas
            Y. Crowell Company (Apollo Edition) (1943).
Jordan, Winthrop D.
    1968   *White Over Black: American Attitudes Toward the Negro,
            1550-1812.* Baltimore: Penguin Books Inc.
King, Martin Luther, Jr.
    1958   *Stride Toward Freedom: The Montgomery Story.* New York:
            Harper and Brothers.
Ladner, Joyce
    1967   "What 'Black Power' Means to Negroes in Mississippi."
            Trans-Action 5:6-15 (November).
Litwack, Leon F.
    1961   *North of Slavery: The Negro in the Free States, 1790-1860.* Chicago:
            University of Chicago Press.
Lomax, Louis
    1962   *The Negro Revolt.* New York: Harper.
Meier, August and Elliott M. Rudwick
    1966   *From Plantation to Ghetto.* New York: Hill and Wang.
Meier, Kenneth J., J. Stewart Jr. and R. E. England
    1989   *Race, Class, and Education: The Politics of Second-
            Generation Discrimination.* Madison, WI: The University of
            Wisconsin Press.
Mezey, Susan G.
    1992   *In Pursuit of Equality: Women, Public Policy, and the Courts.*
            New York: St. Martin's Press.

Motley, Constance Baker
1966   "The Legal Status of the Negro in the United States." In
The American Negro Reference Book. John P. Davis (ed.),
Englewood Cliffs: Prentice-Hall, Pp. 484-521.

Pinkney, Alphonso
1975   *Black Americans.* (Second Edition) Englewood Cliffs, NJ:
Prentice-Hall.

Sigelman, Lee and Susan Welch
1991   *Black Americans' Views of Racial Inequality: The Dream Deferred.*
New York: Cambridge University Press.

Stack, Carol
1974   *All Our Kin.* New York: Harper and Row.

Stamp, Kenneth M.
1956   *The Peculiar Institution.* New York: Vintage Books.
1965   *The Era of Reconstruction,* 1865-1877. New York: Vintage
Books.

Staples, Robert and Leanor B. Johnson
1992   *Black Families at the Crossroads: Challenges and Prospects.*
San Francisco: Jossey-Bass.

Swinton , David H.
1987   "Economic Status of Blacks." In *The State of Black America
1987.* Janet Dewart (ed.), New York: The National Urban
League, Pp. 49-73.
1992   "The Economic Status of African Americans: Limited Owner
ship and Persistent Inequality." In *The State of Black America
1992.* Billy J. Tidwell (ed.), New York: The National Urban
League, Pp. 61-117.

Tidwell, Billy J. (ed.)
1992   *The State of Black America 1992.* New York: The National
Urban League.

U.S. Census
1988   *Statistical Abstract of the United States, 1988* (108th Edition)
Washington, D.C.:USGPO.
1991   *Statistical Abstract of the United States, 1991* (111th Edition).
Washington, D.C.:USGPO.

Williams, Eric
1966   *Capitalism & Slavery.* New York: Capricorn Books.

Woodward, C. Vann
1966   *The Strange Career of Jim Crow.* New York: Oxford
University Press.
1974   *The Strange Career of Jim Crow.* (3rd Revised Edition)
New York: Oxford University Press.

Box Reading 13.1
A Brief Chronology of African Americans

1619	The first Blacks arrived in Jamestown as indentured servants.
1661	The Virginia colony gave statutory recognition of slavery.
1724	There were three times as many slaves in the Carolinas as whites.
1776	Free African Americans were encouraged to enlist in the Continental Army. Over 5,000 served their country.
1783	Massachusetts abolished slavery.
1784	Connecticut and Rhode Island abolished slavery.
1793	The first fugitive slave law was enacted.
1807	Both England and the United States banned the African slave trade. This marked the beginning of the illegal slave trade.
1829	David Walker published his Appeal.
1831	Nearly sixty whites were killed in a slave rebellion lead by Nat Turner.
1850	The Fugitive Slave Act required the federal government to assist in the capture of runaway slaves.
1857	The Dread Scott Decision held that slaves did not become free because they moved to a free state.
1859	John Brown's raid at Harpers Ferry.
1861	The Civil War began following the shelling of Ft. Sumter on April 12.
1862	Lincoln permitted African Americans to enlist in the Union Army.
1863	Lincoln issued the Emancipation Proclamation (January).
1865	More than 186,000 African Americans served in the Union Army. Slavery was legally abolished with the passage of the Thirteenth Amendment to the Constitution.
1866	The Fourteenth Amendment made African Americans U.S. citizens. The Civil Rights Act of 1866 improved the civil liberties of African Americans.
1870	The Fifteenth Amendment gave African Americans the right to vote.
1876	The Hayes-Tilden Compromise allowed the government to remove federal troops from the South.
1896	The Supreme Court ruled in Plessy vs. Ferguson that separate but equal facilities were constitutional.
1905	W.E.B. Du Bois founded the Niagara Movement.

1910	The National Association for the Advancement of Colored People (NAACP) was founded.
1911	The National Urban League was founded.
1914	Marcus Garvey founded the Universal Negro Improvement Association.
1917	Thirty-nine African Americans were killed in a bloody riot in East St. Louis, Illinois.
1919	A number of riots occurred across the country during the Red Summer of 1919.
1933	African Americans were hard hit by the Great Depression.
1943	A race riot in Detroit claimed 34 lives.
1954	The Supreme Court ruled in *Brown vs. Board of Education* that school segregation was inherently unequal.
1955	The Montgomery bus boycott was organized to end segregation in public transportation.
1957	Martin Luther King, Jr., and several Baptist ministers founded the Southern Christian Leadership Conference.
1957	National guardsmen called to Central High School in Little Rock to enforce school integration.
1960	The sit-in movement began in Greensboro, North Carolina.
1961	The Congress of Racial Equality led freedom rides throughout the South to desegregate interstate transportation.
1963	Over 20,000 joined the March on Washington. Civil Rights demonstrators were attacked by police in Birmingham.
1964	The Civil Rights Act of 1964 was signed by Lyndon Johnson.
1965	The Voting Rights Act was passed. This also marked the start of Summer urban riots, as in Los Angeles and Detroit.
1966	Stokely Carmichael called for Black Power and the Black Panther party was organized in Oakland.
1968	Martin Luther King was assassinated in Memphis.

Important Names

Frederick Douglas	Estevanico	Stokely Carmichael
Eugene "Bull" Connor	Hernando Cortez	Medgar Evers
William Lloyd Garrison	Malcolm X	Martin Luther King Jr.
Rodney King	James Meredith	Huey Newton
Rosa Parks	Nat Turner	Bobby Seale
David Walker		

Key Terms

the Abolitionist Movement
Black Codes
Black Power
Central High School
Dred Scott Case
John Brown's raid
Executive Order 9981
gerrymandering
field hands
income gap
middle passage
Montgomery Bus Boycott
Plessy vs. Ferguson
seasoning in the islands
Shelley vs. Kraemer
16th Street Baptist Church
tokenism
triangular trade system
window dressing
Brown vs. the Board of Education
Student Non-Violent
  Coordinating Committee

at-large elections
Black Panther Party
David Walker's Appeal
Congress of Racial Equality
Jim Crow laws
Emancipation Proclamation
Fifteenth Amendment
house servants
freedom riders
indentured servants
manumission acts
New Deal programs
Red Summer of 1919
secondary labor market
sit-ins
slave codes
Thirteenth Amendment
Watts Riot
Southern Christian Leadership
  Conference

1. Discuss five important events in Black history that occurred between the arrival of the first Blacks in America and the American Civil War.
2. Discuss four reasons why the triangular trade system was so lucrative for the European powers.
3. Provide a brief discussion of five ways in which the teachings of Christianity affected the daily lives of Black slaves (these can be either positive or negative aspects).
4. Discuss four important events or personalities involved in the Abolitionist Movement.
5. Discuss five important supreme court decisions or laws that have improved the Civil Rights of African Americans and other minorities since the Second World War.
6. Discuss five important events or personalities involved in the Civil Rights Movement.
7. Discuss the role and contribution of four Black organizations that were active in the Civil Rights Movement.
8. List and discuss five important characteristics of the Black family.
9. Select four socio-economic indicators of social progress in American society and demonstrate whether Black Americans have or have not made social progress in American society.

Part V

The Native American Experience

Chapter 14

The Native American Experience

Introduction

In 1990 there were 1,959,234 Native Americans living on and off reservations, an increase of 37.9 percent from 1980. Between 1970 and 1980 their population increased by half a million (574,000), an increase of 72 percent. This rapid rate of increase can be attributed to natural increase, a more accurate count, and to the simple fact that more people claimed Indian heritage.

In 1990, half (47.6) the Native Americans lived in the West, 29 percent in the South, 17 percent in the Midwest, and six percent in the Northeast. Only four states had Indian populations of more than 100,000, Oklahoma 252,240, California 242,146, Arizona 203,527, and New Mexico 134,355 (Wright, 1992:280).

Many Americans believe that most Native Americans live on reservations, but only one out five (22%) were living on reservations in 1990. In fact two-thirds (63%) live in urban areas, eight percent live in historic areas of Oklahoma, three percent live in Alaskan villages, and two percent live in tribal trust lands. Since the end of the Second World War the trend has been for Native Americans to move to the large cities of the West.

In this chapter we shall examine the historical experience of Native Americans, their removal to barren Western lands, and their incarceration on reservations. Attention also will be given to the systematic destruction of their culture and their struggle to survive in a modern urban society.

The First Americans

The first inhabitants of North America arrived from Asia via a land bridge across the Bering Straits some 35,000 years ago. These were bands of hunters, who followed wild game south into fertile territories that offered an abundance of game and a milder climate. Over thousands of years they settled in every corner of the continent, from the Canadian plains, to the rain forest of Brazil. As a result hundreds of distinct cultural patterns evolved over time, as each tribe adapted to their particular environment.

Various scholars (such as Mooney, Wilcox, Kroeber, Rosenblat, and Steward) have estimated that there were about one million Native Americans living in North America when Columbus landed (Stuart, 1987:Table 3.1). It is estimated that the Indians living here in 1492 spoke over 300 languages and supported more than 300 cultural systems. As early as 1700 the first European settlers on the East Coast were already aware of some fifty or sixty nations of Indians.

Shortly after the Europeans arrived, the Native American population experienced a very significant decline. From an original population of one million in 1500, it is estimate that there were just over half a million (600,000) in the United States by 1800. By 1850 there were just over one-third of a million (388,000) and by 1900 there were fewer than a quarter of a million (237,000) (Stuart, 1987:Table 3.2; Table 34).

The primary cause of this rapid decline in the Native American population was contact with the Europeans, who:

1. exposed them to diseases, like smallpox, measles, mumps, whooping cough, diphtheria, influenza,
2. pressed thousands of them into forced labor,
3. destroyed their villages and their way of life,
4. massacred hundreds of them in Indian Wars,
5. forced them to move from areas of white settlement,
6. destroyed their primary source of food,
7. and incarcerated them on reservations.

First Contact With White Settlers

From the European perspective the idea of discovery meant that an explorer would set foot on a new territory and claim all the land in that region for a European monarch. Obviously this approach assumed that no one lived on the land or otherwise owned the land. But this idea was simply a justification for taking land from indigenous people and removing the native population from areas of white settlement (Oswalt, 1973).

The Dutch were the first to make a treaty with the Iroquois, who were indigenous to New York state. The Iroquois were a formidable military force, as they had formed a League of Five Nations consisting of the Seneca, Onondaga, Cayuga, Oneida, and the Mohawks. They entered a lucrative fur trade agreement with the French. As a nation of warriors the Iroquois fought against other Indian nations, the French, and the British. During the American Revolution the Mohawks and the Onondagas supported the Americans. This resulted in a split among the Five Nations of Iroquois.

Following the Revolutionary War, the Americans retaliated against the Iroquois by destroying their villages and burning their crops. Some Iroquois migrated into Canada and the few who remained in New York signed a treat with the Americans in 1796 (Spicer, 1969:32). The massacre of Indians and the destruction of whole villages set the pattern for American's relations with the Indians.

The traditional territory of the Sioux was the Dakota Territory. Under the provisions of a treaty signed in 1868, the government agreed to ban white settlers from the Great Sioux Reservation (now the state of South Dakota). In exchange they relinquished the rest of their land. But following the discovery of gold in the Black Hills of South Dakota in 1874, a flood of white settlers arrived. Several bloody incidents occurred between the Sioux and white settlers. General George Custer ordered the Sioux off the reservation during the harsh winter, which they refused to do. Custer and his force of 264 men were ambushed by the Sioux at Little Big Horn Creek in 1876. In retaliation for Custer's defeat the Army hunted down and killed every Sioux warrior they could find (Olson, 1965).

At this time the Sioux began a new religion, from which the Ghost Dance evolved. The Ghost Dance was based on the belief that all the buffalo would return, the Indians would recover their land, and the white man would be eliminated from the earth. White settlers were frightened by the Ghost Dance, as they feared its militancy and thought it would instigate another Indian war. In response to the settlers concerns, U.S. Army troops were called to the Pine Ridge Reservation, where they encountered a band of Teton Sioux at Wounded Knee Creek. The soldiers were disarming the warriors when a random shot was fired and they panicked and turned their artillery on the women and children. This resulted in the massacre of 300 Indians (Brown, 1971).

Repression and Control of Native Americans

Following the American Revolution, white settlers were determined to win the battle for land. To achieve their goal they resorted to (1) warfare, (2) organized raids on Indian settlements, (3) blatant massacres, and (4) the destruction of the ecological base of Indian survival (Deloria, 1971:61-63).

Once the Native Americans were defeated on the field of battle, their lives and their future were controlled by government fiat.

In 1789, Congress was authorized to make treaties with the Indians. This was also the year that all Indian matters were turned over to the War Department. Since the 1800's the government has passed numerous laws affecting the lives of Native Americans. A brief review of some of these laws will reveal the relationship between government policies and the subjugation of Native Americans (See Box Reading 14.1).

Perhaps the most important federal law affecting the lives of Native Americans was the Indian Removal Act of 1830. In response to pressure from the American people, Congress passed the Indian Removal Act that authorized the Bureau of Indian Affairs (BIA) to relocate all Indians west of the Mississippi River. Any tribes that resisted were relocated by military force. But resistance was expensive, for both the Indians and the government, in terms of lives and money.

For example, it took ten years (1832-1942), $50 million, and the lives of 1,500 soldiers and countless Indians, to remove the Seminoles from Florida. Similarly the Cherokees were forcibly removed from Georgia, in spite of the Supreme Court decision allowing them to remain on their land. During the forced march from Georgia to the Indian Territory in Oklahoma (1838-1839), nearly one-fourth of the Cherokees died of starvation, disease, and injuries. Their long march is now known as the Trail of Tears (Hagan, 1961). The Creeks were also forcibly removed from their land and half their people lost their lives during their relocation.

This pattern of forcing Native Americans off their land with the arrival of white settlers was repeated throughout the nineteenth century. The U.S. Army was used to protect the rights of white settlers and to insure the removal of the Indians. In 1849 the authority of the Bureau of Indian Affairs was transferred to the War Department. By 1871 the U.S. Congress decided that it would no longer make treaties with the Indians. This meant that all Native Americans were now considered wards of the state (McNickle, 1973).

Getting Out of the Indian Business

For the next seventy years (1887-1953) the government was involved in managing Indian affairs, as opposed to the treaty-military approach of the previous period (See Box Reading 14.1). The stated objective of this new approach was to insure that Native Americans would experience a gradual integration into American society. Their first step in this direction was the passage of the Dawes Act (1887). The intent of the Dawes Act was to make yeoman farmers out of Native Americans by giving them 40 to 160 acres of farm land. The idea was that the ownership of land would civilize the Indians, educate them, and make them hard working citizens, like the white farmers.

However, the results of this policy were disastrous, as it destroyed their tribal culture, dispersed Indian families across hundreds of miles, the excess land was sold to white farmers, and it relieved (at least in theory) the government of its responsibility toward the Native Americans. In the process tribes were disbanded and by the time the Allotment Act was revoked in 1934, Indian lands had dwindled from 138 million acres to only 47 million acres (Deloria, 1969:52-53).

Although Native Americans were granted American citizenship in 1924, they still did not have the right to vote in Arizona and New Mexico. This fluke in the law was not changed until 1948, when the U.S. Supreme Court ruled that these states could not prevent Native Americans from voting. The Indian Reorganization Act of 1934 was an effort by the government to encourage the integration of Indians into American society and to allow for their self government. Obviously the federal government wanted to get out of the Indian business. The Meriam Report, an investigation of the condition of Native Americans, found that they had very serious health problems, very low levels of education, substandard housing, a variety of social problems, and general social depression (Meriam, 1928).

But it was the Termination Act of 1953 (House Resolution 108) that insured that the government would gradually get out of the Indian business. For the clear intent of this legislation was to terminate, as soon as possible, all government obligations to the Indians, as this Act allowed the government to close Indian reservations. As a result of the implementation of the provisions of this Act, Native Americans lost 13 million acres of land.

While more than 100 tribes were adversely affected by the provisions of the Termination Act, the best known were the Klamath tribe in Oregon, who lost 860,000 acres of prime timber land, and the Menominee, who lost 230,000 acres of farm land (Tyler, 1973:161-188). In the final analysis the Termination Act forced thousands of Native Americans to relocate to urban areas, and this resulted in high unemployment rates and universal poverty (Dennis, 1977).

Urban Relocation Programs

Under the direction of the Bureau of Indian Affairs, the government initiated the Voluntary Relocation Program in 1952, which was intended to get the Indians off the reservations and into the cities. This is just another example of the government's attempt to get out of the Indian business. The BIA established relocation centers in major cities close to Indian reservations, such as Los Angeles, Oakland, San Jose, Oklahoma City, Tulsa, Dallas, Denver, and Seattle. This program was expanded in 1957, and again in 1962, under the Employment Assistance Program. By 1968 more than 100,000 Indians had received services from the program and more than 200,000 were relocated to urban centers (Sandefur, 1986; Wax and Buchanan, 1975). Unfortunately, many of the Indians involved in the relocation program were disappointed by what they found in the big cities and were unable to adjust to urban life (Officer, 1971; Price, 1972).

During the 1960's the government's policy toward Native Americans emphasized their civil rights. The Economic Opportunity Act of 1964 was indicative of the new attitude toward Native Americans. This Act allowed the Indians to control their community development programs. Similarly the Indian Civil Rights Act of 1968 extended basic human rights to all Native Americans. The Alaska Native Claims Settlement Act of 1971 guaranteed the right of Native Americans to determine their affairs. The passage of the American Indian Policy Review Commission Act and the Self Determination and Educational Assistance Act in 1975 gave a further demonstration of the new liberal attitude of the U.S. government toward Native Americans.

The BIA and the Reservation System

The Bureau of Indian Affairs (BIA) was established by Congress in 1824 to administer and supervise all activities of Native Americans, to insure their welfare, and eventually plan for their integration into American society. In reality, the BIA was an essential part of the government's long term plan to remove the Indians from the path of progress and to insure that they would be confined to an area where they would not cause any difficulties in the future (Cahn, 1969:5-26).

To this end, the BIA created the first Indian reservations in Oklahoma. Between 1830 and 1880, the territory of Oklahoma served as the official dumping ground for Native Americans forcibly removed from the Mississippi Valley and Eastern settlement areas. As white settlers moved further West, the BIA established reservations in Arizona and New Mexico (Olson and Wilson, 1984). In every case the Indians were removed from the path of progress and were closely supervised and controlled by the government.

Reservation lands were not only selected with the idea that the Indians should be out of the way of progress, but also that they should not be allowed to settle on land that might have any value or economic potential in the future. For this reason most reservations are located off the main routes of travel, on land that is barren and useless for settlement or agricultural purposes, and on land that is absent of any visible natural resources (Kluck-hohn, 1962).

As a result of the policies of the Bureau of Indian Affairs, Native Americans were stripped of their dignity, of any means of supporting themselves, and of their traditional way of life and culture. Consequently, many reservation Indians today are powerless and totally dependent on the government for support and sustenance. The BIA provides for their social welfare, food rations, health care, education, jobs, and insures that they remain powerless and dependent on the government for survival. The BIA's system of population management is the best example of internal colonialism, as Native Americans have been stripped of their culture, land, political rights, and any means of survival.

In 1983 almost six out of ten (755,000) of all Native Americans were under BIA jurisdiction. The largest number lived in Oklahoma (159,852), followed by Arizona (154,818), New Mexico (105,973), Alaska (64,970), South Dakota (46,101), and Washington (39,726). Out of a total of 278 reservations, the majority were in the West (70%), followed by the Midwest (19%), the Northwest (6%), and the South (5%) (U.S. BIA, 1983b; 1985; 1986).

While Indian reservations vary in size, most have a population of less than 1,000. By far the largest reservation is the Navajo reservation, which has a population of 185,661 and is spread across three states (Arizona, New Mexico, and Utah). The second largest reservation is the Cherokee (Oklahoma, 87,059), followed by the Creek (Oklahoma, 56,244), Choctaw (Oklahoma, 26,884), Pine Ridge (South Dakota, 20,206), Southern Pueblos (New Mexico, 18,837), Rosebud (South Dakota, 17,128) and the Tohono O'odham reservation in Arizona (16,531) (Johnson, 1992:805).

Who is an Indian?

If we move beyond the Hollywood stereotypes about Native Americans, we are still left with the question, who is an Indian? For years social scientists have attempted to define the Indian, and so have numerous government agencies.

Essentially there are four basic methods used by government agencies to determine who is a Native American:

1. The Genetic Approach: most often used by the BIA and some Indian organizations to designate membership in a recognized Native American tribe. This requires at least one-quarter Indian ancestry.
2. The Psychological Approach: is simply based on self identification. This approach is used by the Bureau of the Census.
3. The Sociological Approach: based on the acceptance of an individual as Native American, because the majority of friends and social contacts are Native Americans. Thus anyone who is recognized as a member of a tribe or an urban Indian organization is considered a Native American (Wax, 1971:72-73).
4. The Bureaucratic Approach: occurs when a person is on some official list of Native Americans, such as those maintained by the BIA. While they may not identify with the Indian community, these "official list Indians" often

step forward to claim their rights when land settlements occur, to obtain royalties, or any other treaty benefits.

Native Americans usually identify themselves on the basis of a combination of two or more of these approaches, since some Indians are more involved with their culture and community than others. An interesting point in this regard is the consideration that over 80 percent of Mexican Americans today are of Native American ancestry (Forbes, 1973:183).

A Demographic Profile

The population growth rate among Native Americans has increased substantially since the end of the Second World War. In 1950 there were 377,173 Native Americans, a three percent growth rate from 1940. Between 1950 and 1960 their population increased by 46 percent (See Table 14.1 Below). Between 1960 and 1970 their rate of increase was 50 percent, and between 1970 and 1980 they experienced a 71 percent increase. At this rate of growth their population exceeded the two million mark in 1993.

Table 14.1
Native American Population, 1890-1990

Census Year	Total Population	Percent Change
1890	273,607	—
1900	266,732	-2.5
1910	291,014	+9.1
1920	270,995	-6.9
1930	362,380	+33.7
1940	366,427	+1.1
1950	377,273	+3.0
1960	551,636	+42.6
1970	827,273	+50.0
1980	1,420,400	+71.1
1990	1,959,234	+37.9

Source: Modified from Stuart, 1987; Hoffman, 1993:388

As pointed out above, most Native Americans live in the West, primarily in California, Arizona, Oklahoma, and New Mexico. About half live in urban areas (52%), while most of the Indians living in rural areas are on reservations. The four top states of Native American concentration are Oklahoma,

California, Arizona, and New Mexico (Wright, 1992:280) (See Table 14.2). As a result of federal government programs established in the early 1950's, Native Americans were encouraged to move to these urban areas (Sorkin, 1978).

Table 14.2
Ten States With Largest
Native American Population, 1990

Rank	State	Total Number	Percent of Total
1.	Oklahoma	252,240	12.9
2.	California	242,164	12.3
3.	Arizona	203,527	10.4
4.	New Mexico	134,355	6.8
5.	Alaska	85,698	4.4
6.	Washington	81,483	4.2
7.	North Carolina	80,155	4.1
8.	Texas	65,877	3.4
9.	New York	62,651	3.2
10.	Michigan	55,638	2.8
	Total	1,263,788	64.5
	Total Population	1,959,234	100.0

Source: Wright, 1992:280.

Occupational Distribution and Social Mobility

Native Americans, like most minority groups, are concentrated in the lower rungs of the labor force. In 1980, seven out of ten (69.6%) Native American men were active in the labor force, compared with half (48.1%) of the women. Overall their official unemployment rate was 13 percent, but their actual unemployment rate was closer to 20 percent. On some reservations it is not uncommon to find unemployment rates of 50 percent or more (U.S. BIA, 1983a, 1984).

While the general population is equally divided between white collar and blue collar positions, two-thirds of Native Americans (67.3%) are found in blue collar positions and only one-third are in white collar positions. Within the white collar category, most Native Americans are found in sales positions (19.6%), particularly among women (36.1%). Similarly there are more women in the professional-managerial positions than men (See Table 14.3).

Table 14.3
Occupational Distribution Of Native Americans
By Sex, 1980

Occupation	Total Number	Percent	Male Number	Percent	Female Number	Percent
Professional Managerial-Technical	81,840	13.1	42,517	10.9	39,323	16.7
Sales	122,676	19.6	37,480	19.6	85,196	36.1
Craft	76,107	12.1	69,074	17.6	7,033	3.0
Service	91,813	14.6	36,050	9.2	55,763	23.6
Operatives	146,584	23.4	112,695	28.8	33,889	14.4
Laborers	89,326	14.2	77,218	19.7	12,108	5.1
Farm Laborers	18,614	3.0	16,066	4.1	2,548	1.1
Total	626,961	100.0	391,101	100.0	235,860	100.0

Source: U.S. Census, PC8O-1-D1-A, 1984.

Within the blue collar category Native Americans are concentrated in operative positions, followed by service positions, and laborers. Almost one-third of the men are working as operatives and one-fifth are employed as laborers. Women are concentrated in service jobs, while some are employed as operatives.

The movement of Native Americans off the reservations since 1950 is revealed in their labor force distribution. For example, in 1960 one out of four Native American men (23.5%) were farm workers, but in 1980 only three percent worked in agriculture. Similarly in 1960 only 4.9% held professional positions, but this increased to 13.1 percent in 1980. Despite some movement up the occupational ladder, most Native Americans are still heavily concentrated in the secondary labor market.

Poverty and the Income Gap

The official poverty rate among Native Americans dropped from one-third (33.3%) in 1970, to one-fourth (23.7%) in 1980. In 1980 there was a ten percent difference in the poverty rate between urban areas (19.5%) and rural areas (29.2%). This apparent reduction in the poverty rate can be attributed to their movement off the reservations and into urban areas, where there are more job opportunities and social services (Snipp and Sandefur, 1988).

However, the income gap between Native Americans and the general population is still significant, as the median income for Native American families in 1980 was $13,724, compared with $19,917 for all Americans, a difference of $6,000. The median family income for reservation Indians was $9,666, and for families headed by Native American women it was only $7,231. Clearly, life on the reservation is a life of poverty (U.S. BIA, 1986).

A comparison of personal income reveals a significant income gap. In 1980 the median personal income of Native American males was only $8,077, compared to $12,192 for all males (See Table 14.4). In effect this means that Native American males only earn two-thirds (66.2%) of the income earned by men in the general population. But this is a slight improvement over the income earned in 1970, when the income gap was 57 percent. In urban areas the income gap for men improves (74.4%) and is worse in non-farm rural areas (58.8%) (Sandefur and Scott, 1983).

Table 14.4
Median Income of Native Americans,
By Sex 1980

	Males			Females		
Location	Native Americans	United States	Percent of U.S.	Native Americans	United States	Percent of U.S.
U.S.	8,077	12,192	66.2	4,163	5,263	80.9
Urban	9,320	12,526	74.4	4,744	5,527	85.8
Rural-Non-Farm	6,660	11,329	58.8	3,609	4,473	80.7
Rural-Farm	7,075	11,057	64.0	3,969	4,379	90.6

Source: U.S. Census, PC80-1-C1, 1983.

It is interesting to note that in every case the income gap between Native American women and all women is not as significant, as it remains within the 80 percent range. The smaller income gap among women is simply a reflection of the fact that women are consistently paid less for their labor and this tends to reduce the income gap among white and minority women. In effect the range for significant fluctuation in the income gap is not available to women in general, as men, on average, earn twice the income of women.

The Education Gap

The first formal education given to Native Americans was offered by various religious groups in mission schools. The federal government did not become involved in Native American education until the creation of the reservation system, and the founding of the Bureau of Indian Affairs (1834). In 1834, there were sixty mission schools, with 137 teachers, and 2,049 students (Stuart, 1987:164). It was not until 1840 that the federal government worked cooperatively with the mission schools to provide an education to Native American children. By 1860 the BIA schools were independent of mission schools, as federal law prohibited mixing governments funds with sectarian funds for Indian education.

In 1887 the government allocated $1.2 million for the education of 14,000 Indian children enrolled in 227 schools (U.S. BIA, 1975:5). The BIA's emphasis, in these early years, was on Indian boarding schools. Boarding schools were justified on the basis of the isolation of reservations and the great distances involved. Today it is abundantly clear that the real objective of the BIA and mission schools was to rid the children of their heathen culture and civilize them. The results of this misguided policy were tragic, as thousands of Indian children spent nine months out of the year in boarding schools, away from their parents and separated from their cultural environment. Perhaps the worse case occurred when Eskimo children were transported to Oklahoma to attend BIA boarding schools (Lynch, 1973).

Surprisingly universal education among Native Americans is a recent phenomena, as only one-quarter of all Indian children were even enrolled in school in 1948. Since then, their numbers have increased significantly. By 1955 nine out of ten (87.5%) were in school and by 1980 all but four or five percent were attending school.

Another important change in Indian education was the simple fact that most students were enrolled in public schools, as opposed to BIA schools. For example, of the 133,000 Indian students in school in 1960, two-thirds (63%) were attending public schools, while three out of ten (28%) were enrolled in BIA schools (U.S. BIA, 1960). By 1979 eight out of ten (78%) were in public schools, while only one out of five (19%) were in BIA schools (U.S. BIA, 1979). Only a handful (3%-6%) were still attending church sponsored schools.

During the past thirty years the average level of educational achievement among Native Americans has increased. In 1970 their average was 10.9 years, compared to 12.1 years in the general population. This marked an increase from 1960 when their average level of education was only 8.9 years. By 1980 their average level of education was 12.2 years.

In 1970 half the American population had graduated from high school, compared to only one-third of the Native Americans. By 1980, half the Native Americans (55.8%) had also graduated from high school. A review of the educational achievement of Native Americans today reveals that one out of four have at least an elementary education, one third have completed high school, and 7.6 percent are college graduates (See Table 14.5). As is true in the general population, more Native American women graduate from high school as men, but more of the men go on to college. However, the important difference is that more Native American men graduate from college, than women.

Table 14.5
Median Education of Native Americans, 1980

Level of Education	Total Number	Percent	Males Number	Percent	Females Number	Percent
Elementary						
0-4 Years	55,673	8.0	26,978	8.1	28,695	8.0
5-7 Years	56,358	8.1	27,860	8.4	28,498	7.9
8 Years	56,987	8.2	26,790	8.1	30,197	8.3
Total	169,018	24.3	81,628	24.6	87,390	24.2
High School						
1-3 Years	136,872	19.7	59,634	18.0	77,238	21.4
4 Years	216,838	31.3	100,385	30.3	116,453	32.3
Total	353,710	51.0	160,019	48.3	193,691	53.7
College						
1-3 Years	115,266	16.7	58,879	17.8	56,389	15.6
4+ Years	53,456	7.6	30,555	9.2	22,901	6.3
Total	168,722	24.3	89,434	27.0	79,290	21.9
Overall						
Total	691,452	100.0	331,081	100.0	360,371	100.0

Source: U.S. Census, 1980, 1983.

Unfortunately these educational statistics do not tell the whole story behind Native American education today. Two major areas of concern remain, namely: (1) the quality of the teachers and (2) the quality of education that Native Americans receive.

In terms of the quality of the teachers it can be said that (much like our urban ghettos) the teachers that are assigned to Indian schools are not always as culturally aware, or as culturally sensitive as they should be regarding Native Americans. Some have also questioned the qualifications of teachers assigned to Indian schools. In addition the number of Native American teachers is minimal, when compared to the total number of students in any given school (Fuchs and Havighurst, 1972).

The statistics on Native American educational achievement are particularly misleading, since graduation from high school does not mean the same thing for a student in a minority school as it does in a white suburban school. When the test scores of Indian students are compared to white students on verbal skills, reading, and math, it turns out that the scores achieved by Native Americans in the twelfth grade approximate those of eighth grade white students (Stauss, et al, 1982).

Red Power and Pan Indianism

The modern period of Native American activism can be traced to the origins of the Red Power movement. The phrase Red Power is similar in many ways to the phrase Black Power, and was introduced as a guiding force at the 1966 convention of the National Congress of American Indians (NCAI) (Stauss, et al, 1982:254). To some the idea of Red Power referred to the new forms of political demonstrations and protest that were prevalent in the 1960's. But to others it meant that all Native Americans should ban together and fight for their rights. Yet other Native Americans felt that Red Power simply signified a new period of economic development and self determination (Josephy, 1971).

The belief in Red Power is also closely associated with Pan-Indianism and the Pan-Indian movement. Pan-Indianism is based on the philosophy that all Native Americans have similar problems and should put aside any minor differences that may exist, so that they can unify their resources and confront their common enemy. In this case the common enemy is usually the government bureaucracy (specifically the BIA). But some have extended the idea of Pan-Indianism to include Indians in Mexico, and in Central and South America. The more universal interpretation and application of Pan Indianism calls for unity among all indigenous people of the world, who have been the victims of colonial domination and international imperialism (Day, 1972).

The National Congress of American Indians (NCAI) was the first Pan-Indian organization and was founded in Denver, in 1944. Its purpose was to improve the social, economic, and political conditions of all Native Americans. Specifically they monitor government programs affecting Native Americans, lobby for specific bills or programs that might benefit Native Americans, and they monitor the civil rights of Native Americans. The NCAI also played a key role in the creation of the Indian Claims Commission. Many would consider the role of the NCAI as analogous to the work of the NAACP in the African American community.

In 1964 at a Chicago conference, representatives from 67 tribes reviewed the work of the NCAI. This resulted in the founding of The National Indian Youth Council (NIYC). The NIYC was founded by a group of college students, was more liberal and was based on action politics. They used demonstrations and organized protests to influence public opinion. Their first demonstrations were the fish-in protests in Seattle, in 1964.

The best known Pan-Indian organization today is the American Indian Movement (AIM), founded by Clyde Bellecourt and Dennis Banks in Minneapolis during the Summer of 1968. The organization evolved out of a neighborhood police patrol established in Native American communities to report cases of police brutality. AIM also sponsored alcohol rehabilitation programs and fought for local school reform measures. Four years after it was founded, AIM had established 18 chapters across the country, one-third of them on reservations. By 1972 AIM gained national attention primarily as a result of its confrontational policies directed at the Bureau of Indian Affairs and various law enforcement agencies (Mencarelli and Severin, 1975:145-158).

The advocates of Red Power were successful in drawing public attention to the problems and needs of Native Americans. For by attracting attention to their problems, they have been successful in bringing about constructive change. Some of the better known demonstrations of Red Power were,

1. The fish-ins in Washington state (1964), whereby Native Americans had the right to fish for salmon because of the provisions of the Medicine Creek Treaty of 1854. The Supreme Court upheld their treaty rights in 1968 (Steiner, 1968:48-64).
2. A group of 250 Indians landed on Alcatraz Island on November 19, 1969 and claimed the land under a treaty provision that allows Native Americans to claim surplus federal property.
3. Following a three month trans-national march, a group of Native Americans arrived in Washington, D.C., on November 30, 1972 to present their grievances to the government. The BIA closed its doors to the Indians, and this sparked a sit-in and occupation of BIA headquarters that lasted for several days (Burnette and Koster, 1974).
4. Russell Means and 300 supporters occupied the tribal offices at Wounded Knee, South Dakota in February 1973. The 70 day occupation gave their cause national attention.

Naturally there were dozens of demonstrations, sit-ins, and occupations that occurred during this period, but these are the most notable events in the Red Power movement. As with other civil rights organizations and activities, the Native Americans found that their vocal protest often brought about some positive results for their people.

Chapter Summary

Today there are just over two million Native Americans living in the United States, about half of them live in California, Oklahoma, Arizona, and New Mexico. But only one-fourth remain on the reservations, as most have moved to the cities.

It is estimated that the first Native Americans arrived in America some 35,000 years ago. When the first European explorers arrived there were about one million Indians living in this vast wilderness. With the arrival of thousands of white settlers the Native Americans were gradually pushed off the land.

By the nineteenth century the government used the Army to remove the Indians from the land and settled them on barren reservations in the far West. As a result, the Indians were made wards of the state and a pattern of total dependency evolved.

While Native Americans have made some progress since the early sixties, they still have some of the highest poverty rates, are still concentrated in the secondary labor market, have the highest unemployment rates, and are still suffering from the ill effects of a paternalistic educational system.

In recent times Native Americans have formed national organizations to represent their common interest. As with other minority groups, the Native Americans were very active during the Civil Rights Movement and formed their ethnic organizations. The result was the Red Power movement, political activism, mass demonstrations, and confrontations with the authorities. The unifying force among Native Americans today is the philosophy of Pan Indianism, which has allowed Native Americans to overlook minor differences and work in unison toward a collective goal.

References

Brown, Dee
1971   *Bury My Heart at Wounded Knee.* New York: Holt, Rinehart
        and Winston.
Burnette, Robert and John Koster
1974   *The Road to Wounded Knee.* New York: Bantam.
Cahn, Edgar S. (ed.)
1969   *Our Brother's Keeper: The Indian in White America.*
        New York: A New Community Press Book.
Day, Robert C.
1972   "The Emergence of Activism as a Social Movement." In *Native
        Americans Today: Sociological Perspectives.* Howard Bahr, et al
        (eds.), New York: Harper and Row, Pp. 506-531.
Deloria, Vine, Jr.
1969   *Custer Died for Your Sins: An Indian Manifesto.* New York:
        Avon.
Dennis, Henry C.
1977   *The American Indian 1492-1976: A Chronology & Fact Book* (second
        edition). Dobbs Ferry, NY: Oceana Publications.
Forbes, Jack D.
1973   *Aztecas Del Norte: The Chicanos of Aztlan.* Greenwich, CN.:
        Fawcett Publications.
Fuchs, Estelle and Robert J. Havighurst
1972   *To Live on This Earth: American Indian Education.* Garden
        City, NY: Doubleday.
Goodman, James M.
1985   "The Native American." In *Ethnicity in Contemporary
        America: A Geographical Appraisal.* Jesse O. McKee (ed.),
        Dubuque, IA: Kendall/Hunt. Pp. 31-53.
Hagan, William T.
1961   *American Indians.* Chicago: University of Chicago Press.
Hoffman, Mark S.
1993   *The World Almanac and Book of Facts 1993.* New York:
        Pharos Books.
Johnson, Otto
1992   *Information Please Almanac.* Boston: Houghton Mifflin.
Josephy, Jr. Alvin M.
1971   *Red Power.* New York: McGraw-Hill.
Kluckhohn, Clyde and Dorothea Leighton
1962   *The Navaho.* New York: Doubleday & Co.

Lynch, Patrick D.
1973   "Professionals and Clients: Goal Dissonance in Native American Schools". In *Chicanos and Native Americans: The Territorial Minorities*. Rudolph O. De La Garza, et al (eds.), Englewood Cliffs, NJ: Prentice-Hall. Pp. 184-203.

McNickle, D'Arcy
1973   *Native American Tribalism: Indian Survivals and Renewals*. New York: Oxford University Press.

Mencarelli, James and Steve Severin
1975   *Protest 3: Red, Black, Brown Experience in America*. Grand Rapids: Wm. B. Eerdmans.

Meriam, Lewis, et al
1928   *The Problem of Indian Administration*. Baltimore: The Institute for Government Research, John Hopkins Press.

Officer, James E.
1971   "The American Indian and Federal Policy." In *The American Indian in Urban Society*. Jack O. Waddell and O. M. Watson (eds.), Boston: Little, Brown. Pp. 45-60.

Olson, James C.
1965   *Red Cloud and the Sioux Problem*. Lincoln: University of Nebraska Press.

Olson, James S. and Raymond Wilson
1984   *Native Americans in the Twentieth Century*. Provo, UT: Brigham Young University Press.

Oswalt, Wendell H.
1973   *This Land Was Theirs: A Study of the North American Indian* (second edition). New York: John Wiley & Sons.

Price, John A.
1972   "The Migration and Adaptation of American Indians to Los Angeles." In *The Emergent Native Americans*. Deward E. Walker Jr. (ed.), Boston: Little, Brown and Company. Pp. 728-738.

Sandefur, Gary D.
1986   "American Indian Migration and Economic Opportunities." *International Migration Review* 20(1):55-68.

Sandefur, Gary D. and Wilbur J. Scott
1983   "Minority Group Status and the Wages of White, Black, and Indian Males." *Social Science Research* 12:44-68.

Snipp, C. Matthew and Gary D. Sandefur
1988   "Earnings of American Indians and Alaskan Natives: The Effects of Residence and Migration." *Social Forces* 66(4):994-1008.

Sorkin, Alan L.
1978   *The Urban American Indian.* Lexington, MA: Lexington Books.
Spicer, Edward H.
1969   *A Short History of the Indians of the United States.*
        New York: Van Nostrand Reinhold.
Stauss, Joseph, B.A. Chadwick, and H. M. Bahr
1982   "Indian Americans: The First is Last." In *The Minority
        Report.* Anthony G. Dworkin and Rosalind J. Dworkin (eds.),
        New York: Holt, Rinehart and Winston, Pp. 233-261.
Steiner, Stan
1968   *The New Indians.* New York: Delta Book.
Stuart, Paul
1987   *Nations Within a Nation: Historical Statistics of American
        Indians.* Westport, CN: Greenwood Press.
Tyler, S. Lyman
1973   *A History of Indian Policy.* Washington, D.C.:USGPO.
U.S. Bureau of the Census
1983   *1980 Census of the Populations U.S. Summary,* PC80-1- C1
1984   *1980 Census of the Population, U.S. Summary,* PC80-1-D1-A
U.S. Bureau of Indian Affairs (U.S. BIA)
1960   *Statistics Concerning Indian Education.* Washington, D.C.: USGPO.
1975   *Federal Indian Policies.* Washington, D.C.: USGPO.
1979   *Statistics Concerning Indian Education.* Washington, D.C.: USGPO.
1983a   *Local Estimates of Resident Indian Population and Labor
        Force Status, August 1983.* Washington, D.C.: USGPO.
1983b   *Indian Service Population and Labor Force Estimates.* Washington,
        D.C.: USGPO.
1984   *American Indian Areas and Alaska Native Villages: 1980.*
        Washington, D.C.: USGPO.
1985   *A Statistical Profile of the American Indian, Eskimo,
        and Aleut Populations for the United States: 1980.*
        Washington, D.C.: USGPO.
1986   *Indian Health Care.* Washington, D.C.: USGPO.
Wax, Murray L.
1971   *Indian Americans: Unity and Diversity.* Englewood
        Cliffs, NJ: Prentice-Hall.
Wax, Murray L. and Robert W. Buchanan
1975   *Solving "The Indian Problem": The White Man's
        Burdensome Business.* New York: New York Times Book Co.
Wright, John W.
1993   *The Universal Almanac 1993.* Kansas City, KS: Andrews
        and McMeel.

Box Reading 14.1
Important Federal Legislation
Affecting Native Americans

1789	The Constitution granted treaty-making authority.
1789	Congress passed Indian authority to the War Department.
1824	The Bureau of Indian Affairs was founded.
1830	Congress passed the Indian Removal Act.
1849	Indian authority transferred to the Department of Interior.
1871	Congress abolished all treaty making with Native Americans.
1887	Congress passed the Dawes Severalty Act (land allotments).
1921	The Snyder Act authorized welfare services to urban Indians.
1924	Native Americans are granted American citizenship.
1934	The Wheeler-Howard Act allowed for tribal government.
1946	Congress established the Indian Claims Commission.
1948	Indians allowed to vote in New Mexico and Arizona.
1953	Public Law 280 gave courts jurisdiction over Indian lands.
1954	Congressional Act relieved federal government of its obligations to several tribes (Klamath, Menominee).
1964	Economic Opportunity Act, Indian control of community programs.
1968	Indian Civil Rights Act.
1971	Alaska Native Claims Settlement Act.
1974	Indian Financing Act, provided credit and grants to Indians.
1975	Indian Self Determination and Education Assistance Act.
1975	American Indian Policy Review Commission created.
1976	Indian Health Care Improvement Act.

1513	Contact between Native Americans and Europeans began when Ponce de Leon landed in Florida.
1637	Over 500 members of the Pequot tribe were massacred by Connecticut colonists.
1676	The chief of the Wampanoag organized Indian forces and nearly defeated the English colonists in battle.
1680	The Pueblo Indians of New Mexico rebelled against Spanish domination. Hundreds of Spanish colonialists were killed.
1754	The French and Indian Wars lasted until 1763.
1812	The War of 1812 saw Indian tribes fighting for the British and for the United States. Indians who supported the British were punished by the U.S. after the war.
1824	The Bureau of Indian Affairs (BIA) was founded in the War Department.
1831	The Supreme Court held that Native American tribes were domestic dependent nations.
1832	The Supreme Court ruled that Indian nations had a right to self government.
1838	The Trail of Tears, the Cherokee Nation was forcefully removed from Georgia.
1864	The Sand Creek Massacre, in which 300 Cheyennes were killed by the Colorado militia.
1871	Congress passed a law prohibiting the government from negotiating further treaties with the Indians.
1876	The Battle of Little Big Horn.
1886	The Apache warrior Geronimo surrendered to Army troops.
1887	The Dawes Severalty Act was passed by Congress.
1890	The Wounded Knee Massacre.
1828	The Meriam Survey assessed the plight of Native Americans.
1944	The National Congress of American Indians was founded.
1961	The National Indian Youth Council was founded.
1969	The Indians claim Alcatraz Island.
1972	The Menominee tribe was restored to federal-trust status.
1973	The occupation of Wounded Knee, South Dakota.
1974	Native Americans in Washington state won important fishing rights in the Courts.

Dennis Banks
General George Custer

Clyde Bellecourt
Russell Means

Key Terms

Alcatraz Occupation
American Indian Movement
boarding schools
the Cherokees
Economic Opportunity Act
the Iroquois
the Sioux
Indian Reorganization Act
National Congress of American Indians
Pan Indianism
Red Power Movement
Trail of Tears Voluntary
Wounded Knee

Allotment Act
Battle of the Little Big Horn
Bureau of Indian Affairs
Dawes Act
fish-ins
Wounded Knee
the Ghost Dance
Indian Removal Act
National Indian Youth Council
Pine Ridge Reservation
Termination Act
Relocation Program
The Creek Tribe

Sample Test Questions

1. Discuss five ways in which the Native Americans first contact with White settlers was destructive to their way of life.
2. Discuss five important social policies that were imposed on the Native Americans by the U.S. government.
3. What are the four methods that are often used to determine "who is an Indian?"
4. Discuss five major social problems confronting Native Americans today.
5. Discuss four major events in Native American activism.

Part VI

★ ★ ★

The White Ethnic Experience

Chapter 15

The Jewish American Experience

Introduction

Strictly speaking, Jewish Americans are an ethnic group. This is true since their primary identification is based on a cultural definition. But Jews are also an ethno-religious group, for while their identification is based on ethnicity (that is cultural background), it is also anchored in their religious traditions. In American society today their ethnicity is the most prevalent characteristic of their Jewish identification, followed by their religious identification. Obviously it is difficult to separate their ethnic and religious identification, as both are crucial to the maintenance of a Jewish identity. For this reason Jews must be considered an ethno-religious group in American society.

It will surprise some to learn that, strictly speaking, Jews are not a racial group. This is so since they did not evolve from any single biological origin, rather Jews are a genetically diverse group. Although, historically they have been referred to as the Hebrew race. And in view of their heterogeneity it would be impossible to classify Jews as an independent genetic stock. In view of their historical experiences, it is also clear that Jews are not a national group, as they are citizens of many nations. However, most Jews consider Israel their national motherland.

By our definition, Jewish Americans are a minority group since they,

1. have been the victims of prejudice and discrimination,
2. are Jewish by accident of birth,
3. generally marry endogamously,
4. have a strong sense of consciousness of kind,
5. have culturally distinct characteristics,
6. share a common historical experience,
7. and constitute a cohesive religious community.

349

Jewish Immigration to America

While it is said that the first Jews arrived in America a thousand years before Columbus (Sloan, 1971:47), it is a fact that the first Jewish settlers to set foot on American soil were from Racife, Brazil and established a colony in New Amsterdam (New York) in 1654. Although, certain scholars have presented evidence that Columbus himself and several members of his crew were *marranos* (literally pigs), that is, Jews who converted to Christianity during the Spanish inquisition (Feingold, 1982:4).

The first Jews to settle in America were Sephardic Jews, who came from Spain and Portugal to escape religious persecution, as King Ferdinand the Catholic (of Spain) issued a proclamation in 1492 that forced thousands of Jews to either leave the country, convert to Catholicism, or face death. Yet the number of Jews that arrived during the Colonial period (1654-1750) was rather small, as there were only 2,500 in America at the time of the Revolution and by 1820 there were only 3,000. The Jewish population experienced a significant increase between 1850 and 1900 (See Table 15.1).

Table 15.1
The Jewish Population in the
United States, 1654-1990

Year	Population	Year	Population
1654	23	1914	2,933,874
1700	250	1917	3,388,951
1776	2,500	1920	4,200,000
1820	3,000	1927	4,228,029
1840	15,000	1937	4,770,647
1850	50,000	1947	5,000,000
1860	150,000	1957	5,255,000
1877	229,087	1967	5,779,845
1888	400,000	1968	5,868,555
1897	937,800	1980	5,921,000
1900	1,000,000	1987	5,943,700
1907	1,077,185	1990	6,800,000

Source: Brenner, 1986; Diner, 1977; Johnson, 1992:392;
Singer, 1988; Sklare, 1971.

Like thousands of other immigrants the Jews arrived in America in distinct periods, but primarily in response to the religious persecution in Europe and Russia. From their initial settlement in the American Colonies to the present day, five distinct Jewish groups settled in America (Dimont,

1978). The Sephardic Jews arrived during the Colonial period, followed by the Ashkenazic Jews, the modern German Jewish immigration, and the more recent immigration of Soviet and Israeli Jews (See Figure 15.1).

Figure 15.1
Periods of Jewish Immigration to
the United States, 1654-1990

Period	Immigrant Group	Years	Number of Immigrants
Colonial 1654-1776	Sephardic Jews Spain and Portugal	1700-1776	2,000*
Westward Expansion 1720-1860	Ashkenazic Jews Germany and Poland Unskilled Workers	1820-1840 1850-1860	10,000* 80,000*
Industrial Revolution 1880-1924	Yiddish Migration Russia and Poland Garment Workers Unskilled Workers	1881-1910 1881-1924 1904-1908 1915	1,562,800 2,326,458 642,000 136,654
The Great Depression	Modern German Immigration	1925-1932 1933-1937	78,000 33,000
World War II	Elite Immigrants	1933-1945	174,678
Post War Period 1948-1968	Soviet Jews Israeli Jews	1948-1953 1964-1968	132,000 39,000
Immigration Reform Period	Zionists Movement Soviet Jews	1970-1977 1948-1980	15,000 300,000
Modern Period	Israeli Jews	1981-1990	31,600

*Estimated by author
Source: Brenner, 1986:24, 31; Dinnerstein, 1987:15; Lavender, 1977:7; Goldstein, 1973:66, 71; U.S. Census, 1991:Table 7.

The Sephardic Jews (from *Sepharad*, literally Spanish in Hebrew) were well educated, involved in commercial activities, and were very strict in their observance of Jewish religious traditions. In view of their middle class backgrounds they integrated themselves into the life of the community, as many were shopkeepers, merchant shippers, and artisans (Brenner, 1986:17). Although their numbers were small, they established five synagogues in Colonial America, in New Amsterdam (1656), Newport Rhode Island (1678), Savannah (1733), Philadelphia (1745), and Charleston (1750) (Goren, 1980:574).

In the early eighteenth century a new wave of Jewish immigrants arrived. These were primarily German Jews who fled the religious persecution in their homeland. For example, they were denied citizenship, taxed excessively, limited to certain businesses, restricted in their travels, and segregated in their *shtetl* (ghetto) (Mesinger and Lamme, 1985:148).

These immigrants were the Ashkenazic Jews (from *Ashkenaz*, literally German in Hebrew), who spoke German or Yiddish and were not as well educated or skilled as the Sephardic Jews. Initially the Ashkenazic immigrants were shunned by the Sephardic settlers, who considered them working class types. Gradually they were accepted into the upper class synagogues of the Sephardim.

The influx of Ashkenazic immigrants is clearly reflected in the growth of the Jewish population in America. In the early nineteenth century, the Jewish population was only 15,000, but soared to almost a quarter of a million by 1880. By this time the Ashkenazic immigrants were not only the majority, but also constituted the new leadership in the Jewish community.

The most significant flow of Jews occurred during the Great Yiddish Migration (Brenner, 1986:23-31), when 2,326,458 Jewish immigrants arrived between 1881 and 1924 (Lavender, 1977:7). Most of these immigrants were Russian Jews escaping religious persecution, particularly after the assassination of Tsar Alexander II (in 1881 by a group of socialists), when a series of pogroms occurred in which hundreds of Jews were maimed and killed (Dinnerstein, 1987:17). In this regard, it is important to note that in 1880, five million Jews lived in Russia, out of an estimated world population of 7.5 million (Brenner, 1986:24)

In light of the racial violence and the severe limitations placed on their civil rights, thousands of Jews were forced from their homeland. Of the two and a half million Jews who arrived in America, between 1881 and 1924, the largest influx (642,000) occurred between 1904-1908, following a particularly brutal series of pogroms (Brenner, 1986:24).

The Eastern Jews were predominately Russians, and given their very large numbers, their influence on the Jewish community in America was particularly dramatic. By 1900, approximately 70 percent had settled in New York. And by 1915, there were 350,000 Jews living in a two square mile area of Manhattan (Rischin, 1962). In 1927, there were 1,765,000 living in New York City (Brenner, 1986:24; Waxman, 1989).

The credit for the development and success of the garment industry in New York City must be given to the Eastern Jews, as 60 percent were employed as garment workers by 1900 (Leventman, 1969:41). It is interesting to note that many of these Jewish immigrants had been employed in the clothing industry in Russia. Their contribution to the garment industry is clear when we consider that there were only 1,081 garment factories in Manhattan in 1880 (10% of all industries), but there were 11,172 (47% of all industries), in 1910 (Dinnerstein, 1987:22; Moore, 1981).

Following the passage of the Johnson Act (1924), that severely restricted all immigration, only 78,000 Jewish immigrants arrived between 1925 to 1932. In addition, the Great Depression had a negative impact on all immigration (Teller, 1968).

But it was the Nazi Holocaust that stimulated Jewish emigration between 1933 and 1945, when 174,678 immigrants arrived. Of the half million Jews living in Germany in 1933, almost 180,000 immigrated before *Kristalnacht* (Feingold, 1982:49). In spite of the horror stories of persecution and death of Jews in Germany, the Roosevelt administration did not move to repeal the Johnson Act.

The modern German immigration (See Figure 15.1) is unlike all previous Jewish immigration, since these immigrants were social elites escaping from one of the most advanced nations of the world. The restrictions of the Nazi regime forced many Jews out of business. In addition, laws were passed that prohibited Jews from practicing their professions and hundreds of Jewish university professors were fired. By the mid-1930's over 1,100 non-Aryan faculty members had lost their teaching positions. Germany's loss was America's gain, as 2,300 physicians, 1,000 professors, 800 lawyers, 682 journalists, 100 physicists, and hundreds of artists, musicians, and writers immigrated to America during this period (Feingold, 1982:50). Among these immigrants were such distinguished individuals as Albert Einstein, Henry Kissinger, and Edward Teller.

The end of the Second World War marked a new period of Jewish immigration. During the fifteen year period between 1944-1959, a total of 192,000 Jewish immigrants arrived under the provisions of the Displaced Persons Act of 1949. Most of these were Eastern European Jews and several thousand were Chassids, a close knit group of Orthodox Jews (Brenner, 1986:32).

An additional 73,000 Jewish immigrants arrived in America between 1960 to 1968. However, the postwar period is best known for the immigration of Israeli and Soviet Jews (See Figure 15.1). Between 1950 and 1979, more than 96,000 Israelies settled in America. But if the 23,000 Israelies who arrived without proper documents are included, then the actual figure is closer to 119,000. Since 1978, most of the Hebrew immigrants (about 75%) have arrived directly from Israel (Brenner, 1986:32).

While most of the 300,000 Jews who arrived in America between 1948 to 1980 were Israeli Jews, some were Soviet Jews (Gold, 1988:411-413; 1989:411-420, Table 1). It is estimated that between 1971 and 1980 some 80,000 Soviet Jews emigrated to the United States. In 1981, the Jewish Union of Russian Immigrants estimated that there were 100,000 Soviet Jews living in New York City (Orleck, 1987). In view of the current interest in human rights, the immigration of Soviet Jews has received a great deal of attention. Furthermore, the actions of certain Soviet refusenics have served to highlight the plight of all Soviet Jews.

Jewish Religious Beliefs

It is interesting to observe that when most people think of Jewish Americans, they usually think of them in terms of their religion. This is true inasmuch as religion is the socio-cultural cement that has bound the Hebrew nation throughout history. But only half the Jewish Americans today identify with a particular synagogue, and of these only about 15 percent attend religious services regularly (Mesinger and Lamme, 1985:146).

One study of church-synagogue attendance in the United States reveals that only 20 percent of the Jews, compared with 49 percent of the Catholics and 41 percent of the Protestants, attend church services weekly (Hoffman, 1989:593). And a national survey of religious identification found that only two-thirds of the 6.8 million American Jews claimed to practice their religion (Johnson, 1992:392). Therefore, the facts indicate that the level of religiosity (i.e. religious participation) is rather low among Jews. This finding contradicts the popular image of Jews as being highly religious (Glazer, 1990:36-37).

In the United States today there are three distinct branches of Judaism: (1) Orthodox, (2) Conservative, and (3) Reformed. The development of each of these branches can be related to distinct periods in Jewish immigration. The reason for this historic demarcation is that some groups held very traditional beliefs, such as the Sephardic Jews, who were Orthodox. The Eastern Jews were considered conservative in their beliefs, while the Ashkenazic Jews were Reform Jews (See Figure 15.2).

Figure 15.2
Jewish Religious Branches
in the United States, 1989

Religious Branches	Immigrant Group	Estimated Number	Percent of Total
Orthodox	Sephardic Jews	1,000,000	17.0
Conservative	Eastern European Jews	3,000,000	50.0
Reform	German Jews	2,000,000	33.0
Total		6,000,000	100.0

Source: Brenner, 1986:36; Lavender, 1977:3; Mesinger and Lamme, 1985:146.

It is estimated that between 10 to 20 percent of Jewish Americans follow Orthodox beliefs. For Orthodox Jews, traditions, rituals, religious observances, and the teachings of the Torah (the first five books of the Bible) and the Talmud (rabbinic doctrines) form the basis for their lives in the secular world. Fundamentalism and sacred traditions constitute the religious orientation of Orthodox Jews (Danziger, 1989; Heilman and Cohen, 1989).

Some groups within the Orthodox community, like the Hasidic Jews, Chassids, and the Satmarim, are religious fundamentalists who live in close knit sectarian communities (primarily in New York City). They have limited contact with the outside world, dress in traditional garb, observe all the religious laws and rituals, send their children to religious schools, speak Yiddish, and live by the Holy scriptures (Kamen, 1985; Poll, 1969b).

The Reform movement originated in Germany and was transported to America by the Ashkenazic Jews. Today about one-third of the synagogues in the United States follow the Reform movement. The objective of the Reform branch was to adapt Jewish religious beliefs to the changing American environment. Therefore strict adherence to Jewish rituals was not viewed as important, the substitution of English for Yiddish in religious services was allowed, and the strict observation of Jewish dietary restrictions were not considered essential. The secularization of Jewish religious beliefs was achieved by the turn of the century. Today some are of the opinion that the Reform movement has made many services in synagogues as open and liberal as some Protestant churches (Feingold, 1982:56-68).

Conservative Judaism was a reaction to the Reform movement, since it represents the middle-ground position within Judaism. The Conservative movement is associated with the massive influx of Eastern Jews during the late nineteenth century and early twentieth century (See Figure 11.2). Members of the Conservative movement found Orthodox beliefs far too restrictive for their secular goals in American society. In addition, they considered many of the changes promoted by the Reform movement as far too radical for their beliefs, though, most conservative Jews are politically liberal. Today, from 40 to 50 percent of all Jewish Americans identify with the Conservative movement.

In Jewish culture, the synagogue is the focus and the center of Jewish activity. Historically the synagogue was (1) a *Beth T'filoh* (a house of worship), (2) a place were rabbinical students and lay persons gathered for religious study, and (3) a community center. The first synagogue in the United States was built two years after the arrival of the Sephardic Jews in New Amsterdam. By 1880, there were 270 synagogues in America. Ten years later there were 533, and by 1906 there were almost 1,800 (Rosenberg, 1985:54). Today there are 3,416 synagogues in the United States (Hoffman, 1989:591).

Jewish religious beliefs derive from the Torah and the Talmud. For Orthodox Jews these sacred books contain the substance of life, as they guide individual behavior and require certain ritual observances. Perhaps the best known ritual observance is the *Kashrut*, which is the law that either permits or prohibits the consumption of certain foods. Kosher laws prescribe how the food is to be prepared and eaten (Poll, 1969a).

355

Jewish holidays play a very important part in the lives of all Jews, whether they are religious or not. Traditionally Jewish holidays are considered days of rest, when work and economic exchange is prohibited. The observance of the Sabbath is the most common ritual restriction on Jewish activities. Most Jewish holidays mark important religious or historical events.

The *Mitzvahs* restrict the behavior and dress of traditional Jews. For example, among the Hasidic Jews, the yarmulke (the skullcap) is worn at all times and they usually dress in black clothes. On the Sabbath, they are in the synagogue for the entire day. Women are segregated from the men, they marry young, and they have large families. A college education is discouraged among Hasidic Jews, as the men devote their lives to the study of the Torah (Isaacs, 1977).

Today it is not unusual to find Jewish Americans who are not religious and who do not observe Jewish traditions. One study found that most fourth generation Jews are Reform Jews (45%) or are non-religious (31%), that is in ritualistic terms (Cohen, 1988:43-57). This observation is supported by several studies that demonstrate that the younger generation of Jewish Americans tend to be less religious, have more Gentile friends, are less involved in the Jewish community, live in Gentile neighborhoods, and have higher rates of exogamy. Generally they only attend religious services on key holydays and only practice those religious rituals that preserve family ties, such as barmitzvah (Schoenfeld, 1988). In the end, the younger Jewish generation is more interested in symbolic ethnicity, rather than true devotion (Bershtel and Graubard, 1992:93-161).

Anti-Semitism in America

Prejudice, discrimination, and ethnic violence directed at Jews is referred to as anti-Semitism. The origins of anti-Semitism can be traced to the split that occurred between Christians and Jews following the crucifixion of Christ. As a result Jews were often portrayed as Christ killers. For hundreds of years Jews were the victims of ethnic hatred in Europe, as they were denied basic human rights, were the victims of racial violence, were banned from certain cities, and thousands were exterminated in a series of pogroms. Only fifty years ago, some six million Jews lost their lives because of Hitler's final solution.

One reason that Jews have served as the scapegoats for a variety of social ills is that certain stereotypes persist that make Jews a convenient group for social abuse and ethnic violence. Many Americans still believe that Jews control the national economy, are pushy and dishonest, are clannish, and are power hungry (Gordon, 1986; Quinley and Glock, 1979:1-10).

When the first Jewish settlers arrived in New Amsterdam, the governor banned them from the city. Fortunately his order was revoked. In 1762 Jews

356

were denied naturalization rights in Rhode Island and prohibited from conducting business in certain cities (Selzer, 1972:9-15). In fact, one of the reasons for their extreme concentration in the Jewish ghetto in Manhattan was ethnic segregation. Unfortunately their segregation increased their visibility and this only fostered an anti-Semitic atmosphere (Steinberg, 1981:55).

In the United States it was not uncommon for Jews to find their path to higher education blocked by laws that either limited the number of Jewish university students, or prohibited their entry altogether (Higham, 1966). Formal Jewish quotas were published in university policy statements during the 1920's, and became particularly restrictive during the 1930's (Dinnerstein, 1987:35). The use of ethnically restrictive quotas was initiated by Harvard and Columbia in 1922, and shortly thereafter quotas were adopted by Yale and Princeton (Synnott, 1979:14-17).

It was during the twenties and thirties that the alleged conspiracy of world domination by the Jews came into vogue. Jews were also held responsible for the communist conspiracy and were perceived as a threat to democracy (Schaar, 1958:323-346). Similarly, they were blamed for the socialists and communist infiltration of the American labor movement (Dubkowski, 1979). For it was the Eastern Jewish immigrants who accepted socialism as a means to improve the lot of all working people (Mayo, 1988:123-185). The Jewish garment unions were the first to obtain a standard wage, health and pension plans, and educational programs, that eventually served as a model for all unions (Feingold, 1974: 235-236).

The Ku Klux Klan and the German American Bund were the most active racists groups during the Great Depression. The difficult economic times made it is much easier for people to accept racial stereotypes and to find a convenient scapegoat for their problems. Perhaps it was the hatred of these racists groups that prepared the American public for the mass extermination of Jews in Germany, as the American government did little to assist the thousands of Jews who attempted to escape the Holocaust.

In more recent times Jews are still the victims of prejudice and discrimination, as they are restricted from certain occupations, barred from some social clubs, and excluded from certain political circles (Bershtel and Graubard, 1992:62-89; Selznick and Steinberg, 1969:37-52). Contrary to popular belief Jews are still barred from the corporate elite, as they represent less than three percent of the top corporate officials, which has been the case since 1901 (Zweigenhaft and Domhoff, 1982:17-46).

In response to the pervasive anti-Semitism in American society, the Jews have founded several national organizations to monitor acts of discrimination. The first national Jewish organization established to monitor and respond to anti-Semitic acts was the American Jewish Committee, founded in 1906. The Anti-Defamation League was founded by the Independent Order B'nai B'rith in 1913 to monitor and eliminate the publication of any materials that might be slanderous to Jewish Americans. Since then, the Anti-Defamation League has monitored all forms of ethnic discrimination and racial violence. The American Jewish Congress was founded in 1917, by a group of Eastern European Jews in New York City to protect the civil rights of Jewish Americans. The women's division of the American Jewish Congress was founded in 1933 (Elazar, 1990:179-192).

The unanimous conclusion reached by various studies of anti- Semitism in American society is that prejudice against Jews is less likely to occur among the well educated, those with higher incomes, white collar workers, those who belong to liberal Christian religions, and among the younger generation. The most favorable attitudes toward Jews were found in urban areas and in the Northeast and the West (Quinley and Glock, 1979:21-32). By far the South exhibited the most prejudicial attitudes toward Jews (Martire and Clark, 1982:31-45). Overall, the most anti- Semitic attitudes were found among the working class, the less educated, and those in the lower income brackets.

Geographic Distribution

Demographers have encountered several problems in their attempts to enumerate the Jewish American population. First, it is difficult to determine who is Jewish, and secondly the government does not compile data regarding religious affiliation. Nonetheless social scientists have devised several methods to estimate the Jewish population in the United States (Lazerwitz, 1973; Himmelfarb, 1980). One standard method is to count the membership in synagogues and the number of contributors to Jewish philanthropic organizations (Goldstein, 1973).

The United States has the largest population of Jews in the world today (6,800,000 in 1990) (Johnson, 1992:392), followed by Israel (3,562,500), the Soviet Union (1,515,000), France (530,000), and Great Britain (326,000) (Singer, 1988:427). The largest concentration of Jewish Americans occurs in the Northeast (52.5%), with smaller numbers in the North Central region (11.1%), the South (18.8), and the West (17.9%). Most Jews who live in the Northeast live in New York, which still has the largest population of Jews of any state. The second largest concentration of Jews occurs in California, followed by Florida (See Table 15.2).

In view of the historic settlement patterns of Jewish immigrants, New York City has the largest concentration of Jewish Americans today, with an estimated population of almost two million (1,891,400). This represents one third (32%) of the total Jewish population in the United States (Singer, 1988:225-226). In fact, New York City not only has the largest population of Jews in the United States, but also the largest concentration of Jews in the world.

Table 15.2
The Jewish Population in the United States, 1987
By Region and Selected States

Region	Total Population	Percent Distribution
Northeast	3,103,900	52.2
North Central	662,800	11.2
South	1,114,900	18.8
West	1,062,100	17.9
Total	5,943,700	100.0
State		
New York	1,891,400	31.8
California	868,200	14.6
Florida	549,200	9.2
New Jersey	427,700	7.2
Pennsylvania	347,000	5.8
Massachusetts	286,600	4.8
Illinois	259,800	4.4
Maryland	209,700	3.5
Connecticut	113,300	1.9
Texas	97,800	1.6

Source: David Singer (ed.) American Jewish Yearbook 1988.

Today, most New York area Jews live in one of the five boroughs of the city. Although some live in the suburban communities of Nassau, Suffolk, and Westchester. The inclusion of the Jews living in northern New Jersey, southwestern Connecticut, and Rockland County gives the New York metropolitan area a combined population of over two million Jews. (See Table 15.3).

The Los Angeles metropolitan area has the second largest Jewish population in the country, which has more than doubled in the past thirty years. Similarly, the tropical climate of south Florida has attracted thousands of Jewish Americans over the past thirty years, making it the third largest area of Jewish settlement. The fourth largest area of Jewish settlement occurs in New Brunswick and Middlesex Counties, in New Jersey, followed by Philadelphia, Chicago, Boston, and San Francisco (Goldstein, 1980) (See Table 15.3).

Table 15.3
Jewish Population in Selected
Cities and Counties, 1987

City	Total Population	City	Total Population
NewYork Metro Area	1,718,000	Philadelphia Area	250,000
Bronx	85,000	Chicago Metro Area	248,000
Brooklyn	429,000	Boston Metro Area	228,000
Manhattan	282,000	San Francisco Bay Area	196,000
Queens	329,000	Washington D.C. Metro	165,000
Staten Island	34,000	Montgomery and Prince	
Nassau County	320,000	Counties (Maryland)	104,500
Suffolk Count	112,000	Bergen County (NJ)	100,000
Westchester County	127,000	Baltimore	93,000
Los Angeles Metro Area	501,000	Orange County (CA)	80,000
South Florida	481,500	Essex County (NJ)	78,300
Miami (Dade County)	241,000	Cleveland	70,000
Ft. Lauderdale	85,000	Detroit	70,000
Hollywood	60,000	Rockland County	60,000
Palm Beach County	55,000	Atlanta Metro Area	55,000
Boca Raton	52,000	St. Louis	53,500
New Brunswick and		Phoenix	50,000
Middlesex County (NJ)	320,650	San Francisco	45,500
		Denver and Pittsburgh	45,000
		Houston	42,000

Source: David Singer (ed.), American Jewish Yearbook 1988.

Demographic Characteristics

In 1957, the Bureau of the Census found that American Jews were older than the general population, with a median age of 44.5 years, compared to 40.4 years for the general U.S. population (U.S. Census, 1958). By 1970, one out of four Jews were in the 45 to 65 age category, compared to one out of five in the general population. Overall, twelve percent of the Jewish Americans were over 65, compared to ten percent of all Americans (Goldstein, 1980; 1981:77-80).

The concentration of Jewish Americans in the older age categories can be attributed to (1) the impact of immigration over the past fifty years, as 85 percent of the foreign born were 45 years or older in 1960 (Goldstein and

Goldscheider, 1968:42), (2) the greater longevity of the Jewish population, and (3) the lower fertility rate among Jewish women.

Jewish Americans have always demonstrated a low fertility rate, and to this day maintain one of the lowest fertility rates of any ethnic group. Back in 1889, a study of over 10,000 Jewish families discovered that their fertility rate was lower than the general population. A more sophisticated study, conducted in 1905, found that the average Jewish family size in Rhode Island was 2.3, compared to 2.5 among Protestants, and 3.2 for Catholics (Goldstein and Goldscheider, 1968:116). One reason for this early pattern of low fertility among Jewish Americans was the discovery, made in 1930, that a higher proportion of Jewish couples used contraceptives, used them effectively, planned each pregnancy, and introduced family planning methods earlier in their marriages than either Protestants or Catholics (Stix and Notestein, 1940:29).

The more recent studies by Goldstein (1981) and Schmelz and Della Pergola (1983) reveal that fertility rates among Jews are still below the national average. In fact, Jewish fertility is below the zero population growth rate. Several sociological factors have contributed to their reduced fertility:

1. their higher levels of education
2. their higher incomes and occupational positions
3. their concentration in metropolitan areas
4. the greater number of Jewish women in the professions
5. their older age at first marriage
6. the longer delay of first pregnancy following marriage
7. and the universal acceptance of contraception.

Occupation and Income

An examination of the occupational characteristics of Jewish immigrants who arrived during the early phase of the Great Migration (1880-1924) reveals that most were unskilled laborers. But by the turn of the century a large proportion (70%) were skilled workers (Sherman, 1965:98). Most Jews were employed in the notorious sweatshops, where whole families worked 16 hours a day. Men were usually paid $10 to $12 per week, and women and children were payed less (Goldberg, 1947:15-17).

However, the rate of occupational mobility among Jewish immigrants was remarkable. For example, one study found that 60 percent of the Jews were industrial workers in 1900, but only 13 percent were thus employed thirty years later (Goldberg, 1946). Between 1910 and 1950 the number of Jewish white collar workers almost doubled, from 20 to 38 percent. Similarly, a survey conducted between 1948 and 1953 found that the number of Jews in non-manual occupations ranged from 75 to 96 percent, compared to 38 percent in the general population (Glazer, 1958). A Census survey conducted in 1957 found that 75 percent of all Jewish males held white collar positions, compared to 35 percent of the white male population (U.S. Census, 1958).

A survey conducted in 1980, found that 70 percent of Jewish men and 40 percent of Jewish women held professional, technical, or managerial positions. Most of the others were employed in clerical and sales positions (Goldstein, 1981:54). Today, 90 percent of all Jews are employed in white collar positions.

Contrary to the popular stereotype, there are very few Jews in the top positions in banking, as one study (among many) found that only one percent of the senior executives in major banks across the country were Jewish Americans. Furthermore, none of the top twenty banks in America are owned by Jews, as they have never controlled the banking industry (Zweigenhaft and Domhoff, 1982:20-25). Jewish entrepreneurs have been more involved in the American media, such as, film production, television, radio, and publishing. In addition, many of America's most outstanding intellectuals are Jewish writers and scholars.

Educational Achievement

Jewish intellectuals follow a long tradition and respect for learning in the Jewish culture. While the rabbi was the teacher, the members of the Jewish congregation were strongly encouraged to master the passages in the Talmud. With the arrival of thousands of Jewish immigrants in the late nineteenth century, synagogues were quick to organize evening schools for adults and day schools for children. Although the emphasis was on religious studies, these religious schools also offered English language classes.

It did not take long for these pioneers to realize that America offered unlimited opportunities for those who applied themselves and took advantage of an education. A study conducted in the mid-1960's, comparing the educational levels of Jewish Americans with other groups, found that 37.9 percent had graduated from college, compared to 15.9 percent of the general population. Of this group 24.1 percent had obtained advanced degrees, compared to only 9.1 percent of the general population (Sklare, 1971:55). The National Jewish Population Study conducted in 1970 found that only 15.6 percent of the Jewish population had less than a high school education, compared with 45.5 percent of the white population. At the other end of the spectrum four out of ten (41.4%) Jewish Americans had completed college, compared to only one out of ten (11.3%) of white Americans, over the age of 25 (Massarik and Chenkin, 1973:280).

The General Social Survey, commissioned in 1983, found that the median level of education among Jewish Americans was 15.9 years, compared to 12.5 years for the general population. They also found that two-thirds of Jewish Americans were college graduates, compared to only one out of five of the white Protestants in the study (Feagin, 1989:162-163). These data make it clear that Jewish Americans are probably the most highly educated group in American society today.

The Jewish American Family

Like other families in American society, the Jewish American family has also undergone important changes over time. The factors that have most directly affected the Jewish American family are (1) the immigration experience, (2) the diversity among Jewish immigrants, (3) their settlement in close knit ethnic enclaves, (4) the impact of their religious beliefs, (5) the effect of American culture, and (6) the long term process of assimilation (Goldman, 1991).

Given the diversity of the Jewish socio-cultural system today it is difficult to speak of the Jewish family as an ideal type. Obviously Jewish Americans are different in terms of their (1) religious orientation, (2) immigrant experiences, (3) generational level, and (4) current socioeconomic position in American society. Nonetheless Jewish Americans do share some characteristics in common.

Since most Jews were fleeing religious persecution, it is not surprising to discover that most arrived in America in intact family units. These immigrants also realized that they would never return to their homeland, as this was a political impossibility for most of them. As a result, they arrived in America with the knowledge that they, as a family, would have to make the best of their new situation. Furthermore, whole communities of Jewish immigrants settled in American cities and duplicated, as best they could, the family and community structure as they knew it in their homeland. In retrospect it was the Jewish family and community cohesiveness that provided the basis for their social mobility and success in American society.

Despite the social change and turmoil that has occurred over the past thirty years, Jewish Americans still have one of the highest rates of marriage and the lowest divorce rates. For example, a study conducted in the mid-sixties found that only half a percent of the Jewish males were separated or divorced, compared with 2.6 percent of gentile males. While Jewish Americans today still have a very low divorce rate, divorce is the highest among third and fourth generation Jewish couples, as compared to first generation Jewish immigrant couples. Divorce is also higher among Reform Jews, as compared to Conservative Jews. As expected, the Orthodox Jews have the lowest divorce rates among all Jews (Goldstein and Goldscheider, 1968:113). However, more recent studies reveal that even their divorce rate has increased, much as it has in the general population. Nonetheless, the Jewish divorce rate is still among the lowest of all groups (Phillips, 1980).

The sociological studies still confirm the very strong support for marriage among Jewish Americans. One study found that three-fourths of all Jewish males over the age of 14 were married, compared to only two-thirds of all white males (Goldstein and Goldscheider, 1968:102-103). The National Jewish Population Study found that less than five percent of the Jewish Americans in their survey were single (Chenkin, 1972:16). For Jews, marriage and family is a religious obligation, as it is a mitzvah.

One important reason for the enduring stability of their marriages, besides the strong religious prohibitions against divorce, is that Jewish Americans are older when they get married. The Providence, Rhode Island study found that Jewish males were 26 at the time of first marriage, compared to 23 for the total U.S. male population. Similarly, Jewish women married at the age of 23, compared to the age of 20 for the total female population (Goldstein and Goldscheider, 1968:105). A more recent study in Providence, supports these original findings (Kobrin and Goldscheider, 1978:78).

Besides the religious and cultural expectations regarding age at first marriage, it is clear that the higher level of educational achievement serves as an important barrier to early marriage among Jewish Americans. When men and women are compared, Jewish men are three to four years older at the time of first marriage.

As revealed in our previous discussion, Jewish fertility is among the lowest of any group, as a result the size of the Jewish family is small when compared to the general population. The nuclear family is also more prevalent among Jewish Americans, as opposed to the general population. One study found that 90 percent of the Jewish families were of the nuclear variety, as compared to two-thirds in the general population (Goldstein and Goldscheider, 1968:109-110). The percentage of nuclear families usually increases among third and fourth generation Jewish Americans. This is related to their high level of urban concentration and their high socio-economic status.

The prevalence of the nuclear family among Jewish Americans today is offset by their maintenance of strong kinship ties and active involvement in religious, communal, and social organizations (Gordon and Mayer, 1980). For over the years, following their immigration to America, they have accepted the necessity and the advantages of maintaining the nuclear family, but they have also devised social and cultural systems to compensate for the loss of extended family ties. For it was not that many years ago that Jews followed the religious dictum that they live within walking distance of the synagogue.

Intermarriage and Assimilation

Historically sociologists have used the rate of exogamy as an indication of the social acceptability of ethnic or immigrant groups, therefore a high rate of intermarriage would serve as an indication of the increasing social acceptability of a minority group. While the rate of intermarriage is a key indicator of the rate of assimilation, this trend toward higher rates of intermarriage has not always been viewed as a positive sign in the Jewish American community (Farber, et al, 1979).

Historically, it was against the law in most European societies for a Jew to marry a Gentile. Even when it was not illegal, exogamy often met with strong social disapproval, to the point of social ostracism. And in those cases where intermarriage did occur, it was usually when the Jewish partner converted to Christianity. But the teachings of Judaism, and the community consensus, worked against any possibility of intermarriage, as the Jewish elders saw intermarriage as a loss to the community and viewed it as a danger to Judaism, for the following reasons:

1. members of the faith would be lost to the community
2. children from an intermarriage probably would be lost to the community
3. children from an intermarriage are also much more likely to marry exogamously (the multiplier effect)
4. over time intermarriage would destroy the Jewish culture and religion
5. intermarriage reduces the size of the Jewish community
6. an increasing rate of intermarriage results in greater social approval of intermarriage (i.e. among Jews)
7. human capital is reduced in the Jewish community as a result of intermarriage.

While we generally consider Jewish exogamy as a relatively recent phenomena, it is reported that three out of ten (28.7%) marriages involving Jews, were intermarriages between 1776 and 1840 (Stern, 1967:142-143). With the arrival of German Jews the rate of intermarriage declined, and it dropped significantly when Eastern European Jews settled in America. For the rate of exogamy in 1912, was only 1.17 percent (Drachsler, 1920:120-132).

A Bureau of the Census study of 35,000 households in 1957 found that the Jewish rate of exogamy was only 7.2 percent (U.S. Census, 1958). Six major studies conducted in Jewish communities between 1956 and 1966 found that the rate of intermarriage ranged from a low of four percent (in Camden, N.J.), to a high of 18.5 percent (in San Francisco) (Sklare, 1971:187-191). Statistical analysis of the data retrieved from the National Jewish Population Study (1971) found that about one-third of the Jewish Americans who married between 1965 and 1971 had married exogamously (Massarik, 1973; Massarik and Chenkin, 1973).

One study of Denver's Jewish community found that half (52%) of their respondents, between the ages of 20-29, had married Gentile spouses (Cohen, 1988:27). However, the results of this study are discounted and are regarded as an anomaly by many. One expert on Jewish intermarriage in the 1980's estimates that the actual rate of intermarriage among Jewish Americans is closer to 11 percent, particularly on the East coast (Cohen, 1988:40). Nonetheless, the experts predict that the rate of Jewish exogamy will continue to increase in the foreseeable future (e.g. Mayer and Sheingold, 1979; Wertheimer, 1989).

Based on our survey of the literature, we can conclude that exogamy among Jewish Americans will continue to increase because (1) Jews are more integrated into American society, (2) their higher socio-economic positions encourage exogamy, (3) the continued dispersion of Jews in American society promotes higher rates of exogamy, and (4) the decreasing importance of Jewish religious beliefs and practices (Farber and Gordon, 1982:55-59; Sklare and Greenblum, 1979).

However, the effect of intermarriage on the maintenance of Jewish religion and culture is not unilateral, rather its impact is complex. In brief, careful analysis of the effects of exogamy on Jewish American culture reveals that:

1. Jewish men are slightly more likely to intermarry
2. gentile wives are more likely to convert to Judaism (23%), than gentile husbands (11%) (Cohen, 1988:41)
3. Jewish women who intermarry are far more likely to raise their children in the Jewish religion (73%), than are Jewish men (35%) (Cohen, 1988:41)
4. bi-cultural families are less likely to identify with Jewish culture and traditions
5. the younger generation is more likely to accept intermarriage now and in the near future.

Chapter Summary

The first Jewish settlers arrived in America in 1654 and settled in New Amsterdam. They were members of the Sephardic branch, that is Jews from Spain and Portugal. They were followed by Ashkenazic Jews, primarily from Germany. By 1880, the Jewish population in America was approximately a quarter of a million.

The largest influx of Jews occurred during the Great Yiddish Migration, when 2.3 million arrived between 1881 and 1924. These Eastern Jews set the cultural pattern for Jewish life in America. During the Great Depression Americans witnessed the flow of German-Jewish immigrants, who were escaping the terror of the Nazi regime. Most of the recent Jewish immigrants are from the Soviet Union or from Israel.

Jewish Americans are divided into three major branches: the Orthodox, Conservative, and the Reform. Since the turn of the century the Reform Jews have attracted the largest number of followers. The popularity of Reform Judaism can be attributed to their liberal attitudes and their assimilationist orientation.

Today the Jewish American community has the highest level of educational achievement, the highest proportion of men and women in the professions, and one of the highest incomes of any ethnic group in American society. Their success in American society can be attributed to their determination to secure a higher education and their strong sense of community responsibility.

References

Bershtel, Sara and Allen Braubard
   1992   *Saving Remnants: Feeling Jewish in America.* New York:
            The Free Press.
Brenner, Lenni
   1986   *Jews in America Today.* Secaucus, NJ: Lyle Stuart Inc.
Chenkin, Alvin
   1972   "Demographic Highlights: Facts for Planning." In *National
            Jewish Population Study.* New York: Council of Jewish Federa-
            tions and Welfare Funds.
Cohen, Steven M.
   1988   *American Assimilation or Jewish Revival?* Bloomington:
            Indiana University Press.
Danziger, Herbert
   1989   *Returning to Tradition.* New Haven: Yale University Press.
Dimont, Max
   1978   *The Jews in America: The Roots, History, and Destiny of
            American Jews.* New York: Simon and Schuster.
Diner, Hasia R.
   1977   *In the Almost Promised Land: American Jews and Blacks,
            1915-1935.* Westport, CT: Greenwood Press.
Dinnerstein, Leonard
   1987   *Uneasy at Home: Anti-semitism and the American Jewish
            Experience.* New York: Columbia University Press.
Drachsler, Julius
   1920   *Democracy and Assimilation.* New York: MacMillan.
Dubkowski, Michael
   1979   *The Tarnished Dream: The Basis of American Anti-
            Semitism.* Westport, CT: Greenwood Press.
Elazar, Daniel J.
   1990   "Developments in Jewish Community Organization in the
            Second Postwar Generation." In *American Pluralism and the
            Jewish Community.* Seymour Martin Lipset (ed.), New
            Brunswick: Transaction Publishers. Pp. 173-192.
Farber, Bernard, L. Gordon, and A. J. Mayer
   1979   "Intermarriage and Jewish Identity: Implications for
            Pluralism and Assimilation in American Society." *Ethnic and
            Racial Studies* 2:222-230.
Farber, Bernard and Leonard Gordon
   1982   "Accounting For Jewish Intermarriage: An Assessment of
            National and Community Studies." *Contemporary Jewry*
            6(1):47-75

Feagin, Joe R.
1989 *Racial and Ethnic Relations* (third edition). Englewood
  Cliffs, NJ: Prentice-Hall.

Feingold, Henry L.
1974 *Zion in America: The Jewish Experience from Colonial
  Times to the Present.* New York: Twayne.
1982 *A Midrash on American Jewish History.* Albany: State
  University of New York Press.

Glazer, Nathan
1958 "The American Jew and the Attainment of Middle-Class
  Rank: Some Trends and Explanations." In *The Jews: Social
  Patterns of an American Group.* Marshal Sklare (ed.) , New
  York: The Free Press.
1990 "American Jewry or American Judaism." In *American
  Pluralism and the Jewish Community.* Seymour Martin Lipset
  (ed.), New Brunswick: Transaction Publishers. Pp. 31-41.

Gold, Steven J.
1988 "Refugees and Small Business: the Case of Soviet Jews and
  Vietnamese." *Ethnic and Racial Studies* 11(4):411-438.
1989 "Differential Adjustment Among New Immigrant Family
  Members." *Journal of Contemporary Ethnography* 17(4):408-
  434.

Goldberg, Nathan
1946 "Occupational Patterns of Jewish Americans." *Jewish Review*
  3(4):275.
1947 *Occupational Patterns of American Jewry.* New York: Jewish
  Teachers Seminary Press.

Goldman, Ari
1991 "Poll Shows Jews Both Assimilate and Keep Tradition."
  New York Times (June 7).

Goldstein, Sidney
1973 "American Jewry: A Demographic Analysis." In *The Future
  of the Jewish Community in America.* David Sidorsky (ed.), New
  York: Basic Books, Pp. 65-126.
1980 "Jews in the United States: Perspectives from Demography."
  In *American Jewish Year Book, 1981.* New York: American
  Jewish Committee, 1980-1981.
1981 "Jews in the United States: Perspectives From Demography."
  In *Jewish Life in the United States: Perspectives from the Social
  Sciences.* Joseph Gittler (ed.), New York: New York University
  Press

Goldstein, Sidney and Calvin Goldscheider
1968 *Jewish Americans: Three Generations in a Jewish
  Community.* Englewood Cliffs, NJ: Prentice-Hall.

Gordon, Leonard
    1986   "College Student Stereotypes of Blacks and Jews on Two
               Campuses: Four Studies Spanning 50 Years." *Sociology and So-
               cial Research* 70(3):200-201.

Gordon, Leonard and Albert J. Mayer
    1980   "Communal and Pietistic Identification as Related to Size
               and Concentration of Jewish Population." *Journal of Psychol-
               ogy and Judaism* Fall:28-37.

Goren, Arthur
    1980   "Jews." In *Harvard Encyclopedia of American Ethnic
               Groups.* Stephen Thernstrom (ed.), Cambridge: Harvard
               University Press.

Heilman, Samuel and Steven M. Cohen
    1989   *Cosmopolitans and Parochials: Modern Orthodox Jews in America.*
               Chicago: University of Chicago Press.

Higham, John
    1966   "American Anti-Semitism Historically Reconsidered." In *Jews
               in the Mind of America.* Charles H. Stember (ed.), New York:
               Basic Books, Pp. 237-258.

Himmelfarb, Harold
    1980   "The Study of American Jewish Identification: How it is
               Defined, Measured, Obtained, Sustained and Lost." *Journal
               for the Scientific Study of Religion* 19(1):48-60.

Hoffman, Mark S.
    1989   *The World Almanac and Book of Facts 1989.* New York:
               Pharos Books.

Isaacs, Stephen
    1977   "Hasidim of Brooklyn." In *A Coat of Many Colors: Jewish
               Subcommunities in the United States.* Abraham D. Lavender
               (ed.), Westport, CT: Greenwood Press, Pp. 189-194.

Johnson, Otto
    1992   *Information Please Almanac.* Boston: Houghton Mifflin.

Kamen, Robert M.
    1985   *Growing Up Hasidic: Education and Socialization in the
               Bobover Hasidic Community.* New York: AMS Press.

Kobrin, Frances E. and Calvin Goldscheider
    1978   *The Ethnic Factor in Family Structure and Mobility.*
               Cambridge: Ballinger.

Lavender, Abraham D. (ed.)
    1977   *A Coat of Many Colors: Jewish Subcommunities in the
               United States.* Westport, CT: Greenwood Press.

Lazerwitz, B.
1973 "Religious Identification and its Ethnic Correlates."
Social Forces 52:204-220.

Leventman, Seymour
1969 "From Shtetl to Suburb." In *The Ghetto and Beyond: Essays on Jewish Life in America.* Peter I. Rose (ed.), New York: Random House. Pp. 33-56.

Martire, Gregory and Ruth Clark
1982 *Anti-Semitism in the United States: A Study of Prejudice in the 1980s.* New York: Praeger.

Massarik, Fred
1973 "Intermarriage: Facts for Planning." In *National Jewish Population Study.* New York: Council of Jewish Federations and Welfare Funds.

Massarik, Fred and Alvin Chenkin
1973 "United States National Jewish Population Study: A First Report." In *American Jewish Year Book.* Philadelphia: Jewish Publication Society of America.

Mayer, Egon and Carl Sheingold
1979 *Intermarriage and the Jewish Future: A National Study in Summary.* New York: American Jewish Committee, Institute of Human Relations.

Mayo, Louise A.
1988 *The Ambivalent Image: Nineteenth Century America's Perception of the Jew.* Rutherford: Fairleigh Dickinson University Press.

Mesinger, Jonathan S. and Ary J. Lamme III
1985 "American Jewish Ethnicity." In *Ethnicity in Contemporary America: A Geographical Appraisal.* Jesse O. McKee (ed.), Dubuque, Iowa: Kendall/Hunt, Pp. 145-168.

Moore, Deborah D.
1981 *At Home in America: Second-Generation New York Jews.* New York: Columbia University Press.

Orleck, Annelise
1987 "The Soviet Jews: Life in Brighton Beach, Brooklyn." In *New Immigrants in New York.* Nancy Forner (ed.), New York: Columbia University Press, Pp. 273-304.

Phillips, Bruce
1980 *Los Angeles Jewish Community Survey: Overview for Regional Planning.* Los Angeles: Jewish Federation.

Poll, Solomon
1969a "The Persistence of Tradition: Orthodoxy in America." In *The Ghetto and Beyond: Essays on Jewish Life in America.* Peter I. Rose (ed.), New York: Random House, Pp. 118-149.

1969b   *The Hasidic Community in Williamsburg: A Study in the Sociology of Religion.* New York: Schocken Books.

Quinley, Harold E. and Charles Y. Glock
1979   *Anti-Semitism in America.* New York: The Free Press.

Rischin, Moses
1962   *The Promised City: New York's Jews, 1870-1914.* Cambridge: Harvard University Press.

Rosenberg, Stuart E.
1985   *The New Jewish Identity in America.* New York: Hippocrene Books.

Schaar, Howard M.
1958   *The Course of Modern Jewish History.* New York: World.
     Schmelz, U. O. and Sergio Della Pergola
1983   "Population Trends in the U.S. Jewry and Their Demographic Consequences." In *The American Jewish Year Book 1983.* New York: The American Jewish Committee, Volume 83. Pp. 141-187.

Schoenfeld, Stuart
1988   "Integration into the Group and Sacred Uniqueness: Analysis of an Adult Bat Mitzvah." In *Persistence and Flexibility: Anthropological Perspectives on the American Jewish Experience.* Walter P. Zenner (ed.), Albany: State University of New York Press, Pp. 117-135.

Selzer, Michael
1972   *Kike: A Documentary History of Anti-Semitism in America.* New York: World Publishing.

Selznick, Gertrude J. and Stephen Steinberg
1969   *The Tenacity of Prejudice: Anti-Semitism in Contemporary America.* New York: Harper & Row.

Sherman, C. Bezalel
1965   *The Jew Within American Society.* Detroit: Wayne State University Press.

Singer, David (ed.)
1988   *American Jewish Year Book 1988.* New York: The American Jewish Committee, Volume 88.

Sklare, Marshall
1971   *America's Jews.* New York: Random House.

Sklare, Marshall and Joseph Greenblum
1979   *Jewish Identity on the Suburban Frontier: A Study of Group Survival in the Open Society* (second edition). Chicago: University of Chicago Press.

Sloan, Irving J. (ed.)
1971   *The Jews in America, 1621-1970; A Chronology & Fact Book.* Dobbs Ferry, NY: Oceana Publications.

Steinberg, Stephen
1981 *The Ethnic Myth: Race Ethnicity and Class in America.*
New York: Atheneum.
Stern, Malcolm H.
1967 "Jewish Marriage and Intermarriage in the Federal Period
(1776-1840)." *American Jewish Archives* 19:142-143.
Stix, R. K. and Frank Notestein
1940 *Controlled Fertility.* Baltimore: The William & Wilkins Co.
Synnott, M. G.
1979 *The Half-Opened Door: Discrimination at Harvard, Yale,
and Princeton, 1900-1970.* Westport, CN: Greenwood Press.
Teller, Judd
1968 *Strangers and Natives: The Evolution of the American
Jew from 1921 to the Present.* New York: Delacorte Press.
U.S. Census
1958 *Religion Reported by the Civilian Population of the United States.*
Current Population Reports: Population Characteristics,
Series P-2O, No. 79, February 2.
Waxman, Chaim
1989 "The Emancipation, the Enlightenment, and the
Demography of American Jewry." *Judaism* (Fall).
Wertheimer, Jack
1989 "Recent Trends in American Judaism." In *American Jewish
Year Book,* 1989. New York: The American Jewish Commit-
tee, Volume 89.
Zweigenhaft, Richard L. and B. William Domhoff
1982 *Jews in the Protestant Establishment.* New York: Praeger.

1492	The Jews were expelled from Spain.
1492	Several Jews were members of Columbus' crew.
1654	The first Jewish settlement in North America was founded in New Amsterdam (New York).
1730	The first synagogue was founded in New Amsterdam.
1774	Francis Salvador was the first Jew to be elected to a Colonial representative assembly (South Carolina).
1786	Virginia was the first colony to guarantee religious freedom to Jews.
1815	German Jews were denied their civil rights, causing a mass migration to America.
1826	Maryland passed a law ending religious test against Jews.
1848	Revolution in Europe stimulated Jewish immigration from Germany.
1862	Rabbis were allowed to become military chaplains.
1881	Pogroms in Russia resulted in mass Jewish migration to America.
1885	Reform Jews published their principles and beliefs in the Pittsburgh Platform.
1886	Conservative Jews founded the Jewish Theological Seminary.
1914	Louis Brandeis became the leader of the American Zionist movement.
1915	As a result of anti-Semitic hatred in Georgia, Leo Frank was lynched.
1920	The Protocols of the Elders of Zion, an anti-Semitic piece of propaganda was published by Henry Ford.
1924	The Johnson Reed Act drastically limited Jewish immigration.
1930	Nazi propaganda stimulated anti-Semitic acts in America.
1939	Over six million Jews killed by the Nazis during the Second World War.
1948	Israel established as an independent nation. President Truman granted Israel immediate diplomatic recognition.
1967	Israel's Six Day War.
1975	The UN General Assembly declares that Zionism is racism.
1980	Acts of anti-Semitism increase in the United States.

marranos	Sephardic Jews	Ashkenazic Jews
Great Yiddish Migration	pogroms	Johnson Act (1924)
holocaust	Displaced Persons Act (1949)	Kristalnacht
Chassids	Soviet Jews	Judaism
Orthodox	Conservative	Reformed Jews
Torah	Talmud	Hasidic Jews
Chassids	Yiddish	synagogue
Kosher laws	Sabbath	mitzvahs
yarmulke	barmitzvah	anti-Semitism
B'nai B'rith	American Jewish Congress	

Sample Test Questions

---

1. Discuss five reasons why Jewish Americans are a minority group.
2. List and discuss four waves of Jewish immigration. Be sure to note the unique characteristics of each.
3. Provide a brief discussion of the three major branches of Judaism in American society today.
4. List five examples of Jewish culture. Now provide a definition for each.
5. Provide a brief definition of anti-Semitism. Now provide five examples of anti-Semitism in American history.
6. Discuss five reasons why Jewish Americans have one of the lowest fertility rates of any group in American society.
7. Provide five historical or sociological reasons why Jewish Americans have been so successful in American society.
8. Discuss five unique sociological characteristics of the Jewish American family today.
9. List and discuss five characteristics of intermarriage among Jewish Americans today. What is the long term effect of intermarriage on the Jewish American community?

Chapter 16

The Irish American Experience

Introduction

In most studies of American immigration history the Irish would be considered an example of the rapid assimilation of European immigrants. But when the Irish are compared to other white ethnics, it is clear that they did exhibit some unique social and religious characteristics that made them unique among European immigrants.

Perhaps the most distinguishing characteristic of the Irish immigrants was that they were predominately Catholic, and it was this fact that made them stand out in a largely Anglo-Saxon Protestant society. The arrival of the Irish marked the first Catholic invasion of America. As a result they experienced religious discrimination. But it was their religious beliefs that gave them a sense of direction and a sense of community. Furthermore, the church provided the leadership that was essential to their success in overcoming poverty and the sting of discrimination. Over a short period the Irish improved their social and economic conditions, organized themselves into an effective political community, founded and supported parochial schools, and moved from their blue collar jobs into the world of education, business, and politics.

Today, the Irish have demonstrated the most consistent rate of social mobility of any white ethnic gentile group in American society. They have established an admirable record of social mobility in terms of their educational achievements, occupational distribution, and economic standing. In addition, the Irish left their mark on urban politics, education, and American Catholicism.

Pre-Famine Immigration: 1492-1840

According to all historical accounts the first Irishman to reach America was William Ayers, who sailed with Columbus (Griffin, 1973:1). Others believe that a band of Irish monks carried their missionary message to the Indians of North America seven hundred years before Columbus. But these early contacts are unsubstantiated.

However, it is known that substantial numbers of Irish immigrants arrived in America and settled in frontier villages in the seventeenth century. The first national census was conducted in 1790, and it counted 44,000 Irish born residents and half were living in Pennsylvania (Griffin, 1973:11). By the turn of the eighteenth century the Irish American population reached 150,000 (Fallows, 1979:19).

While the actual number of Irish immigrants who arrived before 1820 is unknown, it is an established fact that most of these pre-famine immigrants were Protestants, were from the middle and upper classes of Irish society, and arrived with skills and resources. In contrast, the small number of Irish Catholics that arrived during this early period were either indentured servants or convicted criminals exiled to America.

The Irish Protestant immigrants who settled in America during this early period were primarily Presbyterian farmers from Ulster. While these farmers owned their land and maintained a comfortable living in Ireland, they were suffering from a heavy tax burden, high rents, and tithes imposed by the British. Furthermore, they were weary of the religious conflict in Northern Ireland and the strict laws imposed by the British in an attempt to control the lives of Irish Catholics. In utter frustration, hundreds sold their farms and struck out for the American frontier. As early as 1710 these Irish Protestant immigrants settled in the Blue Ridge Mountains of Virginia, and into the Shenandoah Valley by 1743. In 1775 Irish pioneers blazed the trail into the Kentucky frontier.

These Irish Protestant immigrants did not experience religious prejudice or discrimination, as America was a Protestant society. Consequently their arrival in frontier communities was met with little or no resistance. But with the arrival of Irish Catholics in the early 1820's they began to call themselves Scotch-Irish. This was an attempt to call attention to the fact that they were Protestants. While most were of Scottish ancestry, although some were not, they discovered that this was an effective way to distinguish themselves from the now stigmatized Irish Catholics (Considine, 1961:32-33).

Historical Antecedents to the Famine Immigration

When Pope Adrian IV gave Ireland to Henry II in 1156, the historical die was cast for the social, economic, and political oppression of Irish Catholics for the next eight hundred years. Their oppression was completed during the reign of Henry VIII in the sixteenth century, and they were marked for destruction by Oliver Cromwell. In the war of resistance that followed Cromwell's invasion of Ireland (in 1649), more than half the island's population was massacred, that is about three-quarters of a million people (Greeley, 1972a: 17).

Cromwell's invasion of Ireland was the first example of genocide in modern history. The survivors were reduced to landless peasants. Once victory was achieved, the English Parliament decreed that all land held by Irish Catholics was to be forfeited and given to the English loyalists, while the Irish Catholics were only allowed to remain as renters and servants to their English masters. After the massacre, the Protestants were only ten percent of the population but owned 95 percent of the land. Whereas the Irish Catholics represented 89 percent of the population, but only owned five percent of the land (Fallows, 1979:15). In an agricultural society this meant that the population was reduced to a mass of peasants and serfs (Miller, 1985:35).

Legal oppression began with the introduction of the Penal Laws in the eighteenth century. The Penal Laws were passed by the British to make life in Ireland as miserable as possible. These laws attempted to ban Catholicism from Ireland and to insure that all Irish Catholics remained virtual slaves in their country. The Penal Laws further insured that the plantation system would function in Ireland. In addition, these laws required all priests to register with the authorities and swear their allegiance to the British, or face being branded or castrated.

In 1719, all bishops were banished from Ireland and key religious symbols were prohibited in villages and churches. The Irish Catholics could not vote for members of Parliament, their children were banned from public schools, they were prohibited from establishing their schools, they could not practice law, and were not allowed to serve in the military. Furthermore, Catholics could not deed their land as a whole, could not hold a lease on land for more than thirty years, nor could they own a horse worth more than five pounds (Greeley, 1972a:27-28).

Since Irish Catholics no longer owned their farm land they were subjected to a brutal system of rack-renting, by which English landlord would periodically raise land rents at will. This reduced all Irish tenant farmers to a subsistence level of existence. The fact that made the system even more oppressive was the use of British managers to collect rents and supervise the property for absentee landlords. Consequently Irish farmers were under the constant threat of eviction and were required to provide free labor for all public work projects. Even more devastating they were required to give tithes to the district's Protestant church.

In response to their oppression the Irish formed secret societies, such as the Whiteboys and the Molly Maguires, who intimidated and used violence against their landlords. Marked landlords would have their hay burned, their cattle and pigs slaughtered, and sometimes they were the victims of an assassin's knife. In one year, during the early 1830's, the government reported 9,000 political crimes and 200 homicides in Ireland (Shannon, 1966:17).

Background to the Irish Famine

Following the death and destruction wrought by Cromwell's Army, Ireland was reduced to a subsistence agricultural society based on an economy supported by a plantation system that was dependent on the labor of tenant farmers. Many believe that the great Irish famine was the result of a potato blight, but in fact the mass starvation that swept Ireland was the result of an oppressive system of agricultural production imposed on the Irish by the British (Woodham, 1962).

Since 90 to 95 percent of the agricultural land in Ireland was owned by absentee British landlords, the Irish were reduced to dependent tenant farmers. In effect the Irish became landless peasants, that is serfs, in their homeland. In view of their circumstances Irish farmers only produced two types of crops, one for daily survival, the potato crop, and one for payment of land rent, wheat, barley, and corn. In addition they raised cattle and pigs and supplied milk for export, to pay their rent. Consequently the Irish were forced to eat potatoes, while their cereal crops, milk, and livestock were shipped to England to pay their landlords.

Potatoes were easy to grow, dependable, and provided a substantial yield per acre. One acre of land, in a good year, could produce sixty barrels of potatoes and a family of six could survive on one barrel of potatoes a week. Of course, this meant that they ate potatoes three times a day (Considine, 1961:41-42). Since the average size of the Irish farm was less than fifteen acres (Schrier, 1970:67), this meant that the remaining land was set aside to produce crops to pay their English landlords. Obviously this system of production put the Irish farmers in a very precarious position, as they never knew the quality or the quantity of their potato crop for any given year.

Their forced dependence on potatoes caused nutritional deficiencies and a variety of life threatening diseases, such as rickets, scurvy, beriberi, pellagra, and night blindness, which resulted in birth defects and spread epidemics. In general, malnutrition and disease killed as many people as starvation. The most serious famines occurred in 1800, 1807, 1816, 1839, 1845-1848, 1863, and 1879 (Kennedy, 1973:27).

Clearly it was the system of land tenure, imposed by the British, that insured mass starvation among the Irish. It was not uncommon to find the storerooms of Irish farmers filled with grain, while their families suffered from malnutrition, and a host of diseases. But they knew that their harvest had to go to England to pay their rent. For the British, Ireland was simply a large plantation that provided them with essential agricultural products, that is products that were essential to the maintenance of their economic and military superiority in the world.

Consequently, the Great Potato Famine (1845-1848), was not an act of nature, but rather it was the direct result of the economic exploitation of Irish farmers. Indeed, the Irish famine was viewed by many in England as the solution to the Irish problem. (Greeley, 1972a:36).

It is estimated that the Great Famine resulted in the extermination of over a million Irish Catholics (McCaffrey, 1976: 55). Is it any wonder that the Irish had to ask why the British government, the richest and most powerful nation in the world, allowed Irish meat and grain to be exported to England at a time when thousands of Irishmen were dying of starvation?

The Great Migration: 1841-1900

Like thousands of other immigrants, the Irish were also exposed to many push-pull factors. In addition to the prospect of wholesale starvation, the Irish were also inclined to leave their homeland because of exorbitant rents, mass evictions, pervasive poverty, religious discrimination, agrarian violence, repressive court and penal systems, and very limited opportunities for social improvement. Therefore they viewed their departure for America as an opportunity to escape political and religious oppression, find employment, and marry and have a family.

Most Irish Catholic immigrants were young, as two-thirds were between 15 to 35 years old, 80 percent were single, and there were an equal number of men and women. Half the immigrants were the sons and daughters of Irish farmers from six counties in Munster and Connaught, predominately Catholic regions of the country (Schrier, 1970:4).

It was a common practice for Irish families to save and collect funds to send one of their sons or daughters to America, with the hope that they would find employment and send relief money home. Sometimes farmers would abandon their farms, sell their crops and livestock, and use this money for their passage, which ranged from $12 to $20 per head. In other circumstances, landlords paid the passage for their tenants, as they wanted to rid themselves of the responsibility of impoverished tenants.

The voyage to America took from six to eight weeks and the death toll was high. At the time, these ships were popularly referred to as coffin ships, as they were overcrowded, often ran out of food and water, and were breeding grounds for cholera, typhus, and dysentery (Greeley, 1972a:37). As a result thousands lost their lives during the voyage to the promise land. For example, out of 87,000 emigrants that arrived in Canada in 1847, at the peak of the famine, 6,100 died at sea, 4,100 died in quarantine, and 7,200 died in shore hospitals. Over all about one out of five of the original passengers died (Potter, 1960).

Irish emigration between 1820 and 1900 represents the largest mass movement of people from one country to another in modern history. This is particularly apparent when we consider that for every Irish immigrant in America (in 1860), there were only five compatriots remaining in Ireland. In comparison the ratio for Germany was 1:33 and for England it was only 1:42 (Schrier, 1970:5). The Irish population in America increased rapidly, as they constituted 15.6 percent of the immigrant flow to the United States at the turn of the century, one-third by 1830, and half of all immigrants by 1850.

Table 16.1
Irish Immigration to America, 1820-1990

Decade	Total Irish	Percent of Total	Cumulative Rate	Rate Per Year	All Immigrants	Percent Irish
1820-1830	54,338	1.1	—	5,434	151,824	35.8
1831-1840	207,381	4.4	261,719	20,738	599,125	34.6
1841-1850	780,719	16.6	1,042,438	78,072	1,713,251	45.6
1851-1860	914,119	19.4	1,956,557	91,412	2,598,214	35.1
1861-1870	435,778	9.2	2,392,428	43,578	2,314,824	18.8
1871-1880	436,871	9.3	2,829,299	43,687	2,812,191	15.5
1881-1890	655,482	13.9	3,484,781	65,548	5,246,613	12.5
1891-1900	390,179	8.3	3,874,960	39,018	3,687,564	10.6
1901-1910	339,065	7.2	4,214,025	33,907	8,795,386	3.8
1911-1920	146,181	3.1	4,360,206	14,618	5,735,811	2.5
1921-1930	220,591	4.7	4,580,797	22,059	4,107,209	5.4
1931-1940	13,167	0.3	4,593,964	1,317	528,431	2.5
1941-1950	25,377	0.5	4,619,341	2,537	1,035,039	2.4
1951-1960	57,332	1.2	4,676,673	5,733	2,515,479	2.3
1961-1970	32,966	0.7	4,747,100	2,747	3,321,677	0.9
1971-1980	11,490	0.2	4,758,590	958	4,493,314	0.25
1981-1990	32,823	0.7	4,791,413	2,735	7,338,062	0.44
Total			4,791,413		56,994,014	8.4

Source: Fallows, 1979:48; Johnson, 1992:804.

A review of the average annual rate of immigration, reveals that while only 5,000 Irish immigrants arrived between 1820 and 1830, this increased to 21,000 the following decade (See Table 16.1). During the famine years (1840-1850) an average of 1,500 Irish immigrants arrived each week, for an annual average of 78,000. During this period they represented about half (45.6%) of all immigrants that arrived in America. Of the five million Irish immigrants that arrived between 1820 to 1989, three out of four arrived during the eighty year period between 1820 and 1900.

For the Irish, the voyage to America represented their only means of escape from a life of poverty, or certain starvation. As a result these immigrants saved every cent they earned, in order to send for a relative stranded in Ireland. The remittances sent to Ireland increased from about one million dollars a year in the 1840's to ten million dollars a year by the 1860s (Shannon, 1966:39). While most of the funds were sent to bring another greenhorn over, some families used the money to improve their lives in Ireland. Without these remittances, and the creation of a strong immigrant community in America, the flow of Irish settlers would not have reached such magnitudes.

Irish Settlement In America

Most of the Irish Catholics who came to America settled in the metropolitan areas of the eastern seaboard, primarily as a result of their lack of resources or skills. These were poor farmers who had never traveled more than a half day's walk from their villages. Between 1845 and 1855 almost a million settled in New York City (Fallows, 1979:32). By 1850 almost two-thirds lived in either New York (35.7%), Pennsylvania (15.8%), or Massachusetts (12.0%) (U.S. Bureau of Statistics, 1893:Table 14). By 1870, two-thirds of the foreign born populations of Boston and Providence were Irish, as were half the foreign born living in New York City, Jersey City, Albany, Brooklyn, Pittsburgh, and Philadelphia (U.S. Bureau of Statistics, 1893:Table 15).

In these cities they usually lived in ghetto housing, where they suffered from overcrowding and unhealthy living conditions. Every square foot of tenement space was utilized, as it is estimated that 18,000 immigrants lived in the cellars of New York City in 1863 (Greeley, 1981:75). The lack of clean water and an adequate sewer system meant that such diseases as typhoid fever, cholera, typhus, pneumonia, and bronchitis were common. Of all the recorded deaths in New York City in 1857, two-thirds were children under five. And 85 percent of those admitted to the city's hospital were Irish immigrants (Greeley, 1981:75). So many Irish immigrants died at such a young age in Boston that the expectation was that they would only live an average of fourteen years after their arrival (Considine, 1961:74).

In part, the concentration of Irish immigrants in these slums was the result of their lack of skills and resources. Therefore they had to take jobs at the lowest levels. One survey of eight cities found that two-thirds of the Irish immigrants were employed as laborers in 1870, compared to only 28 percent of the Yankees and Germans. Similarly, only ten percent of the Irish held white collar positions, compared to 37 percent of the Yankees, and 28 percent of the Germans (Erie, 1988:57).

During the 1850's, Irish laborers were payed 75 cents a day and Irish women could expect to obtain room and board, plus a dollar a week as housemaids (Fallows, 1979:33). In the cities the men worked in the factories and mills, and the women worked as laundresses, chambermaids, and waitresses. By 1860, some 70,000 Irish women were employed as domestic servants in New York City alone, and twice as many were thus employed in Boston (Farley, 1961:86; Handlin, 1970). However, the Irish are best known for their work on the thousands of miles of canals and railroads in the East.

The Chesapeake and Ohio Canal, completed in 1840, was built by Irish labor, as was the 350 mile Erie canal. This work was not only extremely difficult but was also very dangerous. For a $1.50 a day they risked their lives, worked from sunup to sunset, lived in shanties, and suffered the effects of cholera, typhoid fever, malaria, pneumonia, and frostbite in the winter. After expenses, the men could expect to earn ten to twelve dollars a month in the summer and only five dollars a month in the winter. In some cases they only worked for their meals (Clark, 1986a:15).

By 1850, the Irish had built over 4,000 miles of canals. Soon their skills in building canals were transferred to railroad construction. In 1830, only 73 miles of rail had been laid, but by 1860 more than 30,000 miles of track were in place (Clark, 1986a:23). In addition, the Irish formed the backbone of the railroad construction projects in the mid-West, the South, and the Southwest. In retrospect it seems like more than simple historical coincidence that the thousands of miles of canals and railroads were constructed during the great Irish migration.

Prejudice and Discrimination

The religious oppression experienced by the Irish was based on seven hundred years of British occupation and oppression. Their religious beliefs were used by the British as a badge for ostracism, that is as a social stigma. Over time their social, economic, and political oppression was formalized into the Penal Laws.

To their dismay, the Anglo Saxon Protestant hatred of Catholics was transferred to American society, primarily as a result of the arrival of large numbers of British immigrants in the previous century. This hatred of Catholics was very much a part of American culture in the 1800's. For this reason the early Ulster immigrants used the term Scotch-Irish to make it clear that they were Protestants. Their fear was that they might be confused with the more recent Catholic immigrants. For it was their religious identification that made the Irish appear suspect, strange, and foreign. Despite the guarantees offered by the Bill of Rights, several states refused to grant

384

religious freedom to all citizens, for example, New York did not repeal its anti-Catholic laws until 1806, Connecticut did not do so until 1818, and Massachusetts waited until 1833 (McCaffrey, 1976:88).

As early as the 1830's employers in New York City and Boston displayed signs in their shops and businesses stating that "No Irish Need Apply." Sometimes the Gaelic name or a strong brogue automatically eliminated the Irish applicant from the employment line. As a result of public pressure against these blatant acts of discrimination, advertisements for domestic help simply specified that "only Protestant women need apply." Similarly some states, under political pressure from the No Nothing Party, and various nativist groups, sought to restrict further immigration and make the naturalization process more difficult for Irish immigrants.

The arrival of Irish immigrants stirred strong anti-Catholic feelings, as many Americans actually believed that Catholics were involved in an international conspiracy in which the Vatican would eventually dominate American society. Some even believed that the Jesuits were in America, often disguised as farmers and workers, to prepare for a Papal invasion. This episode in American history was known as the Mississippi Valley Catholic conspiracy, for which thousands of dollars were collected to protect America from Popery (McCaffrey, 1976:92).

During this period several Protestant organizations distributed anti-Catholic books, pamphlets, and newspapers. These publications not only depicted the Irish as papist traitors but also described them as sexual deviants and social perverts. One woman in particular, Maria Monk, wrote a book and went on a speaking tour, in which she claimed that she had escaped from a convent and told of being seduced by priests and described in some detail the alleged sexual exploits of nuns and priests (McCaffrey, 1976:93).

As expected, this propaganda campaign resulted in numerous acts of violence against Irish Catholics. In 1798 Protestant demonstrators rioted in front of Saint Mary's church in Philadelphia, which resulted in numerous injuries and the destruction of church property (McGee, 1851:88). In 1806, a riot ensued when a group of Protestants attempted to break up a Catholic religious service in New York City (Whittke, 1956:47). The Ursuline convent in Charlestown, Massachusetts was torched in August of 1831. The conflagration set off a wave of random shootings and lynchings of local Catholics that lasted until the late 1860's. When the bishop of Philadelphia sought to obtain public financing for parochial schools in 1844, a Protestant mob set fire to dozens of Irish homes and dynamited the two churches in the Irish ghetto (McCaffrey, 1976:94).

Despite the fact that there were thousands of Jews, Italians, and Blacks in the United States, with clear physical, cultural, and linguistic differences, it is curious that American nativists were able to draw physical and cultural stereotypes of the light-skinned, mostly blue-eyed, English speaking Irish Catholics. Shortly after their arrival the belief emerged that the Irish were a distinct race, with inferior physical and intellectual characteristics. It was during this period that the Paddy stereotype evolved, that portrayed the Irish as immoral, ignorant, prone to violence and criminal activities, poverty ridden, diseased, and guided by superstitious religious beliefs (Knobel, 1986:24-27).

The Irish were further publicly disgraced and ridiculed when the work of the influential political cartoonist Thomas Nast appeared in Harper's Weekly and other national magazines, depicting the Irish as having apelike features, holding a jug of whiskey in one hand and a shillelagh in the other. In other cartoons, Nast depicted Irish and Blacks as apelike figures on election day, posing a threat to informed democracy (Curtis, 1971:59). But Nast did not invent the caricature of the Irish as apelike, as this was an image created by the British, as they considered the Irish the missing link between the gorilla and Black Africans.

The Irish Labor Movement

In any consideration of the numerous contributions of the Irish to American society, their involvement in the labor movement and in politics would have to go at the top of the list. For the Irish arrived with a strong sense of group identification and with a political savvy that grew out of years of resistance to the political oppression by the British. For the Irish understood the effectiveness of political leadership, the importance of the common struggle, and the need for regional and family loyalties.

The involvement of the Irish in the labor movement, and in politics, simply reflects two sides of the same coin. For the Irish were active in the labor movement as a means of protecting their jobs, and they were involved in politics to secure needed social services and to create jobs.

In view of their early concentration in the railroad, canal, and coal mining industries, it is not surprising that the Irish were among the first to organize labor unions. In these industries the work was extremely difficult and dangerous, wages were low, the hours were long, and the men were isolated from their communities. The result was a company town arrangement, whereby the employer had virtual control over every aspect of the production process, wages, working conditions, and their daily lives. This reduced the Irish to wage slaves, inasmuch as they were the victims of a system of debt peonage, in which they often owed their employer money at the end of the month.

In response to these oppressive conditions, the Irish organized themselves. In the early days the call for a strike usually resulted in violence, as the owners would hire their own guards to maintain order. One of the most violent mining strikes, called the Long Strike, occurred in Pennsylvania in 1875. When the owners crushed the strike the Irish organized a secret organization, the Ancient Order of the Hibernians, that resorted to assassinations and sabotage. In the end twenty Irish miners were publicly hanged for their union efforts (Bimba, 1932:70-73).

The Irish also encountered numerous labor abuses on railroad construction projects. Between 1873 and 1874 eighteen different railroads were struck by the Irish, as they were demonstrating against wage cuts and the failure of employers to honor their labor contracts. But it was the railroad strikes of 1877 that caught the nation's attention, as Irish laborers clashed with armed troops in bloody riots in Martinsburg, Chicago, Philadelphia, and St. Louis (Foner, 1977:7-32).

In the end such bitter experiences, and the loss of life, hardened the Irish and spawned the formation of a radical cadre of Irish labor leaders. Their union activities and work experience in these remote locations were soon transferred to the urban labor markets. This resulted in the intermarriage of labor unions and big city politics.

Perhaps the best example of the relationship between organized labor and big city politics occurred in San Francisco. It was the flamboyant labor leader Denis Kearney who first organized the Irish in San Francisco into political wards and then turned out the votes on election day. But Kearney used his bitter hatred of the Chinese immigrants to organize the Irish and to gain political support. He was so effective in his use of the local newspapers and politicians that he founded the Workingmen's Party of California in 1877, which successfully elected the mayor of San Francisco and pushed for a new state constitution (Erie, 1988:49).

The Irish and Urban Politics

One of the reasons for the early political success of the Irish is that they arrived in America with a background in political organization. The few rights that they had in their homeland were only obtained following long legal and political battles with the British. For it was not until 1829 that the last of the Penal Laws were repealed with the passage of the Catholic Emancipation Act.

In light of the thousands of Irish immigrants that arrived during the Great Famine, and their concentration in key cities, it was to their advantage to organize themselves into voting blocks. Consequently, the Irish had the highest rates of naturalization and voter participation (See Table 16.2). For example, in Boston and New York City, one-fifth of the voters were Irish by 1855 (Erie, 1988:33).

While the Irish cannot take credit for inventing the political machine, as it was cultivated by Jefferson and refined by Jackson, they did use it more effectively. To their advantage the Irish had the bodies, and the determination, to make the political machine work. The basis of their political power was the family, the block, and the neighborhood. Every Irish neighborhood had a block captain, a ward captain, and a precinct captain. This was the system that developed party loyalty and this was also the system that delivered the votes (Erie, 1988).

Table 16.2
Irish Born Population in the United States, 1850-1970

Year	Total U.S. Population	Irish Born Population	Percent Irish
1850	23,191,876	961,719	4.1
1860	31,443,321	1,611,304	5.1
1870	38,558,371	1,855,827	4.8
1880	50,155,783	1,854,571	3.7
1890	62,622,250	1,871,509	3.0
1900	75,568,686	1,615,459	2.1
1910	91,972,266	1,352,155	1.5
1920	105,710,620	1,037,233	1.0
1930	122,775,646	923,642	0.75
1940	131,669,275	678,447	0.51
1950	150,697,361	520,359	0.34
1960	179,323,175	406,433	0.22
1970	203,184,772	277,000	0.14

Source: Griffin, 1990:159.

The rewards offered by the Irish political machine were jobs, construction contracts, schools, and social services. For the politicians the machine offered social status, prestige, influence, and political power. Consequently, Irish politicians were responsible for hundreds of public work projects, dozens of social programs, and thousands of jobs in urban America. Naturally, some will point out that the political machine was fueled by graft, but at least it was (as the Irish would say) honest graft. Others point out that the corruption fostered by machine politics was simply a way of redistributing the wealth, for at least it transferred public funds to those in need.

Without any doubt the best known political machine was New York's Tammany Society. For years Irish politicians were barred from Tammany Hall, that is until their block vote could no longer be ignored. By 1860, they had gained important positions in the political organization of the city. Their greatest success was achieved under the leadership of William "Boss" Tweed, who represented the interest of the poor immigrants in the city. He obtained and distributed funds for various public work projects, social programs for the poor, and money for the construction of schools and hospitals.

By the turn of the century the Irish had gained political control in New

York, Chicago, Boston, Philadelphia, New Haven, Jersey City, Albany, and San Francisco (Clark, 1986b; Sarbaugh, 1986; Skerrett, 1986). These political machines formed the basis for the second generation machines of the twentieth century. However, the only political machine to survive well into the post-war period was that of Chicago's mayor, Richard Daley. Since only ten to fifteen percent of the voters in the city were Irish, the Daley machine found it increasingly difficult to appease the needs of the various ethnic factions in the city. To his credit, his son, Richard M. Daley, was elected mayor of Chicago in 1989.

At the national level Alfred E. Smith, the governor of New York, became the first Irish Catholic presidential candidate in American history in 1928. Unfortunately, because of strong anti-Catholic feelings in certain parts of the country he went down to defeat (Reedy, 1991:135-142). Nonetheless, he did attract a majority of votes in eleven of the nation's twelve largest cities. Though Al Smith was defeated, his bid for the presidency meant that neither the Irish nor the Catholic vote could be ignored or taken for granted in the future (Shannon, 1966:151- 181).

It only took a little more than thirty years for Irish Americans to achieve the ultimate goal in American politics with the election of John F. Kennedy to the White House in the fall of 1960 (See Box Reading 16.1). Kennedy's successful run for the presidency not only meant that the Irish had made it, but it also meant that Catholics were now accepted as true Americans, as Kennedy was a Catholic who was only three generations away from the Irish ghetto in Boston. For it was Kennedy's paternal great-grandfather, Patrick, who arrived in Boston as a penniless refugee of the potato famine.

Social Mobility Among The Irish

Three out of four of the Irish immigrants who arrived during the Great Famine were illiterate. While most had full command of the English language, their inability to read, write, or compute was a formidable barrier to upward social mobility. Furthermore the Irish arrived in America without money, resources, job skills, or industrial experience essential for survival in an urban society. In addition, they were also the victims of religious discrimination, that often closed the door to employment and educational opportunities.

Their first real opportunity for social mobility came as a result of their political activities. It was their control of the political machine that gave them their first opportunity to dole out patronage jobs and to offer lucrative public works contracts to Irish businessmen. For example, under the rule of Boss Kelly, Tammany Hall controlled over 40,000 municipal jobs and offered millions of dollars to the local building trades (Erie, 1988:58-59). These building contracts in turn created thousands of jobs in the private sector, which accounted for 90 percent of the jobs available to the machine.

But the political machine could only deliver jobs in the blue collar sector, because the number of white collar jobs available to the machine were limited. In retrospect, the Irish control of urban politics may have slowed their social progress, since they provided job security in blue collar positions in the police, fire, and public works departments, but very few jobs in white collar or professional positions. As a result their representation in white collar positions only increased from ten percent in 1870 to 24 percent in 1900 (Erie, 1978). And their hold on white collar positions was only about half what the distribution was for German and Yankee workers. Furthermore their white collar jobs were primarily in clerical and sales positions, rather than in managerial or professional positions. Hence their relatively small numbers in the white collar labor force were concentrated in low level functionary positions (Thernstrom, 1973:132-133).

With the onset of the Great Depression the Irish, as well as other groups, experienced a drastic reduction in income and a temporary freeze on any opportunities for social mobility. Following the Second World War the Irish took advantage of the new prosperity and the educational benefits offered by the G.I. Bill. As a result, many Irish veterans skipped one, or sometimes two, generations on the mobility ladder, moving from working class occupations to positions in the business and professional world. Indeed, many successful Irish lawyers, doctors, and academics of today are the product of these post-war educational opportunities (McCaffrey, 1976:158-159).

Some believe that the social mobility of the Irish has been exceptionally slow, that is when compared to other groups (Handlin, 1959:26), and others have made the point that their relative failure is simply a reflection of a general Catholic failure (Glazer and Moynihan, 1970:258). However, the available demographic studies reveal that the Irish have not only experienced social mobility, but in fact have surpassed the achievements of other comparable groups in American society today.

The benefits of the educational advances made by the Irish following the Second World War, reveal themselves in several national studies conducted in the early 1960's and 1970's. For example, by 1961 Irish Americans were about twice as likely to graduate from college as any other American, were three times more likely to be lawyers, and twice as likely to be doctors (Greeley, 1972b:4).

When compared to other white ethnics, such as Germans, Italians, Poles, and the French, the Irish had the highest rate of high school graduation (77%) in 1963. Similarly they also held the highest rank in occupational prestige and annual income (Greeley, 1971:Table 4). When the Irish were compared to other American Catholics (such as Germans, Italians, English, French, and the Spanish-Speaking), they had the highest level of high school graduation (84%) and college attendance (49%) in 1964. They also reported the greatest increase in college attendance from the father's generation, to the son's generation (a 34% increase) (Abramson, 1973:Table 8).

In a comparison with WASP (White-Anglo-Saxon-Protestant) Americans, the Irish are also more likely to hold Ph.D.'s or other advanced professional degrees (19% versus 12%). In fact, the Irish are only surpassed in their educational achievement by Jewish Americans (Greeley, 1972a:196-197).

An analysis of the 1970 Census reveals that the Irish matched or exceeded the national average in terms of their education, income, and occupational standing. Their average education was 12.6, compared to 12.2, their average annual income was $8,127, compared to $7,894, and 29.6 percent were in upper level white collar jobs, compared to 28.2 nationally (U.S. Bureau of the Census, 1971:23). Even when Irish Catholics were compared to Irish Protestants, the Irish Catholics were higher in the mean number of years of education (12.5 years compared to 10.9 years), in their occupational prestige (43.7 compared to 36.7), and in their income ($12,426 compared to $9,147) (Greeley, 1976:45, 50, 53). This also would mean, of course, that any general demographic analysis of social mobility among Irish Americans would actually be higher for Irish Catholics.

Table 16.3
Persons Claiming Irish Origin by
Top Ten States, 1980

	State	Number	Percent
1.	California	3,727,925	9.3
2.	New York	2,977,518	7.4
3.	Pennsylvania	2,449,110	6.1
4.	Texas	2,420,367	6.1
5.	Ohio	2,031,751	5.1
6.	Illinois	2,027,692	5.1
7.	Florida	1,617,433	4.1
8.	Massachusetts	1,564,100	3.9
9.	Michigan	1,521,796	3.8
10.	New Jersey	1,444,308	3.6
	Total Irish Population	39,898,006	100.0

Source: Griffin 1990:158.

In a comparative study of occupational distribution among American Catholics, the Irish had the highest proportion in white collar positions (66%). They also experienced the highest level of inter-generational occupational mobility of any of the groups compared (Abramson, 1973:Table 7).

The NORC (National Opinion Research Center) survey, conducted in 1977 and 1978 found that almost half (47%) of the Irish Catholic families reported an annual income of more than $20,000, compared to only one out of four of all American families, 30 percent of all British Protestants, and 46 percent of all Jewish families. One-third (32%) held professional or managerial positions, compared to one-fourth in the general population (Greeley, 1981: 111). In 1970 the median income for Irish American families was on average $2,000 more per year ($11,700) compared to all families in the general population ($9,600) (U.S. Census, 1973:152). By 1980, their annual income had increased by an average of $9,000, that is from $11,700 to $20,719 (U.S. Census, 1983:51).

In conclusion, the Irish have made impressive strides since the early 1960's, particularly in terms of their educational achievements, occupational mobility, and annual income. At the present time the Irish are the most successful white American gentile group. And in view of their recent levels of social mobility, it is certain that they will continue to lead all white ethnic groups in their efforts to achieve the American dream (See Table 16.3).

Chapter Summary

Most Irish immigrants that settled in America before 1800 were from Ulster, and were referred to as Scotch Irish. They called themselves Scotch Irish to distinguish themselves from the new wave of Irish Catholics, who emigrated to America during the Great Famine.

While the Great Famine was caused by a potato fungus, the mass starvation that resulted was more a result of the land tenure system and agricultural production cycles imposed by the British. The British policy in Ireland was to mold Ireland into a plantation economy to serve the needs of Great Britain.

The great Irish migration began in the early 1840's and was stimulated by mass starvation, religious oppression, and by the total lack of opportunities for human survival in Ireland. The flow of immigrants from Ireland between 1820 to 1900 was the largest migration to the United States from any one country.

Upon their arrival in America the Irish Catholics were subjected to various forms of discrimination. In a short time the strong prejudicial attitudes gave way to racial hatred and to organized violence. In response, the Irish organized themselves into effective political units. Their involvement in the American labor movement and in urban politics allowed the Irish to advance themselves.

Today the Irish represent one of the most successful white ethnic groups in American society. When compared to other white ethnics, the Irish have the highest level of achievement in terms of education, occupation, and income. The Irish also have the largest representation of lawyers, doctors, and scholars. Clearly Irish Americans have not only made their mark on American society, but have also made it in American society.

References

Abramson, Harold J.
1973   *Ethnic Diversity in Catholic America.* New York: John
            Wiley & Sons.
Bimba, Anthony
1932   *The Molly Maguires.* New York: International Publishers.
            Clark, Dennis J.
1986a   *Hibernia America: The Irish and Regional Cultures.* New
            York: Greenwood Press.
1986b   "Intrepid Men: Three Philadelphia Irish Leaders, 1880 to
            1920." In *From Paddy to Studs: Irish-American Communities in
            the Turn of the Century Era, 1880 to 1920.* New York: Green-
            wood Press. Pp. 93-115.
Considine, Bob
1961   *It's The Irish.* Garden City, NY: Doubleday & Company.
            Curtis, Lewis P. Jr.
1971   *Apes and Angels: The Irish in Victorian Caricature.*
            Washington, D.C.: Smithsonian Institution Press.
Erie, Steven P.
1978   "Politics, the Public Sector and Irish Social Mobility: San
            Francisco, 1870-1900." *Western Political Quarterly* 31 (2):274-
            289.
1988   *Rainbow's End: Irish-Americans and the Dilemmas of
            Urban Machine Politics, 1840-1985.* Berkeley: University of
            California Press.
Fallows, Marjorie R.
1979   *Irish Americans Identity and Assimilation.* Englewood
            Cliffs, NJ: Prentice-Hall.
Foner, Philip S.
1977   *The Great Labor Uprising of 1877.* New York: Monad Press.
Glazer, Nathan and Daniel P. Moynihan
1970   *Beyond the Melting Pot.* Cambridge: MIT Press.
Greeley, Andrew M.
1971   *Why Can't They Be Like Us?* New York: E.P. Dutton.
1972a   *That Most Distressful Nation.* Chicago: Quandrangle Books.
1972b   "Occupational Choice Among the American Irish: A
            Research Note." *Erie-Ireland* Vol. 7.
1976   *Ethnicity, Denomination, and Inequality.* Beverly Hills:
            Sage Publication.
1981   *The Irish Americans: The Rise to Money and Power.*
            New York: Harper & Row.

Griffin, William D.

 1973 *The Irish in America 1550-1972.* Dobbs Ferry, NY: Oceana
      Publications.

 1990 *The Book of Irish Americans.* New York: Random House.

Handlin, Oscar

 1959 *The Newcomers.* Cambridge: Harvard University Press.

 1970 *Boston's Immigrants.* New York: Antheneum Press
      (revised edition).

Johnson, Otto

 1992 *Information Please Almanac.* Boston: Houghton Mifflin.

Kennedy, Robert E., Jr.

 1973 *The Irish: Emigration, Marriage, and Fertility.* Berkeley:
      University of California Press.

Knobel, Dale T.

 1986 *Paddy and the Republic.* Middletown, CT: Wesleyan
      University Press.

McCaffrey, Lawrence J.

 1976 *The Irish Diaspora in America.* Bloomington, IN: University
      Press.

McGee, Thomas D'Arcy

 1851 *A History of Irish Settlers in North America.* Boston:
      Office of American Celt.

Miller, Kerby A.

 1985 *Emigrants and Exiles: Ireland and the Irish Exodus to North America.*
      New York: Oxford University Press. Potter, George

 1960 To the Golden Door. Boston: Little, Brown & Co.

Reedy, George E.

 1991 *From the Ward to the White House: The Irish in American Politics.*
      New York: Charles Scribner's Sons.

Sarbaugh, Timothy

 1986 "Exiles of Confidence: The Irish-American Community of
      San Francisco, 1880 to 1920." In *From Paddy to Studs: Irish-
      American Communities in the Turn of the Century Era, 1880 to
      1920.* New York: Greenwood Press. Pp. 161-179.

Schrier, Arnold

 1970 *Ireland and the American Emigration, 1850-1900.* New York:
      Russell & Russell.

Shannon, William V.

 1966 *The American Irish.* New York: MacMillan Publishing.

Skerrett, Ellen

 1986 "The Development of Catholic Identity among Irish
      Americans in Chicago, 1880-1920." In *From Paddy to Studs:
      Irish-American Communities in the Turn of the Century Era, 1880
      to 1920.* New York: Greenwood Press. Pp. 117-138.

Thernstrom, Stephan
  1973   *The Other Bostonians: Poverty and Progress in the*
              American Metropolis, 1880-1970. Cambridge, MA: Harvard
              University Press.
U.S. Bureau of the Census
  1971   *Characteristics of the Population by Ethnic Origin:*
              November 1969. Washington, D.C.: USGPO. Current Popula-
              tion Report, Series P-2O, No. 221.
  1983   *Census of Population: 1980 General Social and Economic*
              Characteristics. Washington, D.C.: USGPO PC8O-1-C1.
U.S. Bureau of Statistics
  1893   *Arrivals of Alien Passengers and Immigrants in the United*
              States from 1820 to 1892. Washington, D.C.: USGPO. Pages
              90-133.
Whittke, Carl
  1956   *The Irish in America.* Baton Rouge: Louisiana State
              University Press.
Woodham-Smith, Cecil
  1962   *The Great Hunger.* New York: Harper & Row.

Important Names

William Ayers	Pope Adrian
Oliver Cromwell	Maria Monk
Thomas Nast	Denis Kearney
William "Boss" Tweed	Richard Daley
Alfred E. Smith	John F. Kennedy

Key Terms

Scotch-Irish	penal laws	the whiteboys
Molly Maguires	rack-renting	Irish Famine
coffin ships	the Long Strike	block captain
Ancient Order of the Hibernians	Workingmen's Party	Tammany Hall

Sample Test Questions

1. Prepare a brief discussion of five factors that contributed to the Irish Famine.
2. Discuss five of the living or working conditions that existed in Ireland prior to the Great Famine.
3. List and discuss four of the push-pull factors that resulted in the Great Migration.
4. Apply the soft-spot theory of the labor market to the types of jobs that attracted the Irish immigrants during their initial period of settlement in America.
5. List and discuss five examples of prejudice and discrimination experienced by Irish immigrants during their initial period of settlement in America.
6. Provide five sound historical reasons why the Irish were successful in establishing the labor movement and in creating an effective political base in urban America.
7. Prepare a short essay in which you identify five historical or sociological reasons for the rapid upward social mobility of Irish Americans.

Box Reading 16.1
U.S. Presidents of Irish Origin
(Direct Paternal Line)

---

1. Andrew Jackson (1829-1837), son of Andrew Jackson, who emigrated from County Antrim to South Carolina in 1765.
2. James Polk (1845-1849), great-great grandson of William Polk, who emigrated from County Donegal to Maryland in 1690.
3. James Buchanan (1857-1861), son of James Buchanan, who emigrated from County Donegal to Pennsylvania in 1783.
4. Chester Arthur (1881-1885), son of William Arthur, who emigrated from County Antrim to New York in 1815.
5. William McKinley (1897-1901), grandson of James McKinley, who emigrated from County Antrim to Pennsylvania in 1800.
6. Thomas Woodrow Wilson (1913-1921), grandson of James Wilson, who emigrated from County Antrim (via Scotland) to Virginia in 1807.
7. John Fitzgerald Kennedy (1961-1963), great-grandson of Patrick Kennedy, who emigrated from County Wexford to Massachusetts in 1848.
8. Richard Nixon (1969-1974), great-great-great-great-grandson of James Nixon, who emigrated from County Kildare to Delaware in 1705.
9. Ronald Reagan (1981-1989), great-grandson of Michael Reagan, who emigrated from County Tipperary (via England) to New York in 1853.

---

400 B.C.	Celtic tribes invaded Ireland.
432 A.D.	St. Patrick brought Christianity to Ireland.
795	Vikings began raiding Ireland.
1492	William Ayers was a member of Columbus' crew.
1541	Henry VIII forced Ireland to accept him as their king.
1603	English law extended to cover all of Ireland.
1609	The Ulster Plantation begins.
1649	Oliver Cromwell crushed an Irish revolt, took land and political rights away from Irish Catholics.
1695	Beginning of Penal Laws against Catholics.
1698	South Carolina passed laws discouraging the entry of Catholics.
1737	The Charitable Irish Society was founded on St. Patrick's Day in Boston by 26 Irish immigrants.
1762	First celebration of St. Patrick's Day in New York City (first parade in 1779).
1775	Daniel Boone, and other Irish pioneers, began the settlement of Kentucky.
1776	The Declaration of Independence was signed by three men born in Ireland and five men of Irish origin.
1790	The Hibernian Society of Philadelphia was founded.
1793	The Catholic Relief Act gave Catholics the vote.
1801	Ireland became part of the United Kingdom.
1803	The Benevolent Hibernian Society of Baltimore was organized.
1807	James Sullivan was elected governor of Massachusetts.
1810	*The Shamrock*, the first Irish American newspaper, was published in New York City, Thomas O'Connor editor.
1814	The Irish Emigrant Society was founded in New York City by Dr. Robert Hogan.
1815-1835	Great era of road and canal building in the United States, primarily by Irish immigrants.
1824	Seven Irish Americans were serving in the U.S. House of Representatives.
1833	New York City had an estimated 40,000 Irish born residents.
1834	Anti-Catholic riot in Charlestown, MA. An Ursuline Convent was burned.
1837	Bond Street (anti-Irish) Riot in Boston.
1844	Anti-Catholic riots in Philadelphia, resulted in 30 deaths, 150 wounded, 200 families burned out.
1845-1847	A potato famine in Ireland kills 1,000,0000.
1949	Ireland declared itself a republic.

Source: Griffin, 1973; 1990:11-22, 378.

Chapter 17

The Italian American Experience

Introduction

Few Americans realize that the bulk of Italian immigrants arrived in this country a hundred years ago. These pioneer immigrants were illiterate farm workers who arrived with few resources, could not speak English, and were unfamiliar with the ways of an urban industrial society. And in less than four generations they have integrated themselves into the mainstream of American society. But in the process many have relinquished important aspects of their culture, blended into American society, intermarried at an ever increasing rate, failed to pass their language on to their children, and have lost their sense of ethnic identity.

Today Italian Americans have established an enviable record of success in terms of their educational achievement, occupational mobility, economic success, and political participation. Consequently, names like Geraldine Ferraro, the Democratic vice presidential candidate in 1984 and New York senatorial candidate in 1992, Mario Cuomo, the governor of New York, and Lee Iacocca, the former head of Chrysler Corporation, are commonplace today.

Of the estimated 12 million Italian Americans, two-thirds are concentrated in the metropolitan areas of the Northeast, 20 percent live in the South, ten percent in the West, and five percent in the mid-West (Juliani, 1987:62). With an estimated population of two million, New York state has the largest population of Italian Americans, followed by Massachusetts (430,000), Illinois (323,000), Rhode Island (119,000), Ohio (258,000), and California (567,000) (Allen and Turner, 1988:224-304). Today their greatest concentration occurs in New York City, followed by Boston, Philadelphia, Providence, Chicago, Cleveland, Buffalo, Rochester, and San Francisco.

In this chapter we shall outline the immigration and settlement patterns of Italian Americans, consider the discrimination that they encountered, review their occupational distribution, and follow their gradual movement up the socio-economic ladder. We shall conclude with a brief review of the major contributions of Italian Americans to American society.

The Flow of Italian Immigrants

A consideration of the immigration data reveals that the flow of Italian immigrants was negligible before 1880. For during the sixty year period between 1820 and 1880 only 81,277 Italians arrived in America, that is less than 1,400 per year (See Table 17.1). But it is clear that the dramatic increase in Italian immigration began in 1880, as over 300,000 arrived between 1881 and 1890. Their flow doubled during the following decade and between 1901 and 1910 over two million Italian immigrants arrived. Of the more than five million Italians that immigrated between 1820 and 1989, eighty percent arrived during the 40 year period between 1880 and 1920 (Linkh, 1975).

Table 17.1
Italian Immigration to America, 1820-1990

Decade	Total Italian	Percent of Total	Cumulative Rate	Rate Per Year	All Immigrants	Percent Italian
1820-1830	439	.008	—	44	151,824	0.30
1831-1840	2,253	.04	2,692	225	599,125	0.38
1841-1850	1,870	.035	4,562	187	1,713,251	0.11
1851-1860	9,231	.17	13,793	923	2,598,214	0.36
1861-1870	11,725	.22	25,518	1,172	2,314,824	0.51
1871-1880	55,759	1.0	81,277	5,576	2,812,191	2.0
1881-1890	307,309	5.8	388,586	30,731	5,246,613	5.9
1891-1900	651,893	12.2	1,040,479	65,190	3,687,564	17.7
1901-1910	2,045,877	38.4	3,086,356	204,587	8,795,386	23.3
1911-1920	1,109,524	20.8	4,195,610	110,952	5,735,811	19.3
1921-1930	455,315	8.5	4,650,925	45,531	4,107,209	11.1
1931-1940	68,028	1.3	4,718,953	6,803	528,431	12.9
1941-1950	57,661	1.1	4,776,614	5,766	1,035,039	5.6
1951-1960	185,491	3.5	4,962,105	18,550	2,515,479	7.4
1961-1970	214,111	4.0	5,176,216	21,411	3,321,777	6.4
1971-1980	129,367	2.4	5,305,583	12,937	4,493,000	2.9
1981-1990	32,894	0.45	5,338,477	2,741	7,338,062	0.44
Total			5,338,477		56,994,014	9.4

Source: Alba, 1985:21; Statistical Yearbook of the INS, 1987:6; Johnson, 1992:804.

As with other groups, the flow of Italian immigrants was affected by changing conditions in the homeland and by the myriad opportunities offered in America. The flow of Italian immigrants to America occurred in four stages:

1. The Northern Italian Immigration (1776-1879)
2. The Great Migration (1880-1929)
3. The Great Depression and Second World War (1930-1945)
4. The Post War Period (1946-1989)

The flow of Italian immigrants during the first period was negligible, as less than 14,000 arrived between 1820 and 1860. While Italians lived in every state of the Union before the Civil War, most lived in California (2,805), New York (1,862), and Louisiana (1,134) (Nelli, 1983:40; Schiavo, 1934). These pioneers arrived as permanent settlers, 90 percent were from Northern Italy, and most arrived with skills, resources, and capital. Many were artisans, craftsmen, teachers, seamen, merchants, artists and political exiles (diFranco, 1988:43). In California, they were the first to plant and harvest grapes, and in both Louisiana and California they bought farm land and became prosperous members of the community (diLeonardo, 1984:54-64; Gumina, 1978; Scarpacci, 1979). Between 1860 and 1880 nearly 68,000 Italians settled in such places as New York City, New Orleans, Galveston, San Francisco, Boston, Charleston, Key West, Memphis, Mobile, and Philadelphia (Rolle, 1968:110-125).

The Italians who flocked to America during the Great Migration were different from the pioneer immigrants. Perhaps the most distinctive characteristic of this second wave of Italian immigrants was that they were predominately (80% to 90%) southern Italians, from the provinces south of Rome or from Sicily or Sardinia (Mangano, 1917:54-57). Most of the Mezzogiorno (Southern Italians) immigrants were farmers or landless peasants, two out of three were illiterate (Gambino, 1974:78-79), four out of five were between the ages of 18 to 45 (Lord, et al, 1905:14), four out of five were men (Gambino, 1974:78), and many arrived in America as sojourners (Lopreato, 1970:14-16). One study found that 1.2 million immigrants returned to Italy between 1908 and 1916 (Wittke, 1939:437). Overall, almost half the 4.5 million Italian immigrants who arrived between 1876 and 1924 returned home at some point (diFranco, 1988:87). Although many of these were returning for their wives and children.

The Mezzogiorno settled in the urban ghettos of America at the turn of the century and they had to bear the brunt of America's discrimination. The resistance to their arrival was prompted by inherent nativists feelings in America and by the very large flow of immigrants during this period.

Immigration restrictions were first applied directly on Italian immigrants in 1882, with the imposition of a fifty cent head tax on new immigrants. But the most damaging piece of legislation was passed in 1917, when Congress approved a law that required all immigrants to pass a literacy test. This law had a deleterious impact on the flow of Italian immigrants, since almost half the Mezzogiorno were illiterate in their language (Gambino, 1974:79).

The initiation of hostilities during the First World War resulted in an abrupt decline in the flow of immigrants from all countries, but it was the passage of the Johnson-Reed Act of 1924 that imposed official government quotas on all immigrants. The Act set a two percent immigration limit on all countries, based on their numbers in the United States in 1890 (Lopreato, 1970:17). By 1929, Italy's quota was limited to only 5,802 per year, compared to Germany's 25,957 and Great Britain's 65,721. Clearly the government's immigration policy favored Anglo-Saxon and Germanic immigrants of the pre-1880 immigration period. This discriminatory policy was not altered until 1965.

In the end it was the Great Depression, and not U.S. immigration laws, that severely limited the flow of immigrants from all countries. During this period a total of 90,355 Italian immigrants arrived, for an annual average of only 8,214 (See Table 17.1). Of equal importance, the ravages of the Second World War caused the immigration rates to plummet, as only 935 Italians arrived during this entire period (i.e., from 1941- 1945).

The last group of Italian immigrants arrived after the Second World War. Many of these immigrants were war refugees, while others were part of a family reunification effort. After 1965, the new wave Italian immigrants began to arrive. Since the end of the war the flow of Italian immigrants has fluctuated between 25,000 and 30,000 per year.

Immigration To America

Following the unification of Italy in 1870, the Northern provinces gained the upper hand in the political and economic structure of the country. Northern Italy was urban and industrial, while the South was rural and agriculturally based. Over the years, the landless peasants in the South had suffered from political oppression, poor soil, draught, poverty, overpopulation, unemployment, excessive taxes, and corruption in the government. These are the primary factors that prompted the Italians to search for new opportunities abroad.

Italian immigration during this period can best be described as a diaspora, as some 25 million Italians emigrated between 1860 and 1920. This from a country with a population of 35 million, at the turn of the century (Monticelli, 1970:3). In addition to the five million that emigrated to America, millions more emigrated to northern Europe, North Africa, Argentina, Brazil, Australia, and Canada (Nelli, 1983:31-32; Pisani, 1957:48). They departed in search of new opportunities and in a desperate attempt to escape the poverty of southern Italy.

The introduction of steamship service during the 1880's, made the voyage from Italy to America an economic reality for thousands of Italians. The passenger ships departed from the major Italian ports of Genoa, Naples, Palermo, and Messina. The voyage took from ten to fifteen days (Nelli, 1983:33), and the fare, in steerage, was between $27 to $39, at the turn of the century. At the time the cost of the fare was equivalent to four months pay for a peasant from Calabria or Basilicata (Gambino, 1974:87).

After their voyage across the Atlantic, 97 percent of the Italian immigrants disembarked at Ellis Island (Nelli, 1983:47). About 95 percent answered all the immigration questions correctly and passed their medical examinations (diFranco, 1988:80). The Italian immigrants arrived in America with very limited resources, as most had about $8.84 in their pockets, compared to $41.51 for Scottish immigrants (Gambino, 1974:78). This was slightly more than a week's wages for a common laborer in New York City at the turn of the century.

The Urban Village

In view of their limited resources, most Italian immigrants settled in New York City, or in cities no more than a few hours train ride away. By 1900, New York City had an Italian Population of 145,433, Philadelphia 17,830, Boston 13,738, Newark 8,537, Providence 6,256, Pittsburg 5,709, and Buffalo 5,669 (Lord, et al, 1905:8). Overall, seven out of ten (72%) of the 484,207 Italians in the United States in 1900 lived in New England, New York, New Jersey, or Pennsylvania (Iorizzo and Mondello, 1971:60- 61).

The nine out of ten Italian immigrants who settled in American cities at the turn of the century brought their village culture with them (Briggs, 1978; Firey, 1947:193). Their return migration pattern insured that close family ties were maintained with relatives remaining in Italy and guaranteed that their native culture was systematically rejuvenated. In addition, family and cultural ties were strong since it was their custom to share their homes with relatives and compatriots. Before long their concentration in American ghettos resembled an urban village (Gans, 1962).

The urban village phenomena was further assured in view of their practice of taking in boarders, who were often from their village. For a four room apartment, in a dumbbell tenement in Lower Manhattan, Italian immigrants were paying from $12 to $18 a month (i.e., half a month's wages) (Freeman, 1987:225). Normally, a family of five or six would sleep in one of the bedrooms and five to ten boarders would sleep in the other bedroom. It was the responsibility of the woman of the house to prepare the meals and wash clothes for everyone (Alba, 1985:53-54).

The Italian settlement in the urban village of Lower Manhattan was clearly demarcated, so that one side of Mott street was reserved for the Napolitani and the other side for the Basilicati. The Siciliani lived on Prince street, while Hester street housed the villagers from Apulia (Kessner, 1977:20-21). It was not long before this area was commonly referred to as Little Italy, the seventeen-block neighborhood that was home for more than 40,000 immigrants by 1910 (Nelli, 1983:64; Russo, 1970).

As their settlement patterns within the urban village indicate, the Italian immigrants were keenly aware of regional, cultural, and linguistic differences (Lopreato, 1970:40-41). Over a short period the Italians reproduced close village and regional ties, created fictive-kin relationships (the *compariggio*), and celebrated traditional festivals, national holidays, and holydays of obligation (Johnson, 1985:29-31). Their concentration in the urban village allowed them to live and work in an Italian speaking sociocultural environment, obtain cultural foods, wear traditional clothes, and purchase Italian books and newspapers. In addition they received a continuous flow of news from the motherland, as they often received letters and packages from relatives (La Sorte, 1985:117-124).

The *Padrone* and Self Help

Besides the merchants in the urban village, the Italian immigrants also could engage the services of ethnic specialists. Perhaps the most important of these was the *padrone*. The *padrone* was a labor contractor who found work and housing for new immigrants. The *padrone's* advantage was that he could speak English and had the right connections with employers who needed cheap Italian labor. For his services the immigrants paid the *padrone* a commission, which ranged from one to fifteen dollars, depending on the wages and the length of the job (Nelli, 1983:79). By 1897, two out of three Italians in New York City worked for a *padrone* (Koren, 1897). By 1900, there were over 2,000 small bosses in New York City alone (La Sorte, 1985:74).

The *padrone* usually met the immigrant ships at the docks and offered the men jobs in building, railroad, tunnel, canal, or road construction. Unfortunately, some *padrone* were unscrupulous and took advantage of the naivete of their fellow countrymen by charging exorbitant rates for their services, collecting fees and not finding them jobs, or by paying them less for their labor than they promised (Nelli, 1964; Iorizzo, 1970).

Sometimes the *padrone* also operated Italian banks, located in store fronts or in markets. These were not really banks in the traditional sense, as they functioned as an informal social service agency. Often these banks would simply hold an immigrant's money, as a special favor, but would not pay any interest on deposits. These banks rarely made loans, and when they did it was at an exorbitant rate (Koren, 1897). By 1900, there were 412 chartered Italian Banks in New York City, and many more operated without charters (Brandenburg, 1903:21).

The bank's most popular service was the collection of weekly payments from immigrants, for the eventual purchase of steamship tickets. Once sufficient funds were collected the banker would purchase, for a fee, the tickets and mail them to the depositor's relatives in Italy. The bank also provided the immigrants with such services as letter writing, sending and receiving mail, forwarding money to relatives in Italy, and giving free advice on a whole variety of issues affecting their customers. Occasionally an unscrupulous banker would abscond with all the funds (La Sorte, 1985:72-74).

Mutual Benefit Associations

The mutual benefit association provided the Italian community with basic social services. The primary purpose of the association was to offer assistance in time of illness and to provide death and burial benefits (Park and Miller, 1921:119- 126). The immigrants were required to make weekly deposits, usually ten cents, into the association's coffers. With a membership of up to two hundred, this was a substantial amount of money from which one could draw in time of need. In return, the association guaranteed relief in the event of illness or an accident, in which case they usually payed the association member about $3 per week (half a week's wages). The association also would guarantee an appropriate burial (which all association members were required to attend), and provide a lump sum death benefit to surviving family members.

By 1912, there were 258 mutual benefit associations in New York City alone, and over 200 in Chicago by 1927 (Iorizzo and Mondello, 1971:95; Nelli, 1970). In 1920, there were more than 2,500 mutual benefit associations or fraternal organizations in the hundreds of Italian American communities throughout the United States (diFranco, 1988:100). These mutual benefit associations formed the basis for the development of various lodges, orders, fraternal, and recreational organizations. The largest and most influential of these organizations, the Order of the Sons of Italy in America, was founded in New York City in 1905, by Dr. Vincent Sellaro. By 1923, the Order claimed a membership of almost 300,000 (Nelli, 1983:117; Pisani, 1957:126).

Prejudice and Discrimination

The most blatant acts of discrimination against Italian Americans did not surface until the flow of Italian immigrants increased dramatically during the 1880's. Clearly, it was this massive influx of Italian immigrants and the economic depression that hit the nation during this period that agitated the nativists (LaGumina, 1973:135-147; 157-162). In addition, there was labor strife in the cities, a growing fear of anarchism and communism, agrarian unrest in the Midwest, and an increase in racial violence in the South (Higham, 1971).

Since most Americans were of German, British, or Irish ancestry, the Italians were looked down upon as swarthy diminutive aliens who did not fit the popular conception of an American. However, a clear distinction was made between Northern Italians and Southern Italians, as the Northern Italians had fair complexions and were perceived as more Germanic and more refined. In contrast, Southern Italians were often considered illiterate, superstitious peasants who were low class, ignorant, unassimilable, and prone to violence. Therefore the Southern Italians were not considered appropriate material to make good Americans, for these were the unwashed hordes of southern Europe who were invading lily-white America (diFranco, 1988:83-84). Even the U.S. Immigration Commission bought into this stereotype and not only kept separate records for Northern and Southern Italians, but also classified them as distinct races (Pisani, 1957:116).

In an effort to avoid the sting of discrimination, the Northern Italians tried to distinguish themselves from the Southern Italians (Rolle, 1968:94-95). The newspapers exacerbated the situation by promoting the stereotype of Italians as fun loving, thriftless, irresponsible, noisy, musical, childish, high spirited, hot blooded, and prone to violence (Pisani, 1957:118-120). Italian men were depicted as cynical, calculating, hard-bitten, vengeful, lustful, and violent (Gambino, 1974:117-118; Martinelli and Gordon, 1988). Furthermore, many believed that they were taking jobs from American citizens, serving as cheap labor and as strike breakers, and depressing wages (Rolle, 1980:61).

Xenophobia and Ethnic Violence

During the economic downturn of 1883, Italian immigrants in New York City were used as convenient scapegoats for a whole host of social problems, such as the high unemployment rate, the deterioration of the slums, an array of public health problems, crime in the streets, and even for the graft and corruption in city hall (Rolle, 1980:66). The following year Italian immigrants were blamed for an attack on a police officer in Chicago. The *Chicago Tribune* attributed the crime to Italians, since the officer was stabbed with a wooden dagger (Iorizzo and Mondello, 1971:64). Four years later, the *Tribune* published a story that Chicago had a Mafia. The basis for this allegation was simply the fact that Chicago had a large Sicilian community.

By the mid-1880's Italians were considered armed and dangerous. Major newspapers across the country had convinced the public that Italians were to be avoided and it did not take long for the public's prejudice against Italians to turn to violence. During the summer of 1886, an Italian immigrant was lynched in Vicksburg, Mississippi, on suspicion of child molestation. In the spring of 1888, the police chief of Buffalo arrested every man in the Italian community, following the murder of one Italian by another. Of the 325 arrested, only two men had concealed weapons (Iorizzo and Mondello, 1971:66). This wholesale incarceration was but one indication of the public's disdain for Italian immigrants.

During the 1890s, the public's xenophobia manifested itself as mob violence. The most infamous incident occurred in the spring of 1891, when eleven Italians were slain by a white mob. This incident followed the murder of the chief of police of New Orleans, who had been investigating alleged gang activities among Italian dock workers. Since the Italians were accused of his murder, one hundred were immediately arrested, and after questioning all but 19 were released. Of these, ten were accused of murder and nine were held as accomplices. The jury found six of the nine accomplices innocent and the other three were held for a new trial.

Frustrated at the turn of events, the local Vigilance Committee took matters into its own hands. Committee members stormed the jail, but did not encounter any resistance from the police, and killed eleven of the Italian prisoners (Coxe, 1937; Karlin, 1942). The next day the newspapers and the politicians praised the work of the Vigilance Committee. The *New York Times* characterized the victims as "sneaking and cowardly Sicilians," as "bandits and assassins," and as "lawless and uncivilized" (Iorizzo and Mondello, 1971:70). At a diplomatic gathering Theodore Roosevelt made the comment that the mob violence in New Orleans was "a rather good thing" (Gambino, 1974:109).

Later the same year several Italians were lynched by a mob in West Virginia. In 1893, one Italian was lynched in Denver and two years later six Italians were killed by a mob in Walsenburg, Colorado, on suspicion of murdering a saloon keeper (Gambino, 1974:109). The following year two hundred Italians were driven out of Altoona, Pennsylvania by a crazed mob. In 1895, six *padroni* were lynched in a mining town in Colorado, as they were labeled labor agitators. The same year a mob stormed the jail house in Hahnville, Louisiana, attacked and brutalized six Italian inmates, and lynched three of them. In a similar incident, five Italians were lynched in Tallulah, Louisiana in 1899, after a mob stormed the jail. The murdered men were Sicilian merchants who refused to conform to Jim Crow laws in their treatment of African American customers (Cunningham, 1965).

The Italian American community was outraged by these acts of indiscriminate violence and by the fact that the perpetrators were able to proceed with impunity. The irony is that the victims themselves were depicted as criminals bent on violence. The result was the creation of a stereotype that viewed Italians as a criminal element, when in fact they were the innocent victims of crime in the streets.

Italians in the Labor Market

Like thousands of other immigrants, Italians were forced to take the least desirable jobs and they entered the labor market at the point of least resistance. To their detriment, many were ill prepared for employment in an industrial society. Consequently most worked at pick and shovel jobs, moved dirt, mixed cement, and carried bricks. These immigrants built the first transportation systems in America, as they worked in constructions gangs on roads, subways, in sewers, canals, and tunnels. They also erected the buildings, built the bridges, laid the tracks, and paved the streets of America (Fenton, 1975).

While most Italians who arrived between 1899 and 1910 were unskilled laborers, one out of five were craftsmen or professionals. For every thousand Italians that arrived during this period, 35 were carpenters, painters, or masons, five were stonecutters, 34 were shoemakers, 23 were tailors, and one was a barber (La Sorte, 1985:63). Among the professionals the largest group were musicians, followed by sculptors, artists, teachers, engineers, clergy, and physicians (Lord, et al, 1905:63-64). Of the 1,768,281 Italian immigrants who came to America during this period (1899-1910), and reported a record of previous employment, 768,811 were common laborers and 563,200 were farm laborers (Kessner, 1977:33-34). Of the million and a half Italian residents in the United States in 1909, only 800 were physicians and 500 were lawyers (La Sorte, 1985:64).

Italian women ranked second among all immigrant women as contributors to the family income in 1910 (Daniels, 1986:96). Most worked in the burgeoning garment industry of New York City, or established cottage industries manufacturing lace, candy, artificial flowers, or tobacco products. By 1910, Italian women represented the largest ethnic group (36.2%) employed in the garment district of New York City (Nelli, 1983:87). One-third of all married women in Little Italy (New York) were employed outside the home in 1911 (Pleck, 1979:373).

In addition to the 277,000 immigrant women who were gainfully employed in New York City in 1910, it is estimated that some 200,000 were contributing to the family income in the homework system (Cohen, 1977; Daniels, 1986:96). Under this system the women sewed garments at home, did embroidery, made artificial flowers, arranged feathers, and even cracked nuts. Homework was suited to Italian wives as they could stay home with their children, who also contributed to the process (Femminella and Quadagno, 1976). Needless to say this was a very abusive system.

Italian immigrants were not only relegated to the lowest levels of the labor market, but they also experienced wage discrimination. For example, in the construction of the Croton Reservoir the city of New York paid Anglo American laborers an average of $1.40 per day, while it paid Italian workers $1.20 per day (Gambino, 1974:70). Similarly, in 1906 Italians were paid $1.46

for a ten hour day, while Irish laborers were paid $2.00 per day. In tunnel work the Irish were paid $3.00 to $5.00 per day, while Italians received $1.75 to $3.00 per day (La Sorte, 1985:65). Italian women employed in the garment industry earned an average of $1.00 per day, while those employed in the homework system earned about 60 cents a day (Daniels, 1986:100).

A study of family income between 1900 and 1910 found that the Italian immigrant family had an average annual income of $600, which was about half the income of Anglo American families (Gambino, 1974:80). This was true, despite the fact that almost two-thirds of the Italian families had two or more members in the labor force. The fact that is even more remarkable is that 95 percent of the Italian immigrants saved an average of $29.00 per month in 1910 (Gambino, 1974:91). Life for the first generation was spent at the bottom of the labor market and at the first rung of the economic ladder.

Social and Economic Mobility

When compared to other immigrants, the Italians had a slow start in terms of their socioeconomic mobility. However, there are several good reasons why they were concentrated in the lower socio-economic brackets. Most Italians were trapped in the least desirable jobs because of discrimination, lack of skills, educational deficiencies, illiteracy, their rural backgrounds, and the language barrier. The Italians also arrived in America at a time when the nation was expanding and growing, and though the construction industry provided thousands of jobs, it also meant that most would live out their lives in America as common laborers.

Their general lack of skills, illiteracy, and low levels of education were unfortunately passed on to the second generation. It was a common practice for the sons of Italian laborers to follow in their father's footsteps. As a result, very little or no mobility was experienced between the first and second generations (Child, 1943; Martinelli, 1989:49-50). Their most serious problem was the language barrier, and their lack of education. A study conducted in 1910 found that half (53.9%) of the Southern Italians were illiterate (Nelli, 1983:146).

To make matters worse, many Italian immigrants thought that a formal education was a waste of time, as they encouraged their children to find a job as soon as possible. Indeed, the common practice was for parents to take their children out of school at the age of 14 (which was legal with a work permit). As a result less than one percent of Italian children were attending high school in 1917 (Nelli, 1983:147). Furthermore, Italian children had the highest truancy rate of any European group and the highest level of after school employment (Nelli, 1983:146-147). When education was set as a goal, it was perceived in terms of a vocational education, that is as a means of learning a skill that could be applied in one of the manual trades (Gallo, 1974:154). Based on personal experience, Italian immigrants believed that obtaining a practical education was far more important than receiving academic training (Lopreato, 1970:164-165).

The need for industrial workers during the boom years of the First World War only served to draw more second generation Italians into unskilled jobs. Unfortunately, the onset of the Great Depression sealed the fate of many Italian Americans and guaranteed that most would remain in the blue collar labor force for yet another generation. At the time of the great crash only eleven percent of the Italian American students who entered New York City's high schools graduated, compared to 40 percent of all other students in the city (Covello, 1972: 285). In short, the Great Depression further delayed their movement out of the blue collar labor force. But even during this bleak period there were signs of progress, as half of all Italians were laborers in 1916, but only 31 percent were laborers in 1931. In addition, more Italians were employed as electricians, plumbers, contractors, and as foreman than ever before (Lopreato, 1970:148).

In retrospect the Second World War offered Italian Americans an opportunity to learn new skills (Vecoli, 1978). The war also provided many Italians with their first opportunity to attend college. And returning veterans took advantage of the training and educational opportunities offered by the G.I. Bill. Whereas only 15 percent of the college aged youth were enrolled in college in 1940, by 1954 their rate of attendance doubled, and increased to 38 percent by 1960 (Alba, 1985:82).

By the 1960's, second generation Italian Americans began to take advantage of the educational opportunities that were available after the war. Their median years of education was 10.9, compared to 11.0 for all second generation Americans, and 10.7 for all Americans (Lopreato, 1970:161). At the same time the number of Italians attending college increased to 21 percent, compared to 29 percent in the general population who were enrolled in college during the war. Their college enrollment increased to 45 percent, compared to 43 percent overall, during the 1960's (Greeley, 1977:44). Similarly, when Italian Americans were interviewed in a 1964 study, only seven percent of their fathers had graduated from high school, while almost half (48%) of the respondents were high school graduates. While 17 percent of the respondents had graduated from college only four percent of their fathers were college graduates (Abramson, 1973:Table 8).

Though Italians did make some progress in their educational achievement during the sixties, half (52%) were still in blue collar jobs in 1964, more than the national average for other European or white Protestant groups (Thernstrom, 1973:171). But when compared to their fathers' positions in the labor market social mobility was evident, as 71 percent of their fathers were in blue collar jobs (Nelli, 1983:185).

Italian Americans Today

While social mobility among Italian Americans was a slow process during the late fifties and sixties, they have advanced significantly during the seventies and eighties. In one study of the social position of White ethnics, conducted in the early seventies, Italian Americans were third from the top in income ($11,748), surpassed only by the Jews ($13,340) and Irish Catholics ($12,426) (Greeley, 1974:51). Their average annual family income was $9,590, about two thousand dollars higher than the national average. This pattern continued into the eighties, when their annual income was $21,842, compared to $19,917 for all U.S. families (U.S. Census, 1983:177).

By the early seventies, it was evident that the Italians were following the pattern of social mobility established by Jewish Americans, as the sons and daughters of small entrepreneurs and businessmen were entering college in greater numbers. For example, one-third of the students in the City University system (of New York) were of Italian descent, as were half those attending Fordham University (Nelli, 1983:186). One reason for this dramatic increase in college attendance was the open enrollment policy instituted by City University in the early seventies and the determination of Italian Americans to take advantage of the opportunity to obtain a higher education (Krase, 1986:217-218).

Nonetheless, a detailed study of their academic achievement, conducted in the late seventies, found that they fell behind the WASPs (White Anglo-Saxon Protestants) in college attendance and college graduation, as only a quarter of the Italians had ever attended college, compared to over 40 percent of the WASPs. And only 13 percent had graduated from college, compared to one out of five of the WASPs (Alba, 1985:118-124).

In 1980, 13.7 percent of Italian Americans were in professional and technical positions, compared to 15.4 percent of the total population, and 15.4 percent held managerial positions, compared to 10.4 percent in the general population. A larger proportion of Italian Americans were also found in clerical-sales (30.9%) and craft positions (13.9%) than in the general population. But fewer were in operative and laborer positions (15.8%), than in the general population. Their lower representation in blue collar positions is a significant change from their representation in 1960 and 1970. As a result there were more Italian Americans in white collar positions, than in the general population (U.S. Census, 1983:174).

The sanguine prediction is that more Italian Americans will move into higher paying white collar positions as the third and fourth generation become the majority of the ethnic group, and as the number of mixed marriages increases (Alba, 1981; 1985:129). Italian Americans also will experience a steady increase in educational and occupational achievement as a result of the greater number of Italian American women in higher education and in white collar positions (Crispino, 1980). Women were historically denied educational and employment opportunities and their entry into higher education will certainly increase the socio-economic position of Italian Americans as a group (Egelman, 1987:148).

Chapter Summary

While several thousand Italians lived in the United States before the Civil War, it was not until 1880 that they began to arrive in significant numbers. The period between 1880 and 1920 is often referred to as the Great Migration, as 80 percent of the more than five million Italians that arrived in America came during this period. They were forced to take those jobs that required strong backs and a determination to succeed. Their only solace was the security and support that they found in the urban village and the intimacy and support of their families.

With an increase in their numbers, there was also an increase in the level of discrimination. The newspapers played a very significant role in developing and perpetuating the stereotype of the Italian immigrants as criminals. Unfortunately they were more often the victims of mob violence and crime in the streets.

Any improvement in the social status of Italian Americans did not take place until the end of the Second World War. By the 1980's Italian Americans demonstrated higher levels of education, income, and occupational distribution when compared to other European immigrant groups. As a result of their gradual progress many Italian Americans today hold positions of power and prestige in government, business, and education.

References

Abramson, Harold J.
1973   *Ethnic Diversity in Catholic America.* New York: John Wiley
        & Sons.

Alba, Richard D.
1981   "The Twlight of Ethnicity among American Catholics of
        European Ancestry." *The Annals* 454:86-97.
1985   *Italian Americans.* Englewood Cliffs, NJ: Prentice- Hall.

Allen, James P. and Eugene J. Turner
1988   *We The People: An Atlas of America's Ethnic Diversity.*
        New York: MacMillan Publishing Co.

Brandenburg, Broughton
1903   *Imported Americans.* New York: Stokes.

Briggs, John W.
1978   *An Italian Passage: Immigrants to Three American Cities,*
        1880-1930. New Haven: Yale University Press.

Child, Irwin L.
1943   *Italian or American? The Second Generation in Conflict.*
        New York: Russell and Russell (1970).

Cohen, Miriam
1977   "Italian American Women in New York City: 1900-1950:
        Work and School." In *Class, Sex and the Woman Worker.* Mil-
        ton Cantor and Bruce Laurie (eds.), Westport, CT: Green-
        wood Press. Pp. 120-143.

Covello, Leonard
1972   *The Social Background of the Italo-American School Child.*
        Totowa, NJ: Rowman & Littlefield.

Coxe, John E.
1937   "The New Orleans Mafia Incident." *Louisiana Historical*
        Quarterly, 20:1067-1110.

Crispino, James
1980   *The Assimilation of Ethnic Groups: The Italian Case.* New
        York: Center for Migration Studies.

Cunningham, George E.
1965   "The Italians, a Hindrance to White Solidarity in Louisiana,
        1890-1898." *Journal of Negro History* 50:22-36.

Daniels, Cynthia R.
1986   "No Place Like Home: A Pictorial Essay on Italian American
        Homeworkers in New York, 1910-1913." In *Support and Strug-*
        gle: Italians and Italian Americans in a Comparative Perspective.
        Joseph L. Tropea, et al (eds.), Staten Island, NY: The
        American Italian Historical Association, Pp. 93-113.

diFranco, Philip
1988   *The Italian American Experience.* New York: Tom Doherty
            Associates.
diLeonardo, Micaela
1984   *The Varieties of Ethnic Experience: Kinship, Class, and
            Gender Among California Italian Americans.* Ithaca, NY: Cornell
            University Press.
Egelman, William
1987   "Italian Americans in the Year 2000: The Impact of
            Education." In *The Melting Pot and Beyond: Italian Americans
            in the Year 2000.* Jerome Krase and William Egelman (eds.),
            Staten Island, NY: The American Italian Historical Associa-
            tion, Pp. 137- 174.
Femminella, Francis X. and Jill Quadagno
1976   "The Italian American Family." In *Ethnic Families in
            America.* Charles Mindel and Robert W. Habenstein (eds.),
            New York: Elsevier. Pp. 61-87.
Fenton, Edwin
1975   *Immigrants and Unions: Italians and American Labor,
            1870-1920.* New York: Arno.
Firey, Walter
1947   *Land Use in Central Boston.* Cambridge: Harvard University
            Press.
Freeman, Robert C.
1987   "The Development and Maintenance of New York City's
            Italian-American Neighborhoods." In *The Melting Pot and
            Beyond Italian Americans in the Year 2000.* Jerome Krase and
            William Egelman (eds.), Staten Island, NY: The American
            Italian Historical Association, Pp. 222-237.
Gallo, Patrick J.
1974   *Ethnic Alienation: The Italian-Americans.* Rutherford, NJ:
            Fairleigh Dickinson University Press.
Gambino, Richard
1974   *Blood of My Blood: The Dilemma of Italian-Americans.*
            Garden City, NY: Doubleday & Co.
Gans, Herbert J.
1962   *The Urban Villagers: Group and Class in the Life of Italian-
            Americans.* Glencoe, IL: The Free Press.
Greeley, Andrew M.
1974   *Ethnicity in the United States: A Preliminary Reconnaissance.*
            New York.
1977   *The American Catholic: A School Portrait.* New York:
            Basic Books.

Gumina, Deanna P.
1978   *The Italians of San Francisco, 1850-1930.* New York: Center for Migration Studies.
Higham, John
1971   *Strangers in the Land, Patters of American Nativism, 1860-1925.* New York: Atheneum.
Iorizzo, Luciano J.
1970   "The Padrone and Immigrant Distribution." In *The Italian Experience in the United States.* Silvano M. Tomasi and Madeline H. Engel (eds.), New York: Center for Migration Studies. Pp. 43-76.
Iorizzo, Luciano J. and Salvatore Mondello
1971   *The Italian-Americans.* New York: Twayne Publishers.
            Johnson, Colleen L.
1985   *Growing Up and Growing Old in Italian-American Families.* New Brunswick, NJ: Rutgers University Press.
Juliani, Richard N.
1987   "The Position of Italian Americans in Contemporary Society." In *The Melting Pot and Beyond: Italian Americans in the Year 2000.* Jerome Krase and William Egelman (eds.), Staten Island, NY: The American Italian Historical Association, Pp. 61- 71.
Karlin, Jules A.
1942   "The Italo-American Incident of 1891 and the Road to Reunion." *Journal of Southern History,* 8:242-246.
Kessner, Thomas
1977   *The Golden Door: Italian and Jewish Immigrant Mobility in New York City, 1880-1915.* New York: Oxford University Press.
Koren, John
1897   "The Padrone System and Padrone Banks." *U.S. Department of Labor Bulletin* 9(2):113-129.
Krase, Jerome
1986   "Educational Attainment and Educational Values of Italian Americans Over generations." In *The Italian Americans Through The Generations.* Rocco Caporale (ed.), Staten Island, NY: The American Italian Historical Association, Pp. 212-225.
LaGumina, Salvatore J.
1973   *Wop! A Documentary History of Anti-Italian Discrimination in the United States.* San Francisco: Straight Arrow Books.
LaSorte, Michael
1985   *La Merica: Images of Italian Greenhorn Experience.* Philadelphia: Temple University Press.

Linkh, Richard
  1975   *American Catholicism and European Immigration,*
            1900-1924. New York: Center for Migration Studies.
LoGatto, Anthony F.
  1972   *The Italians in America 1492-1972: A Chronology &*
            Fact Book. Dobbs Ferry, NY: Oceana Publications.
Lopreato, Joseph
  1970   *Italian Americans.* New York: Random House.
Lord, Eliot, et al
  1905   *The Italian in America.* New York: B.F. Buck & Co.
Mangano, Antonio
  1917   *Sons of Italy.* New York: Missionary Education Movement
            of the United States and Canada.
Martinelli, Phylis C.
  1989   *Ethnicity in the Sunbelt: Italian American Migrants in*
            Scottsdale, Arizona. New York: AMS Press.
Martinelli, Phylis and Leonard Gordon
  1988   "Italian Americans: Images Across Half A Century."
            Ethnic and Racial Studies 11(3) 319-331.
Monticelli, Guiseppe L.
  1970   "Italian Emigration: Basic Characteristics and Trends With
            Special Reference to the Post-War Years." In *The Italian Ex-*
            perience in the United States. Silvano M. Tomasi and Madeline
            H. Engel (eds.) Staten Island, NY: Center for Migration
            Studies.
Nelli, Humbert S.
  1964   "The Italian Padrone System in the United States."
            Labor History 5:153-167.
  1970   *Italians in Chicago, 1880-1930.* New York: Oxford University
            Press.
  1983   *From Immigrants to Ethnics: The Italian Americans.* Oxford:
            Oxford University Press.
Park, Robert E. and Herbert A. Miller
  1921   *Old World Traits Transplanted.* New York: Harper & Row.
Pleck, Elizabeth
  1979   "A Mother's Wage: Income Earning Among Married Italian
            and Black Women, 1896-1911." In *A Heritage of Her Own.*
            Elizabeth Pleck and Cott (eds.), New York: Simon and
            Schuster.
Pisani, Lawrence F.
  1957   *The Italian in America.* New York: Exposition Press.

Rolle, Andrew F.

1968   *The Immigrant Upraised: Italian Adventurers and Colonists in an Expanding America.* Norman: University of Oklahoma Press.

1973   *The Other Bostonians.* Cambridge: Harvard University Press.

1980   *The Italian Americans.* New York: The Free Press. Thernstrom, Stephan

Russo, Nicholas J.

1970   "Three Generations of Italians in New York City: Their Religious Acculturation." In *The Italian Experience in the United States.* Silvano M. Tomasi and Madeline H. Engel (eds.), New York: Center for Migration Studies. Pp. 195-211.

Scarpacci, Jean

1979   "Immigrants in the New South: Italians in Louisiana's Sugar Parishes, 1880-1910." In *American Working Class Culture.* Milton Cantor (ed.), Westport, CT: Greenwood Press.

Schiavo, Giovanni

1934   *The Italians in America Before the Civil War.* New York: Arno Press (1975).

Thernstrom, Stephan

1973   *The Other Bostonians.* Cambridge: Harvard University Press.

U.S. Census

1983   *U.S. Census of Population, 1980: General Social and Economic Characteristics.* Washington, D.C.: USGPO PC80-1-C1.

Vecoli, Rudolph J.

1978   "The Coming of Age of the Italian Americans: 1945-1974." *Ethnicity* 5:119-147.

Wittke, Carl

1939   *We Who Built America: The Saga of the Immigrant.* Englewood Cliffs, NJ: Prentice-Hall.

Geraldine Ferraro   Mario Cuomo
Lee Iacocca   Dr. Vincent Sellaro

Key Terms

Mezzogiorno	literacy test	Johnson-Reed Act
diaspora	Ellis Island	urban village
compariggio	*padrone*	Italian banks
mutual benefit associations	Order of the Sons of Italy	xenophobia
vigilance committee	cottage industries	homework
G.I. Bill		

Sample Test Questions

1. Provide a description of the key characteristics of each of the four waves of Italian immigration.
2. Discuss five characteristics of life in the urban village for Italian immigrants.
3. Discuss the role of Italian immigrant women in their community and the family. Select four examples of their contributions.
4. List and describe four functions served by the *padrone* in the Italian immigrant community.
5. Provide five examples of ethnic stereotypes or ethnic violence used against Italian Americans during their settlement period in American society.
6. List and discuss four areas in American industry where Italian immigrants made a significant contribution to the development of American society.
7. Discuss four areas where Italian Americans have made significant progress in their socio-economic status since the end of the Second World War.

Part VII

The Experience of Ethnic Women

Chapter 18

Ethnic Women
in America

Introduction

Women have historically been considered the second sex, that is they have been treated as second class citizens as a matter of practice and have systematically been denied access to the source of power in society. Like other minorities, women have also experienced social oppression and have felt the effects of prejudice and discrimination. The term that was coined in the mid-sixties to describe the prejudice and discrimination experienced by women was sexism. With the publication of *The Feminine Mystique* (1963), Betty Friedan raised the consciousness of women across the country and made them aware of their subordinate status and the negative impact of sexism on their daily lives.

The awareness of their inferior position in American society resulted in the evolution of the modern women's movement. The National Organization of Women (NOW) organized women in an attempt to make them aware of their social, economic, and political oppression. As a result of the indefatigable efforts of the National Organization of Women, and other women's organizations, the social position of women has improved in almost all areas of American life and more men are now aware of the negative effects of sexism, not only on the lives of women but also on their lives.

This chapter will provide an overview of the current social position of women in terms of their economic gains, educational achievements, and occupational positions. Special attention will be given to those areas where women have not experienced social progress. The plight of ethnic women today will serve as the focus of our review of the social and economic condition of women in American society. As minorities, ethnic women not only suffer from prejudice and discrimination because they are women, but they also experience ethnic and racial oppression. Therefore ethnic women are the victims of double jeopardy, since they experience both racism and sexism in American society.

Women In America Today

In view of the changes that have occurred since the Civil Rights Movement and the Women's Movement in the early sixties, women have made progress in most areas of American life, particularly in education, the labor market, and in the political arena. Unfortunately their economic progress has not matched advancements in other areas of society.

Between 1950 and 1990 the labor force participation rate of women increased from one-third (33.9%), to one-half (57.4%) (U.S. Census, 1991:Table 632). However, their actual labor force participation rate varies by age, marital status, race, and education. Today half (57.4%) the women 16 years and over are in the labor force, compared to three out of four men (76.4%) (U.S. Census, 1991:Table 636) (See Table 18.1).

Table 18.1
Women in the U.S. Labor Force,
1900 to 1990

Year	Number of Women in Labor Force	Percent Women in Labor Force
1900	5,319,000	18.3
1910	7,445,000	19.9
1920	8,637,000	20.4
1930	10,752,000	22.0
1940	12,845,000	24.3
1950	18,408,000	29.0
1960	23,268,000	32.5
1970	31,580,000	43.3
1980	45,611,000	51.5
1990	56,554,000	57.4
2000*	66,800,000	62.6

*population projections
Source: Johnson, 1992:54; U.S. Census, 1991:Table 632.

The data also reveals that almost every woman will work at some point in her life. The likelihood of women entering the labor market is even greater today as more women are becoming the primary wage earner in their families, as 90 percent of the single parent families are headed by women.

Today, seven out of ten employed women are working full-time and many of those who are working part-time would take a full-time position, if it were available.

The labor force participation rate of women is directly affected by their marital status, as divorced women are the most likely to be employed (75.5%), followed by single women (68%), women with absent husbands (61.1%), and women with husbands present (57.8%) (U.S. Census, 1991:Table 642, Table 643). Even the traditional deterrent for women who work outside the home, that is having children at home under six years old, is not a significant barrier (Hayghe, 1984), as half these women (58.2%) were employed in 1990, compared to only 18.6 percent of the women in the same situation in 1960 (U.S. Census, 1988:Table 623 and 624; Johnson, 1992:54) (See Table 18.2 Below).

Table 18.2
Women with Children in the Labor Force,
1955 to 1990

Year	Under 18 Years	6 to 17 Years	Under 6 Years
1955	27.0%	38.4%	18.2%
1965	35.0	45.7	25.3
1975	47.4	54.8	38.9
1980	56.6	64.4	46.6
1985	62.1	69.9	53.5
1990	66.7	74.7	58.2

Source: Johnson, 1992:54.

A key indicator of women's minority status is income, as women only earn about 60 percent of what men earn. Despite the apparent social progress that has occurred in American society since the sixties, the 60 percent wage ratio has only varied by only a few percent since 1950 (Goldin, 1990). While only 16.7 percent of men employed full-time in 1989 earned under $15,000 per year (at or near the poverty level), 33.3 percent of white females, 36.7 percent of African American females, and 40.1 percent of Latinas fell into this income category (Johnson, 1992:57). Although one out of six (57%) of the working men earned more than $25,000 per year (1989), only 29.3 percent of the women did (See Table 18.5).

Despite their apparent progress, women with a college degree only earn as much as white men with high school diplomas (Paul, 1989:15). Even more discouraging is the fact that the longer women remain in the labor force, their proportional earning of the white male's income decreases. In 1960 working women only earned 60 percent of what working men earned and thirty years later they were only earning 68 percent of what men earned (Acker, 1992:57-62; Cherry, 1989:135-139). The wage gap between working men and women was $2,100 in 1960, but it increased to $8,600 by 1989 (See Table 18.3).

Table 18.3
Median Earnings of Full-Time Workers
15 and Over, by Sex, 1960-1989

Year	Median Earnings Women	Men	Earnings Gap	Women's Earnings as % of Men's
1960	$3,257	$5,368	$2,111	60.7
1970	5,323	8,966	3,643	59.4
1975	7,504	12,758	5,254	58.8
1980	11,197	18,612	7,415	60.2
1985	15,624	24,195	8,571	64.7
1987	16,911	25,946	9,035	65.2
1989	18,778	27,430	8,652	68.0

Source: Johnson, 1992:57, U.S. Census, 1991:Table 678.

Another indication of women's minority status is reflected in the blatant sex segregation that occurs in the work place today. According to the Department of Labor, half the employed women (52%) are found in clerical or service positions and half are employed in occupations that are 75 percent female. One out of five are in jobs that are more than 95% female (Paul, 1989:15-16).

These highly segregated pink collar jobs include, secretaries, dental hygienists, kindergarten teachers, dental assistants, practical nurses, etc. (See Table 18.4). In contrast, slightly more than half the men are in occupations that are at least 80 percent male (Reskin and Hartmann, 1986:7, Table 2-2; Paul, 1989:21).

In addition to their loss of opportunities for occupational mobility, sex segregation in the work place also means that women are paid less for their labor, as the wages paid in any given industry decrease with the percentage of women employed (Acker, 1992; Chafetz, 1990:45-63, 178-198; Reskin and Roos, 1990). For example, a survey of the median weekly earnings of full-time workers reveals that women are payed less than men in every occupation (See Figure 18.1).

In effect women are paid less because they are in women's jobs, and women's jobs are paid less because they are performed by women (Cherry, 1989: Table 8-3; England and Browne, 1992:24-26; Roos, 1992:79-86).

Table 18.4
Highest Concentration of Women
in Segregated Jobs, 1990

Occupation	Percent	Occupation	Percent
Secretaries	99.0	Data Entry Keyers	93.6
Dental Hygienists	98.6	Welfare Service Aides	92.5
Kindergarten Teachers	98.2	Personnel Clerks	91.1
Dental Assistants	98.1	Bank Tellers	91.0
Practical Nurses	97.0	Bookkeepers	91.0
Child Care Providers	96.9	Dietitians	90.8
Receptionists	96.8	Speech Therapists	90.5
Private Household	96.1	Telephone Operators	90.4
Registered Nurses	95.8	Clerks	88.9
Cleaners and Servants	95.8	Waiters and Waitresses	87.8
Typists	95.6	Hairdressers	88.7
Sewing Machine Operators	94.0	Nursing Aides, Orderlies	88.7
Teachers Aides	93.7	Librarians	87.3

Source: 1991 Census:Table 652.

On average each percentage point increase in the number of women in an industry reduces their annual earnings by $42. Overall women's work pays $8,600 less per year on average than men's work (U.S. Census, 1991:Table 678). More than half of the women working full time in the labor market earn less than $20,000 a year, but almost six out of ten (57%) of the men earn more than $25,000 a year (See Table 18.5).

The very high level of occupational segregation among women results in fewer opportunities for promotions, less frequent and smaller raises, higher layoff rates, and the lack of job security. Consequently, women are far more likely to suffer economic hardships (Eitzen and Baca Zinn, 1992). Even when women are employed they are twice as likely as men to receive poverty wages (60.8% compared to 31.9%) (U.S. Census, 1988:Table 710). As a result, two out of three (61%) of the adults who live below the poverty level are women and half the poor families are headed by women (Sparr, 1986:61), as compared to only one out of ten (10.3%) of the male headed households (Burnham, 1986:77). This trend has been referred to as the feminization of poverty.

Even more noteworthy is the finding that while only 7.8 percent of white families fell below the poverty level in 1990, 23.4 percent of the Latino families and 27.8 percent of the African American families were plagued by poverty. Today, two-thirds (67.2%) of poor African American families and seven out of ten (70.3%) of poor Latino families are headed by women. Of those living below the poverty level who are under 21 years of age, three out of four (76.4%) of the African American children, two out of three (65.1%) of the Latino children, and one out of three (35.4%) of the Anglo children live below the poverty level (U.S. Census, 1991:Table 748). This despite the fact that two-thirds of all mothers with children under eighteen years of age are in the paid labor force (Vannoy and Philliber, 1992:390-393).

Figure 18.1
Median Weekly Earnings of Full-Time Workers
by Selected Occupation and Sex, 1989

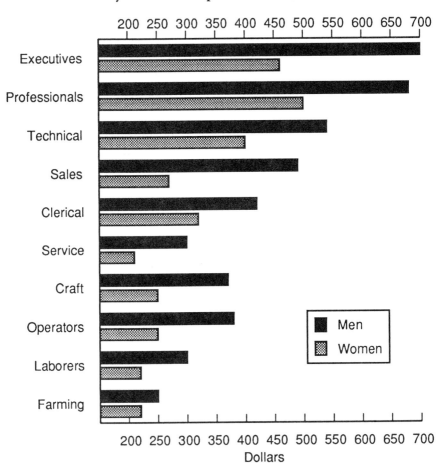

Source: U.S. Census, 1991: Table 678.

Table 18.5
Earnings of Year-Round, Full Time Workers,
by Sex, 1989

Earnings in Dollars	Distribution (percent)		Difference Women to Men
	Women	Men	
Less than 10,000	13.2 %	6.5%	+6.7
10,000 to 14,999	20.1	10.2	+9.9
15,000 to 19,999	20.9	12.9	+8.0
20,000 to 24,999	16.5	13.4	+3.1
25,000 to 49,999	26.3	42.1	-15.8
50,000 and over	3.0	14.9	-11.9
Total	100.0	100.0	

Source: Johnson, 1992:57.

As is true among Mexican American farm workers, women are not poor because they do not get out and work, rather they are poor because the wages that they are paid for their labor drive them into poverty (England, 1992; Sawhill, 1976). In effect women, like Mexican American farm workers, are relegated to a life of poverty primarily because they are paid poverty wages.

Minority Women:
A Case of Double Jeopardy

Patriarchy, that is male domination, has fostered institutional sexism and has relegated women to inferior positions in society. As with other minorities, women were encouraged to enter the labor market as a new source of cheap labor, that could be drawn upon in time of need and dispensed with during economic downturns. While the needs of American capital drive the system of labor exploitation, it is the pervasiveness of male dominance and the ideology of institutionalized sexism that maintain the system.

The realization and understanding that minority women were subjected to two distinct systems of social oppression was made clear in the early 1970's, when it was demonstrated that women of color were not only the victims of racism but were also the victims of sexism. As a result, minority women not only experienced prejudice and discrimination because of their ethnicity and race, but were also treated as second class citizens because of their gender. Frances Beale (1970) was among the first to suggest that the African American woman was really a slave to a slave and therefore lives under the threat of double jeopardy. Others have since pointed out that women of color suffer from the double effects of discrimination in the labor market, the educational system, and in the economic market place (Almquist, 1979; Cortera, 1980; Cole, 1986; Jameson, 1988; Baca-Zinn, 1987).

The analysis of the oppression of women of color is now viewed as a triple system of domination, based on (1) racism, (2) sexism, and (3) social class oppression (Collins, 1986; Hooks, 1981; Steady, 1981). This perspective provides an important modification in the theory of women's oppression in society, as this analysis provides for variations in the system of social stratification, which can either increase or decrease the level of oppression.

Therefore racism and sexism cannot be perceived or understood as independent forces working in the greater society, rather they must be viewed as dual aspects of one process, that is the social oppression of women. Within this oppression one also finds social class distinctions that affect the level of oppression. Obviously the forms of racism are variable, that is the impact of racism is different for certain people and for certain groups, as it affects minority men and women, and as it is felt by the rich and the poor within these social categories.

Likewise, sexism is a function of a woman's race and ethnicity, as neither racism nor sexism exist in a pure form (i.e., as independent forces in society), but rather they constitute a synergistic constellation of social variables that are affected by social class differences (Smith and Stewart, 1983:1-2). For example, high social status can ameliorate the deleterious effects of racism or sexism. In sum, even a person's position in the system of social stratification can never completely obliterate the sting of racism or sexism (Glass, 1990).

Unfortunately much of the work on the status of women in American society today has failed to focus on the lives of minority women, with the result that the research data and studies on women of color are sparse. Most of the research on women seems to share the assumption that all women are white (Dill, 1983; Palmer, 1983; Jameson, 1988). But careful analysis of the available data reveals that when white women are compared to women of color, minority women are at a much greater disadvantage in terms of their occupational distribution, wages, educational achievement, and overall economic well being (Mezey, 1992:91-108).

The Lives of African American Women

Racial issues have often overshadowed the plight of African American women, since the racial question has primarily focused on the lives of African American men, and the feminist's movement is primarily concerned with the goals and objectives of white women. Even the Civil Rights Movement focused on the social and economic condition of African American men and not on the concerns of African American women.

When the modern women's movement was launched, many African American feminists portrayed it as a petty bourgeois white fad that failed to address the issues that were important to them (King, 1971). Other critics have made the point that the women's movement usurped key issues that served as the foundation of the Civil Rights Movement, such as affirmative action (Hood, 1978). Indeed, some are of the opinion that the Women's Movement was launched from the platform of the Civil Rights Movement.

Before long some African American feminists felt that the objective of the women's movement was to satisfy the needs of white middle-class women. For example, African American women found it difficult to relate to the white women's emphasis on greater labor force participation or their interest in escaping the confines of their homes, since the proportion of African American women in the labor force has historically exceeded that of white women, and being a housewife was a luxury they could ill afford. Furthermore, African American women were fearful that the women's movement would only make headway at the expense of the African American movement and that eventually the issue of racism would pale against the importance of sexism (Dill, 1983:175).

Since the days of slavery, African American women have worked in and outside their homes to provide for their families. As a result they have always worked a double shift, and their labor force participation rate has always exceeded the national average. For example, as early as 1890 one-third (36%) of African American women were employed outside the home, compared to only fourteen percent of white women (Marable, 1983:Table VIII). By the turn of the century 41.2 percent were employed, and by 1920, 43.7% were in the labor force, that is at almost twice the rate for all women (Dill, 1979:Table I). Today, African American women have a labor force participation rate of 58.7 percent, compared to 57.2 percent for white women and 53.5 percent for Latinas (U.S. Census, 1991: Table 632).

African American women have historically worked in either agriculture or domestic service, which was a carry-over from slavery and a reflection of pervasive racial discrimination. For example, in 1880 half (52%) were employed in domestic service and almost half (44%) in agriculture (Marable, 1983:Table IX). By 1930 almost two-thirds (62.6%) were domestic servants and only one-fourth (26.9%) were in agriculture. Their distribution in the labor force did not change significantly until the post-war period (1950) when two out of five (40.9%) were domestic servants and only 8.7 percent were in agriculture. By 1960, one-third were domestic servants and in 1970 only one out of five were thus employed. In 1980 the number of African American domestic servants dropped to less than ten percent. In comparison the distribution of white women in domestic service ranged from one to four percent between 1950 and 1980 (Higginbotham, 1983:Table 1).

Since the time of slavery African American women have provided for their families as wage earners (Aldridge, 1989:132-137). For example, there are more married African American women in the labor force than married white women, and they are also more likely than white women to be the sole support of a household. In 1989 half (55.6%) the African American households were headed by women, compared to only 18.1 percent of white households (Schick and Schick, 1991:46). Consequently their income is essential to the support of their families, as African American women seldom have access to the resources of the highest paid employees, that is white men.

While women in general earn about 60 percent of what men earn, African American women only earn about one-third (36.9%) of what white men earn (Farley and Allen, 1987:Table 10.4). Since African American men only earn 63 percent of what white men earn, this means that a dual income African American family only earns about as much (per year) as the average white man.

It is also important to note that minority women contribute about one-third of the family income, as compared to one-fourth by white women. Since more African American families are low income, the wages of working wives are critical, as working wives contribute two-thirds (69%) of the family's income if the annual family income is less than $10,000 per year, 56 percent if it is between $10,000 and $14,999, and 46.6 percent if it is between $15,000 and $19,000 (U.S. Dept. of Labor, 1983).

Even when African American women obtain an education, they are still underpaid for the positions that they hold (Aldridge, 1989:Table 3). For example, a white male high school graduate had a higher annual income ($20,968) in 1981 than an African American male college graduate ($19,892) and earned more money than an African American female with a graduate degree ($19,395) (Felder, 1984:Table 15). By 1984 white male high school graduates ($19,600) still earned more than African American female college graduates ($18,400) (Farley and Allen, 1987:Table 10.7). Even more discouraging is the fact that the more education that African Americans obtain, the greater their income gap when compared to whites.

A comparison of the annual income of African American women with white men reveals the long term effects of racism and sexism in the work place. For example, in 1989 the median annual income of full-time employed African American women was $15,652, or about three-fifths (62%) of what white men earned ($25,064). In the professional and technical fields African American women earned 52 percent of what white men earned, 66 percent in clerical positions, 55 percent as operatives, and 66.6 percent as service workers (U.S. Census, 1991:Table 678).

In view of increasing divorce rates, high unemployment rates, the cost of housing, and high inflation, it is clear that African American women will remain an important source of economic support for the African American family (Wojkiewicz, et al, 1990). Today, African American women serve as the lifeline of support for their families, for without their wages an even greater number of African American families would sink into poverty. On

430

average their income provides more than half their family income (Hunter and Ensminger, 1992:421-424; Swinton, 1988:136-138).

La Chicana: The Mexican American Woman

Like African American women, Mexican American women have also had a long history of labor force participation. During the early period of settlement in the Southwest, Chicanas supported their families by cooking, washing, and cleaning in the homes of Spanish land barons and Anglo cattle ranchers. Furthermore, Mexican women have a long history of bringing outside work into their homes. For example, they earned money by cooking for others, washing and ironing clothes for others, selling prepared foods, and providing child care for other families. Yet these women are rarely counted in the official records as employed, or as contributing to the support of their families. Indeed this is still true today.

Although Mexican women have contributed to the economic survival of the family since pre-Columbian times (Cotera, 1977) and during the colonial period (Hart, 1980:151-157), they did not officially enter the American labor market until the early 1880's. According to the historical accounts, Mexican women constituted six percent of the Los Angeles labor force in 1860, which doubled (13%) by 1880 (Griswold del Castillo, 1979:65-69). By 1880 Chicanas were officially in the paid labor force in Santa Barbara, where they worked as domestic servants, fruit and nut harvesters, and as cannery workers (Camarillo, 1979:90-93). In El Paso, Mexican women had a high rate of labor force participation by 1890, when they were employed as domestic servants, laundresses, sewers and stitchers, cooks, dishwashers, and common laborers (Garcia, 1980; 1981).

As Chicano families settled in the Southwest, communities sprang up in those areas where jobs were available, usually in the agricultural valleys of Texas and California, or at the intersection of major rail lines. As in the past, Chicanas supported their families by bringing work into their homes or by offering their services as domestics (Romero, 1987, 1992; Ruiz, 1987). They also had to take the least desirable jobs, at the lowest pay (Barrera, 1979:131; Ruiz, 1984:1-4; Segura, 1984). This was not only the result of the discrimination that they experienced as Chicanas and as women, but also a result of the fact that their work as domestics was greatly undervalued, as it was considered an extension of housework (Garcia-Bahne, 1981:39).

With the introduction of year-round agricultural production in the Southwest, a new demand for female labor evolved. Mexican migrant workers were encouraged to bring their wives and children with them, as the growers discovered that the women could pick almost as much fruit, vegetables, and cotton as the men. Growers discovered that having women in the fields improved the dependability of their labor force. And as agricultural production increased after 1910, so did the number of women in the fields. By the 1920's growers found that Mexican women were the ideal labor force in the food processing and canning industries, for they found that they could work them for long hours, at low pay, and under physically oppressive conditions, without any major problems.

Chicanas dominated the canning and garment industries of the Southwest during the 1930's. Employers preferred to hire Mexican American women in the garment industry, canneries, and packing houses, as they found that they were docile, unlikely to complain, and easy to manage. As a result, Chicanas not only experienced occupational segregation by sex, but also by ethnicity, as they were always assigned to the most tedious, dirty, and lowest paying job in the factory. During this period most of the garment factories were located in Los Angeles, El Paso, and San Antonio. For example, Los Angeles had about 150 dress factories, employing about 1,500 Mexican women, out of a labor force of 2,000. They were paid about a dollar a day (Taylor, 1980). In 1934, San Antonio garment workers were paid from six to eleven cents an hour, for a 45 hour week and pecan shellers, also predominately women, averaged less than $2.00 a week (Acuña, 1988:224).

Historically, Chicanas were concentrated in factories and assembly plants, primarily because of discrimination, labor market segmentation, and limited employment opportunities, (Garcia, 1975). But their concentration and ethnic identification contributed to the early unionization of Chicana factory workers (Blackwelder, 1984). Before long they assumed leadership positions in the International Ladies Garment Workers Union, the Needle Trades Workers Industrial Union, and the pecan shellers union *El Nogal*, which was 4,000 strong in the mid-1930's (Green, 1971).

Unfortunately, thousands lost their jobs and many were left without resources during the Great Depression. In some cases mass deportations were ordered, as in Los Angeles (Hoffman, 1974), and employers demonstrated a distinct preference to hire their kind. During the Second World War Chicanas were encouraged to enter the fields, canneries, processing plants, garment factories, and the various war time assembly plants. For the first time Chicanas were allowed to enroll in government training programs, were allowed to work in the factories, and some were even allowed to enroll in apprenticeship programs.

Following the war, Chicanas, like all women, were encouraged to give their jobs to the veterans and return to their lives as housewives. Unfortunately many advances made during the war were lost. Nonetheless some found work in the new production, processing, and fabrication plants established in such cities as Los Angeles, Phoenix, El Paso, San Antonio, and Houston. In response their concentration shifted to operative and service positions. As in the past, many Chicanas worked out of their homes, washing and ironing, providing child care, and cleaning and cooking for others. In addition, some began to do small assembly and piece work out of their homes

(Fernandez and Garcia, 1986).

The two most important changes for Chicanas in the early seventies was their shift into white collar positions (primarily into clerical jobs), and their movement into the electronics industry (Segura, 1992:163-168). By 1970 almost half were white collar workers, with just over one-third of these in clerical and sales positions, while four out of ten were employed as operatives or service workers. During the seventies, the electronics industry discovered that Chicanas were ideal for the tedious and endless task of manufacturing and assembling electronic parts, at minimum wage. Therefore, it is no surprise that the four major electronic plants in the United States are located in Anaheim, Los Angeles, San Jose, and Dallas, areas known for their heavy concentration of Mexican Americans (Fernandez and Garcia, 1988:Table I).

According to the 1990 census Chicanas had a labor force participation rate of 52.7 percent, compared with 56.6 percent for white women. Of the 5,477,000 Mexican Americans in the labor force in 1989, three out of ten (30%) were women (Schick and Schick, 1991:186). Although 12.8 percent held professional or managerial positions, this was only half the rate for white women (26.3%). Four out of ten (36.8%) held technical or sales positions, one out of four (24.6%) held service jobs, three percent in craft positions, and one out of five (20.9%) worked as operatives or laborers. Overall half (50.4%) were employed in white collar positions, compared to three out of five (60.4%) white women. Among those in blue collar positions most were in service (24.6%) or in operative positions (20.9%). This compares with 17.5 percent service workers and 8.9 percent operatives among white women (Schick and Schick, 1991:186).

While all women earn 60.8 percent of what men earn, Chicanas ($8,110) only earn one-third (32.4%) of what white men earn per year ($25,064). Obviously Chicanas are the victims of both racism and sexism. In professional positions Latinas earn 54 percent of what white men earn, as managers 46 percent, in sales 25.6 percent, as clerical workers 57 percent, as operatives 50 percent, and as service workers 69 percent (Schick and Schick, 1991:186). Overall the average annual income of a white male ($25,064) is considerably higher than the annual income of two Chicanas employed full-time ($16,220). Similarly a Mexican American husband and wife employed full-time earn $20,217 a year, that is $5,000 less than the average white male earns in a given year (Schick and Schick, 1991:186; U.S. Census, 1991:Table 659).

One out of five (26%) Mexican American families live below the poverty level, compared to only ten percent of non-Latino families. More than one out of four (27.4%) of the heads of poverty families were active in the labor force and half (47%) of the poverty families are supported by women. Clearly Latinas are overrepresented among the ranks of the poor. But they are not poor because they do not work, rather they are poor despite the fact that they do work, as three out of five (59.8%) employed Chicanas earned less than $10,000 in 1989 (Schick and Schick, 1991:186).

While half the Chicanas are employed outside the home, and countless others earn money by bringing work into the home, a significant number still fall below the poverty level (Gimenez, 1990:26-29). This is not only the result of the poverty wages they receive but also a result of segregation in the labor market, their concentration in the lowest paying jobs, and their inability to secure positions that would insure their upward social mobility (Zavella, 1987). Most are employed in clerical positions, as operatives, or on assembly lines, that is in the lowest paying and most insecure positions (Ybarra, 1988). Therefore it should come as no surprise to discover that three out of five (59.8%) of all Chicanas employed full-time earn less than $10,000 per year (Schick and Schick, 1991:186).

Chinese American Women

During the first fifty years of Chinese settlement in America the Chinese woman was a rarity. Between 1850 to 1900 the arrival of Chinese women was limited by the cost and difficulty of the journey, the dangers of such a trip, and by strong cultural prohibitions against female emigration. As a result only 8,848 women arrived during the peak period of Chinese immigration (i.e., 1850-1882), while over 100,000 men arrived during this period (Goldman, 1981:95).

During this period most Chinese women were prostitutes. The 1870 Census counted 2,018 Chinese women in San Francisco, seven out of ten of whom were listed as prostitutes (Cheng, 1984:421). Chinese women were sold, kidnapped, or otherwise lured into prostitution, and then sold for a contract to an agent or brothel owner. Most were indentured for four years and were required to work a minimum of 320 days per year. A brothel owner could expect to earn a net profit of $10,000 over a four year period from the labor of one prostitute, that is at a time when Chinese laborers were doing well to earn a dollar a day (Cheng, 1984:412).

By 1880 the number of prostitutes in Chinatown decreased dramatically, as only one-third were listed as so-called daughters of joy. This dramatic reduction was primarily the result of the work of Christian missionaries who rescued many Chinese women and the determination of American authorities to stamp out this problem. By 1920 very few prostitutes remained in Chinatown.

Many former prostitutes married Chinese laborers and became productive members of the community as seamstresses, laundresses, domestic servants, and cooks. Others worked beside their husbands in family businesses as unpaid laborers in laundries, restaurants, grocery stores, and lodging houses. By the early 1920's Chinese women were already a primary source of labor in the canneries and in the garment factories (Kim, 1983:121).

By the turn of the century there were only 4,522 Chinese females in America, compared to 85,000 males. Chinese men had few options, as they were not permitted to return home to marry and they were not allowed to marry white women. Therefore, they could either return home permanently or remain single in America. The few Chinese women who did marry, produced the first generation of Chinese American children. At the turn of the century only nine percent of the Chinese were native born, but by 1920 almost one-third (30%) were native born (Glenn, 1983:Table 1).

Without any doubt it was the strict immigration restrictions that prevented the Chinese from establishing families in America. The Chinese Exclusion Act was passed by Congress in 1882, and was extended indefinitely in 1904. In 1922 the Cable Act insured that any American citizen, particularly women, who married an alien who was ineligible for citizenship (i.e., Chinese, Japanese, Koreans, and Asian Indians) would loose their U.S. citizenship. The Immigration Act of 1924 placed further restrictions on the immigration of alien wives of U.S. citizens (i.e., native born Chinese men). The clear intent of U.S. immigration laws were to forestall the formation of Chinese families in America. In the end they were effective, as the average annual flow of Chinese women between 1882 and 1943 was only 215 per year (Yung, 1986:42).

Often American born Chinese women were forced by their families to marry an older Chinese bachelor, as the custom of arranged marriages was maintained into the late 1920's in America. But as the second generation gained independence and became more westernized, they often rebelled against tradition and the wishes of their parents, and married the man of their choice (Wong, 1945:130). Unfortunately these American born Chinese women found that while they were fluent in English and had completed their educations, they still experienced discrimination in the labor market. Even those Chinese American women who held graduate and professional degrees found it difficult to establish themselves. In the end some relocated to an area where the Chinese were unknown, and discrimination was not an integral part of the social environment, while others had to establish themselves in Chinatown.

Between 1920 and 1940 Chinese American women were active in their communities and were at the forefront of the new women's liberation movement. With the support of Protestant churches, they founded organizations that sponsored social programs, recreational activities, English language classes, legal counseling, and community health care programs. They worked for women's rights, became more independent and worked outside their homes, and they taught their daughters the ideals of freedom and democracy. In 1938 Chinese American women went on strike for union representation in the garment factories and established their own chapters of the International Ladies' Garment Workers' Union (Yung, 1986:61).

The crisis of the Second World War offered Chinese Americans their first opportunity to work in factories, assembly plants, and shipyards, where they learned new skills. In total, more than 12,000 Chinese Americans served in the armed forces, some of whom were women. While in the military Chinese American women served their country in a variety of capacities: as teletype operators, clerks, communication specialists, nurses and medical technicians, and even as pilots. Back on the home front Chinese American women held dances, parades, and raffles to sell war bonds, and did volunteer work for the USO.

In view of China's support of the United States during the war, the restrictions of the Chinese Exclusion Act were finally lifted in 1943. The most important change occurred in 1946, with the passage of the War Brides Act. This act allowed the alien wives and children of veterans or U.S. citizens to enter the United States as non-quota immigrants. As a result, over three thousand Chinese women immigrated in 1948 alone. Between 1944 and 1953 over 80 percent of the Chinese immigrants were women. Before long their sex ratio began to move toward a more balanced distribution and new families were created. These immigrant wives were either women who had been separated from their husbands for many years (in some cases for up to 30 years), or the brides of veterans or U.S. citizens who married in China (Lee, 1956).

By the mid-sixties the Chinese American family had changed from a small producer type of family structure (i.e., one based on a family run business), to a dual wage family that required equal involvement of both the husband and wife in the labor force (Glenn, 1983). This transition meant that women played a more important role in the maintenance of the family, as they now contributed equally to its economic survival. In the past they were usually employed in the family business as unpaid family workers. Naturally this meant that Chinese American women were involved in the major decisions of the family and their husbands had to do some of the housework. The pooling of income and their participation as a team member contributed to their social equality in the family and liberation in the community.

In 1920, two-thirds (64%) of Chinese American women were employed as domestics or in manufacturing, that is primarily in the garment industry. Before the Second World War most were employed as domestic servants (29%), as operatives (26%), and in clerical positions (26%). Only eight percent were professionals. In 1960, half (55%) were employed in white collar positions, predominately in clerical and sales positions (38%) and one out of six held professional positions (17%). By 1980, two out three (65%) were white collar workers, and one out of four (25%) were in professional and managerial positions. Chinese American women also have the highest labor force participation rate among women at 58.3 percent, compared to

49.4 percent for white women (Yung, 1986 Appendix G & H). But their actual labor force participation rate is even higher when unpaid family members working in family businesses are included.

Although Chinese American women have the highest rate of college completion (29.5%, compared to 13.3% for white women and 21.3% for white men), they are still not earning salaries commensurate with their educations. For example, a California study found that while only one out of six (16.3%) of Chinese American women with college degrees earned more than $21,000 a year, more than half (51.1%) of the white men did (Woo, 1985:316). As with all women, Chinese American women are the victims of sex discrimination in the labor force and in the market place, but they are also the victims of silent racism in American society.

But it also should be understood that not all Chinese American women are employed in professional and white collar positions, as one out of five (18%) are factory workers and one out of seven (14%) are domestic servants. During the past decade, thousands of Chinese immigrant women have taken the worst jobs, at the lowest pay, just to survive in America. Therefore, the representation of Chinese American women in the labor force has taken a bi-polar distribution, with a large group holding white collar positions and an equally large number working in low wage factory jobs.

Today Chinese American women are organizing themselves and working to improve their social and economic positions. In addition, they are active in dozens of organizations that are working to improve conditions in their communities. Of particular importance is their involvement in the Women's Movement and the large number of Chinese American women who are successful and now serve as effective role models for the younger generation of Chinese Americans.

Japanese American Women

The flow of Japanese women to America shares two basic similarities with that of Chinese women, as there were very few Japanese women in America before the turn of the century, and the few that did arrive during this period were primarily prostitutes (Ichioka, 1977). By the turn of the century Japanese prostitutes were reported working in Hawaii, California, Oregon, and Washington (Ichioka, 1977:203). Prostitution among the Japanese immigrants declined significantly after 1910, partly as a result of the strict laws passed against the immigration of prostitutes, and as result of the introduction of picture brides.

The number of Japanese women in the United States before the turn of the century is unclear, but there were only 985 in 1900, compared to over 23,000 Japanese men. Of these, less than half (410) were married. In 1910 there were only 9,000 women, compared to 63,000 men. Of this number three out of five (61.4%) were married. As a direct result of the picture bride program the number of Japanese women increased significantly between 1910 and 1920. By 1920 the number of women increased to 38,303, sixty percent (22,193) of whom were married. In 1920 women represented one-third (34.5%) of the Japanese immigrant population (Ichioka, 1980:341; Thomas, 1952:575; Yamoto, 1932:70-72).

Overall a total of 45,706 Japanese women arrived in America between 1909 and 1923, of whom 33,628 (73.6%) were listed as wives. This influx was the result of the arrival of picture brides (Glenn, 1986:31; Matsui, 1922:15-17). The picture bride program was initiated in response to the Gentleman's Agreement of 1908, that terminated all immigration from Japan, with the exception of wives. Since most of the Japanese immigrants were single males they decided to send for wives. Given the great expense of travel to Japan they simply relied on the traditional system of proxy or arranged marriages. The Japanese men in America allowed their families to make all the arrangements and they met their new wives at the docks in San Francisco (Ichioka, 1980: 342-348). Because of public agitation against their immigration, the Japanese government stopped issuing passports to picture brides in February of 1920, and the United States banned all immigration from Asia in 1924.

The introduction of women into the Japanese immigrant community not only insured the survival of the family, but also insured that the Issei (first generation Japanese immigrants) would produce a second generation of American citizens. The effectiveness of the picture bride program is clear when we consider that only one percent of the Japanese immigrant population was native born at the turn of the century, and only increased to six percent by 1910. As a result of the rapid influx of Japanese women, there were 26.7 percent native born children in 1920 and almost half (47.3%) were native born by 1930. By 1940 almost two out of three (62.7%) of the Japanese in America were native born (Hale, 1945:173).

The period following the termination of immigration from Asia (1924), until the onset of the Second World War is recognized as a stabilization period for Japanese Americans. During this period many Japanese immigrants purchased farms and businesses. Issei women often worked side by side with their husbands, on the farms, in the fishing villages, and in the boarding houses and restaurants (Hanawa, 1982).

Their Nisei (second generation) daughters were exposed to a mixture of Japanese and American culture, as they grew up in the 1920's and reached adulthood in the late 1930's or early 1940's. They were bilingual and bicultural, as they attended Japanese language and cultural schools. But at the same time they were Americanized, as they attended Anglo high schools, celebrated all the national holidays, and belonged to all the teenage and young adult clubs. In effect the Nisei were as American as they could possibly be during this period (Matsumoto, 1984).

Like their mothers, about one-fourth of the Nisei daughters worked in agriculture, one-fourth in domestic service, and one out of five in clerical and sales in 1940. A smaller proportion worked in family run businesses. A few were employed in light manufacturing and in the garment industry. Only three percent worked as professionals, primarily as teachers and nurses (Glenn, 1980).

As a result of their internment during the Second World War Japanese American women were forced to give up their jobs. In the camps, some were allowed to use their skills, such as doctors, nurses, and teachers, but most worked on camp projects and in community gardens. After spending a year in the internment camps, some of the more fortunate Nisei women were allowed to leave the camps to attend colleges in the East.

Upon their release from the camps Nisei women found employment in industry (26.5%), in domestic service (12.4%), and in clerical work (34.6%). This was in contrast to their heavy involvement in agricultural work and family run businesses before the war. They were also faced with the fact that they had lost their financial resources, homes, and businesses as a result of their internment, and therefore sought employment in the private sector, where they expected to accumulate capital. Indeed their labor force participation rate was 55 percent higher in 1950, than it was in 1940 (Glenn, 1986:79).

In 1950 most Issei women (85.2%) were still employed in blue collar positions as farmers (28.1%), as operatives (27%), as domestics (15.8%), and as service workers (11.5%). During this period their labor force participation rate was higher than most women, as 47.3 percent were in the labor force in 1950, compared to 38.7 percent of all women. In 1960, 56.3 percent were active in the labor force, compared to 37.9 percent of white women. In 1970 their rate increased to 57.5 percent, compared to 49.3 percent among white women (Glenn, 1986:Table 6).

By 1960, half (54.5%) of the Nisei women held white collar positions, with most in clerical jobs (31%) and a few in the professions (12.5%). Very few (6.5%) were employed as domestics and only one out of four (27.8%) were working in manufacturing or service jobs. Very little change occurred in the occupational distribution of Nisei women between 1960 and 1970, as they were still concentrated in white collar positions.

In the 1990's the Sansei women (the third generation) are moving into the higher white collar and professional positions. This is in direct response to their higher levels of college graduation. As a result, most Sansei women hold white collar positions. However, as is true among other Asian women, they are still underpaid for the work they perform and the positions they hold in management and in the professions. In addition, Japanese American women still find that it is very difficult to break the dual barriers of sexism and racism in American society.

Chapter Summary

Ethnic women are a minority not only because of their gender, but also because of their ethnicity or race. Consequently they are the victims of double jeopardy, since they experience discrimination as a result of their ethnicity and race, and because of their gender. In addition they experience oppression as a result of social class discrimination.

While women are more likely to be active in the labor force today, they are also more likely to live in poverty, primarily as a result of the poverty wages that they receive. Economic data reveal that more employed women live below the poverty level than men. Historically, African American women have had a higher rate of employment than white women. They also exhibit the greatest income gap between white men and women, as they only earn about one-third of the wages that the average white man earns. As a result, working African American women are far more likely to fall below the official poverty level than any other group in society.

Mexican American women have taken factory jobs and are found extensively in the garment industry, processing plants, the service industry, and most recently in electronic assembly plants. While the official statistics reveal that half the Chicanas are active in the labor force, their true level of labor force participation is higher, as they tend to work in the informal labor market and bring work into their homes.

Chinese American women have long suffered from the effects of discrimination and only recently have they experienced social mobility in the labor market. In view of their high levels of education many have established themselves in the professions. But many of the more recent immigrants are employed in production plants and in the garment industry.

As with Chinese American women, Japanese American women are also well represented in the upper echelons of the labor market, primarily because of their higher levels of education. But like other Asian women, they are often underpaid for their level of education, skills, and job experience.

Today ethnic women are making the point that they are willing to work and want to obtain an education. However, they also want to be treated equally and receive their just rewards, not only in the labor market, but also in other institutions of American society.

References

Acker, Joan
    1992   "The Future of Women and Work: Ending the Twentieth Century." *Sociological Perspectives* 35(1):53-68.

Acuña, Rodolfo
    1988   *Occupied America: A History of Chicanos.* New York: Harper & Row (Third Edition).

Aldridge, Dolores P.
    1989   "African American Women in the Economic Marketplace: A Continuing Struggle." *Journal of Black Studies* 20(2):129-154.

Almquist, Elizabeth M.
    1979   *Minorities, Gender, and Work.* Lexington, MA: Lexington Books.

Baca-Zinn, Maxine
    1987   "Minority Families in Crisis: The Public Discussion." Memphis, TN: Center for Research on Women, Memphis State University. Research Paper No. 6.

Barrera, Mario
    1979   *Race and Class in the Southwest: A Theory of Racial Inequality.* Notre Dame, IN: University of Notre Dame.

Beale, Frances
    1970   "Double Jeopardy: To be Black and Female." In *The Black Woman.* Toni Cade (ed.), New York: Signet. Pp. 90-110.

Blackwelder, Julia K.
    1984   *Women of the Depression; Caste and Culture in San Antonio, 1929-1939.* College Station: Texas A & M Press.

Bureau of Labor Statistics
    1985   *Employment and Earnings.* Washington, D.C.: USGPO

Burnham, Linda
    1986   "Has Poverty Been Feminized in Black America?" In *For Crying Out Loud: Women and Poverty in the United States.* Rochelle Lefkowitz and Ann Withorn (eds.), New York: The Pilgrim Press. Pp. 67-83.

Dill, Bonnie T.
    1979   "The Dialectics of Black Womanhood." *Sings* 4(3):543-555.
    1983   "Race, Class, and Gender: Prospects for an All Inclusive Sisterhood." *Feminist Studies* 9(1):131-150.

Camarillo, Albert
    1979   *Chicanos in a Changing Society.* Cambridge: Harvard University Press.

Chafetz, Janet S.
1990 *Gender Equity: An Integrated Theory of Stability and Change.* Newbury Park, CA: Sage Publications.

Cheng, Lucie
1984 "Free, Indentured, Enslaved: Chinese Prostitutes in Nineteenth Century America." In *Labor Immigration Under Capitalism.* Lucie Cheng and Edna Bonacich (eds.), Berkeley: University of California Press. Pp. 402-434.

Cherry, Robert
1989 *Discrimination: Its Economic Impact on Blacks, Women, and Jews.* Lexington, MA: D.C. Heath and Company.

Cole, Johnnetta B.
1986 "Commonalities and Differences." In *All American Women.* Johnnetta B. Cole (ed.), New York: Free Press. Pp. 1-30.

Collins, Patricia H,
1986 "Learning From the Outsider Within: The Sociological Significance of Black Feminist Thought." *Social Problems* 33(6):1429

Cortera, Marta
1977 *Diosa y Hembra: The History and Heritage of Chicanas in the U.S.* Austin, TX: Information Systems.
1980 "Feminism: The Chicana and Anglo Versions." In *Twice a Minority: Mexican American Women.* Margarita B. Melville (ed.), St. Louis: C.V. Mosby. Pp. 217-234.

Eitzen, D. Stanley and Maxine Baca Zinn
1992 "Structural Transformation and Systems of Inequality." In *Race, Class, and Gender.* Margaret L. Andersen and Patricia H. Collins (eds.), Belmont, CA: Wadsworth. Pp. 178-182.

England, Paula
1992 *Comparable Worth: Theories and Evidence.* New York: Aldine.

England, Paula and Irene Browne
1992 "Trends in Women's Economic Status." *Sociological Perspectives* 35(1):17-51.

Farley, Reynolds and Walter R. Allen (eds.)
1987 *The Color Line and the Quality of Life in America.* New York: Russell Sage Foundation.

Felder, Henry E.
1984 *The Changing Patterns of Black Family Income, 1960-1982.* Washington, D.C.: Joint Center for Political Studies.

Fernandez-Kelly, Maria and Anna M. Garcia
1986 "The Making of an Underground Economy: Hispanic Women, Home Work, and the Advanced Capitalist State." *Urban Anthropology* 14:1-3.

1988   "Invisible Amidst the Glitter: Hispanic Women in the Southern California Electronics Industry." In *The Worth of Women's Work: A Qualitative Synthesis.* Anne Statham, et al (eds.), Albany: State University of New York Press. Pp. 265-290.

Friedan, Betty
1963   *The Feminine Mystique.* New York: Norton.

Garcia, Mario T.
1975   "Racial Dualism in the El Paso Labor Market, 1880- 1920." *Aztlan* 6(2):197-218.
1980   "The Chicana in American History: The Mexican Women of El Paso, 1880-1920: A Case Study." *Pacific Historical Review* 49(2):315-337.
1981   *Desert Immigrants: The Mexicans of El Paso, 1890-1920.* New Haven: Yale University Press.

Garcia-Bahne, Betty
1981   "La Chicana and the Chicano Family." In *Essays on La Mujer.* Rosaura Sanchez and Rosa Martinez Cruz (eds.), Los Angeles: Chicano Studies Center Publications, University of California. Pp. 30-47.

Gimenez, Martha E.
1990   "The Dialectics of Waged and Unwaged Work: Waged Work, Domestic Labor and Household Survival in the United States." In *Work Without Wages: Comparative Studies of Domestic Labor and Self-Employment.* Jane L. Collins and Martha Gimenez (eds.), Albany: State University of New York. Pp. 25-45.

Glass, Jennifer
1990   "The Impact of Occupational Segregation on Employment Conditions." *Social Forces* 68:779-796.

Glenn, Evelyn N.
1980   "The Dialectics of Wage Work: Japanese American Women and Domestic Servants, 1905-1940." *Feminist Studies* 6(3):432-471.
1983   "Split Household, Small Producer and Dual Wage Earner: An Analysis of Chinese-American Family Strategies." *Journal of Marriage and the Family* 45:35-46.
1986   *Issei, Nisei, War Bride: Three Generations of Japanese American Women in Domestic Service.* Philadelphia: Temple University Press.

Goldin, Claudia
1990   *Understanding the Gender Gap: An Economic History of American Women.* New York: Oxford University Press.

Goldman, Marion S.
1981   *Gold Diggers and Gold Miners: Prostitution and Social Life on the Comstock Lode.* An Arbor: University of Michigan Press.

Green, George N.
1971   "The ILGWU in Texas, 1930-1970." *Journal of Mexican American History* 1(2):144-169.

Griswold del Castillo, Richard
1979   *The Los Angeles Barrio, 1860-1890: A Social History.* Berkeley: University of California Press.

Hale, Robert M.
1945   "The United States and Japanese Immigration." Chicago: Ph.D. Dissertation, Division of Social Sciences, The University of Chicago.

Hanawa, Yukiko
1982   "The Several Worlds of Issei Women." Long Beach: M.A. Thesis, California State University.

Hart, John
1980   "Working-Class Women in Nineteenth Century Mexico." In *Mexican-American Women in the United States.* Magdalena Mora and Adelaida R. Del Castillo (eds.), Los Angeles: University of California, Chicano Research Center Publications.

Hayghe, Howard
1984   "Working Mothers Reach Record Number in 1984." *Monthly Labor Review* 107:31-34.

Higginbotham, Elizabeth
1992   "We Were Never on a Pedestal: Women of Color Continue to Struggle With Poverty, Racism, and Sexism." In *Race, Class, and Gender.* Margaret L. Andersen and Patricia H. Collins (eds.), Bellmont, CA: Wadsworth. Pp. 183-190.

Hoffman, Abraham
1974   *Unwanted Mexican Americans in the Great Depression: Repatriation Pressures, 1929-1939.* Tucson: University of Arizona Press.

Hood, Elizabeth
1978   "Black Women, White Women: Separate Paths to Liberation." *Black Scholar* 9:45-46.

Hooks, Bell
1981   *Aint' I a Woman: Black Women and Feminism.* Boston: South End Press.

Hunter, Andrea G. and Margaret E. Ensminger
1992   "Diversity and Fluidity in Children's Living Arrangements: Family Transitions in an Urban Afro American Community." *Journal of Marriage and the Family* 54:418-426.

Ichioka, Yuji
1977   "Ameyuki-San: Japanese Prostitutes in Nineteenth Century America." *Amerasia Journal* 4(1):1-21.
1980   "Amerika Nadeshiko: Japanese Immigrant Women in the United States, 1900-1924." *Pacific Historical Review* 49:339-357

Jameson, Elizabeth
1988   "Toward a Multicultural History of Women in the Western United States." *Signs* 13(4):761-791.

Kim, Elaine H.
1983   *With Silk Wings: Asian American Women at Work.* Oakland: Asian Women United of California.

King, Helen
1971   "The Black Woman and Women's Lib." *Ebony* (March) Pp.68-76.

Lee, Rose Hum
1956   "The Recent Immigrant Chinese Families of the San Francisco-Oakland Area." *Marriage and Family Living* 18(1):14-24.

Marable, Manning
1983   *How Capitalism Underdeveloped Black America.* Boston, MA: South End Press.

Matsui, Shichiro
1922   "Economic Aspects of the Japanese Situation in California." Berkeley: M.A. Thesis, Department of Economics, University of California.

Matsumoto, Valerie
1984   "Japanese American Women During World War II." *Frontiers* 8(1):6-14.

Mezey, Susan G.
1992   *In Pursuit of Equality: Women, Public Policy, and the Federal Courts.* New York: St. Martin's Press.

Palmer, Phyllis M.
1983   "White Women/Black Women: The Dualism of Female Identity and Experience in the United States." *Feminist Studies* 9(1):151-170.

Paul, Ellen F.
1989   *Equity and Gender: The Comparable Worth Debate.* New Brunswick: Transaction Publishers.

Reskin, Barbara F. and Heidi I. Hartmann (eds.)

1986   *Women's Work, Men's Work: Sex Segregation on the Job.*
        Washington D.C.: National Academy Press.

Reskin, Barbara F. and Patricia Roos

1990   *Job Queues, Gender Queues: Explaining Women's Inroads
        into Male Occupations.* Philadelphia: Temple University
        Press.

Romero, Mary

1987   "Domestic Service in the Transition From Rural to Urban
        Life: the Case of La Chicana." *Women's Studies* 13:199-222.

1992   *MAID in the U.S.A.* NY: Routledge.

Roos, Patricia A. and Barbara F. Reskin

1992   "Occupational Desegregation in the 1970s: Integration and
        Economic Equality?" *Sociological Perspectives* 35(1):69-91.

Ruiz, Vicki L.

1984   "Working for Wages: Mexican Women in the American South-
        west, 1930-1980." Tucson: Southwest Institute for Research
        on Women, University of Arizona, Working Paper No. 19.

1987   "By the Day or Week: Mexicana Domestic Workers in El
        Paso." In *To Toil the Livelong Day: America's Women at Work,
        1780-1980.* Carol Groneman and Mary Beth Norton (eds.),
        Ithaca: Cornell University Press. Pp. 269-283.

Sawhill, Isabelle

1976   "Discrimination and Poverty Among Women Who Head
        Families." In *Women and the Workforce.* M. Blaxall and B.
        Regan (eds.), Chicago: University of Chicago Press.

Schick, Frank L. and Renee Schick (eds.)

1991   *Statistical Handbook on U.S. Hispanics.* Phoenix, AZ: Oryx
        Press.

Segura, Denise

1984   "Labor Market Stratification: The Chicana Experience."
        Berkeley Journal of Sociology 29:57-91.

1992   "Chicanas in White-Collar Jobs: 'You Have to Prove Yourself
        More'." *Sociological Perspectives* 35(1):163-182.

Smith, Althea and Abigail J. Stewart

1983   "Approaches to Studying Racism and Sexism in Black
        Women's Lives." *Journal of Social Issues* 39(3):1-15.

Sparr, Pamela

1986   "Reevaluating Feminist Economics: 'Feminization of Poverty'
        Ignores Key Issues." In *For Crying Out Loud: Women and Pover-
        ty in the United States.* Rochelle Lefkowitz and Ann Withorn
        (eds.), New York: The Pilgrim Press. Pp. 61-66.

Steady, Filomina C.
1981   "The Black Woman Cross-Culturally: An Overview."
In *The Black Woman Cross-Culturally.* Filomina C. Steady
(ed.), Cambridge, MA: Schenkman. Pp. 7-42.

Swinton, David H.
1988   "Economic Status of Blacks 1987." In *The State of Black
America 1988.* Janet Deward (ed.), New York: The National
Urban League. Pp. 129-152.

Taylor, Paul S.
1980   "Mexican Women in Los Angeles Industry in 1928." *Aztlan*
11(1):99-131.

Thomas, Dorothy S.
1952   *The Salvage.* Berkeley: University of California Press.

Treiman, Donald and Heidi Hartmann
1981   *Women, Work and Wages: Equal Pay for Jobs of Equal
Value.* Washington, D.C.: National Academy of Sciences.

U.S. Census
1982   *Persons of Spanish Origin in the United States: March 1982.*
Current Population Reports: Population Characteristics,
Series P-20, No. 396.
1988   *Statistical Abstract of the United States: 1988.* 108th Edition.
Washington, D.C.:USGPO.
1991   *Statistical Abstract of the United States, 1991* (111th edition).
Washington, D.C.: U.S. Department of Commerce.

U.S. Department of Labor
1983   *Handbook on Women Workers.* Washington, D.C.:U.S.
Department of Labor, Women's Bureau, Bulletin 298.
1985   *Employment and Earnings.* Washington, D.C.:U.S.
Department of Labor, Bulletin 32, January.

Vannoy, Dana and William W. Philliber
1992   "Wife's Employment and Quality of Marriage." *Journal of
Marriage and the Family* 54:387-398.

Wojtkiewicz, Roger A., S.S. McLanahan, and I. Garfinkel
1990   "The Growth of Families Headed by Women: 1950-1980."
Demography 27:19-30.

Wong, Jade S.
1945   *Fifth Chinese Daughter.* New York: Harper and Row.

Woo, Deborah
1985   "The Socioeconomic Status of Asian American Women in
the Labor Force: An Alternative View." *Sociological Perspectives* 28(3) 307-338.

Yamoto, Ichihashi
1932   *Japanese in the United States.* Stanford, CA: Stanford
University Press.

Ybarra, Lea

    1988   "Separating Myth from Reality: Socio-economic and Cultural Influences on Chicanas and the World of Work." In *Mexicanas at Work in the United States*. Margarita B. Melville (ed.), Houston: Mexican American Studies Program, University of Houston. Pp. 12-23.

Yung, Judy

    1986   *Chinese Women of America: A Pictorial History*. Seattle: University of Washington Press.

Zavella, Patricia

    1987   *Women's Work and Chicano Families: Cannery Workers of the Santa Clara Valley*. Ithaca, NY: Cornell University Press.

Key Terms		
National Organization of Women	sex segregation	pink collar jobs
poverty wages	poverty level	patriarchy
institutionalized sexism	sexism	triple domination
double shift	bi-polar distribution	picture brides
bicultural families		

Sample Test Questions

1. Provide a brief discussion of five areas where women experience social or economic discrimination in the labor market. Include examples for each.
2. Have the social and economic conditions of women in American society improved in the past 30 years? If you believe that conditions have or have not improved, support your response with specific examples and information from the assigned reading.
3. List and discuss five ways in which minority women are the victims of "double jeopard."
4. Discuss five problem areas that have made it difficult for African American women to improve their social and economic conditions over the past 30 years. Give examples of each problem area.
5. In view of the history of Chicanas in the labor force, discuss four areas where Chicanas have worked to support their families despite the long term effects of prejudice and discrimination.
6. Prepare a succinct discussion where you demonstrate five areas where Chinese American and Japanese American women share common social and historical experiences.

Appendix A

The Immigration and Naturalization Service
Visa Preference System: 1988

Preference	Use Rate	Designation
First	20%	Unmarried sons and daughters of U.S. citizens who are at least 21 years of age.
Second	20%	Spouses and unmarried children of permanent resident aliens.
Third	10%	Members of the professions, scientists, and artists of exceptional ability.
Fourth	10%	Married children of U.S. citizens.
Fifth	24%	Brothers and sisters at least 21 years of age of U.S. citizens.
Sixth	10%	Skilled or unskilled workers who are in short supply.
Seventh	6%	Political refugees who enter conditionally and are allowed to adjust their status.
Eighth		Nonpreference category, includes other qualified immigrants as visa numbers are not required for application in this category.

Source: Immigration and Naturalization Service, 1988 Statistical Yearbook, Pp. xiv-xv.

451

Immigration by Country of Last Residence 1820-1991 (thousands)

Country	Total 1820-1991	Total 1961-1970	Total 1971-1980	Total 1981-1990
All countries*	58,821	3,321.7	4,493.3	7,338.0
Europe	37,248	1,123.5	800.4	761.5
Austria[1]	1,832	20.6	9.5	18.9
Hungary	1,669	5.4	6.6	5.9
Belgium	211	9.2	5.3	6.6
Czechoslovakia	146	3.3	6.0	5.4
Denmark	371	9.2	4.4	2.8
France	792	45.2	25.1	92.1
Germany[1]	7,094	190.8	74.4	159.0
Greece	707	86.0	92.4	31.9
Ireland	4,730	33.0	11.5	67.2
Italy	5,403	214.1	129.4	12.3
Netherlands	376	30.6	10.5	4.2
Norway	802	15.5	3.9	83.2
Poland[1]	623	53.5	37.2	40.3
Portugal	506	76.1	101.7	20.5
Spain	288	44.7	39.1	11.1
Sweden	1,286	17.1	6.5	8.0
Switzerland	360	18.5	8.2	57.6
USSR[1,3]	3,475	2.5	39.0	18.7
United Kingdom[2]	5,136	213.8	137.4	159.2
Yugoslavia	139	20.4	30.5	37.3
Other Europe	183	9.1	18.9	7.7
Asia	6,361	427.6	1,588.2	2,738.1
China[4]	938[4]	34.8	124.3	298.9
Hong Kong	318[4]	75.0	113.5	98.2
India	498	27.2	164.1	250.7
Iran	187[4]	10.3	45.1	116.0
Israel	143[4]	29.6	37.7	44.2
Japan	468[4]	40.0	49.8	47.0
Korea	668[4]	34.5	267.6	333.8
Philippines	1,095[5]	98.4	355.0	548.7
Turkey	416	10.1	13.4	23.4
Vietnam	473[6]	4.3	172.8	281.0
Other Asia	1,157	36.5	176.1	631.4
America	14,365	1,716.4	1,982.5	3,615.6
Argentina	135[7]	49.7	29.9	27.3
Canada	4,316[7]	413.3	169.9	158.0
Colombia	315	72.0	77.3	122.9
Cuba	758[8]	208.5	264.9	144.6
Dominican Rep.	552[7]	93.3	148.1	252.0
Ecuador	166[7]	36.8	50.1	56.2
El Salvador	322[7]	15.0	34.4	213.5
Haiti	282[8]	34.5	56.3	138.4
Jamaica	452[12]	74.9	137.6	208.1
Mexico	4,837[7]	453.9	640.3	1,655.7
Other America	2,231	264.4	373.8	639.3
Africa	368	29.0	80.8	176.8
Oceania[13]	212	25.1	41.2	45.2
Unknown or Not Reported	268	0.1	——	1.0

Immigration by Country of Last Residence 1820-1991—(Continued)

1988	1989	1990	1991	Percent			
				1820-1991	1961-1970	1971-1980	1981-1990
643.0	1,090.9	1,536.5	1,827.2	100.0	100.0	100.0	100.0
71.8	94.3	124.0	146.7	63.3	33.8	17.8	10.4
2.5	2.8	3.8	3.5	3.1	.6	0.2	0.3
0.7	0.7	1.0	0.9	2.8	.2	0.1	0.1
0.7	0.7	0.8	0.7	0.4	.3	0.1	0.1
0.7	0.5	0.6	0.6	0.2	.1	0.1	0.1
0.6	0.6	0.7	0.6	0.6	.3	0.1	0.1
3.6	4.1	4.3	4.0	1.3	1.4	0.6	1.3
9.7	10.4	12.1	10.9	12.1	5.7	1.7	2.2
4.7	4.6	3.9	2.9	1.2	2.6	2.1	0.4
5.1	7.0	9.7	4.6	8.0	1.0	0.3	0.9
5.3	11.1	16.2	30.3	9.2	6.4	2.9	0.2
1.2	1.2	1.5	1.3	0.6	.9	0.2	0.1
0.4	0.6	0.6	0.6	1.4	.5	0.1	1.1
7.3	13.3	18.4	17.1	1.1	1.6	0.8	0.5
3.3	3.9	4.0	4.6	0.9	2.3	2.3	0.3
2.0	2.2	2.7	2.7	0.5	1.3	0.9	0.2
1.2	1.2	1.4	1.2	2.2	.5	0.1	0.1
0.9	1.1	1.3	1.0	0.6	.6	0.2	0.8
1.4	4.6	14.8	31.6	5.9	.1	0.9	0.3
14.7	17.0	19.1	16.8	8.7	6.4	3.1	2.2
2.0	2.5	2.8	2.8	0.2	.6	0.7	0.5
0.8	0.7	0.9	1.2	0.3	.2	0.2	0.0
254.7	296.4	321.9	342.2	10.8	12.9	35.2	37.3
34.3	39.3	40.6	24.0	1.6	1.0	2.8	4.1
11.8	15.2	14.4	15.9	0.5	2.3	2.5	1.3
25.3	28.6	28.8	42.7	0.8	.8	3.7	3.4
9.8	13.0	14.9	9.9	0.3	.3	1.0	1.6
4.4	5.5	5.9	5.1	0.2	.9	0.8	0.6
5.1	5.4	6.4	5.6	0.8	1.2	1.1	0.6
34.2	33.0	31.0	25.4	1.1	1.0	6.0	4.5
61.0	66.1	71.3	68.8	1.9	3.0	7.9	7.5
2.2	2.5	3.2	3.5	0.7	.3	0.3	0.3
12.8	13.3	14.8	14.8	0.8	1.1	3.8	3.8
53.7	74.5	90.6	126.4	2.0	1.1	3.8	8.6
294.9	672.6	1,051.0	1,297.5	24.4	51.7	44.3	49.3
2.6	3.8	6.0	4.2	0.2	1.5	0.7	0.4
15.8	18.3	24.6	19.9	7.3	12.4	3.8	2.2
10.2	14.9	23.8	19.3	0.5	2.2	1.7	1.7
16.6	9.5	9.4	9.5	1.3	6.3	5.9	2.0
27.2	26.7	42.1	42.4	0.9	2.8	3.3	3.4
4.7	7.6	12.5	10.0	0.3	1.1	1.1	0.8
12.0	57.6	79.6	46.9	0.5	.5	0.8	2.9
34.8	13.3	19.9	47.0	0.5	1.0	1.3	1.9
20.4	23.6	23.7	23.0	0.8	2.3	3.1	2.8
95.2	405.6	680.2	947.9	8.2	13.7	14.3	22.6
55.3	91.6	128.8	128.4	3.8	7.9	8.3	8.7
17.1	22.5	32.8	33.5	0.6	.9	1.8	2.4
4.3	5.0	6.8	7.1	0.4	.8	0.9	0.6
0.1	0.1	0.5	0.2	0.5	—	—	—

Source: U.S. Immigration and Naturalization Service, 1992.

Name Index

Subject Index

458

459